Library of
Davidson College

Perspectives on Bilingualism and Bilingual Education

James E. Alatis
John J. Staczek
editors

Perspectives on Bilingualism and Bilingual Education

Perspectives on Bilingualism and Bilingual Education

James E. Alatis
John J. Staczek
editors

Georgetown University Press, Washington, D.C. 20057

Copyright © 1970, 1978, 1980, 1985 by Georgetown University Press.

All rights reserved

Printed in the United States of America

Library of Congress Cataloging in Publication Data
Main entry under title:

Perspectives on bilingualism and bilingual education.

    1. Bilingualism--Addresses, essays, lectures.
2. Education, Bilingual--Addresses, essays, lectures.
3. Multilingualism--Addresses, essays, lectures.
4. Language and languages--Study and teaching--
Addresses, essays, lectures. I. Alatis, James E.
II. Staczek, John J.
P115.P47   1985   404'.2   85-5457
ISBN 0-87840-192-X

Contents

Preface   ix

I. Linguistics and Sociolinguistics

Einar Haugen
Linguistics and Dialinguistics   3

Dell Hymes
Bilingual Education: Linguistic vs.
Sociolinguistic Bases   10

William F. Mackey
Interference, Integration, and
Synchronic Fallacy   18

II. The Multicultural Community and Policy

E. Glyn Lewis
Types of Bilingual Communities   49

Eric P. Hamp
Problems of Multilingualism in Small Linguistic
Communities   65

Shirley Brice Heath
Bilingual Education and a National
Language Policy   75

III. Bilingualism, Thought, and Cognition

John Macnamara
Bilingualism and Thought   91

Vera John
Cognitive Development in the
Bilingual Child   107

Wallace E. Lambert
Some Cognitive and Sociocultural Consequences
of Being Bilingual   116

IV. Ethnicity and Multilingualism

Charles A. Ferguson
   Patterns of Literacy in Multilingual
   Situations   133

Robert J. Di Pietro
   Culture and Ethnicity in the Bilingual
   Classroom   142

Courtney B. Cazden, Robert Carrasco, Abdil Abel Maldonado-Guzman, and Frederick Erickson
   The Contribution of Ethnographic Research
   to Bicultural Bilingual Education   153

Joshua A. Fishman
   Bilingual Education in the United States
   under Ethnic Community Auspices   170

V. Language Proficiency

John B. Carroll
   International Comparisons of Foreign Language
   Learning in the IEA Project   179

Heidi Dulay and Marina Burt
   The Relative Proficiency of Limited English
   Proficient Students   185

James Cummins
   The Construct of Language Proficiency in
   Bilingual Education   205

John W. Oller, Jr.
   A Language Factor Deeper than Speech: More
   Data and Theory for Bilingual Assessment   228

VI. Curriculum, Materials, and the Profession

María Medina Swanson
   Bilingual Education as a Profession   247

Robert Lado
   Linguistics and Preparation of
   Bilingual Materials   255

Mary Finocchiaro
Classroom Practices in Bilingual Education   266

VII. Communication and Bilingualism in the Classroom

Carolyn Kessler and Mary Ellen Quinn
Positive Effects of Bilingualism on Science
Problem-Solving Abilities   279

John J. Gumperz
Verbal Strategies in Multilingual
Communication   293

Deborah Tannen
Implications of the Oral/Literate Continuum for
Cross-Cultural Communication   308

Muriel Saville-Troike
Cross-Cultural Communication in
the Classroom   330

VIII. Evaluation and Bilingualism

G. Richard Tucker and Gary A. Cziko
The Role of Evaluation in Bilingual
Education   341

Robert L. Cooper
Research Methodology in Bilingual Education   365

Noel Epstein
Bilingual and Bicultural Education:
The Role of the Scholar   374

IX. Case Studies

Merrill Swain
Bilingual Education for the English-Speaking
Canadian   381

H.H. Stern
Bilingual Schooling and Foreign Language Education:
Some Implications of Canadian Experiments
in French Immersion   395

Joan Rubin
  Toward Bilingual Education for Paraguay 419

Lily Wong Fillmore
  Learning a Second Language: Chinese Children in the American Classroom 432

PREFACE

Bilingualism and bilingual education, in national and global settings, are generic themes that appear almost universally in the literature of linguistics, education, sociology, and psychology. The significance of their relationship is hardly accidental as both deal with the human, community, societal, and national conditions of two or more languages in contact.

Reflective of major historical contributions to the fields, the present volume is a collection of research and thought over a period of some eleven years. The first public forum for each of the articles was the annual Georgetown University Round Table on Languages and Linguistics, and the subsequent volumes of proceedings: **Bilingualism and Language Contact** (1970), **International Dimensions of Bilingual Education** (1978), and **Current Issues in Bilingual Education** (1980).

In republishing selected papers from these volumes, we hope to provide a research perspective on the principal thematic issues that are the foundation of continuing research in bilingualism and bilingual education. To describe the papers as important contributions to these fields is perhaps to understate their contemporary value. Indeed, the body of knowledge, ideas, and research strategies that constitutes the fields themselves are due in large part to the framework and agenda these authors provide.

To the authors whose work appears in this volume we are indebted for the direction they have given to bilingualism and bilingual education.

James E. Alatis
John J. Staczek

I. Linguistics and Sociolinguistics

LINGUISTICS AND DIALINGUISTICS

EINAR HAUGEN

Harvard University

Abstract. Efforts are being made to establish a new interdisciplinary field under the name of sociolinguistics. In an article entitled 'Sociolinguistic perspective on the study of bilingualism' (1968) Joshua Fishman has charged linguists with 'methodological and theoretical rigidity,' specifically in their conception of language as a 'pure, monolithic' structure, and of language contact as resulting in 'harmful' interference. It will be the purpose of this paper to determine to what extent this charge is justified.

One of the problems that has concerned some of us for a number of years is to ask what contribution linguists could make to the study of bilingualism. In the rapid growth of linguistics that we see taking place before our eyes, there is a danger that the kind of problems which bilinguals face may be neglected. The topic of bilingualism has interested psychologists and educators a good deal more than it has linguists, and much of the literature on the subject is written by non-linguists. This is surprising in view of the fact that linguists are (or ought to be) bilingual by definition, and one would expect them to take an interest in their own problems.

The situation has been acutely pointed up in a free-swinging article by Joshua A. Fishman, who accuses linguists of not being 'truly impartial to the language of bilinguals' (Fishman 1968a: 29). We are told that linguistic research on bilingualism 'has but two basic notions to it, the first being that of two "pure" languages and the second, that of "interference" between them.' The concept of 'languages in contact' is characterized by Fishman as 'the interaction of two entities that normally exist in a pure and unsullied state and that have been brought

4/ Einar Haugen

into unnatural contact with each other.' 'The underlying model of
pure, monolithic langue leads the linguist to assume that the interaction or fusion of two such is "interference", that is, deleterious,
harmful, noxious.' The linguist's ferreting out of interference is
described as being like that of 'a housewife looking for smears of
wet paint ... what structures of language X have rubbed off on language Y and vice versa?' As a result, we are told, linguists have 'frequently failed to familiarize themselves with the communities and
speakers from which they have obtained their corpuses of speech'
and have overlooked the fact that 'in many ways bilinguals are people
like other people' (Fishman 1968a: 29-30).

At first sight one is inclined to take this salvo rather lightly, as
a piece of science fiction, since it does not correspond to any con-
ceptions harbored by those of us who have carried on research in
bilingualism over the past generation. Happily, Fishman does not
footnote his charges, so that no one needs to feel hurt. If Joshua's
trumpets are going to bring the walls of Jericho down, one would be
happy not to be living in that particular city.

Among the linguists who have dealt seriously with bilingualism in
America, Uriel Weinreich certainly is preeminent. He introduced
the terms that are the particular targets of Fishman's critique,
namely 'interference' and 'languages in contact' (Weinreich 1953).
As I read Weinreich's book, these terms are entirely neutral and
dispassionate designations of important aspects of bilingual behavior. He defined languages as being in contact 'if they are used alternately by the same persons.' Interference phenomena were 'those
instances of deviation from the norms of either language which occur
in the speech of bilinguals as a result of their familiarity with more
than one language' (Weinreich 1953: 1). I find no reference to these
norms as being 'pure' or to interference as being 'noxious'. Instead,
Weinreich notes that to the bilingual a 'partial identification' of the
two systems is 'a reduction of his linguistic burden'. He discusses
the possibility of systemic merger, but for most bilinguals he pre-
fers to speak of 'two coexistent systems' (Weinreich 1953: 8). In
long-established bilingual communities, however, he recognizes that
'there is hardly any limit to interference' (Weinreich 1953: 81), so
that some speakers might be said to have 'only one language with two
modes of expression' (Weinreich 1953: 9). As for familiarity with bilingual communities, one could hardly overlook the fact that Weinreich lived in New York and did field work in Switzerland.

As one who from time to time has written on this subject, perhaps
I may be so bold as to quote a sentence or two from my own writings.
More than thirty years ago, in my first article in Language, I wrote:
'When the speakers of [Norwegian] were transplanted to American
soil ... a more or less gradual transformation of their speech became

inevitable... [This process is] generally referred to under the inaccurate metaphor of "borrowing", and the result is called a "mixed language"... These terms obscure the fact that what has really taken place is a shift in structure ... correlated to a shift in cultural and social form.' (Haugen 1938: 113) In a 1950 article published in Language I demonstrated that 'the process of learning changes the learner's view of the language' (Haugen 1950: 216). In my Norwegian Language in America I documented the rise of new linguistic norms in bilingual communities; I called them 'bilingual norms' or 'bilingual dialects' (Haugen 1953: 60). (I was therefore somewhat surprised to read in an article by Ma and Herasimchuk [in Fishman 1968b: 644] that linguists had not noticed that 'speakers generate their own bilingual norms of correctness'.) In the same work I inveighed against the views of educated native speakers who rejected the emigrant's language as either 'comical or offensive' (Haugen 1953: 57). The book was based on memories of participation in bilingual communities since childhood and active field work over a period of years. As for admitting that 'bilinguals are people,' I can only say that I am one myself.

The point of these quotations has merely been to demonstrate that Fishman's charges can hardly be based on the work of linguists who have actually concerned themselves with bilingualism. Knowing his writings and his outlook, I suspect that he would exonerate us and other linguists who have worked firsthand with these problems and say that we were not writing as linguists, but as sociolinguists.

The charge is therefore more properly directed at the linguists proper, those who are generally recognized as being in the mainstream of American linguistics. In their writings we find precious little either about bilingualism or any other kind of linguistic variability. If we peek in the standard textbook of American structuralism, H. A. Gleason's Introduction to Descriptive Linguistics (1955, revised 1961), we find that only one of its twenty-eight chapters deals with what he calls 'variation in speech'. Under this heading he throws together borrowing, dialectology, levels of speech, etc. These are all marginal to his definition of descriptive linguistics, which is concerned only with 'minimal contrastive elements and their combinations', i.e. the synchronically defined structure of a single idiolect. If we turn hopefully to the linguists of the New Grammar, who speak freely of 'creativity' in language, there is little change on this point. On the very first page of Chomsky's Aspects we read that linguistic theory is 'concerned primarily with an ideal speaker-listener, in a completely homogeneous speech-community' (Chomsky 1965: 3). Since the bilingual by definition lives in a nonhomogeneous speech community and usually (if not always) falls short of being an ideal speaker, there is little encouragement to bilingual study in this pronouncement.

Any scholar is of course entitled to exclude from his research strategy any set of data he chooses if this enables him to make more powerful generalizations. Sooner or later, however, the excluded data will rise up to haunt him. The appeal to the speaker's native intuition for judgments on grammaticality has shown that each speaker has his own distinct competence, and that this can vary with time and place. Gleason recognized the limitations of his approach and suggested that it might be a valid objective to make 'an empirical description of the range and significance of variation' and to make 'generalizations about linguistic variation as a characteristic feature of language'. He even suggested that such generalizations might become 'the basis for a second type of linguistic science', but found that 'we lack a general term for this discipline as a whole' (Gleason 1961: 392).

In the meanwhile, 'sociolinguistics' has offered itself as a candidate for such a term. William Bright declared linguistic diversity to be the essential criterion of the field in his introduction to the UCLA symposium on sociolinguistics (Bright 1966: 11). From the hardcore linguist's point of view, however, the prefix socio- compromises the term by identifying variation with its social correlates, which he feels are not his primary business. In 1956 I proposed 'dialinguistics' as a possible name for the kind of interlingual confrontation that is now often known as 'contrastive' or 'differential' linguistics (Haugen 1956: 41). I was impressed by the number of linguistic terms in this area that begin with the Greek prefix dia-, all of which suggest variation: 'diachronic' linguistics studies variations in time, 'dialectology' variations in space. Weinreich proposed 'diasystem' for the compound system of bilinguals. In 1954, at a Georgetown lecture, I suggested the use of 'diaphones' and 'diamorphs' to identify interlingually defined phonemic and morphemic units. Recently Dingwall (1964) has used the term 'diaglossic' for a similar operation; the step is short to 'diaglossics' or 'diaglottology'. The disjecta membra are present to constitute a field of dialinguistics, if only a coherent theory and terminology could be developed.

Within such a theory seen from an entirely linguistic point of view, the concept of the 'nonunique' or 'variable' structure would seem to be central. Perhaps the very word 'structure' is unfortunate as suggesting a rigidity which is not characteristic of human behavior. We would certainly have to examine once more whether Meillet's famous dictum of the coherence of language systems is really true. If a language is really un système ou tout se tient, how does it happen that bilinguals find it so easy to accept novel elements into their systems?

There are other well-known linguistic dogmas that require reexamination in the light of the data furnished us by bilingual speakers. One of them is the distinction between langue and parole, now reformulated into English by Chomsky as 'competence' and 'performance'. Mackey began his description of bilingualism (1962: 51) by assigning bilingualism to the domain of parole, as a characteristic of the individual rather than of the group. But every time a bilingual draws upon the resources of his other language, he is by ever so little altering the nature of his competence in both. Every performance alters one's competence by the increment of what one has learned or unlearned during the performance. Our linguistic competences are changing from moment to moment throughout our lives, and there is no set of data which reveals this more clearly than the life cycle of bilinguals.

What I have called a 'bilingual dialect' in the bilingual speech community may prove to be either stable (as in India) or unstable (as in the United States). This is a matter for empirical examination in each given instance. The main thing is that bilinguals exhibit in principle a succession of variable competences, which may be infinite in number, since they represent points on a continuum from one language to another. The concept of the variable competence is one that needs to be developed in order to account not only for the interferences of bilinguals, but for all kinds of idiolectal, dialectal, social, and historical variation. Only in this way can we get away from the stultifying logico-mathematical formalism and devise models that reflect more accurately what speakers actually do.

It is not my intention here to outline a full-scale theory of bilingualism, only to suggest a few lines of inquiry, some of which are well represented in the literature, and others less so. The characteristic features of bilingual behavior include the complementary processes of learning and unlearning one's two codes, and one's success in switching from one to the other. While a first language is learned step by step as the child matures, a second language has to establish its structure under constant reference to the first. If we recognize that every item and every rule that is established in the second language adds to the competence of the speaker, which grows and expands with each successful performance, we will accept the concept of variable competence. On the way from monolingualism to bilingualism the learner passes through stages that may be called (with Nemser 1969) 'learner's systems', some of which can be studied in children and an entirely different set in adolescents or adults. Generative linguists speak glibly of 'adding' or 'deleting' rules, as if one could just write it into the learner's system. But each item and each rule in a second language is somehow related to those of the first, and each one is the response to an opportunity and a need for learning.

The gradual 'build-up' of competence in the second language may be matched by a gradual 'unlearning' of the first language. An extreme example of this occurs in aphasics, which as Roman Jakobson showed many years ago (1941) proceeds in the inverse order to the learning. A mild form of it is observed in immigrants who lose fluency in their native language after some years in a new linguistic environment. To some extent the first language is dismantled—by the forgetting of words, complex sentence structures, subtleties of meaning. The same person may be building up one language and partly tearing down another; or better still, he is rebuilding his first language to suit the occupancy of a new personality. The German language can here provide us with a handy set of tags: if we call the building-up a language an <u>Aufbau</u> and the aphasic dismantling an <u>Abbau</u>, the bilingual's restructuring can be called an <u>Umbau</u>. This is the goal of all the studies of bilingual interference: in what way has a language been rebuilt or <u>umgebaut</u> because of the coexistence with another language in the minds of bilingual speakers?

This conception of the symbiosis of languages and the ever varying competences of individual speakers and speech communities is as far as possible from the rigid conception of monolithic systems for which linguists were castigated, and not without reason, by Joshua Fishman. Linguists have an opportunity to study the infinite variability of language more clearly and easily among bilinguals than among monolinguals. I would be glad to scuttle the word 'interference' if it is felt to imply a condemnation. It would have been nice if someone had started calling the same phenomenon 'enrichment', for it can easily be argued that the bilingual who reaches into his other language for an expression is in fact enriching his effective range of communication, for he is using a word or a form that feels right to his interlocutors. However, the term 'enrichment' is as loaded as 'interference', and if we want a really neutral word, we will have to accept some such term as 'transfer', originally launched by Zellig Harris. Only in normative grammar does it make sense to speak of 'interference', for then the speaker is violating a rule laid down by fiat and not by custom. But that is another problem entirely.

It is my conviction that linguistics can profit by becoming dialinguistic, and that the problems of bilinguals can receive a linguistic solution if linguists are willing to settle for a variable rather than a static competence.

REFERENCES

Bright, William, ed. 1966. Sociolinguistics: Proceedings of the UCLA Sociolinguistics Conference, 1964. The Hague: Mouton.
Chomsky, Noam. 1965. Aspects of the theory of syntax. Cambridge, Massachusetts: The M.I.T. Press.
Dingwall, William Orr. 1964. Diaglossic grammar. Ph.D. dissertation, Georgetown University. Washington, D.C.

Fishman, Joshua A. 1968a. Sociolinguistic perspective on the study of bilingualism. Linguistics 39.21-49.
_____ et al. 1968b. Bilingualism in the barrio. Final report, U.S. Department of Health, Education and Welfare. New York: Yeshiva University.
_____. 1968c. Readings in the sociology of language. The Hague: Mouton.
Gleason, Henry A. 1955 (rev. ed. 1961). An introduction to descriptive linguistics. New York: Holt, Rinehart and Winston.
Haugen, Einar. 1938. Phonological shifting in American Norwegian. Language 14.112-120.
_____. 1950. The analysis of linguistic borrowing. Language 26. 210-231.
_____. 1953. The Norwegian language in America: a study in bilingual behavior. Philadelphia: University of Pennsylvania Press (reprinted 1969, Indiana University Press).
_____. 1954. Problems of bilingual description. Georgetown University Monograph Series on Languages and Linguistics, No. 7, 9-19.
_____. 1956. Bilingualism in the Americas: a bibliography and research guide. University, Alabama (Publications of the American Dialect Society, No. 26).
Jakobson, Roman. 1941. Kindersprache, Aphasie und allgemeine Lautgesetze. Uppsala. (Språkvetenskapliga Sällskapets i Uppsala Förhandlingar 1940-1942).
Mackey, William F. 1962. The description of bilingualism. Canadian Journal of Linguistics 7.51-85. (Reprinted in Fishman 1968c, 554-584).
Nemser, William. 1969. Approximative systems of foreign language learners. Yugoslav Serbo-Croatian-English Contrastive Project, 3-12. Zagreb, 1969.
Weinreich, Uriel. 1953. Languages in contact. Findings and Problems. (Publications of the Linguistic Circle of New York, 1). New York.

BILINGUAL EDUCATION: LINGUISTIC VS. SOCIOLINGUISTIC BASES

DELL HYMES

University of Pennsylvania

Abstract. The objectives of the Bilingual Education Program are in part to develop greater competence in English among children of limited English-speaking ability. There are children who need the Program's help, but who may be missed if the Program is permitted to make the same fundamental mistake as does much linguistic theory: to equate competence in a language with competence in ways of speaking.
Children may enter school with English as their first and only language, but with the communicative norms of a different cultural background (and ultimately, language community) governing their use of English in the school situation. In her paper Mrs. Philips presents data from an American Indian case. Here I shall discuss briefly how the linking of 'Cartesian' and 'Herderian' linguistics compounds the confusion cited above, and how a sociolinguistic perspective on the notions of 'language' and 'speech community' may help to resolve it, and to provide a conceptual basis adequate to the empirical problem.

(When Dr. Alatis invited me to participate in this Round Table Meeting, I suggested that he invite Mrs. Philips instead. She is doing empirical research on the problem of the meeting, as I am not. He very kindly asked us both. I see my role as one of sketching the theoretical background to Mrs. Philips' work. I shall try to underscore the significance of the sort of research in which she is engaged.)

Bilingual education is a sociolinguistic subject par excellence. The skills of linguists are both necessary and insufficient. The role of linguistics in research on bilingual education may seem to be a matter only of application of a linguistics already given. The contrary is the case. Research on bilingual education requires a kind of linguistics not yet fully constituted. The use of linguistics in such research challenges linguistics to develop conceptual and methodological tools able to deal adequately with the place of speech in human life—with the place of actual speech competencies in actual lives.

A goal of education, bilingual or other, presumably is to enable children to develop their capacity for creative use of language as part of successful adaptation of themselves and their communities in the continuously changing circumstances characteristic of contemporary life. And linguistics indeed has already addressed itself to this goal, as witnessed by the concern within descriptive theory for the 'creative aspect of language use' (Chomsky 1965, 1966) and the recognition of the role of the child's first language long advocated by many linguists and anthropologists. In both respects, however, linguistics falls short until it is able to deal with ways of speaking in relation to social meanings and situations, until, in short, the starting point of description is not a sentence or text, but a speech event; not a language, but a repertoire of ways of speaking; not a speech community defined in equivalence to a language, but a speech community defined through the concurrence of rules of grammar and rules of use.

The leading view of the nature of linguistic competence and creativity has been dubbed 'Cartesian linguistics' (Chomsky 1966), not as a historically exact label, but in recognition of a direction given to theory of language in the period following Descartes by an emphasis on the nature of mind as prior to experience, and an analytic, universalizing, reconstituting methodology (cf. Cassirer 1955, Ch. I, 'The Philosophy of the Enlightenment'). In similar vein, one may dub a subsequent tradition of thought 'Herderian linguistics' (Hymes 1970a), not as a historically exact label, but in recognition of a direction given to theory of language in the period following Herder (1744-1801) by an emphasis on language as constituting cultural identity (cf. Barnard 1965: 117, 118, 142), and on a methodology of sympathetic interpretation of cultural diversity sui generis—Herder coined the German verb einfühlen—if within a larger universal framework. (The two traditions might be labelled 'Enlightenment' and 'Romantic', but the individual names perhaps are better, in that they less imply two mutually exclusive periods, or simple uniformity within each.)

'Cartesian' and 'Herderian' approaches have contributed much to our knowledge of language. In the past the differences between the two approaches have been salient, but here what matters most is what they have fundamentally in common: isolation of a language as the object of linguistic description; equation of a language with a speech community (or culture); taking of the social functions of language as external, given, and universally equivalent; restriction of study of the structure of language to units and relations based on reference.

The emergence of sociolinguistics is in important part a response to social needs; but as an intellectual stage in the history of linguistics, the recent history of sociolinguistics can be seen as a response to the hegemony of 'Cartesian' and 'Herderian' assumptions, first, by critical analysis of the assumptions themselves, and, secondly, by effort to replace them. Just as Boas, Sapir, Bloomfield, Pike, and others can be seen as concerned to develop concepts and methods adequate to the description of all languages, so the current work of Ervin-Tripp, Fishman, Gumperz, Labov, and others can be seen as concerned to develop concepts and methods adequate to the description of speech communities. And where Boas, Sapir, Bloomfield, Pike, and others had to empty some concepts of normative or ethnocentric content (e. g. 'inflection', 'incorporation' vis-à-vis compounding), extend some (e. g. morphème), and invent others (e. g. phoneme), with regard to grammars, so have contributors to sociolinguistics today the task of emptying, extending, and inventing with regard to the identification and organization of ways of speaking.

Mrs. Philips' work is a contribution to the empirical task. In the rest of my remarks I shall sketch some of the critical analysis associated with it, with regard to 'Cartesian' concepts of competence and creativity, and 'Herderian' concepts of language in the speech community.

The concern with competence and creativity in Chomsky's 'Cartesian' linguistics is an advance toward sociolinguistics, but, on analysis, an advance more nominal than real. To make competence central, rather than la langue, to reconcile the sphere of creativity with that of structure, does focus discussion on actual human beings and their abilities, and regard them as acquirers and shapers of culture, rather than merely as 'culture-bearers'. Just such a transformation was projected for anthropology and linguistics by Sapir in his last writings (see discussion in Hymes 1970b). But whereas Sapir turned attention to 'living speech', understood as requiring that received categories be reconsidered within the matrix of social interaction, Chomsky's 'Cartesian' linguistics seems a cogent, thoroughly thought out perfection of the impulse to the autonomy of language that spurred so much of structural linguistics and in an earlier stage, Sapir himself. From origin as possibly a physico-chemical accident to the assumptions of wholly fluent use free of situation in a homogenous community, any dependence of language on social interaction and adaptation is excluded.

In brief, Chomskyan 'competence' is restricted to knowledge and, within knowledge, to knowledge of grammar. Much of what would normally be considered part of a speaker's knowledge and ability is excluded. Much of what one would need to study to understand actual individual competence is not 'competence' but 'performance'. In effect, two senses of 'performance' are confounded: a negative sense, in which 'mere' performance is that superficial behavior which linguistics must seek to go beneath, and an implicitly positive sense, in which 'performance' is everything other than grammar that contributes to acceptable speech. The confusion tends to give the positive contents of 'performance' the negative association, and in any case, the dichotomy is used to relegate all but grammar to a secondary status. The constitutive role of social factors is ignored, as is knowledge of them, yet identification and motivation are found to be key factors in sociolinguistic change (Labov 1966, Le Page 1969). Performances, as events, have no admitted structure of their own.

The 'creative aspect of language use', like 'competence', promises more than it contains. It is analyzed (Chomsky 1966) in terms of the possibility of producing an indefinitely large number of sentences, free of immediate stimulus control, that are yet appropriate. But a sentence might be new, free of stimulus control, and bizarre. Appropriateness entails a relation to situation. Competent speakers have knowledge of the structure and meaning of sentences and of the structure and meaning of situations and the relations between the two as well. Just as 'Cartesian' linguistics reduces competence to knowledge of grammar, so it reduces 'creativity' to novelty.

Those concerned with linguistic aspects of education and with sociolinguistic theory must thank Chomsky for making competence and creativity central to linguistic theory, but must reconstruct the concepts for themselves.[1]

Cartesian and 'Herderian' linguistics differ most obviously with regard to the place of differences among languages. There is not, to be sure, a complete opposition. The most celebrated early figure in the 'Herderian' tradition, W. von Humboldt, was concerned with universals as well as specific difference, as were Boas, Sapir, and Whorf later. Indeed, what Herder, von Humboldt, and Goethe are linked by is a conception of form that links the individual and universal. The notion of form is linked to that of creativity, and individuality, both, so that in contrast to the 'Cartesian' sense of particularity and uniqueness of personality (language, culture) as negative limitation, such limitation is seen as positive. It is not the absence of universality, but realization of a universal power. The universal finds realization only in the actuality of the particular; form is truly acquired only through the power of self-formation (Cassirer 1961: 20-25). (On this development, see Cassirer 1950: 224-5, 252; 1955: 32-36; 1961: 20-26. On von Humboldt as having found his way into the study of language through his concern with the characterization of individuals and individual peoples, see Lammers 1936 and Leroux 1958: 69, n. 2).

Chomsky treats von Humboldt in terms of his continuity with the general approach of the Enlightenment; he acknowledges but omits much of that aspect of von Humboldt which, according to Cassirer, is his distinctive achievement. He follows von Humboldt in concern with the universal power, but neglects von Humboldt's understanding of form as something not given, but historically emergent and acquired.[2] The treatment of von Humboldt is in keeping with the treatment of competence and creativity.

The 'Herderian' approach, as developed by von Humboldt is indeed the approach needed in sociolinguistics. The focus, however, must be changed from a language, as correlate of a people, to persons and their ways of speaking. The inadequacy of a monolingual approach has long been recognized and, indeed, no one has ever denied the obvious facts of multilingualism, the prevalence of linguistic diversity in the world. The difficulty remains that in informal thought one tends to fall back on the Herderian model of one language, one people, one culture, one community—the Hopi and their language, etc., (on the persistence of 'savage anthropology' of this sort, see Fontana 1968), because we are only beginning to have sociolinguistic models and taxonomies adequate to thinking in terms of multilingual situations. But, as the work of Gumperz, Labov, and others has shown, more than plurality of languages is involved.

First of all, what counts as a language boundary cannot be defined by any purely linguistic measure. Attitudes and social meanings enter in as well. Any enduring social relationship or group may come to define itself by selection and/or creation of linguistic features, and a difference of accent may be as important at one boundary as a difference of grammar at another. Part of the creativity of users of languages lies in the freedom to determine what and how much linguistic difference matters. The alternative view, indeed a view often taken, conceals an unsuspected linguistic determinism. (For a recent issue of this sort, involving the notion of ethnic unit and mutual intelligibility, cf. Hymes 1968.)

Secondly, speech communities cannot be defined in terms of linguistic features alone in another respect. Their definition must comprise shared knowledge both of one or more primary varieties, and of rules for their use. Differential knowledge of a linguistic variety aside (and that is of course of importance), a person who is a member of a speech community knows not only a language but also what to say. A person who can produce all and any of the sentences of a language, and unpredictably does, is institutionalized. For some range of situations, itself to be empirically determined and perhaps varying significantly across communities, a competent member of the speech community knows what to say next. And just as there are Sprachbunde, defined by linguistic features shared across language boundaries, so there are Sprechbunde, defined by shared rules of speaking. (I owe this notion to J. Neustupný). And such sharing of speech rules across languages may extend not only in space but also through time. The Ngoni of Africa, for example, mostly no longer speak Ngoni, but use the language of the people in Malawi whom they conquered. However, they use it in Ngoni ways, ways whose maintenance is considered essential to their identity. Analagous situations obtain in some American Indian communities.

In general, both theory and relevance to education require that one break with the equation between a named language and a functional role. Functional role is primary and problematic (cf. argument of Hymes 1966). The means that serve a given function are to be empirically determined. Beyond cognitive differences possibly attributable to differences of language, there are cognitive differences due to differences in speaking. There is interference not only between phonologies and grammars, but also between norms of interaction and interpretation of speech. One must take the vantage point of the person acquiring competence in speech in a community, and discover the number and organization of ways of speaking that result.

The notions of rules of cooccurrence and rules of alternation, recently developed by Ervin-Tripp are general and neutral concepts for discovering the organization of linguistic features in a community, comparable to concepts developed for discovering phonological and grammatical structure. They rely upon the fundamental notion of contrastive relevance, but generalize it to the contrastive relevance of 'stylistic' features as well as features of reference. (Vowel length for emphasis is as much a contrastive feature of English or Wasco Chinook as /m/ : /n/ to distinguish morphemes.) And the step from the identification of features to organized sets of features is, to repeat, an empirical one, governed by analysis of other components of speech events as well. The step is not, repeat not, taken by automatically referring features to a 'named' language known externally and prior to investigation. Rules of cooccurrence identify styles; rules of alternation identify their social meanings and contrastive relevance in use. (This last is the step that the approach to styles of Pike (1967) fails to take.) The notion 'ways of speaking' calls particular attention to the fact that members of a speech community have a knowledge such that speech is interpretable as pertaining to one or another genre, and as instancing one or another speech act and event.

In sum, there is no quarrel with the 'Cartesian' concern for universals and the human mind. There is much concern with the 'Herderian' concern for individuation and emergent form. Only the focus of theory and description changes, from rules of language to rules of speaking. It is the latter that are fundamental, embracing the former as one constituent. And an understanding of rules of speaking is indispensable to understanding failures and to increasing success in bicultural education.

NOTES

[1] A sociolinguistic critique of 'Cartesian' linguistics is markedly parallel to the critique by Marx of Feuerbach. By substituting 'Chomsky' (or 'Cartesian linguistics') for 'Feuerbach', and 'linguistic' for 'religious', one has a remarkably applicable statement:

> 'Chomsky resolves the linguistic essence into the human essence. But the essence of man is no abstraction inhering in each single individual. In its actuality it is the ensemble of social relationships.
> 'Chomsky, who does not go into the criticism of this actual essence, is hence compelled:
> (1) to abstract from the historical process and to establish linguistic intuition as something self-contained, and to presuppose an abstract—isolated—human individual;
> (2) to view the essence of man merely as "species", as the inner dumb generality which unites the many individuals naturally' (i.e. not socially).
> (Quoted from Easton and Guddat 1967: 402.)

I do not think one can abandon some conception of a generic human nature (human essence), as the thesis might be taken as saying; but the man for whom Chomsky's competence and theory is a model is indeed an isolated man in the abstract. There is nothing to be said about men (or women).

[2] One might argue that transformational generative grammar ought by rights to be especially concerned, as was von Humboldt, with individual form. By establishing that marked departures from universal, or natural, features and relations entail costs, it is able to recognize the great extent to which languages, or rather their speakers, pay such costs, and to appreciate the power of the sociohistorical forces that motivate such payment.

REFERENCES

Barnard, F. M. 1965. Herder's social and political thought, from enlightenment to nationalism. Oxford, Clarendon Press.
Cassirer, Ernst. 1950. The problem of knowledge. Philosophy, science, and history since Hegel. New Haven, Yale University Press.

_____. 1955. The philosophy of the enlightenment. Boston, Beacon Press. (Princeton University Press, 1955; German original, Tübingen, 1932).
_____. 1961. The logic of the humanities. New Haven, Yale University Press. (German original, Göteborg, 1942.)
Chomsky, Noam. 1965. Aspects of the theory of syntax. Cambridge, M.I.T. Press.
_____. 1966. Cartesian linguistics. New York, Harper and Row.
Easton, Lloyd D. and Kurt H. Guddat, eds. 1967. Writings of the young Marx on philosophy and society. Garden City, New York, Doubleday.
Ervin-Tripp, Susan M. 1971. On sociolinguistic rules: alternation and co-occurrence. In John J. Gumperz and Dell Hymes, eds., Directions in sociolinguistics. New York, Holt, Rinehart, and Winston.
Fontana, Bernard L. 1968. Savage anthropologists and unvanishing Indians in the American Southwest. Paper read before the 67th Annual Meeting of the American Anthropological Association, Seattle, Washington, November 21.
Hymes, Dell. 1966. Two types of linguistic relativity: some examples from Amerindian ethnography. In William Bright, ed., Sociolinguistics, 114-158. The Hague, Mouton.
_____. 1967. Why linguistics needs the sociologist. Social Research 34 (4): 632-647.
_____. 1968. Linguistic problems in defining the concept of 'tribe'. In June Helm, ed., Essays on the problem of tribe, 23-48. (Proceedings of the 1967 annual spring meeting of the American Ethnological Society). Seattle, University of Washington Press.
_____. 1970a. Linguistic aspects of comparative political research. In Robert T. Holt and John E. Turner, eds., The methodology of comparative research, Ch. VII. New York, The Free Press.
_____. 1970b. Linguistic method of ethnography. In Paul Garvin, ed., The problem of method in linguistics. The Hague, Mouton.
_____. 1971. On communicative competence. Philadelphia, University of Pennsylvania Press.
Labov, William A. 1966. The social stratification of English in New York City. Washington, D.C., Center for Applied Linguistics.
Lammers, Wilhelm. 1936. Wilhelm von Humboldts Weg zur Sprachforschung 1785-1801. Berlin.
Le Page, R.C. 1969. Problems of description in multilingual communities. Transactions of the Philological Society, 1968, 189-212. London.
Leroux, Robert. 1958. L'anthropologie comparée de Guillaume de Humboldt. (Publications de la Faculté des lettres de l'Université de Strasbourg, Fascicule 135.) Paris, Société d'éditions.
Pike, K.L. 1967. Language in relation to a unified theory of the structure of human behavior. The Hague, Mouton.

INTERFERENCE, INTEGRATION AND THE SYNCHRONIC FALLACY

WILLIAM F. MACKEY

International Center for Research on Bilingualism
Université Laval

Abstract. One of the most difficult operations in analyzing the language behavior of bilinguals is that of separating the integration of foreign elements into their code from the interference of such elements in the messages. The operation is made more difficult if it has to be performed within the framework fashioned by the fictitious synchronic/diachronic dichotomy. In place of this, the concept of language as an evolving code is more applicable to the analysis of the speech of bilinguals. A method is suggested to help distinguish interference from integration. Results of preliminary experimentation with the method are discussed.

The purposes of this paper are (1) to examine the effects of synchronic description in distinguishing between interference and integration in cases of language contact, and (2) to suggest alternative methods of description suitable for the analysis of systems in motion.

0. Introduction

Let me begin by adopting the now old-fashioned practice of introducing and defining my key terms. By interference, I mean the use of elements of one language or dialect while speaking or writing another; it is characteristic of the message. By integration I mean the incorporation into one language or dialect of elements from another; it is characteristic of the code. What I shall call the 'synchronic fallacy' is the belief that one can describe a language as if at any one point in time its code were stable.

We shall first consider the implications of (1) this 'synchronic fallacy', see how it relates to the distinction between (2) integration and interference, study the possible ways of (3) measuring integration, and analyse the quantitative relationship between (4) integration and availability with sample measurements.

1. The synchronic fallacy

A code is a convention. In language it is a social convention adopted by a speech community. But at any one point, certain elements of the code are preferred to others. At any one point in time, some language signs entering the code will be adopted quickly while others will be integrated gradually; any of these may disappear quickly or gradually, independently of their rate of adoption. Since the language code and its systems are in constant motion, the most appropriate description is not a synchronic analysis but a quantum description. Because a detailed treatment of this question would lead us into a discussion of general linguistic theory, which is evidently beyond the concern of this conference, I shall be content to refer to a recent paper which I have called 'Toward a Quantum Linguistics' (Mackey 1970b), and (1) to reproduce a remark which I made at the International Seminar on the Description and Measurement of Bilingualism in 1962 (Kelly 1969) on the limitations of synchronic description before explaining why it is not suited for describing (2) the entropy of evolving codes.

1.1 Limitations of synchronic descriptions

Almost all modern linguistic theories of language, including those of Saussure, Bloomfield, and Hjelmslev, have postulated a dichotomy between diachronic and synchronic linguistics. This postulate has been workable with the type of analysis made up to now—descriptive and historical grammars. But it is a fiction, ignorable only under two conditions: (a) where language change is so slow and minute as to be imperceptible within the same generation, and (b) where the refinement of analysis does not go beyond distinctive features.

Since language must evolve, there must be variation and vacillation; otherwise we would always be dealing with dead languages. The speed of language evolution through vacillation varies according to the social elements of control—likely to be different in illiterate and bilingual communities.

In bilingual communities, the incidence of interference contributes to the degree of vacillation, and consequently to the speed at which one or more of the languages or dialects evolve. So that degrees of change which in an unilingual situation will take many generations may, under the impact of bilingualism, be realized in one.

If this is the generation whose language use is being described, the investigator is faced with what appears to him either as interference or as a code with a high degree of free-variation. Both are illusions conditioned by the postulate that we are dealing with one or two synchronic codes. And the treatment of bilingual material as synchronic becomes more and more complex as one multiplies cases, because in any evolving code the degree of individual variation is a function of the rate of change.

And it is precisely the speed of this evolving code in situations of language contact that makes its description and measurement so difficult. What has to be described and measured is a two-dimensional continuum, one of which is continually alternating at the moment the other is inconsistently vacillating.

The point I want to make here is that this fiction of the synchronic, which has served so well in generating the abstractions of descriptive and transformational grammars, becomes quite unreal when used to describe the unstable and rapidly evolving systems of nonliterate communities and of languages in contact. This fallacy which assumes a fixed code or norm has led the students of language contact up a blind alley at the end of which was the impossibility of distinguishing between the two fundamental notions in the linguistic study of bilingualism, namely between integration and interference or, if you will, between interference in the code and interference in the message—since the same term has been used for both. This fiction of synchronic description has also made it difficult to determine when interference in the code is no longer interference, that is when it becomes part of the language. At what point, for example, did French words like *ignorance*, *nation*, *page*, *lingerie*, and *liqueur* become part of the English language?

Let us now go back to Saussure's original analogy where he compares a language to a game of chess, in which the state of the board is constantly changing according to certain fixed rules which the players must follow (Saussure 1915: 125-27). This is an often quoted analogy used to explain the classical dichotomy between diachronic and synchronic linguistics. The game can be described diachronically in terms of the moves of the players according to the rules, or synchronically in terms of the resulting distribution of the pawns on the board at any given point in time. The analogy and the dichotomy have indeed been useful as a basis for the elaboration of descriptive grammars and dictionaries of standardized languages, the very standardization of which is a factor in attenuating the natural variation and evolutionary tendencies of language.

Since few speakers will deviate greatly from the norm, and these may be limited to groups that are peripheral in space and time—dialects speakers, the very young and the very old—the number of people so deviating will not be in the majority, especially in those few languages which have a long tradition of standardization. Even for these highly standardized languages, the analogy is far from perfect, since if one were to freeze this linguistic game of chess at any point in time, in addition to finding some pawns in some squares and others in others, one would find a number of pawns between squares, some emerging ones on one edge and entering ones on the other edge of a number of squares, squares of different sizes and dimensions, pawns of different sizes, shapes and colors—bishops with the features of horses and horses becoming bishops—and procedures which were laxer or stricter than others in a game where the rules are forever changing.

1.2 The entropy of evolving codes

In other words, we would find a state of entropy, of continual transformation within the system. For all living languages are in a perpetual state of entropy—some more than others, and at some times more than at other times.

Repeated interference from another code tends to increase this entropy, whereas literacy and standardization tend to decrease it. Two related unwritten languages will tend to blend into one more quickly than will two equally related languages with standardized written forms used by most of their speakers. And in formally standardized codes, interference will reach the point of resistance earlier than in nonstandardized languages, for the gap between what speakers of standard languages say and what they know they should be saying becomes quickly more apparent and tends to promote in the literate community such formalized defenses as purism, irredentism, and language repression.

In the permissible range of variation in usage, the entropy of a language is affected by the degree of tolerance of the people who speak it. Some communities tolerate interference more than do others. This tolerance may have historical determinants; but it is also related to literacy, standardization and language contact. In nonliterate communities it may be wider than in literate societies. In unilingual communities, it may be less than in multilingual groups where the incidence of use of linguistic features from several languages by any individual may actually form a single continuum (Le Page 1968). And in nonliterate, multilingual groups, the range of tolerance may even become identical to mutual intelligibility achieved by a speech economy whose norm is the sum of all operant codes. In such situations, the new elements entering the speech of individuals from another language or dialect may do so entirely by chance and never be heard again; or they may be repeated with such consistency as to give the impression that

they have been transferred to the other language and integrated into
its code. Yet there is no indication in the occurrence of these elements
in the stream of speech whether they represent such cases of integration or cases of interference. How then can one distinguish between integration and interference?

2. Integration and interference

One of the most difficult puzzles in the study of bilingualism has
been the separation of cases of integration (borrowing) into the code
from cases of interference in the message. It involves two problems:
(1) the problem of identification, and (2) the problem of relativity.

2.1 The problem of identification

When we listen to an item from another language used in a stretch
of speech, we have at first no direct way of knowing whether the item has
been integrated into the code of the speaker or whether he is bringing it
in from another code. We do not know whether the presence of the foreign item is the result of integration into the code or interference in the
message.

It is indeed possible to study one independently of the other. The
sorts of integration into the code, generally called language borrowing,
have been masterfully classified and analysed by Haugen in a much
quoted article (Haugen 1950). It has also been the subject of some extensive treatises (Deroy 1956).

Some indication of the integration of a word into the code may be had
by observing the way it is used in the message. If it is combined with
the native morphology and phonology it is likely to be more integrated
than if it is not so used. For example, the English verb check when
used in the French sentence, Il l'a checké hier, would indicate some
degree of integration. So could a word whose pronunciation is made to
conform to the phonological structure of the native language (e.g. Spanish estek from steak). But integration into the morphological and phonological systems is very often impossible to observe in any stretch of
speech containing items from another language. For example, the English word cute in the French sentence, Elle est bien cute, could be a
case of borrowing or a case of interference, if we had to rely only on
textual evidence. Witness also the pronunciation of integrated trade
names in the radio advertising of bilingual communities.

If a French-speaking bilingual uses the word sweater in a stretch of
speech, we have no way of knowing whether the word sweater has replaced chandail in his French, or whether he is simply introducing this
word from his English code for anyone of many possible social or psychological reasons. If we discover that he does not know the French

word for <u>sweater</u> and that the word <u>sweater</u> is his French way of saying <u>chandail</u>, we know that we are not up against a case of interference. On the other hand, if he does know how to say <u>chandail</u> in French, this may or may not be an indication that his use of the word <u>sweater</u> is a case of interference. Here we are up against the question of bilingual doublets such as were common in 13th and 14th century England, where English words, like <u>help</u>, and their French equivalents, like <u>aid</u>, were used indifferently and sometimes together. For the desire of the bilingual speaker to make himself understood by his fellow bilinguals can induce him to use both his codes as an extra guarantee. We find this even in the writings produced during the bilingual periods of a country's history; in the literature of Medieval England, for example, we can read such French-English stretches of bilingual redundancy as <u>ignoraunce, thet is unwisdom (The Ancren Riwle, c. 1225), lord and sire, faire and fetisly</u> (Chaucer), <u>olde and auncyent doctours, glasse or mirrour</u> (Caxton). Were these cases of integration or of interference?

2.2 The problem of relativity

Even in highly literate communities there is a permissible range of variation in usage, and on close examination we find that instead of a fixed code and a positive norm, we have an unstable code and a relative norm. The word 'norm' of course, can be ambiguous, meaning either what people expect or what people do. Here we will take the norm to mean what people do and say, not what they say they do. And since all people do not always do the same things in the same ways, the norm is relative. If it were not, languages would be eternal; they would never change.

New elements are continually entering a language and old elements are dropping out. But this intake and fallout is not sudden; it does not happen the day a new grammar or dictionary comes off the press to consecrate its contents as the norm. It is a gradual process which is observable but not observed. It takes place in time at a rate which is highly variable. And the variability of the rate is a function of numerous factors—some stable and others unstable.

The stable factors are all internal; that is, they have to do with the nature of language and the nature of numbers. Their stability depends on the characteristics of the system in which they operate and on its dependence upon the other systems of the language. The fewer elements there are in the system, the more stable the system. A phonological system with less than a hundred units and a limited number of structures is inherently more stable than a grammatical system with a thousand units and more structures. For the number of phonemes in a language constitutes a very small class—usually much less than a hundred items. The loss or addition of a single phoneme, therefore, is likely to disturb the system more than the loss or addition of a grammatical form. For example, if the English language were suddenly to be deprived of the /t-d/ phoneme distinction, the whole system of systems which makes up the language would be affected more than it would by the loss of the -<u>ive</u>/-<u>ove</u> grammatical distinction between present (<u>drive</u>, <u>dive</u>, <u>strive</u> ...) and past (<u>drove</u>, <u>dove</u>, <u>strove</u> ...).

This is perhaps why most items entering the code into its larger classes have both low redundancy and high information content. In the smaller classes of linguistic items, the probability of integration of a foreign element into the code is necessarily lower; but its probability of interference in the message is correspondingly higher. Because of this, its redundancy is high and its information content low. For example, when getting the hang of a foreign accent, the strange sound which consistently replaces a certain allophone in the stream of speech does not on each recurrence add much new information to the message. We come to expect it and to take it for granted, for it can be predicted. In other words, the more predictable the interference, the less it interferes. Grammatical items, in turn, are more stable than items of the vocabulary, which may contain more than ten thousand active elements. These are much more loosely systematized than are elements of the grammar and are consequently less stable.

The inherent degree of stability of a language element, which depends on its function in the system or subsystem to which it belongs, is modified by external factors such as social change and dialect or language contact.

In bilingual communities there will be those who always use certain forms from their other language and who know no other, and yet are always understood because most of their interlocutors are bilingual. There will be for a given concept, those who know both terms and use only one. Those who know both forms and use them indifferently. In other words, the question of whether or not a given element belongs to both codes or only to one does not take a yes/no answer. It is also a matter of degree. If everyone uses one and only one form, that form—even though it comes from and still exists in the other language—is part of the bilingual's languages. It can be said to have been 100% integrated into the other languages (e.g. the word <u>wrench</u> in the French of some Acadians is almost as integrated as is the word <u>sugar</u> in English).

On the other hand, if only half of the population have integrated the form into their code, it can be said to be 50% integrated. The percentage may range anywhere from near zero to 100%. Integration into a code is a matter of degree. But if integration is a matter of degree, what we need are techniques for determining the extent to which the use of a foreign item may be considered normal. In other words, we need methods for measuring the degree of integration.

3. Measuring integration

By what criteria can we measure the extent to which a foreign item has become part of a language code? We can take our measures either (1) from the message or, (2) from the code.

3.1 Measuring from the message

By collecting samples of the speech of bilinguals, it is possible to identify and quantify the foreign elements that are introduced. This can be done from the point of view of their frequency or from the point of view of the range of occurrence.

From the point of view of frequency, it seems reasonable to suppose that, if the norm is what people use, the more frequently people include a foreign element in their speech, the more normal it is. How can we then determine the number of times people use a given word or form? One way of finding out is by counting the number of times that word or form comes up in suitable samples of speech or writing. With this in mind, we obtained samples of the free speech of some fifty Acadian bilinguals. After making extensive tape recordings of the unrehearsed conversation of these bilinguals, we computed the frequency of occurrence of English items in their French speech (Mackey 1966).

It soon became evident, however, that the occurrence of an item from the other language depended largely on what the bilingual happened to be talking about at the time his conversation was being recorded. When he was talking about airplanes, the word <u>wing</u> was likely to occur more often than it did when he was talking about horses, in which case, the word <u>hoof</u> was more likely to occur. On the other hand, a very small but important part of the vocabulary always recurred, no matter what he was talking about; it included words like <u>est</u>, <u>à</u>, <u>de</u>, and <u>je</u>— most of them grammatical words. If one of these words were to be replaced by its equivalent in the other language, the number of times it was so replaced could presumably be used as a measure of its degree of integration into the receiving language. But such words—partly because they are the most highly related to the most systematic and structured areas of the language—were seldom replaced. The few that did occur belonged to classes, like conjunctions, representing the least structured of the structure words. If they ever did enter the language, structure words did so only after many of the content words of the general vocabulary had already been affected. Moreover, the criterion of frequency of occurrence is valid for only a small portion of the total number of elements in the language, and these include the grammatical units. For the bulk of the vocabulary, the frequencies depending as they do on the field or the situation, are unstable and therefore unreliable (Mackey 1965a).

An approach making use of frequency of occurrence is the measurement of the degree of consistency of usage. If a foreign form is consistently used to the exclusion of any other, it may be assumed that the form has been completely integrated into the code. But how can one prove that the usage of such a form is one hundred percent consistent? Another difficulty arises when the degree of consistency varies continually from one situation to the next. This makes the degree of consistency difficult to measure, especially when one considers the multiplicity of situations in which individuals in a multilingual community may be involved. Yet the possibility of measurement has been demonstrated in a study distinguishing consistency of usage in various socioeconomic classes of society using as many as five different styles per person (Labov 1966).

Another way of determining the degree of integration would be by counting the number of texts in which a word occurs (range). Although the most frequent words are also those which occur everywhere (have the greatest range), some words are likely to occur in certain texts more than in others. If a man is talking about the production of eggs, the words hen and chicken are more likely to occur than they would if he were talking about the production of light bulbs, paper cups, or iron ingots. But the fact that these words did not occur when talking about eggs would not indicate that they were unimportant to the speaker.

Many important words are seldom used, even in situations to which they are relevant. We do not often write or talk about our tongues or our noses, but this does not mean that we have little knowledge of or use for these words. When we need them, they are available. Secondly, the number of texts is no indication of the complete range of coverage; it would be difficult to cover all the multitude of possible things about which each individual in a population may want to talk. Finally, with range as with frequency, we are dealing with the usage—with the message as it were, rather than directly with the code which produces the message out of an infinite number of possible messages.

What we need is a criterion of integration that deals directly with the code and is likely to expose the bulk of the vocabulary covering the maximum number fields in which it is likely to be used.

3.2 Measuring from the code

Attempts have been made to suggest ways of finding evidence of integration into the code. These include tests of availability, acceptability, and translatability. Let us first examine the uses of availability.

Availability is a measure of the potential of the items in a code. Whereas frequency of textual occurrence is a suitable measure of language forms which must be used, availability is the appropriate measure for words which may be used. These include the thousands of nouns, verbs, adjectives and adverbs which are more or less at the disposal of the bilingual speaker. How can we get at this storehouse of vocabulary? One way is by asking the subject to supply an inventory. This can be accomplished through a formal test. This availability test has the speaker list items on each code according to any number of semantic fields. To return to the above example of sweater/chandail, we have seen that the occurrence of one in the context of the other language was no indication of integration into the other language. What then would an availability test indicate? If a bilingual includes sweater on top of the list of French words for clothing, and chandail at the bottom of the list, we know that both items are part of his French code; if he lists only sweater in his French code, it is likely that it may have replaced the word chandail, unless that term is used with a different meaning, which is often the case for integrated items in bilingual communities. If in a recorded text therefore, we were then to find the word sweater, we could discount it as a probable case of interference. In other words, we first ask the bilinguals to identify their codes before analyzing samples of their speech to decide the extent to which there is interference or switching between codes.

Availability is not integration, but it can be used as a measure of the degree to which an item comes to mind as belonging to one code or the other of the bilingual. It has been used only for the nongrammatical elements of a language—those which serve as labels for concept categories, especially concrete nouns. Although this does not mean that we exclude abstractions, it does seem fitting that a new measure should start as close as possible to the concrete in order to permit easier evaluation. But how can such a measure be applied to a whole population and its language codes?

One way of measuring the availability of an item in a population is to take a representative sample of that population and have each person supply an inventory of the items in each conceptual, or semantic field (for example, food, clothing, housing, etc.). The type and number of conceptual fields depend on the detail and amount of information desired (Mackey 1969). For example, in the field of clothing we ask each person to supply a list of words he uses for clothing in a given language. Some words will appear on most lists, others on only a few. The number of lists on which a word appears indicates the number of people to which the word has most readily occurred within the time limit (in this case, a quarter of an hour per field). This can be stated as a percentage of the population including the word in their vocabulary of that particular field. In the case of a bilingual population, if one asks for the vocabulary of one language, one may get certain items which really belong to the vocabulary of the bilingual's other language. This may indicate a number of possibilities. The bilingual may know only the item in his other language, or not know to which language the item belongs.

Or he may know both items, but remember one of them more readily than the other.

If he indicates items of the other language in the list, they may well be the only items he knows for the concept that comes to his mind. But we do not have enough evidence to assume that this is always the case. We can only say that these items come more readily to his mind than do the others.

We can assume that you can get at the code which a person has in his head by asking him to write it down. If he does not include an item, however, it does not necessarily mean that it is excluded from his code. Its exclusion or inclusion may be a function of the number of responses, which, in turn, is a function of the time taken to produce the inventory, up to the limit of the total vocabulary of the individual in a given field (Mackey 1969a).

From the inventories, we know the number of persons who have indicated a foreign word as part of their code. We do not yet know the number of persons who understand the native word and yet list the foreign word. This, however, can be checked through a test of translatability (see below). Such a test would tell us whether or not a person knows a word, but not how well he knows it. Persons with an effort of memory and enough time may be able to retrieve the native word. This is borne out in interviews with bilinguals. In such interviews, we find the subjects saying such things as: 'My grandmother used to say something like this'. But because the native word is not uppermost in their minds, they will use the foreign word instead. Forgetting is relative, gradual, and a matter of degree.

It seems safe to assume, therefore, that in the bilingual, French-English Acadian materials that we have analyzed and will use as examples, any given French word is understood and remembered to a certain degree. In a given field, the possibilities are the following: (i) the French word can be excluded (E. = zero), (ii) the English word can be excluded (F. = zero), (iii) both can be excluded (E. + F. = zero), and (iv) either can be dominant.

How can we measure this dominance? We assume that in any given field the inclusion of one word rather than another is an indication that that word has been better remembered. There is a whole literature on word association which seems to bear out this assumption (cf. Marbe's law, Thumb and Marbe 1901). For example, if a person includes the words <u>sweater</u> and <u>scarf</u> and excludes <u>leggings</u>, as types of clothing, we can assume that when thinking or talking about clothing, the corresponding words and the objects to which they refer come more readily to mind.

If for the thing 'sweater' however, the bilingual can remember only the name used in the second language, we can assume that although the object comes to mind, it is associated more readily with its name in the other language. In a group of bilinguals, some will include the concept 'sweater', others will not. Of those who include it some will give the French word (chandail) in the French list; others will include the English word (sweater) in the French list, indicating that it is uppermost in their mind. If all do this, it is that word and not its counterpart in the native language that is uppermost in the minds of most people.

If a hundred people were to include the concept 'sweater' in an inventory of their clothing, it may be assumed that that concept is available to 100% of that population. Out of this hundred who have included the concept if fifty were to put the word sweater in the French list, it may be assumed that the English word is uppermost in the minds of half the people. It has been integrated to that extent into the vocabulary likely to be available. Its degree of integration is 50%, meaning that a person taken at random from those who are likely to use either sweater or chandail is just as likely to use the one as he is to use the other. The probability of sweater being the word is .5 and the probability of chandail is also .5 in situations in which the concept is going to be expressed.

What is true for a hundred people is also true for a thousand, or for any number. And if this number is a valid sample of the population, it can be said that in the given bilingual population the word sweater, no matter what its degree of availability, or its importance in a given semantic field, would have just as much chance of coming to the mind of any person chosen at random as would the word chandail. The words are equally probable and their degree of integration (as expressed by this probability), is equal. This probability (.5) is neither a measure of its likelihood of occurrence (frequency), nor of the number of spoken or written texts in which it is likely to occur (range), nor its importance for a given field (availability). It simply says for a given population in a given field that a specific concept ('sweater') is just as likely to be expressed in English as it is in French. It does not say how many people use both words and to what extent, although this is information that could be obtained with a slight refinement of the technique (see below), which could also indicate for those using such doublets whether they are given different or the same roles as far as meaning or domain is concerned (for example, distinctions between les gars, les garçons, les gosses, and les boys).

The availability test is not the only possible technique enabling us better to distinguish integration from interference. There are also the tests of acceptability and translatability.

The acceptability test was suggested a few years ago by Nils Hasselmo at the Unesco International Seminar on the Description and Measurement of Bilingualism (Kelly 1969: 121-41), and later developed by him in a study of American-Swedish bilinguals (Hasselmo 1970).

The purpose of the test is to obtain a range of possible variation of selected items likely to occur in the normal, everyday speech of the bilinguals. The degree of acceptability of an item is indicated by the average score of a given group of subjects judging recorded sentences on a four-point scale. It is obtained by having each subject in a representative group of bilinguals rate constructed and actually observed test sentences containing elements from the other language. Each sentence is rated as to whether, speaking to a friend in the community, the subject would 'say it that way' almost always, sometimes, never (but others would), or never (and others neither). The results reported showed a complete range of degrees of acceptability.

Another access to the code of the bilingual may be had through a test of translatability, also suggested by Hasselmo. It tests the bilingual's ability to furnish equivalents in his other language. Testing procedures are similar to those used for obtaining indices of acceptability. Here the bilingual hears words from one of his languages in the context of the other and is asked to supply the equivalent form in the language of the text. The equivalent must cover essentially the same content as the test item. If the bilingual is unable to supply a suitable equivalent, it may perhaps be assumed that the item actually belongs to his other code, or to both. For example, in the French sentence, <u>Je voulais enlever la roue, mais j'ai perdu mon wrench</u>, one bilingual whom I tested was unable to find the French equivalent of <u>wrench</u>, insisting that it was after all a French word. Preceding translatability, Hasselmo has a test of identification to find out in which language the bilingual classified a selected group of items, identifying those which he thinks had been taken over from the other language. The results also showed a continuum, ranging from complete identification with one language to complete identification with another.

To sum up, we can try to separate a bilingual's codes in three different ways: (i) by asking him what items each code contains (availability), (ii) by asking him to separate items according to the code to which they belong (acceptability), and (iii) by asking him to transfer items from one code to the other (translatability). These different tests may really be measuring different things. An item which is not very acceptable may yet be the most readily available. We find such conflicts in situations of language contact and dialect contact, like the one exemplified in Stephen Leacock's remark before an audience in England whom he suspected of despising his Canadian accent—'I don't like it any better than you; but it's the best I can do.' A word may also be easily translated and identified as belonging to one language, and yet be more highly available than its equivalent in the other language.

Before any of these measures are used extensively, it would be important to find out the extent to which they are related and in what respect one might be used as a check on the others. It would seem, for example, that translatability could be inversely proportional to acceptability.

Interference, Integration /31

By correlating the results of such tests it seems possible to determine the borrowed items in the bilingual's codes. This would add precision to the quantitative immediate-constituent analysis of recorded samples of typical speech behavior of individual bilinguals to determine the pattern and degree of interference and alternation (Mackey 1965b). It would mean giving the same three tests to representative samples of the bilingual population and calculating the percentage of integration of each item into the other language. Since I have not yet replicated acceptability or translatability tests on a group, I can supply here only an example of the use of the availability test on a sample bilingual population to obtain indications of the degree of integration of items from one code to the other.

4. Integration and availability: Sample measurements

Let us now see how these proposed measurements from the code would work on a sample population. We shall limit our demonstration to the use of availability indices as a measure of integration. The indices will be taken from a survey of the French of almost 2,000 young Acadian (French-English) bilinguals out of a bilingual population of some 200,000 representing about a third of the inhabitants living in an area of 28,000 square miles (New Brunswick). We shall describe (1) the scope and method of investigation before treating, and (2) the types of analysis and the results obtained in establishing integration probabilities.

4.1 Scope and method

The investigation covered a sample population of some 2,000 (1,745) bilinguals under 19 years of age. This sample population produced 33,510 pages of French vocabulary inventory which yielded a total of 887,550 word tokens in 27 semantic fields.

Because of the great volume of material gathered, we decided to limit the first analysis to the responses of the youngest age-group (under 13) in twelve areas and to 16 semantic fields (see Table 1).

This involved the analysis of 11,456 questionnaires which represented the responses of 702 informants in 16 semantic fields, yielding 286,400 tokens.

An analysis of these word tokens, with the aid of a computer, yielded 64,031 different written forms, each of which had to be brought together by hand under the appropriate word type. For example, the forms quetelle, quettil, quitel, and ketel, along with their frequencies, had to be rewritten under their word type, kettle.

The net result of this work was a list of 10,521 word types representing the total available French vocabulary of the 700 young bilinguals in the 16 semantic fields, as supplied by them in the five to seven hours of cumulative testing time. Most of this vocabulary (about 90%) was indeed French; but there were significant numbers of English words, and also loan-blends, Canadianisms, and even neologisms of the bilingual's own creation (see Table 2).

Each of these 10,521 word types was then put on a punch-card along with the number of bilinguals in each age-group supplying the word. A computer program was then elaborated which would: (i) arrange the words in semantic fields, (ii) total the frequencies for each word type, (iii) within each semantic field arrange the words in decreasing order of frequency, (iv) calculate for each word its percentage of the total response, (v) list the rank of each word, and (vi) print out the results with all words grouped according to the semantic fields and ranked according to percentage of total response.

The results, as printed out by the computer, appeared in some 250 pages of tables. Each table had 12 columns which successively indicated the word, its rank, its percentage of the total population listing it, and the totals and percentages for each age-group (see Table 3).

4.2 Analysis and probabilities

The 702 informants aged 8 to 12 (reduced for some fields to 661), completed a total of 11,456 questionnaires in 16 semantic fields, produced a total of 286,400 word tokens representing 64,031 word forms, which were later reduced to 10,521 word types.

Of these 10,521 different word types, 4,731 (44.1%) appeared only once. The number varied according to the semantic field, the fewest being in the field of clothing (128) and the greatest number being in the field of pastimes (536).

On top of each list, word types with the highest response, which accounted for 75% of the total, were all in French. Most of the code integration from English into French was found in the lower 25% of the list, indications that the commonest words in the French language of these bilinguals were still French.

The proportion of words replaced to words retained was about 3/17, that is, the lists supplied an average of 3 English words to 17 French words. But the proportion varied according to the semantic field. For the parts of the body, it is one English word for 26 French words (English 11, French 285); whereas for the field of cooking, the proportion of English to French is 1/5 (111/540) (see Table 2).

Some words, however, were counted as neither English nor French. These included 20 so-called loan-blends, 165 Canadianisms, and 418 neologisms. Under loan-blends were listed such French expressions as station à feu, constructed on an English model (fire station). Under Canadianisms, we included those items constructed from French materials but peculiar to the area from which they came, for example, moulin à coudre. Under neologisms, we listed all unidentified forms, many of which seemed to be of the informant's own invention; for example, words like licerpitant. For the distribution of these three categories by semantic field, see Table 2.

But this distribution of the everyday vocabulary of the young Acadian bilinguals between English and French is not sufficient to reveal the relative importance of the French or English terms in the community. We are interested in knowing what this large percentage of English replacements actually represents, of determining the extent to which English, the transmitting language, has entered the French, the receiving language, of the community. It is evident that not everyone has replaced the French term by the English word, because for most English words we have also the French equivalents. For each word we are able to tell the percentage of our bilingual population preserving the French word when speaking in French. For most words, these form a majority of the population. For example, whereas 95% of the bilinguals speaking French would use the word manteau, only 3% would use the word coat. There were some terms, however, like flashlight, mixer, map, pickles, office, and manager, where the English term seems to be ousting the French in the speech of the community.

We were now in a position to determine the extent to which (Lt) the transmitting language (English) had been integrated into the (Lr) receiving language (French) of the bilinguals.

4.2.1 Probabilities

The first step was to extract all available English items (At) from the French inventory, and then to search the inventory for French equivalents (Ar). In each case we listed the percentage of the population which included the words and compared both figures. For example, in the semantic field of clothing 94.7% included manteau, and only 3.1% listed coat. Whereas in the field of cooking, three times more people listed mixer or mix-master (6.9%) as included the French equivalent (mélangeur 1.8%). For other items, like flashlight, there was no French word listed by a single person.

Knowing the percentage of the bilingual population which include in their inventory of one language (Lr) a given item from the other (Lt) or another language (if more than two languages are involved), it is possible to calculate the probable degree of integration (pI) of a vocabulary item (V) of the transmitting language (Lt), in this case English, as a replacement for a vocabulary item in the receiving language (Lr), in this case French, since it would be equal to the availability of the transmitted item (At) over the sum ( ) of the availability of both items ($At + Ar$). Or,

$$pI\ (VLt > VLr) = \frac{At}{A}$$

In other words, we divide the combined percentages (A = At + Ar) by the percentage listed for the transmitting, or lending, language and state the results as a proportion of 100. For example, in the inventories of French words for clothing, 11.4% of the bilinguals listed foulard, and 6.6% included scarf. The latter has therefore an integration probability of

$$pI = \frac{At}{A} = \frac{6.6}{6.6 + 11.4} = \frac{6.6}{18} = .367$$

This would mean that if the word scarf were to appear in a stretch of French speech recorded in the area, the probability that it is part of the code would be .367. If, on the other hand, the word flashlight were to appear there would be a probability of almost 1.00—that is, it is almost certain that it had been completely integrated into the local code. If the word head appeared, however, the converse would be true; it is almost certainly not part of the local code and the probability would be almost 1.00 for a case of interference—not of integration. In other words, interference would be inversely proportional to integration. The more an item is integrated into a code, the less likely that its appearance in the message—in the speech of a bilingual—would be a case of interference.

4.2.2 Relationships

Finally, what is the relationship between integration and availability? Are they completely independent, or are they related? If so, to what extent?

A first approximation to an answer may be studied by plotting the one against the other. If we therefore take all the words in the sample selected from the 16 semantic fields and plot their degrees of availability (At + Ar) (first two columns in Table 4) against their probability of integration (last column of Table 4), we can see that the distribution of the points of relationship is not haphazard (see Figure 1 on Integration as related to Availability). There is an observable tendency for these points to cluster low in the availability scale. In the sample examined, most items entering the code are the least readily remembered.

If we take a closer look at the appended Figure, we notice the following: (a) None of the words from the transmitting language (English) represents concepts that are highly available (upper right corner of Figure). Is this necessarily so, or does it reflect the fact that the basic French vocabulary of these young bilinguals is still exclusively French? (b)

Few highly available words have entered the code from the other language (upper half of Figure). Is this because a highly available item is more strongly associated with its most usual form, or is it simply an indication of the fact that few of the important French words have been replaced? (c) The great majority of the replacements occurred in words supplied by less than a third of the sample population (lower third of Figure). (d) More than 90% of the correlations are below the diagonal line leading from the highest degree of availability to the lowest probability. Most of those above the line represent pairs which pose special semantic problems, like those of imbalance in semantic diversity (e.g. E. map = F. carte géographique; carte = map, postcard, card) (Mackey 1969). These should be checked against the results of translatability tests.

An overall glance at the figure might give the general impression that the probability of a foreign item being integrated into the other code of the bilingual is inversely proportional to its degree of availability. These figures are quite insufficient to enable one to come to such a conclusion. In the first place, they are based on only 10% of the integrated data to be found in the analysed part of the sample, since the intention is simply to illustrate a method of expressing the relativity of integration. Secondly, the data are taken from only 16 general semantic fields in a single geographical area, and within a limited age-group.

What the figure does illustrate, however, is that, for this particular age-group within the particular geographical area and language community, the probability of integration of their most important (available) concrete words is in general not high enough to oust the native equivalents. If, however, we were to present a breakdown by semantic field, some fields might show a line of a different angle, a different delineation of the pattern of relationships, in which many important words might show a high probability of integration. If we were to use subjects speaking highly mixed languages we would presumably get other patterns. In other words, the analytic procedure illustrated here might be useful to indicate the degree of mixture of languages and dialects in contact.

It may be that most items entering the code of a language start at a low level of availability, but only after the probability of remembering the native word has declined sufficiently to make the probability of the foreign equivalent dominant. Whether or not this is always the case can be decided only after extensive surveys and widespread experimentation with different semantic fields, different populations and different languages.

The results presented here are valid only for the Acadian areas of the Canadian Maritimes, particularly those in New Brunswick, for a limited age-group, and for a few of the most concrete and universal semantic fields. It would now be necessary to extend the analysis to other semantic fields and other age-groups in order to find out whether or not the relationship between integration and availability changes with age and area.

Conclusion

Until then, we may hazard the following general conclusions on the analysis of integration as distinct from interference:

(1) Conventional synchronic analysis is unsuited to the description of mixed and rapidly changing codes.
(2) Code integration is relative.
(3) Its relativity can be measured.
(4) Interference can be stated in terms of this relative integration.

This may not be the only way out of the dilemma; but I should be satisfied if this paper gives some indication that a way can be found.

TABLE 1.

Sample Population: Age and Area Distribution

Age-group	Town	County	No. of bilinguals
8-9	St-Jacques	Madawaska	35
8-9	Bathurst	Gloucester	26
9-10	St-Jacques	Madawaska	35
9-10	Bathurst	Gloucester	25
9-10	Shippegan	Gloucester	100
9-10	Petit Rocher	Restigouche	90
9-10	Drummond	Victoria	36
10-11	Bathurst	Gloucester	31
10-11	Shédiac	Westmorland	26
10-11	Rivière-du-Portage	Gloucester	40
10-11	Rogersville	Kent	33
10-11	Tracadie	Gloucester	37
10-11	Ste-Anne	Madawaska	35
10-11	St-François	Madawaska	28
11-12	Bathurst	Gloucester	27
11-12	Campbellton	Restigouche	29
11-12	Tracadie	Gloucester	83
Total			702

TABLE 2.

Semantic Fields: Distribution of Vocabularies

Semantic Field (in French)	French	English	Canadian	Blends	Neol.	Totals
1. The body	285	11	3	0	24	323
2. Clothing	248	94	5	0	13	360
3. Housing	569	84	10	0	13	676
4. Furniture	474	80	16	0	9	579
5. Food	346	104	3	2	33	488
6. Meals	332	61	2	4	9	408
7. Cooking	549	111	11	0	14	685
8. Schooling	597	83	11	0	13	704
9. Heating and light	477	56	4	0	41	578
10. City life	760	109	2	0	33	904
11. Town and village	605	112	8	1	18	744
12. Transport	501	103	5	0	37	646
13. Farming	688	64	16	4	36	808
14. Animals	249	44	3	0	41	337
15. Games	874	189	30	5	45	1,143
16. Occupations	951	106	36	4	39	1,138
Totals	8505	1401	165	20	418	10,521

TABLE 3. Sample Page of Computer Print-out

Cuisine

Age Population	rank	9 – 12 700		9 61		10 267		11 203		12 123	
		%	pop.	%	pop.	%	pop.	%	pop.	%	pop.
Poêle	1	92.5	605	68.8	42	95.8	256	94.5	192	93.4	115
Table	2	82.2	538	86.8	53	85.3	228	74.8	152	85.3	105
Chaise	3	78.1	511	70.4	43	80.8	216	72.4	147	85.3	105
Armoire	4	74.3	486	63.9	39	79.7	213	59.6	121	91.8	113
Cuillère	5	68.3	447	26.2	16	48.6	130	110.3	224	62.6	77
Couteau	6	64.5	422	32.7	20	50.1	134	92.1	187	65.8	81
Fourchette	7	62.8	411	29.5	18	48.3	129	93.1	189	60.9	75
Assiette	8	52.9	346	22.9	14	41.1	110	75.3	153	56.0	69
Chaudron	9	39.6	259	26.2	16	47.1	126	36.4	74	34.9	43
Tasse	10	37.6	246	18.0	11	32.5	87	48.2	98	40.6	50
Plat	11	35.0	229	18.0	11	42.3	113	34.4	70	28.4	35
Verre	12	35.0	229	21.3	13	27.7	74	43.8	89	43.0	53
Frigidaire	13	30.1	197	9.8	6	36.7	98	25.1	51	34.1	42
Réfrigérateur	14	29.9	196	32.7	20	22.4	60	31.0	63	43.0	53
Radio	15	24.1	158	8.1	5	29.2	78	20.6	42	26.2	33
Laveuse	16	22.4	147	8.1	5	23.9	64	19.7	40	30.8	38
Sink	17	22.0	144	9.8	6	29.9	80	20.1	41	13.8	17
Boite	18	21.8	143	1.6	1	19.4	52	21.1	43	38.2	47
Evier	19	21.4	140	24.5	15	13.8	37	25.1	51	30.0	37

Table 3 is continued on pp. 216–217.

TABLE 3 (Cont.)

Cuisine

Age Population	rank	9 - 12 700		9 61		10 267		11 203		12 123	
		%	pop.	%	pop.	%	pop.	%	pop.	%	pop.
Porte	20	17.7	116	34.4	21	19.4	52	5.4	11	26.0	32
Horloge	21	16.6	109	4.9	3	13.8	37	13.7	28	33.3	41
Bol	22	15.2	100	13.1	8	11.6	31	24.6	50	8.9	11
Soucoupe	23	14.5	95	3.2	2	13.8	37	15.2	31	20.3	25
Fenêtre	24	14.3	94	32.7	20	12.7	34	5.4	11	23.5	29
Tiroir	25	14.3	94	1.6	1	20.9	56	9.8	20	13.8	17
Pan	26	13.9	91	8.1	5	20.2	54	8.3	17	12.1	15
Lumière	27	13.7	90	19.6	12	17.6	47	6.8	14	13.8	17
Salière	28	12.8	84	.0	0	8.2	22	22.6	46	13.0	16
Can	29	11.4	75	6.5	4	13.1	35	14.7	30	4.8	6
Grille-pain	30	11.3	74	8.1	5	4.4	12	21.1	43	11.3	14
Poivrière	31	11.1	73	.0	0	6.7	18	20.6	42	10.5	13
Sécheuse	32	11.1	73	3.2	2	9.3	25	13.7	28	14.6	18
Pompe	33	10.8	71	3.2	2	8.2	22	9.3	19	22.7	28
Balai	34	10.5	69	6.5	4	10.8	29	5.9	12	19.5	24
Bombe	35	10.3	68	6.5	4	11.6	31	10.3	21	9.7	12
Rideau	35	10.3	68	9.8	6	11.2	30	5.9	12	16.2	20
Vaisselle	37	9.7	64	6.5	4	10.1	27	6.8	14	15.4	19
Télévision	38	9.4	62	9.8	6	13.4	36	6.4	13	5.6	7
Planche à repasser	39	9.3	61	8.1	5	8.2	22	7.8	16	14.6	18

Toaster	39	9.3	61	1.6	1	10.4	28	9.3	19	10.5	13
Cafetière	41	9.0	59	4.9	3	8.9	24	9.3	19	10.5	13
Portrait	42	8.7	57	4.9	3	7.4	20	5.4	11	18.6	23
Batteur d'oeufs	43	8.5	56	8.1	5	10.8	29	7.8	16	4.8	6
Sucrier	43	8.5	56	1.6	1	4.8	13	16.2	33	7.3	9
Téléphone	43	8.5	56	3.2	2	9.3	25	8.3	17	9.7	12
Pot	46	8.4	55	1.6	1	2.9	8	16.7	34	9.7	12
Miroir	47	8.2	54	6.5	4	8.6	23	5.4	11	13.0	16
Thépot	48	7.9	52	.0	0	6.3	17	14.7	30	4.0	5
Lavabo	49	7.7	51	1.6	1	9.7	26	4.9	10	11.3	14
Beurrier	50	7.1	47	1.6	1	4.1	11	12.3	25	8.1	10
Fauteuil	51	7.0	46	4.9	3	2.2	6	3.9	8	23.5	29
Chaise berceuse	52	6.8	45	4.9	3	10.4	28	4.4	9	4.0	5
Bouilloire	53	6.4	42	.0	0	7.4	20	3.4	7	12.1	15
Couteau à pain	53	6.4	42	1.6	1	1.4	4	15.2	31	4.8	6
Nappe	53	6.4	42	3.2	2	3.3	9	9.8	20	8.9	11
Banc	56	5.9	39	1.6	1	9.2	25	3.4	7	4.8	6
Casserole	56	5.9	39	9.8	6	6.3	17	6.4	13	2.4	3
Garde-robe	56	5.9	39	3.2	2	7.1	19	3.4	7	8.9	11
Fourneau	59	5.8	38	19.6	12	5.2	14	1.9	4	6.5	8
Calendrier	60	5.6	37	3.2	2	4.8	13	2.4	5	13.8	17
Fer à repasser	60	5.6	37	1.6	1	5.2	14	6.4	13	7.3	9
Crucifix	62	5.5	36	.0	0	6.3	17	3.9	8	8.9	11
Chantepleure	63	5.0	33	1.6	1	6.7	18	5.4	11	2.4	3
Machine à laver	63	5.0	33	.0	0	2.9	8	6.4	13	9.7	12
Couteau à viande	65	4.8	32	.0	0	2.2	6	10.3	21	4.0	5
Cup	65	4.8	32	.0	0	2.9	8	11.8	24	.0	0
Eau	65	4.8	32	6.5	4	4.8	13	5.9	12	2.4	3

TABLE 4.

Integration Probabilities: English into French

English (At) >	French (Ar)	pI
1. The body		
brain .3%	cerveau 15.2%	0.019
jaw .1%	mâchoire 1.6%	0.058
2. Clothing		
sweater 8.7%	chandail 86.9%	0.091
jumper 1.1%	_____ 86.9%	0.012
suit 8.1%	habit 13.6%	0.373
scarf 6.6%	foulard 11.4%	0.366
belt 5.2%	ceinture 17.5%	0.229
slacks 5.2%	pantalons 78.1%	0.062
coat 3.1%	manteau 94.7%	0.031
skirt 2.3%	jupe 61.1%	0.036
overalls 1.6%	salopettes 5.9%	0.213
tie 1.1%	cravate 46.2%	0.232
boots .2%	bottes 29.7%	0.006
_____ .2%	bottines 18.3%	0.108
slippers .1%	pantoufles 13.6%	0.007
3. Housing		
sink 4.8%	évier 6.0%	0.444
attic 2.3%	grenier 26.3%	0.080
plug .7%	prise de courant .4%	0.636
4. Furniture		
sink 12.2%	évier 18.0%	0.403
_____ 12.2%	lavabo 13.5%	0.474
fridge 3.7%	réfrigérateur 28.8%	0.113
_____ 3.7%	frigidaire 31.0%	0.106
desk 3.2%	pupître 17.9%	0.151
bathtub 2.8%	bain 11.7%	0.193
lights 2.5%	lumières 18.2%	0.120
chesterfield 2.3%	sofa 41.6%	0.052
_____ 2.3%	divan 8.6%	0.211
washer .7%	laveuse 44.3%	0.001
_____ .7%	machine à laver 5.9%	0.010
5. Food		
bean 4.7%	fève 30.0%	0.013
pickle 2.6%	cornichon 1.0%	0.722
corn .5%	blé d'Inde 25.7%	0.019
radish .1%	radis 4.7%	0.020
6. Meals		
cup 10.2%	tasse 84.9%	0.107

TABLE 4 (Cont.).

English (At) >	French (Ar)	pI
napkin 6.6%	serviette 18.3%	0.265
glass 1.0%	verre 87.9%	0.001
salt .4%	sel 9.3%	0.041
fork .3%	fourchette 99.7%	0.030
7. Cooking		
sink 22.0%	évier 21.4%	0.506
_____ 22.0%	lavabo 7.7%	0.740
can 11.4%	boîte 21.8%	0.343
toaster 9.3%	grille-pain 11.3%	0.451
mixer 2.7%	mélangeur 1.8%	0.600
mix-master 4.2%	_____ 1.8%	0.700
8. Schooling		
map 40.3%	carte géographique 21.1%	0.656
_____ 40.3%	carte 13.5%	0.749
pen .1%	plume 63.9%	0.001
_____ .1%	stylo 6.0%	0.016
pencil .1%	crayon 90.3%	0.001
9. Heating and light		
flashlight 19.1%	lampe de poche 0%	1.000
bulb 7.8%	ampoule 15.3%	0.337
heater 2.5%	chaufferette 10.1%	0.198
fireplace 2.1%	foyer 4.5%	0.318
oil 1.3%	huile 73.5%	0.173
furnace 1.2%	fournaise 68.7%	0.171
stove .4%	poêle 94.3%	0.004
10. City life		
office 11.5%	bureau 3.1%	0.787
post office 6.5%	bureau de poste 21.3%	0.233
fire station 1.5%	poste de pompier 4.4%	0.254
barber 1.3%	barbier 10.2%	0.113
_____ 1.3%	coiffeur 6.2%	0.173
11. Town and village		
bowling alley .4%	salle de quilles 5.2%	0.070
bank 1.8%	banque 14.3%	0.111
drugstore .6%	pharmacie 2.7%	0.181
fire station .4%	poste de pompiers 1.5%	0.210
_____ .4%	station de pompier .6%	0.400
_____ .4%	bâtisse à incendie .2%	0.666
liquor store .4%	commission des liqueurs 2.5%	0.137
city hall .2%	hôtel de ville .9%	0.188
12. Transport		
truck 19.8%	camion 74.8%	0.209

TABLE 4 (Cont.).

English (At) >	French (Ar)	pI
trolley 3.2%	tramway 4.0%	0.444
streetcar .2%	_____ 4.0%	0.047
boat .6%	bateau 89.7%	0.006
steamer .4%	bateau à vapeur 1.2%	0.250
13. Farming		
digger 1.5%	bêcher 1.8%	0.454
bin .3%	bacul .3%	0.500
row .1%	sillon 9.8%	0.010
flower .1%	fleur 12.6%	0.007
weeding .1%	esherbage 5.0%	0.019
spray .1%	arroseur 5.2%	0.018
14. Animals		
buffalo 2.8%	bison 10.7%	0.207
raccoon 1.2%	raton laveur 5.3%	0.187
cat .9%	chat 98.1%	0.090
lamb .6%	agneau 7.8%	0.071
beaver .4%	castor 27.8%	0.141
pig .4%	cochon 72.1%	0.005
deer .3%	chevreuil 56.0%	0.005
monkey .3%	singe 33.3%	0.008
15. Games		
basketball 11.3%	ballon-panier 21.0%	0.349
race 3.8%	course 25.1%	0.131
bowling 2.6%	quilles 24.1%	0.097
checkers 2.3%	dames 32.8%	0.065
volleyball 2.3%	ballon-volant 5.1%	0.310
cards .3%	cartes 48.0%	0.006
16. Occupations		
manager 4.6%	gérant 3.4%	0.575
boss .3%	_____ 3.4%	0.081
nurse 2.6%	garde-malade 37.5%	0.064
_____ 2.6%	garde 2.1%	0.553
engineer 2.5%	ingénieur 8.5%	0.227
cook 2.1%	cuisinier 14.8%	0.124
plumber 1.0%	plombier 26.5%	0.037
farmer .9%	fermier 36.7%	0.023
_____ .9%	cultivateur 8.5%	0.095
driver .6%	chauffeur 23.2%	0.252
garageman .6%	garagiste 15.3%	0.037
milkman .4%	laitier 9.5%	0.040
lumberjack .3%	bûcheron 24.5%	0.012
reporter .1%	journaliste 6.4%	0.015
secretary .1%	secrétaire 9.6%	0.010

INTEGRATION AS RELATED TO AVAILABILITY

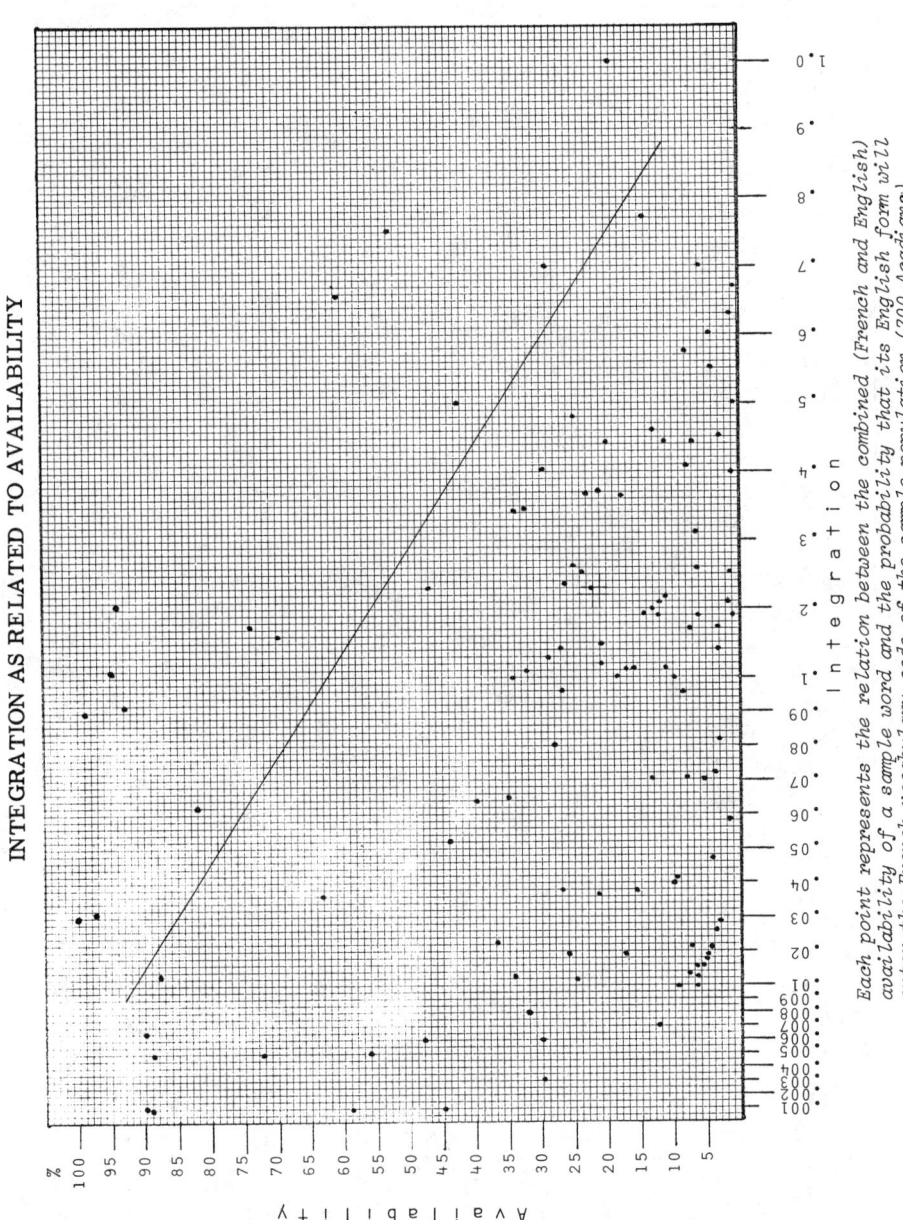

Each point represents the relation between the combined (French and English) availability of a sample word and the probability that its English form will enter the French vocabulary code of the sample population (700 Acadians).

REFERENCES

Bousfield, W. A., and W. D. Barclay. 1950. The relationship between order and frequency of occurrence of restricted associative responses. Journal of experimental psychology 40: 643-647.
Brotsky, S. J., D. C. Butler and M. L. Linton. 1967. Association time, commonality, and the test-retest reliability of free association responses. Psychonomic science 9: 319-320.
Chomsky, N. 1964. Degrees of grammaticalness. The structure of language: Readings in the philosophy of language. Jerry Fodor and Ferrold Katz, eds. Englewood Cliffs, New Jersey: Prentice-Hall.
Coleman, E. B. 1965. Responses to a scale of grammaticalness. Journal of verbal learning and verbal behavior 4: 521-527.
Deroy, L. 1956. L'emprunt linguistique. Paris: Les Belles Lettres.
Diebold, A. R. 1961. Code-switching in Greek-English bilingual speech. Georgetown University Monograph Series on Languages and Linguistics 15: 53-59.
Fishman, J. A. 1964. Language Maintenance and language shift as a field of inquiry; a definition of the field and suggestions for its further development. Linguistics 9: 32-70.
Green, E. 1963. On grading phonic interference. Language Learning 13: 85-96.
Gumperz, J. J. 1964. Linguistic and social interaction in two communities. American anthropologist 66 (6, Part 2): 137-153.
Hasselmo, Nils. 1970. On diversity in American-Swedish. (Unpublished paper). Mimeographed, University of Minnesota.
Haugen, E. I. 1950. The analysis of linguistic borrowing. Language 26: 210-231.
Herdan, G. 1966. How can quantitative methods contribute to our understanding of language mixture and language borrowing? Statistique et analyse linguistique. Paris: Presses universitaires de France, 17-39.
Hill, A. A. 1961. Grammaticality. Word 17: 1-10.
Jakobovits, L. A. and Lambert, W. E. 1961. Semantic satiation among bilinguals. Journal of experimental psychology 62: 576-582.
Kelly, L. G., ed. 1969. Description et mesure du bilinguisme/ Description and measurement of bilingualism. Toronto: University of Toronto Press (for the Canadian Unesco Commission).
Labov, W. 1969. Contraction deletion and inherent variability of the English copula. Language 45: 715-762.
Lambert, W. E. 1955. Measurement of the linguistic dominance of bilinguals. The journal of abnormal and social psychology 50: 197-200.
Le Page, R. B. 1968. Problems of description in multilingual communities. Transactions of the Philological Society of Great Britain 1968: 189-212.

Mackey, W. F. 1965a. Language teaching analysis (chapter 6). London and Bloomington: Longmans and Indiana University Press.
──────. 1965b. Bilingual Interference; its analysis and measurement. The journal of communication 15: 239-249.
──────. 1966. The measurement of bilingual behavior. Canadian psychologist 7: 75-92.
──────. 1967. Bilingualism as a world problem. Montreal: Harvest House.
──────. 1969. Concept categories as measures of culture distance. Quebec: I.C.R.B. (prepared for Man, language and society. The Hague: Mouton (in the press).
──────. 1970a. Optimization of the population-response ratio in lexicometric sampling. Quebec: I.C.R.B. (To appear in Tijdeschrift voor Toegepaste Linguistiek).
──────. 1970b. Toward a quantum linguistics. Quebec: I.C.R.B. (prepared for the Linguistic Department Seminar of McGill University).
──────. Theory and method in the study of bilingualism. London: Oxford University Press (in the press).
Maclay, H., and M. D. Sleator. 1960. Responses to language: Judgment of grammaticalness. International journal of American linguistics 26: 275-282.
Quirk, R , and J. Svartvik. 1966. Investigating linguistic acceptability. The Hague: Mouton.
Saussure, de F. 1915. Cours de linguistique générale (5 ed., 1960). Paris: Payot.
Thumb, A. and Karl Marbe. 1901. Experimentelle Untersuchungen über die psychologischen Grundlagen der sprachlichen Analogiebildung.
Weinreich, U. 1953. Languages in contact; findings and problems. New York: Linguistic Circle of New York (Series: Linguistic Circle of New York, Publications, No. 1).
──────. 1957. On the description of phonic interference. Word 13: 1-11.

II. The Multicultural Community and Policy

TYPES OF BILINGUAL COMMUNITIES

E. Glyn Lewis

0. Introduction. For practical purposes my discussion will be limited to mass or societal bilingualism as distinct from that which characterizes an individual in an otherwise homogeneous community. Second, though it is advisable to bear in mind the fact that a collection of individuals associated in any one place with a particular institution such as the United Nations or the EEC may be construed to be a community, I shall limit my discussion to historical rather than contrived groups--the bilingualism of the latter is elitist rather than societal. Third, while it is possible to consider bilingual communities on one of two levels--that is, the maximum level of the national community (which may be bilingual without necessarily all the local communities being bilingual), I shall have regard in the main for the minimum level of the local community or cluster of communities. A typology of states like that produced by Falch (1973) according to the types of language policy they pursue in respect of their minorities is useful, but since it does not set out to consider how far such policies are implemented, it has only a limited value for educationists and administrators. The minimum level or microlevel analysis stands at the point of intersection of policy and implementation.

But, it may be asked, why bother about a typology at all? Why not consider each local problem as it arises? The answer is that a typology facilitates comparison and without comparison we cannot generate sufficiently general hypotheses--we remain in the field of ad hoc programs, limited tactics with little value for prediction. Science is based on comparison because science is measurement and classification. Nevertheless, I concede that comparison may be achieved without resorting to the production of a typology. Indeed, one may achieve more sophisticated comparisons by ignoring the name given to a type of community and comparing the operation of a number of selected variables irrespective of how they cluster to constitute a type of community. Instead of comparing names (such as segregated or diffused bilingual communities) one may deal with such variables as size, stability, geographic location, indigenousness, length of residence, etc. Such a multivariate approach (cf. Carroll 1975 and Lewis and Massad 1975) would certainly be more incisive than one which relies on a given typology, but from the standpoint of a teacher and administrator it is both time-consuming and uneconomical. A blunt instrument is often more effective than one which is razor sharp. Furthermore, bilingual education in any community is 'structure dependent': the form of education is only one of the institutions which characterize the community. Each of those other institutions is itself a cluster of variables and each institution would have to be taken into account in analyzing the bilingual characteristic of the community.

1. Motivation of the advocacy of bilingual education. At the present level of studies of bilingual education, in attempting to identify types of bilingual communities we have to rely on more or less educated experience rather than hard evidence provided by analytical studies, and all this paper offers is a target for criticism which may enable us to emerge with more satisfactory suggestions. Fundamental to this approach is the belief that the important variables are more often than not historical, and have to do very much with the nonlinguistic sources of heterogeneity within the community. Insofar as we are by definition concerned with bilingual communities, the most salient source of such heterogeneity is obviously linguistic. But consciousness of linguistic differences may be, and very often is, a surrogate for the consciousness of other sources of difference, a symbol of them, or a means of reinforcing consciousness of nonlinguistic differences. I believe that advocacy of bilingual education--valuable and indeed necessary though such an education may be in and for itself--has been used, legitimately, as a means of drawing attention to what in my view are possibly more vital needs. Before bene esse comes esse; before a community can live well, it has first simply to survive. Bilingual education has been advocated ostensibly for entirely pedagogic reasons, while the fundamental rationale for the proposal is to bring about greater political, economic, and social equality. Language is a convenient focal issue because it is a more categorical marker of difference than material deprivation. In any community poor and ill-fed people are to be found in all language groups, majority and minority alike, though the incidence may be greater among the former. Language is a recognizable and unequivocal marker and can therefore fully reflect and reinforce consciousness of the other disparities. This approach to bilingual education is perfectly justifiable because all forms of education are concerned with the redistribution of power or the maintenance of its current distribution. Consequently, to ensure

the possibility of any fruitful outcome a consideration of types
of bilingual communities, though it presupposes the existence
of linguistic differences, should give at least equal weight to
the resolution of associated sources of heterogeneity. Greatly
though we may value a particular language, as humanists we do
not, in the last resort, aim to teach the language so much as
to enable the speakers of that language to develop their full
potential as persons.

2. **Sources of heterogeneity in bilingual communities: Relevant variables.** That being the case, we need to discuss the
sources of heterogeneity which may be associated with differences of language in any significant way (Linz and Miguel 1975).
First, there are differences in economic development between
groups in contact. Declining differences in economic and social
levels between the speakers of Welsh and the English has coincided with the decline in linguistic heterogeneity which has been
brought about partly and negatively by assimilation, but also
affirmatively by the expansion of bilingual education among
speakers of English. Another source of heterogeneity is the
extent to which a language is regarded as central to the maintenance of its way of life or culture, or as is the case with very
many groups simply as one of the traits associated with that
culture. Another source of heterogeneity, the degree of political participation, characterizes local communities in Southern
Africa, the United States, and the USSR, for instance, though
to a lesser extent if at all in the Netherlands (except with immigrant groups), in Switzerland, or Britain. These are only a
very few of the sources of heterogeneity which are associated
with the historical development of many bilingual communities.
They constitute a set of variables which are important primarily
because they affect attitudes.

There are other historical or diachronic variables which could
be exemplified, but I turn now to variables which simply reflect
the current situation of the community. They are synchronic
variables. The first of these we may term 'diffusion' variables
since they have to do with the openness or the occlusive, closed
character of the community. Some communities welcome contact,
and members of some ethnic groups in contact are known to
have changed their ethnic affiliation or character not once but
twice or thrice on account of the fluidity of the group. Other
communities, because of authoritarian attitudes, dogmatism, a
feeling of self-sufficiency, pride, or indifference, are opposed
to contact and are virtually closed communities. Local groups
of immigrant communities in Britain are seldom motivated to advocate bilingual programs on the model of those already existing
in the traditional minority areas of the country. The replication in the United States of types of programs for Canadian bilingual communities is evidence of the value of an open society.
The same was true at one time of the Republic of South Africa,

which was keenly interested in developing educational programs for varying European types of bilingual communities.

Diffusion variables also have to do with the impact of foreign policy on the local communities. In the USSR bilingual education, which is an aspect of 'nationalities policy', has changed direction on more than one occasion, according to the state of the country's foreign relations. When the state is threatened, the rights of minorities are apt to be ignored. Bilingual education affecting German and Asian communities in the United States has been affected by two World Wars. Nor was it only the languages actually spoken by enemy nations that suffered, but the validity of the concept of bilingual education was put at risk. In England the idea of bilingual education for the majority English-speaking children was canvassed as a possibility only with the imminence of British entry into the European Economic Community.

A second set of variables differentiating bilingual communities we may term 'settings', since they concern the present context of contact. The most obvious variable in this class is the indigenousness or nonindigenousness of one or other or both groups. The United States has two such indigenous communities: on the one hand, those which are primordial or autochthonous, the Amerindians; and on the other hand, those which are incorporated by the purchase of their land or by more violent means--Mexican Americans. Of the nonindigenous or immigrant groups, there are also two types: those like the Cubans who are tied by language to indigenous groups, and the 'free-floating' groups like the Scandinavians, Italians, or Germans, who have no such ties with the indigenous. The differences between such groups are not unimportant because the indigenous of either type are historically and closely tied to large and identifiable territories in the United States, the existence of which serves to reinforce attachment to native languages. Territorial bases have always been important for minorities in Europe, including those of the USSR, Yugoslavia, Switzerland, and Belgium. It is the basis of pressure by Quebec.

Another 'setting' type of variable concerns the institutional structure of the community. If we take education as one such institution, we find that two groups in contact may have entirely different views concerning the structural dependence of bilingualism on other institutions. For instance, when two languages are being used in the community, one possibility is that one of them may be ignored institutionally. If both languages are included in the system of education of a particular community, the bilingual system may be entirely independent of the mainstream structure, as tends to be the case with Amerindian Contract Schools. Or the local system may be totally integrated with the mainstream (or unmarked system), as is the case in Wales or Ireland, where few schools are not completely bilingual. Or the local system may be parallel to or exist as an alternative to the mainstream system, as is the case in the USSR, where nationality schools may coexist with Russian medium schools in any part of the country. Or the local system may be peripheral, a loose adjunct, as is the case in the United States with very many programs for the Italians, or Greeks, or French. Or, finally, the form of bilingual education may be eccentric to, or outside the orbit of, the mainstream system, as is the case with elitist schools like the United Nations International School in New York.

But irrespective of the kind of relationship which exists between the local community provision and the mainstream system, the former will invariably be affected by important characteristics of the mainstream. Some of the most important of these characteristics have to do with the degree to which the mainstream has catered and continues to cater for the material aspirations of the minority without taking language differences into account. Attitudes to bilingual education were affected in Wales for a long time by the fact that the nonmarked system, without acknowledging, to any significant degree, the existence of the Welsh language, was successful in catering for the upward mobility of speakers of Welsh. This is equally true of the United States (so far as concerns the earlier immigration groups especially) and is the case at present in the USSR, where political as well as economic aspirations are promoted by the existence of Russian medium schools.

Another way in which the unmarked system may influence the kind of provision made within the local bilingual community is the extent to which the mainstream system is characterized by 'status rigidity'. High and low status groups within the same community may be involved differentially with bilingual education. Status may work in opposite directions for different groups. In the United States low or negative status determines selection for bilingual education. This is equally true of the French majority groups but not of the English minority groups in Quebec. So far as concerns European-Bantu education in South Africa, low status is a condition of bilingual education; but so far as English-Afrikaans bilingual education is concerned, status is irrelevant or tends to favor Afrikaans. Status is relevant to the USSR in the sense that the dominant group, the Russians, do not favor bilingual education for themselves and, in fact, interpret bilingual education exclusively in terms of learning Russian as a second language. In British schools status may not be associated or be associated only very loosely with type of education, selection for it, and retention within it of the immigrant ethnic group involved in any community. On the other hand, in Wales, which is also associated with the total system of British education, status tends to be correlated with bilingual education of native speakers of English. It is irrelevant to speakers of Welsh.

3. Types of bilingual communities

3.1 Relatively stable communities. Though I can only touch on some of the relevant variables which tend to distinguish types of bilingual communities, I ought now to embark upon the task of formulating a tentative typology of such communities. The first distinction is between those which consist of relatively stable components, and those with relatively mobile ones. Stability or mobility may be cultural-linguistic or demographic. For instance, a community may be split three ways: two groups which remain fairly distinct from each other, and another which for several reasons is marginal to either or to both. The marginal group may have been produced by assimilation of the minority or, on the other hand, it may have been produced by a system of bilingual education which, though it is oriented to the maintenance of both groups, cannot avoid creating a third culture. I doubt whether most of those who, like myself, have been bred bilingually, realize the extent to which we are the inheritors of a marginal culture and belong to a marginal community for that reason. The tendency has been to attach negative value judgments to the concept of marginality as if it affected only individuals who during their lifetime lose their exclusive contact with this or that language, culture, and community, and are stigmatized as deviant. There exist marginal cultures which have contributed greatly to the enrichment of civilization and their historical development entitles them to be regarded as the equals of so-called exclusive or pure cultures in any community. One of the tasks of bilingual education is to enable young people to take a pride in such cultures and to regard them as natural cultural environments. There is no necessary relationship between maintaining a language and the maintenance of the culture with which it may be associated historically. There are bilingual communities which are relatively homogeneous culturally.

By stable communities what is also meant in this discussion is geographic and demographic stability. Such communities tend to be fairly small, though the example of Switzerland, where the different but large communities have remained fairly stable over many decades, suggests that size alone is not all important. The communities I have in mind are stable because they are isolated for one of four reasons. They may be geographically isolated like those of the North Caucusus, the Irish of the Gaeltacht, the Scots of the Highlands and Islands, and the most thoroughly Welsh-speaking groups of the North and West of the Principality. Some of these geographically isolated communities may exist on the frontiers of a majority language, as is the case with the Celts of Britain, Ireland, and France. Other isolated groups may be 'enclaves' within much larger groups by whose influence they are surrounded. Some enclaves are vestigial remains of much larger linguistic groups: for example, speakers of Turkish introduced into the Crimea by the Ottomans; Albanians, Croats, and Greeks in the southern areas of Italy; the Sorbs of Lausitz (Lausatia) within East Germany; and speakers of Rumanian dialects who are bilingual in Serbian, Bulgarian, or Greek in Balkan countries. Other enclavic communities have been created by restrictive language policies, as is the case with the Basques of Southern France and Northern Spain. Other enclaves are the consequence of shifting political boundaries, as is the case of the Danes and the Germans, respectively, south and north of the Schlesvic line, or the Hungarian minorities in Yugoslavia. So far as the United States is concerned, Amerindian communities on reservations constitute important examples of linguistic enclaves.

Some bilingual communities, though they may be geographically isolated on frontiers or within enclaves, are isolated to a large extent because of their own tradition of restricted culture contact. Following Edward Dozier's example, we may term them 'bounded' communities. Dozier refers to the Pueblos, but historically much younger groups like the Amish come within this category. The characteristic of boundedness becomes apparent when we consider other Amerindian communities. Wick Miller speaks of these nonbounded communities, even though they might belong to the same linguistic community, as nonpermanent, 'the largest permanent social unit being the family, larger groupings being temporary and ephemeral'. There was considerable shifting from one group to other groups in contact (Sherzer 1973), especially on account of intermarriage. Barth (1969) and Leach (1954) refer to similar groups in Southern Asia.

Isolation of the kind I have described is not a characteristic of rural communities only. Segregated urban communities, isolated for social and cultural reasons, may also be regarded as bounded. The barrios and ghettos tend to be closed, relatively stable communities, the involuntary product of generations of social, psychological, linguistic, and cultural introversion.

One characteristic which distinguishes the bilingualism of communities which are isolated for whatever reason--geographic enclavic restrictiveness, boundedness, or urban segregation-- is its peripheral or local character. Bilingualism exists either in very small pockets or on the boundaries of contact. Such peripheral bilingualism, characteristic of European communities, differentiates itself from the diffused bilingualism of mobile groups of the United States. In Europe, language differences have been associated with distinguishable territories and later with nation states occupying such territories. Because of the identification of territorial or national entities with linguistic integrity, heterogeneity tended to be limited to the frontiers and was for that reason local and peripheral. In Belgium, the problem is to stabilize the boundaries of the two main groups. In Wales, too, it has been a question of attempting to maintain such boundaries. In Yugoslavia, bilingual education is not a substantial characteristic within any of the major language territories but is fairly well restricted to the frontiers between them and, within some of them, to the immigrant groups or incorporated minorities. In the USSR, peripheral or exclusively minority bilingualism--i.e. bilingualism which involves non-Russians-- is far more prevalent than it is in the United States, partly because of the almost total diffusion of the lingua franca (English) in the one compared with the limited diffusion of Russian in the other. Bilingualism involving two minority languages tends to be eroded by the spread of the dominant lingua franca. The other reason for difference between the bilingual communities of the two countries is that while language differences (apart from the indigenous Amerindian and Mexican American) tend not to be associated with territories in any stable fashion in the United States, there is an essential association between language and territory in the USSR, which is within the historical European pattern.

3.2 Mobile populations

3.2.1 Introduction. It must be conceded that the bilingualism of the physically isolated, enclavic, bounded, or segregated communities is quantitatively and possibly qualitatively much less significant than that which has resulted from movement within and across linguistic, ethnic, and national boundaries. Such mobility has taken several forms, although very few studies have been made of the differential effects of those several types of movement on types of language communities (see Kasdan 1970:1).

As an aspect of social and linguistic anthropology the study of kinds of population movement and their differential effect has to be undertaken within a wide context. Migration is a demographic problem; it influences sizes of populations. It is an economic problem because a shift in density of population is often due to or results in imbalances in standards of living. It takes in considerations of social psychology since issues of motivation and attitudes are involved. It is also a sociological problem because migration may influence social structures and cultural systems (Jansen 1969:60; cf. also Volkova 1967:19). Then again, historical factors are involved, for example, in the differential ethnic growth rates which exist in the United States, Canada (Quebec especially), and the USSR, and which help to maintain some bilingual communities like the French in Quebec, or Central Asians in the USSR against the pressure of dominant languages. It is significant and somewhat surprising that hardly any migration studies are concerned with education as a dependent or independent variable.

Among the aspects of population movement which are intimately involved in considerations of language contact and bilingual communities are the functions which mobility fulfills. Zastavskaya (1970) distinguishes three main functions. First

Types of Bilingual Communities /57

there is an accelerating function, exemplified in Wales and the Soviet Union, where in both cases movement of populations increased the rate at which linguistic contact had been proceeding for centuries. The second function is to redistribute populations, and one of the major differences between the Soviet Union and the United States is that while this redistributive function predominates over all others in the USSR, in the United States, relatively speaking, it is the 'receptive' or accumulative function which is most characteristic in establishing bilingual communities. The final function is selective: there are differences in the age and sex compositions of migrant groups and these differences, important for language, characterize bilingual communities everywhere.

Another aspect of the wider context of the study of migration and its effects on language is the motivation of mobility. Usually, migration has been regarded as exemplifying the results of the push of unfavorable economic conditions at home and the pull of more favorable circumstances elsewhere, which was the view of A. C. Haddon (1912) and Numelin (1937). Duncan (1958:90) saw 'migration as the main mechanism of adjustment to the re-distribution of economic opportunity caused by national resource development and technological change which impinge unequally on industries and areas'. Students of the Soviet Union tend towards the same conclusion (Parming 1972: 64).

However, migration and the processes of demographic and linguistic assimilation which may result from it are not simple phenomena. If communities which are initially bilingual become eroded, it may be the product of less material aspirations and motivations. Economic motivations, while they may be sufficient explanations of some migrations, cannot account entirely for the early settlement of the English in the United States, nor of Dutch, German, Swedish, Norwegian, and French attempts at colonization and later immigration. Personal and group freedom, and civic as well as religious freedom counted for as much or more with many of the migrants and helped to make an indelible mark on their communities. The behavior of migrants in their new communities towards their native languages and to the languages of those they met in conflict or otherwise, cannot but have been influenced by the attitudes which impelled them to migrate in the first place.

Furthermore, according to his motivation the migrant does not simply react to his new surroundings--geographical, cultural, or linguistic. A large number possess a 'cognitive model ... as to the nature and goals of migration' (Philpott 1968:474). These goals affect valuations of the areas they leave just as much as of their new social environment. 'The composite memory of things past is a significant variable in any analysis of immigrant experience, yet it has often been ignored or given scant significance' (Jackson 1969:2). For instance, the immigrant may continue to express a lively and practical concern for the

politics of his homeland. This is undoubtedly the case of the
Cubans. Lebanese migrants to the United States have been
known to have had a similar active interest in their native conflicts (Sweet 1967:180). Whatever their commitments to their
areas of origin (and they are far from being exclusively political or even broadly social), there is no doubt that concentrations of immigrants in the United States--Asians in California,
Italians in New York, Puerto Ricans in New Jersey--constitute
networks of relationships with the homeland, with families and
friends whom they assist to migrate and settle, and whom they
attract to specific localities, thus reinforcing the original culture and language in strategic 'closed' communities.

Although the degree of their importance varies, such considerations affect most linguistically heterogeneous communities. But
there are some considerations which help us to differentiate
fundamentally between them. For instance, it is customary to
refer to Russian mobility as being almost exclusively territorial,
and that of Britain as only partly territorial (affecting the Celts)
but oceanic or maritime in respect of emigration to America and
other countries, and in respect of current immigration from
former colonies. There are other considerations of a political nature with considerable relevance to the study of the
linguistic aspects of mobility. The Soviet Union is a confederation of territorially and linguistically distinct and colonized
nations and nationalities, while (apart from the indigenous
peoples) the United States is not. Unlike the United States
and Britain, in the Soviet Union international migration is entirely synonymous with internal mobility. Furthermore, in the
Soviet Union there is a closed ethnic and linguistic society:
migration results only in their redistribution, whether within
or across the frontiers of Soviet nationalities. The United
States, Canada, most countries of Europe, and Britain are
linguistically open societies; the nature of the frontier in each
case is such as to ensure that to a large degree mobility allows
for the receptivity of new groups.

Such differences focus on the relative importance of different
kinds of frontiers, of which one can distinguish first those that
are to all intents and purposes objective. These include those
created or sanctioned by history--politically and therefore in
most areas ethnically determined, or frontiers which are physically objective, created by seas, rivers, and mountains. Other
kinds of frontiers are social and psychological, imposed or
acquiesced in for ideological or emotional reasons. Language
differences in the USSR tend to be related to objective boundaries (save in the case of the Jews); languages are identified
with territories and these territories have geographically or historically determined objective frontiers. This is also the case
in Britain so far as the Celts are concerned, but not where
new minorities are involved for whom linguistic frontiers ignore
territorial boundaries and are more often than not coincidental
with social-psychological or attitudinal divisions. This tends to

be the case in the United States also except for the Southwest,
and even there, strictly speaking, only in respect of the Amerindian population. In Canada, the provincial status of the
French-speaking population approximates to the status of territorially defined nationalities in the USSR. Differences between
objective and subjective frontiers are associated with ease or
difficulty of linguistic-group mobility. In the United States,
what linguistic frontiers there are tend to be impermanent and
shifting, corresponding little if at all to administrative boundaries. In the USSR, they have tended to be permanent, determinate, and to coincide with national boundaries. Within-group
mobility in the USSR is greater than cross-national mobility
and so tends to localize bilingual communities.

3.2.2 **Type of movement.** In studying the factors which
affect bilingualism, the first requirement is to identify, distinguish, and define the various types of movement; it is proposed
here to consider first within-national mobility in its several
forms and to follow this by considering forms of international
migration. Because some countries like the Soviet Union,
Yugoslavia, and Switzerland are federations of nations and for
that reason migration may be simultaneously intranational and
international, the distinction is not categorical.

The most primitive form of migration is 'nomadism', which has
been misconceived as unplanned or irregular wandering; however, its most salient characteristic is cyclical movement of
groups within a limited geographical compass. Soviet nomads,
such as Kazakhs and Tatars of the Steppe, followed regular
patterns from a winter camp through a spring route to a summer pasture and so back over an autumn passage to the winter
camp again. In the United States, the Apache were such a
nomadic group. They were without systems of agriculture or
permanent habitation but lived in temporary symbiotic relations
with the Pueblos (Dozier 1976:3). Although, in a limited fashion, it still persists among some small Indian and Eskimo groups,
nomadism is no longer a significant cause of heterogeneity in
North America.

Examples of such nomadic peoples still remain in the Soviet
Union, and until fairly recently were an important aspect of
life in Central Asia and the Far North. So far as the nomads
of the Soviet Far North are concerned, this type of movement,
while it prevailed as their characteristic mode of life, facilitated the maintenance of their language against the pressure
of Russian. A large proportion of them are reindeer herders
and remain nomads, visiting settlements only at long intervals.
Their grasp of Russian tends, even on an official reckoning,
to be relatively low. Only 29 percent of the Yukagirs and
32.5 percent of the Itelmen, for instance, claim to have learned
some Russian. In fact, the level of competence of that proportion is low: children of these nomads, when they are placed
in boarding schools, need to have intensive preliminary

instruction in 'zero grades' before being allowed into the regular classes. Not only has nomadism been a factor in avoiding the pressures exerted by the presence of any one major language, like Russian; it has also been a powerful force, as was the case with Semitic languages in the Middle East, in promoting the diffusion of a tribal language among those with whom they came into contact (Whatmough 1933:21). Seafaring (a variant of nomadism) has been responsible for the diffusion of Austronesian languages.

Seasonal migration differs from nomadism insofar as the former usually involves the movement of only a very few members of the total group, who tend to be motivated by individual, sometimes idiosyncratic goals rather than by group traditions. Because it involves a small number, such seasonal migration has been thought to lack much significance for language change and bilingualism. Yet the migration of seasonal workers from agricultural Welsh-speaking areas had a profound effect on the maintenance of the Welsh language in new industrial centers during the first phase of industrial development. The Welsh language of the receiving industrial area was reinforced because the temporary workers were themselves Welsh. It was the sending areas from and to which the Welsh-speaking migrants departed and returned cyclically which experienced the eroding influence of migration. They might stabilize the proportion of Welsh to English in the industrial areas but their regularly repeated cycles of migration and return changed the situation of the Welsh language in their original homes. Whether we are concerned with seasonal migration or with nomadism, the effects of such types of migration on language contact, compared with the influence within settled communities, cannot be ignored. So far as the United States is concerned, Voegelin and Voegelin (1973:1107) refer to this in considering the languages of the Great Basin:

> The vagueness or indeterminateness in establishing language barriers in the Great Basin may be accounted for in part by seasonal migrations and, more generally, a fondness for moving about in 'wider areas' whether economically motivated or to relieve the isolation of living (otherwise) in contact with none other than members of a few families ... One suspects less vagueness in determining where the language barriers lie in Pueblo societies.

Commuting is a variant of nomadism and seasonal migration, where the cycle of migration is more rapid--daily or weekly rather than seasonal. Partly because of its frequency and regularity, as well as because the commuter tends to be involved with large numbers of speakers of other languages in urban areas, commuting has had and is having significant influences on language maintenance and in promoting bilingualism. In due course the commuter becomes a 'culture broker', an

Types of Bilingual Communities /61

intermediary between groups, usually at different levels of sociocultural development. Tabouret-Keller (1972) points to situations of the linguistic hinterland of Toulouse. Cooper's studies of the interaction of different linguistic groups in Ethiopian market places point to the same results on the languages of the 'market migrants' (Cooper and Carpenter 1969). The commuting practices of American Indians on the reservations usually involve not only adults who travel to work but also children who travel to school. The effect of such commuting is all the greater because it involves not only differences between languages, e.g. Navajo and English, but the very basis of the language's survival, the way of life of the tribe. The effect of commuting must be considered in its relationship to the individual commuter as well as to the community to which he belongs. Studies of language contact generally have regard for the groups in contact: here is a case where the contact is primarily established by individuals acting outside the group but affecting it nevertheless.

3.3 Permanent migration

3.3.1 Voluntary migration. A more significant population movement is relatively permanent migration--a moving away of a collectivity from one location to another, where it is ultimately dispersed or if it is not, becomes enclavic.

At present, such movements in the USSR may be restricted within the boundaries of an ethnic group, or may proceed across such boundaries without, however, crossing national or administrative frontiers; or they may involve moving into a different national republic. But it is necessary to emphasize that crucial though such migrations are to the promotion of bilingual communities in the Soviet Union, at present the main type of population movement has been local and the main source of urban growth has been the surrounding linguistically homogeneous rural population. Two-thirds of new urban populations come from such rural areas (Perevedentsev 1965:34).

The frequent migrations of Amerindian tribes is well attested historically, and so is the movement of other ethnic groups within the United States--for instance, speakers of Spanish within and from the Southwest.

However, not all such migrations in the United States involve changing the habitat of the rural indigenous Amerindian or Spanish populations. Interstate movements have been a continuing characteristic and such movements involve both native and foreign born, so that the flux which international immigration represents is intensified by subsequent movement. In fact, for more than a century the ratio of stable to migrant population in the United States has not changed significantly, nor has the proportion of the population who have migrated across state boundaries--although after an early reduction at the turn of the first half of the last century, the tendency is for interstate migration to accelerate slightly each decade, thus reinforcing the diffused (as opposed to the peripheral) character of American bilingual communities.

Such high ratios of migrant to stable population, and the relatively high ratios of foreign-born migrants in the total migrant ratio over such a long period, makes for considerable ethnic and linguistic convergence and is contrary to the experience of the Soviet Union until very recently.

Another feature of migration making for such convergence is second-stage (or urban to suburban) migration of the foreign-born and/or their children in the United States. Such a movement also implies the abandonment of relatively closed urban communities, where the ethnic language is heavily reinforced, for more open or at least more dispersed suburban locations, where that reinforcement is less evident.

3.3.2 Involuntary migration. Deportation, evacuation, forcible resettlement, and slavery are all forms of involuntary migration and their impact on language has been recorded often enough. In some cases communities--sometimes whole nations-- may be involved; in others, only individuals. Even when communities or whole ethnic groups are involved they may be resettled as groups or dispersed in very small numbers. The nature of the language contact and the type of bilingual community that ensues depend on the size and cohesiveness of the group relative to the area of settlement and the status of the cultures associated with the languages.

The part played by slaves in the historical progress of bilingualism, while it should not be overestimated, cannot very well be ignored. In some areas their numbers were very large. Philip of Macedon colonized Thrace with Greek and Macedonian slaves--the large settlements bearing such titles as 'the city of slaves' or 'the city of adulterers' (Jones 1937:4). Such colonies tended to be linguistically and ethnically heterogeneous. Intermarriage, involving slaves, facilitated a complete intermixture of races in bilingual communities. They were assimilated, but not before periods of bilingualism. Their influence varied according to their occupations. The proportion of them in domestic service must have been considerable at all times: they were employed in secretarial and managerial posts as bank managers, interpreters, tutors, and teachers (Jones 1956:185). Their impact on bilingual education was significant (Lewis 1976).

So far as concerns the United States, Africans migrated involuntarily to North America to be used as chattel slaves on plantations, in mines, forests, small towns, and cities, on roads and small farms. The Afro-American element of the population of the United States is large and influential. As a dynamic minority, developing its own ideology which reflects its own culture nurtured in Afro-American 'bounded' communities, it has had a great influence on the thinking of linguistic minorities without, I believe, being itself a 'linguistic minority' and so capable of posing a strictly 'bilingual' as distinct from a 'minority' problem. But their exclusion from the category of linguistic minorities is due not to the 'difficulty posed by forced migration to the preservation of any or all cultural and social continuities' (Mintz 1961:1970). Forced migration of cohesive Indian bands and tribes did not prevent them from maintaining their languages. Nor has the forcible removal of some Soviet nationalities killed off their languages (Lewis 1972). The enslavement of Greeks in Rome produced a rich bilingual society (Lewis 1976). However, the particular circumstances of African slavery did make it virtually impossible for their languages to be maintained and the kind of linguistic heterogeneity characterizing their communities may be regarded as bidialectal rather than bilingual.

REFERENCES

Barth, F. 1969. Ethnic groups and boundaries. Boston: Little, Brown.
Carroll, J. 1975. The teaching of French in ten countries (=International Studies in Evaluation). New York: John Wiley.
Cooper, R. L., and S. Carpenter. 1969. Linguistic diversity in the Ethiopian market. In: Fishman (1972).
Dozier, E. P. 1976. The Pueblo Indians of North America. New York: Holt, Rinehart and Winston.
Duncan, O. D. 1958. Population redistribution and economic growth. Economic Development and Cultural Change 7.90-94.
Falch, J. 1973. Contribution à l'étude du statut des langues en Europe. Quebec: Laval University Press.
Fishman, J. A., ed. 1972. Advances in the sociology of language, Vol. 2. The Hague: Mouton.
Fishman, J. A. 1976. Bilingual education: An international sociological perspective. Rowley, Mass.: Newbury House.
Haddon, A. C. 1912. The wandering peoples. Cambridge: Cambridge University Press.
Jackson, J. A. 1969. Migration: Sociological studies, Vol. 2. Cambridge: Cambridge University Press.
Jansen, C. 1969. Some sociological aspects of migration. In: Jackson (1969).
Jones, A. H. H. 1937. The cities of the Eastern Province. Oxford: Clarendon Press.
Jones, A. H. H. 1956. Slavery in the ancient world. Economic History Review 6.185-199.
Kasdan, L. 1970. Introduction. In: Spencer (1970).
Leach, E. R. 1954. Political systems of highland Burma. Cambridge: Cambridge University Press.
Lewis, E. Glyn. 1972. Multilingualism in the Soviet Union. The Hague: Mouton.

Lewis, E. Glyn, with Carolyn Massad. 1975. The teaching of English as a foreign language in ten countries (=International Studies in Evaluation). New York: John Wiley.
Lewis, E. Glyn. 1976. Bilingualism and bilingual education in the ancient world. In: Fishman (1976).
Linz, J. J., and A. Miguel. 1975. Differences and comparisons: The eight Spains. In: Merrit and Rokkan (1975).
Merrit, H. L., and S. Rokkan. 1975. Comparing nations: The use of quantitative data in cross-national research. New Haven: Yale University Press.
Mintz, S. W. 1961. Review article: Slavery. American Anthropology 63.iii.
Mintz, S. W. 1970. Some aspects of involuntary migration. In: Spencer (1970).
Numelin, R. 1937. The wandering spirit: A study in human migration. London: Macmillan.
Parming, T. 1972. Population changes in Estonia 1935-1970. Population Studies 26.i.55-78.
Perevedentsev, V. I. 1965. Relation of population migration and ethnic convergence. World Population Transactions 513-518. London: Oxford University Press.
Perevedentsev, V. I. 1970. Population migration and utilization of labour resources. Voprosy Ekonomiiciya, 9 September.
Philpott, S. B. 1968. Remittance obligations, social networks and choice among Montserration migrants in Britain. Man 3.iii.465-476.
Philpott, S. B. 1970. The implications of migration for sending societies. In: Spencer (1970).
Sebeok, T. A., ed. 1973. Linguistics in North America. Vol. 10 of: Current trends in linguistics. The Hague: Mouton.
Sherzer, J. 1973. Area linguistics in North America. In: Sebeok (1973).
Spencer, R. F. 1970. Migration and anthropology. American Ethnological Society Proceedings, Spring. Seattle: University of Washington Press.
Sweet, L. E. 1967. The women of Ain ad-Dayr. Anthropological Quarterly 40.167-183.
Tabouret-Keller, A. 1972. A contribution to the sociological study of language maintenance and shift. In: Fishman (1972).
Voegelin, C. F., and F. H. Voegelin. 1973. The South West and the Great Basin. In: Sebeok (1973).
Volkova, N. C. 1967. Problems of bilingualism in the North Caucasus. Sov. Etn. 1.27-40.
Whatmough, J. 1933. Prae-Italic dialects in Italy. 2 vols. Cambridge: Harvard University Press.
Zastavskaya, V. 1970. Quoted in: H. I. Safa and B. M. Du Toit, Migration and development. The Hague: Mouton.

PROBLEMS OF MULTILINGUALISM IN SMALL LINGUISTIC COMMUNITIES

Eric P. Hamp
University of Chicago

*To the memory of my old friend
John G. Hawthorne*

There are small linguistic communities on most of the continents of the earth, and nearly all of them, at least today, are destined to be bi- or multilingual. The study of such situations, both in their social and autonomous linguistic dimensions, offers rich opportunities for linguistic theory, quite apart from the important problems of the practical world presented in these communities. There are many more such communities in North America than most Americans would guess--if they ever thought about it.
  In this paper I will be drawing my material from Europe because the cases I speak of are familiar to me in detail. To illustrate, however, that such cases are far from rare or arcane, the Appendix to this article lists the nearly three score languages of the USSR which do not at present serve as administrative or official vehicles of any politically constituted unit. I base my data on M. I. Isayev (1977).
  We are dealing here with languages which are very small or miniscule in point of number of speakers.
  From Western Eurasia one can mention as comparable minorities the Celtic of Britain and France, Frisian, Basque, Lusatian, Friulian, south-Italian Greek, Aromân, Tsakonian, and the discontinuous speech groups of Judeo-Spanish and Romany. The recognition status and educational opportunities of these have changed enormously in the past two decades, and differ greatly in their development and present standing from region to region. But, as I hope to make clear, the background considerations for each of these, politics and policy aside, are far from equivalent.

There are problems that one is led to reflect upon without
having originally intended to. I have long been interested in
the phenomena of language contact and diffusion, of bilingualism and areal linguistics, of convergence and its role in diachronic genetic studies. Even these interests emerged somewhat accidentally, as by-products, as it were, of original goals
in the traditional fields of historical and comparative linguistics
and of dialectology. As an Indo-Europeanist I wished to fill
in some of our worst gaps in the study of that family, chiefly
in the Celtic and Albanian areas. This led me to the descriptive study of dialects, peripheral varieties, and enclaves, of
these languages--a study which I have never really abandoned.
As time went on I realized that I had accumulated in the course
of my fieldwork an unintended knowledge of contact phenomena
for the areas in question. Thus my attention shifted more and
more to problems of language interference, a quest with which
I have become incurably fascinated. Eventually, I arrived at
the view that I have held for some time, and elaborated in my
unpublished 1971 presidential address to the Linguistic Society
of America, that correct genetic comparative linguistics cannot
be practised without constant heed and reference to areal data
analysis, and vice versa. As a matter of fact, in recent years
I have become increasingly occupied with the possibility of using diachronic areal formulations directly as a means of evolving chronologies for the statement of conventional genetic
changes.

Such studies have perforce involved me in the observation of
situations of multilingualism where at least one of the languages
in question is of small size in relation to the contact language.
It is in such situations of interaction that one is privileged to
observe conditions of contact that otherwise might not be accessible. The result--originally unintended--is that I have accumulated a dossier of cases of unequal language contact, of situations where a numerically small (unpopulous) language or dialect abuts a relatively widespread, or highly valued, or institutionally organized language. The result varies enormously in
a number of parameters and is instructive for our grasp of language as a social or cultural phenomenon. My purpose in this
paper is to outline something of what I have learned from direct
field observation. This brief study is in the nature of a casebook contribution.

The impact of unequal language contact can be noted in at
least two major ways. One consists in the substantive alterations that can be detected in one or both of the grammars involved; that is to say, certain aspects of one grammar are adjusted in the direction of corresponding aspects of the other
grammar. This is the typical case of what has been called
'interference'. But the effect is also visible in what may be
regarded as the limiting case of the latter phenomenon: the
speed with which the smaller language is given up entirely,
i.e. the process of language death. However, it seems to me

Problems of Multilingualism /67

that there are senses in which language death is not best
viewed as a simple limiting case of interference; this distinction will come out in some of the cases to be reviewed. It is
easily possible to find instances of only mild interference,
where death rapidly ensues; contrariwise, there are clear cases
of a notably long survival of a language with remarkably deep
and extensive interference.

There are cases where the effects of interference can be
attributed to highly specific social mechanisms. In Mandritsa,
in southeast Bulgaria, there is a single village which speaks a
dialect of Albanian as its home language; it once formed part
of a cluster of about half a dozen such villages, the balance
of which have vanished from sight and scholarly record on the
other side of the Turkish border. There is also a splinter of
Mandritsa surviving in Mándres, near Kilkís in Greece, which
was resettled at the time of the First Balkan War; until the
last war kinfolk used to visit back and forth, and the dialect
of Mándres is little different from that of Mandritsa. Mandritsa
is a Tosk dialect of Albanian, and has been separated from the
main body of the language for perhaps several centuries. The
dialect is far from dying out, isolated though it is. However,
the grammar is the most divergent of all Albanian dialects I
know (which comprise all those in existence save one variety
in the Ukraine). It is warped heavily in the direction of Turkish and Bulgarian, and perhaps also of Greek, betraying its
long contact with all of these. Now, thanks to the excellent
ethnographic work of the Bulgarian linguist Bojka Sokolova,
the specific social reasons for this are not far to seek. Mandritsa has traditionally enjoyed a successful and lucrative silkworm industry; it has therefore not been in a position of inferiority conducive to abandoning its own traditions, such as
its home language. Marriages were frequently made outside,
as well as inside, the village. However, a man who married
into Mandritsa normally moved into his wife's household and
ultimately was expected to learn Albanian; yet, of course, a
Balkan family is strongly patriarchal. The net effect of this
marriage pattern is clear: many authoritarian fathers in
Mandritsa have been handing on imperfectly learned Albanian,
their least strong language.

Alongside the last case we may place an instance of differential survival which may be traced, at least in part, to the
specifics of culture traits. During the present century, the
Albanian enclaves of Greece and of Italy are undergoing a
highly dissimilar fate. The dialects of what we may conveniently call Arvanítika in Greece are dying out rapidly in our
own day. Though there has indeed been a flow of population
into the major urban centers, no drastic depopulation has
occurred in the Arvanítika areas. In fact, major regions of
rural depopulation in Greece (e.g. the mountains of the north)
are not Arvanítika, and while one can point to some parts of
meager subsistence level (e.g. in Arkadía), most of the

concentrations of Arvanítika lie in well-favoured, more southerly
territories (the Pelopónnesos, Attica, Boeotia, Locris, Andros,
etc.). Thus Arvanítika is dying by the route of acculturation
--transfer to the dominant language. Let us pause here to note
a converse case, that of Scottish Gaelic. While all speakers of
Scottish Gaelic are today bilingual, the language has not been
receding for the past two centuries by a parallel simple acculturation. As a matter of fact, in the north of Scotland (including the northern portion of the Outer Hebrides) there is
still a sufficient proportion of Gaelic speakers so that, in the
wake of the recent redistricting of British shires, the most
northerly one has declared itself as officially Gaelic speaking
for purposes of a governmental and legislative first language.
Actually, the dramatic drop in Scottish Gaelic over the past
two centuries quite simply reflects the massive depopulation of
the Highlands; this emigration, forced or otherwise, represents
one outcome of the tragic developments which were beginning at
the time of Boswell and Johnson's journey through the region.

Quite the reverse of the doom of Arvanítika, most of the enclave villages of Arbëresh in Italy have suffered no such re-
cession of their language, if any at all. Indeed, some of these
villages are now witnessing an enthusiastic local revival in the
schools, stimulated by the modern-day currents of minority
movement sweeping throughout Europe and the world. The reverse trend in survival of these two enclave groups is all the
more striking when one recalls their spread and distribution
at the beginning of the present century. At that time, the
villages of Italy numbered about 45 (with the loss of some four
or five Arbëresh villages by the present day), and these are
scattered in about a dozen clusters, mostly numbering a few
villages or a single village apiece strewn over the southern
third of Italy. The Arbëresh are strikingly isolated groups,
and many of their dialects are highly unintelligible one to the
other; I have played recordings from Barile (Potenza) in
Vaccarizzo Albanese (Cosenza), and the hearers could not
guess for a half-hour what language it was ... they imagined
it was American! Such fragmentation and exposure might lead
one to expect the worst.

The geographic distribution of Arvanítika has been completely
different. Here, my village list for the past few centuries runs
to several hundred names, and at the turn of the century there
were a good few hundred surviving Arvanítika villages. It is
true that the total population of these, or at least the average
per settlement, was nowhere like that of the Italian enclaves; a
village of 3,000 is very large for Arvanítika (500 to 1,000 is frequent), but modest or median for Arbëresh. But this is perfectly proportionate; villages of Italy are generally many times
more populous than the sparse settlements of Greece. Moreover, the Arvanítika areas comprise sizeable solid clumps of
villages: in the Pelopónnesos we have (or had) all of Korinthía,
most of the Argolid, much of Akhaía (except for Patras and

Kalávrita), virtually all of Triphylía, not to mention smaller
residues in Lakonía, Arkadía, and Elis. North of there, we
find all of Attica except Athens itself, all of Boeotia except
Thebes, solid blocks of Euboea and Andros (i.e. the adjacent
ends of these two islands). To look at the map, one would
think these sturdy and resilient continua, after five to six
centuries of survival since the Byzantine collapse.
   It is possible to argue that accessibility has had much to do
with the differential survival of Arvanítika and Arbëresh. It
is true that the Arbëresh villages in the long Italian peninsula
lie far to the south of the center, and especially far from the
important northern centers; the Arvanítika settlements, on the
other hand, somewhat encircle Athens and the older capital
area of the Argolid (Náuplion). Yet, I know from personal
experience that in many cases, as recently as 20 years ago,
the condition of roads and transport did not make these Greek
villages, any more readily reached than those of the Mezzo-
giorno, where Italy's advanced technology (when not blocked
by simple poverty) has penetrated for a good century.
   It seems apparent, however, as one moves about among these
villages that the survival of Arbëresh and the absorption of
Arvanítika both depend to a great extent on the natural ground
prepared by their different 'distancing' from the surrounding
major culture. From the very beginning, when the Arvanítes
moved south in the peninsula into what is now Greece, their
south Tosk culture must have differed little from that of their
late Byzantine neighbours the Greeks; their belief system must
already have been largely that of Orthodoxy. Since for a long
time under the Turks, membership in the Orthodox church was
the main feature that defined an ethnic Greek, the Arvanítes
understandably came to think of themselves as Greeks who
merely differed in a detail of speech. That they have long
considered themselves Greeks--the unsophisticated villagers
were until recently dimly aware that what is now national Albania shares their language--is illustrated by the fact that
several of the famous names of the Greek Revolution were in
fact Arvanítes. By contrast, all the Arbëresh up to a century
or two ago, and a fair number up to the present day, preserve a considerable cultural distance from the surrounding
Italians. Most noteworthy is their Orthodox religion, but other
traits of dress, food, and folklore go along with this. These
villages are highly endogamous; I have lived in a village for
extended periods where every Calabrese (non-Arbëresh) person in our quarter of town was routinely identified to me as
such. In the nineteenth century, a local indigenous (to be
sure, Western-influenced) Arbëresh literature grew up before
anything comparable arose in Albania itself; nothing of the
sort has ever happened among the Arvanítes.
   Let us quickly note one more case of differentially preserva-
tive cultural specifics, this time among the Celts. It seems to
me clear that the vanishing current state of the Irish language,

despite the heroic efforts of a century of nationalism, and the
present weak and retreating position of Breton, despite recurrent minority efforts grounded in traditional French liberty and
factionalism, can be correlated to a certain degree with the
Roman Catholicism of these countries. Per contra, Protestant
Wales and Scotland (where the Church of England is rejected)
show proportionately far more life linguistically. Now, it is a
fact that the Catholic Church does not foster independent devotional or family Bible reading; the latter, until a generation
ago, constituted the only occupation on Sunday in Scotland
after one had trudged home from divine service. Children may
have nodded asleep at these ordeals, but the entire process,
as well as its values, impressed them. I recall from work on
the Scottish Gaelic dialect survey the constant problem of keeping good native speakers from substituting Biblical forms (or
their favourite minister's outside dialect pronunciation) for their
own; they not only wanted to 'give you the best' (social climbing), but they relished these stylistic variants. In Wales, in
addition to such Bible reading and the like, when native literature took a slump for other reasons (as it also did in Ireland),
marathon sermons stepped into the breach. These sermons, the
dominant form of literature at the time, cultivated all the ornate
embellishment and institutionalized style in which Celtic literature has long outstripped the rest of Western Europe. The result of this, oversimplified, is the modern Welsh literary language and the common nondialect spoken form used today
equally in the North and South. What linguists have lost in
the dialect record of Welsh and Scottish Gaelic has been gained
in the survival of these languages alongside the powerful domination of English.

The differential role of cultural exclusionism. Up to now we
have been considering the differential effect of selected categories of factors in conserving or depressing minority languages
in situations of contact. The factors discussed above are in
some cases noncultural (e.g. geography), and in other cases
are specific culture traits which have been brought into accidental juxtaposition. But in all these instances there is nothing
inherent in the factor that is specifically designed for survival
or assimilation, i.e. that has such a result as its overt cultural goal. That is to say, there is nothing about one or the
other Christian religion that has literacy as a basic portion of
its content; what we observe is simply the accident of a combination of attendant traits.

However, cultures also have as a part of their complex of
traits a specific view or policy concerning integrity of the culture and the role of diversity. This in itself has important
consequences for language contact, and the more so to a dramatic degree in the case of small communities.

To start with a case which is surely familiar to all of us,
French-speaking culture can be ranked high on the scale of

built-in cultural exclusionism. It is the common experience of
Americans arriving in France that they not only have trouble
segmenting phonetic bursts of French to discover which words
they actually don't know, but that the French seem to show no
mercy toward their plight. What the American does not realize
is that the French are really not being nasty or difficult; a
Frenchman simply knows that certain things are eternally true
and not subject to debate: French culture (and language) is
not merely best--it is there, it is logical, it is French. One
does not make concessions to the foreigner, because he also
must realize that there is only one way to speak--logically, à
la française. Americans also think that the English are sometimes cold (even though here they share the same language for
practical purposes); but actually English behaviour that operates as if other languages scarcely exist is not a specimen of
the exclusionism just caricatured for French. English culture
is simply oblivious, insular--provincial, if you will. I have
heard it remarked that the Italians presumably are reduced to
eating such filthy oil and drinking that heavy wine because
they make such an abominable cup of tea.

Surely the fate of Breton has much to do with the fact of the
all-pervading centralized view that French culture fosters--
quite apart from the question (which I explicitly ignore here)
of whether and at what periods political discouragement has
been employed. By comparison, Welsh has fared much better
alongside the forgetful English. One meets narrowly educated,
nonintellectual Englishmen who can recite a catalogue of institutionalized prejudices against the Welsh, but who feel that
Aberystwyth is so far towards Thule and so unpronounceable
that it really can't be worth bothering about. The pragmatic
English view is that if trade is prospering and if law and
government are exercising an orderly noninterference, people
like the Welsh and the Nepalis are entitled to their funny little
habits. Meanwhile, the Welsh--with their jabbering clanishness,
in the English view--practice a considerable degree of structured exclusionism, confident in the sublimity of their morals,
poetry, and music. The fact that Europe scarcely knows these
is Europe's loss.

Even more striking--indeed, a case of classic contrast--is the
interplay of these parameters in the instances of Arvanítika vs.
Arbëresh. Greek culture probably exceeds French, if that is
possible, in the respect we are considering. In fact, the Greek
combines French exclusionism with British oblivion. One highly
effective trait which enhances Greek isolation is its solitary
possession (like Georgian or Armenian, two other well integrated
and insulated cultures) of a distinct alphabet--an object itself of
the reverence due only to heirlooms of antiquity. Consider
that an average Greek villager would never even recognize the
name of Hamlet or Plato if he saw it on a pan-European book
cover; I have witnessed the ubiquitous policeman of a village
stare at my passport upside-down before handing it back

gravely to me after an appropriate interval. But beyond the alphabet, Greek culture is exclusionistic, tenacious, proud, retrospective. Arvanítika speakers, who are Greek citizens, unflinchingly and happily accept the axioms that Greek is the oldest culture, Greek literature the first, the benefits of modern civilization Greek inventions with Greek names (democracy, physics, atomic fission--and bombs), and that the Greek language is the oldest, the richest (two or more words for every notion), the hardest (even we make mistakes often!), the only one with a true grammar. Why indeed should they persist with a crude tool that does not even have a grammar!

Now consider Italy. It is a modern nation, but despite the Risorgimento, the attitudes of the old city-states have never completely left. Bolognesi are intensely proud of Bologna, and not only because it is the gastronomic Mecca. Patricians of the city, proud of an erudition that they trace back to Rome, speak a Ciceronian standard Italian--but carefully preserving vowel qualities and substituting z/zz for standard č/ǧ to betray their origin. This is not provincialism, it is deliberate. The last is demonstrated a fortiori because they also, amongst themselves, write books and deliver learned formal papers in their local dialect. It is simply a fact of Italian culture that localism, including local dialect, is cultivated and highly valued; as foreigners, we note, as a corollary to this, that we are always treated with what we think is politeness and toleration. But, of course, the Italian is not inherently more polite and goodhearted than the Frenchman or Englishman; he simply accounts routinely for what he expects to be our own localism.

Placed in this framework, we see now that the alloglot Arbëresh enclaves fit neatly into Italian culture. These villages are not provincial objects of shame; each has its own honourable home speech--it is a mere detail that genetically the language happens not to be a divergence traced to Imperial Latin. After all, Pugliese is totally opaque to a north Italian. We also see how, in the intensely literary and antiquarian Italian culture of polite letters, a tiny literature (largely of poetry) grew up in the nineteenth century in many of these enclaves. They were simply behaving in a more modest way like their richer Bolognese countrymen.

Finally, from the foregoing we should be able to predict, even if we did not know it, that immigrant Greeks in the United States will cling to their language to the third generation, while Italians in populous neighbourhoods lose theirs and embrace English in a remarkably short time.

APPENDIX

A. LANGUAGES OF THE USSR WHICH DO NOT AT PRESENT SERVE AS ADMINISTRATIVE OR OFFICIAL VEHICLES OF ANY POLITICALLY CONSTITUTED UNIT

From the Iranian family

Talysh
Yagnobi
Ishkashimi

Yazgulami
Shugni

From the Turkic family

Gagauz (146,000 speakers in the Moldavian SSR)
Crimean Tatar (in the Uzbek SSR)
Karaim
Urum (a transfer of Greek to Turkic)
Krymchak

Shor (17,000)
Chulym (4,500)
Karagas (600)
Kamasin (200)

From the Tungusic family

Evenki (12,899)
Nanai or Goldi (6,911)
Even or Lamut (6,736)
Negidal

Ulcha
Orok
Oroch
Udege

From the Uralic family

Veps
Izurian
Vod
Livonian
Khanty or Ostyak (14,562)
Mansi or Vogul (4,037)

Saam (1,058; these are the Lapp of the Kola)
Nenets or Yurak (23,952)
Selkup or Ostyak-Samoyed (2,186)
Nganasan or Tavgi (953)
Enets or Yenisei-Samoyed (300)

From the Caucasus group

Zan or Mingrelian
Svan
Bats
Plus about 12 languages from the Avar-Andi-Tsez (Dido) and Lezgin groups

From Luoravetlan

Chukchi (13,597)
Koryak or Nymyllan

Itelmen or Kamchadal
Kerek
Alyutor

Other languages

Siberian Eskimo and Aleut
Nivkh or Gilyak (4,420)
Ket (1,182)
Yukagir (615)

B. LANGUAGES WITH A RECOGNIZED WRITING SYSTEM (AN ADOPTED ORTHOGRAPHY) [From List A]

Evenki	Nenets
Nanai	Selkup
Even	Chukchi
Khanty	Eskimo
Mansi	Nivkh

and a few of the Caucasus languages

REFERENCE

Isayev, M.I. 1977. National languages in the USSR: Problems and solutions. Translated by Paul Nedov. Moscow: Progress Publishers.

BILINGUAL EDUCATION
AND A NATIONAL LANGUAGE POLICY

Shirley Brice Heath
University of Pennsylvania

1. National language policies. Critical to the planning and
implementation of any national language policy is the definition
of 'national language' either spelled out or assumed by policy-
makers. The particular definition chosen derives in large part
from the historical background of the nation. For those countries once part of a colonial empire, but independent in the
nineteenth century, there was a strong tendency to equate
national language with the European language of domination.
For example, throughout the nineteenth century and well into
the twentieth, Peru, Mexico, Bolivia, and Ecuador continued
the policy of Castilianization which had been initiated during
the colonial period. Nations which gained their independence
in the early part of the twentieth century followed this policy
also. In the period between the World Wars, the new European
nations which resulted from the break-up of empires and re-
alignment of political boundaries chose an indigenous language
as their national language in opposition to the language previously imposed on them. Similarly, in post-colonial nations after
World War II, there has been a widespread tendency to promote
indigenous languages as national languages. The language
rights of minority populations have, in the past three decades,
become a predominant concern of many nations, and new interpretations of the term 'national language' have resulted.
In Peru, for example, 'national languages' refers to all the
indigenous languages of the nation (Peru 1972a, 1972b; Wölck
1972); the General Education Law of 1972 specifically recognizes
the indigenous languages of Peru and endorses the concept of
bilingual education for its potential in bringing the communities of Peru an opportunity to have access to a meaningful education. Recently, the 'Universal Declaration of Human Rights'

was published in 24 indigenous languages of Peru (La Nueva Crónica 1974). The official declaration that all indigenous tongues are national languages is, however, primarily a symbolic gesture acknowledging the existence of the nation's minority peoples. There is no plan for all these languages to be used in any instrumental sense by the government or any of its agencies (Albo 1977). In Peru, only Quechua is receiving serious attention for use in publications, political and educational; and there is an attempt to determine a supradialectal norm of Quechua which can be spread through education.

Another use of the term 'national language' is that which designates an official language recognized as the norm for governmental, educational, and international relations, political and commercial. The declaration of French as the national language for the Ivory Coast is such an example. In this situation, the official norm is spread to speakers of indigenous languages through the educational system; and accessibility to professional occupations depends in part on knowledge of French.

In the Soviet Union, the term 'national language' is used to refer to any language which has become standardized and is identified with a nationality. Lewis (1972) provides a summary of the extent of linguistic diversity among the national minorities of the Soviet Union which, since the eighteenth century, has created several waves of national language policies. Stalin's approaches are perhaps best known in the Western world (Stalin 1934, 1942).

Yet another use of the term 'national language' is one in which a former colony which has achieved independent status declares one of its indigenous tongues the national language. English or some other European language may or may not remain the official language in use for international affairs and the predominant tongue of business, government, and higher education. The indigenous tongue declared the national language takes on the role of 'lingua franca' for language groups within the country in numerous daily interactions across groups. Swahili in Tanzania is such an example (Whiteley 1969). A related example is the use of the term 'national language' in Morocco, where Classical Arabic is the national (official) language; yet Berber and spoken Moroccan Arabic must be known for participation in internal commercial affairs. French is the language necessary for entrance into the highest social strata.

It follows that national language policy depends in large part on the particular definitions of the term assumed, historical precedent in language decisions, and the diversity and relative socioeconomic resources of the different language groups in a nation. The extent and type of corpus and program planning and implementation vary greatly, as does the process of planning (Rubin et al. 1977). Bilingual education is for some countries only a part of the policy and the process. In some nations, language policy is specifically articulated and subject to highly specialized planning by groups or institutions charged with this task. The Soviet Union, the Peoples Republic of China, Norway, Malaysia, and Sweden represent the wide range of nations in which language policy, program implementation and maintenance, and materials production are included among the duties of particular divisions of the government and national nongovernmental agencies. In other nations, supra-polity decisions in response to issues or events for which the relevance of language is not considered may, at the local level, be interpreted as pertinent to language. However, at the federal level, implications of the policy for language choice or change may not have been considered at the point of decision making. Economic, political, or educational policies may contain provisions which affect language choice; but language per se need not be a primary area of consideration. Often, in these cases, supra-polity decisions provide a configuration in which local groups recognize the relations to language of the constituent elements; and they reshape higher level decisions to influence local institutions to respond to language issues (Heath 1976a).

Motivations and results of national language policies are also highly varied. In some cases, local-level interpretations of language policy center on particular institutions, such as education or specific industries. The goal of a language policy is usually to spread one particular language or language variety. However, this spread may be either replacive or additive. The goal of replacive programs is to encourage the spread of the official norm over all other varieties in the nation. Programs supporting replacive goals are often termed transitional, since the policy assumes the chosen national language will be used in coordination with other languages for only a generation or so until the national language replaces indigenous tongues. An additive policy is designed to encourage the population to supplement their indigenous language(s) or variety(ies) with the official language or variety. Some additive programs foster the spread of European languages of wider communication; others promote the spread of indigenous languages to new functions associated with higher education, public record-keeping, and vocational opportunities in an industrialized work force. When a language is slated for addition to other codes, the result is usually extension of the linguistic repertoire to include formal and public registers, written and oral. Primary emphasis is most frequently given to extending reading and writing skills in the chosen language or variety. Programs supporting the additive goal in language policy are sometimes interpreted as tolerant, even occasionally supportive, of languages other than the official variety. In some situations, however, if social and economic advancement depend on learning the official code and using it in a wide range of functions, an avowedly additive program may be interpreted by some groups as transitional in the long run.

Bilingual education is usually associated with additive programs. Materials and instructors provide for the use of both indigenous languages and the designated official norm. Additive programs, including those which depend on policies declaring an indigenous tongue as a national language, often enlist cooperation of members of minority groups for participation in bilingual education efforts. In addition, these programs often force the integration of some minority members into government programs. The relatively recent revitalization of minority languages in many nations has created some changes in the composition of decision-makers in institutions such as education, transportation, and the mass media. These movements vary greatly in the intensity of efforts made by minority language speakers to have their language spread across institutions. For example, the Welsh language movement has penetrated not only education--across the curriculum from kindergarten through college--but it has also created changes in public advertising, in TV and radio, in road signs, and in the customer services of some commercial firms.

In some cases, a bilingual education movement may exist without the support of a national language policy. For example, throughout Great Britain in recent decades, the provision of bilingual education or early instruction in the indigenous languages of immigrants derives not from a national language policy, but from educational rulings which guarantee parents that, within the limits of reasonable expenditure, their children may have instruction appropriate to their needs. Other bilingual services or situations permitting use of languages other than English may derive from specific local statutory laws. National laws may not go so far as to place indigenous languages on a footing of equality with the official norm; but they may guarantee specific rights. For example, the Welsh Language Act passed in English Parliament in 1967 granted equal validity to Welsh on any document or declaration in court (Welsh Cymdeithas yr Iaith Gymraeg 1974). Many movements to promote the revival, maintenance, and/or spread of minority languages have no official policy supporting them, but they are instead allowed to grow in democratic countries because there are no laws prohibiting their existence. In addition, many such movements are ways of obtaining recognition of the speakers of a minority language as a viable national culture, and recognition of the language in specific institutional functions is only a minor goal of what is ostensibly billed as a language movement. Examples are to be found in the revival of Scottish Gaelic and Breton where there are, in the first case, no monolingual speakers of the language, and, in the second case, relatively few. Some young people are learning these languages as second tongues and promoting wide-sweeping rights of these groups to recognition of a viable heritage (Dressler and Wodak-Leodolter 1977).

2. The United States approach. Currently, within the United States, the term 'national language policy' is invoked in response to bilingual education. Those who favor bilingual education argue that such an educational policy is appropriate to the guarantee of equal opportunity and of certain freedoms provided in the Constitution. In effect, groups at the local level interpret the Constitution and statutory laws covering equal educational opportunities as providing a national language policy which supports bilingual education. Those who oppose bilingual education argue that the national language of the United States has always been English, unquestionably, and that federally funded efforts to support bilingual education serve to maintain minority languages and to discourage the young of these groups from learning standard English. This argument also maintains that, given the course of assimilation of minority language groups in United States history, today's minority language groups will also find it necessary to learn English for socioeconomic advancement. In the climate of controversy surrounding bilingual education, other types of linguistic awareness have arisen; and educators, policy-makers, and human services delivery personnel are reassessing uses of language in their professions. New approaches to simplifying public language, clarifying regulations, and improving writing skills are seen as both democratizing and rehabilitative for traditionally valued skills in the use of standard English.

The numerous forces behind these trends recognize the need for political support; thus they often relate their desire for particular linguistic aims to other political or social goals and hope to gain institutional support from existing governmental agencies. These bodies have built-in mechanisms of social change for specific areas of national life, such as education, government printing, and distribution of social services; and language goals can thus be incorporated into other changes in these areas. Seeing multiple weaknesses in this piecemeal approach to language choice and language change, some groups advocate serious consideration of a national language policy. Close attention to the historical background of language decisions in the United States may provide useful information for undertaking such a proposal.

2.1 Historical precedents. The United States approach to language policy must be seen as deriving in large part from traditions and philosophies set by the history of Great Britain. Once English was established over French in the fourteenth century in England, Englishmen did not initiate policies to insure maintenance of English. Language was a matter of individual choice or chance. If born into poor circumstances where one learned another language or a substandard variety of English, one was expected to seek out exposure to the acceptable language variety. Those born in certain geographical or social settings were guaranteed exposure to the proper language variety. For Englishmen, achievement of the prestige dialect was a matter of concern for socially mobile individuals, not policy-makers. Schoolmen, intellectuals, and artists promoted extension of English; but, in general, policy-makers assumed that individuals would see the merits of adopting the prestige variety and would do so (Heath 1976a).

The colonial and early national philosophies related to language were strongly influenced by the British approach. In spite of diversities of populations and languages variously distributed and aggregated at times and places in the United States, a national language policy was never seriously considered (Heath 1976b). Recognizing any such proposals as a possible constriction of freedoms of choice in linguistic and cultural matters, political and legal leaders often pointed out that governmental support of a standardized official English language norm conflicted with not only democratic ideals, but also the realities of language change. In a geographically and socially mobile nation, the constant interaction of individuals across groups would 'preserve an identity of language throughout the United States', views expressed by John Marshall (Marshall to Webster, January 14, 1831, Noah Webster MSS.). Throughout the first three-quarters of the nineteenth century, popular response and reasoned intellectual leadership recognized the occasional calls for a national language policy as all too frequently deriving from self-interests, political, economic, or social.

Several leaders proposed language(s) as resources in the United States. These voices suggested that bilingualism and bilingual education were consistent with national goals. Perhaps it is most important that support of bilingual education during this period came not from a national language policy, but in response to local community needs. 'Don't loose [sic] your vernacular tongue in which ... you have to make your way one of these days ...' Thus the German-born, but 'thoroughly Americanized', editor of the first edition of Encyclopedia Americana wrote his son in 1842 (Francis Lieber MSS.). Officials of the Philadelphia Public Schools extended this idea in 1852 when they proposed that instruction in both English and German be available, because of the presence of a 'large and increasing German population with whom almost every educated man is at some time thrown into business relations' (Annual report 1853). In 1865, William Harris, superintendent of schools in St. Louis, maintained that retention of one's native language provided a consciousness of the history of one's ancestry and access to influence from the oldest members of the family; these abilities were very potent in giving tone to the individuality of youth (Kluwin forthcoming). This wide variety of responses to language differences was possible because the United States had not endorsed a national language policy.

A similar flexibility existed with respect to defining standard English. In the earliest days of the common school and state mandated compulsory attendance laws, grammar books called for memorization of rules of grammar, but they also stressed flexibility in language uses (Heath forthcoming). The concern of these early American grammarians was that form not take precedence over substance in writing and speaking. During the next decades as common schools and compulsory attendance were becoming more and more widespread in the United States, grammar books increasingly stressed standardization, and flexibility in language use and knowledge of different languages or varieties of language were increasingly downgraded. By the late 1880s, some school systems became intolerant with the emphasis on 'basic skills' and rule recitation. In 1884, for example, the superintendent of the Philadelphia schools called for a change in the course of language study. The change resulted from a belief that the study of grammar as a subject was not appropriate until the high school level. The recommended course was one which required increased use of language in writing, speaking, and reading. Students were to be held accountable for facts supporting generalizations and they were to express their thoughts clearly. A later report from the superintendent condemned earlier practices and explained his own recommendations: 'The application of what the pupils had learned of the principles of language to the elucidation of prose and poetry was rarely practiced. The result was facility in talking about grammar without the ability to use it' (Philadelphia Annual report 1889:24). Other reasons for the curricular change sound strikingly similar to theoretical statements which have recently come out of sociolinguistic approaches to language in education. Annual reports stressed that language was the heart of the curriculum because through language, students learned both knowledge and rules of functioning in classrooms; language study was to be not a single subject of study, but integrated throughout all subjects (Philadelphia Annual reports 1883, 1892, 1895, 1898-99, 1903).

The uses of language, and the need to have variety in language(s) extended to the curriculum of commercial high schools in Philadelphia and other cities such as Cleveland, St. Louis, and San Francisco. The teaching of foreign languages was a central portion of the curriculum in a commercial high school in Philadelphia in 1896. In comparison with business rivals in Europe, American businessmen lacked foreign languages, and commercial high schools stressed knowledge of Spanish, German, and French, as well as practical approaches to the uses of English in business (Philadelphia Annual report 1899).

The emphasis to be made here is that in the face of problems very similar to those generally lumped in consideration of a national language policy for the United States today, policymakers, educators, and business leaders planned and implemented local responses in accordance with local needs. Without

the current reliance on federal funding, and consequently the
abundance of statutory laws and regulations coming from the
national level, bilingual education, foreign language promotion,
and highly varied integrated programs of language skills were
planned and maintained at local levels.

2.2 Current issues in bilingual education. Since the middle
of the nineteenth century, proponents of bilingual education
and flexibility in definitions and approaches to standard English have been countered with arguments for an English-only
policy which supported rigid prescriptions of standard English.
The two camps fought out their battles at the local level until
the xenophobia of the second decade of the twentieth century
which led some local groups to support state legislation declaring English the official language of the state (Geffert et al.
1975). The two forces have only recently brought their differences to the national level, and the Bilingual Education Act of
1968 has caused many of the conflicts which formerly occurred
at local and state levels to reappear on the national level.
Proponents of bilingual education want a national language
policy to protect and maintain bilingual education and the
rights of minority language speakers. Those who oppose bilingual education want, if not a national policy, at least a
national commitment to English monolingualism and to the maintenance of past standards in use of the English language. The
push for minimal competency laws at the state level comes from
these forces, who wish tests of English usage, particularly
composition skills, to determine awarding of a high school
diploma.

For these groups, national language embodies a unifying symbol to numerous values. If asked what is the national language
of the United States, the man in the street will say English.
If asked further questions such as why, when, and how, that
person will offer folk notions as historical and social facts:
the founding fathers, including Webster, had a hand in the
decision; the particular kind of English which is American has
been standardized by schools and other public forces; a good
citizen's responsibility includes knowledge of 'good English';
the man who talks right acts right, is predictable in behavior
and conforming as a citizen (Heath forthcoming). Many citizens
assume that use of English is somehow official in the United
States, and is the result of decisions made at some point in the
past. In addition, the term 'national language' carries with it
the connotation of not only English, but a particular kind of
English, which is standardized and spoken according to norms
of usage established by particular groups within the population. English as the national language is seemingly supported
by the reliance in public schools on English literature and English history. The notion of standard English is supported by
a concern with American English, the Webster tradition, and
teachers' and grammar books' adherence to the positive

correlation between successful composition skills and clear, logical thinking. During the 1920s when there were increasingly frequent moves by individual states to mandate English as the official language of the states, there was a simultaneous trend in English grammar books stressing that the writing of good English was one way of illustrating one's character. Correct usage of English was believed to correlate with honesty, dependability, hard work, thrift, and other characteristics of predictable citizens. For many adults in the United States who received their public schooling during the period from the 1920s through the 1940s, the choice of English as the national language was not only a political necessity, but a moral need. There were powerful convictions that proper English predicts proper behavior, and the use of English referred not only to a linguistic choice, but to a selection of values and to ways of behaving. Implicit in this is the view that language is the basis of nationality, a cohesive force, and that control of language choice will and should carry over into control of other types of behaviors.

Those who favor bilingual education are quick to point out that opposition to bilingual education and promotion of English only is often a way not only of proscribing languages other than English, but also ways of behaving which do not conform to mainstream norms. Thus, as long as a monolingual language choice is tacitly sanctioned in national policies which do not center on language per se, but affect language choices at the local level, there is no way of guaranteeing freedom of choice in numerous social and cultural matters. If ballots are available in different languages, so should warrants and warranties be. Carpenters should be allowed to use their native language in tests for licensing. Social services, travel information, financial information, and government regulations and applications should be as accessible to those who speak a language other than English as they are to English speakers. However, since the impact of Civil Rights legislation has been greatest in education, bilingual education is at the heart of proposals for a national language policy. Once the guarantee of bilingual education is as secure as other educational approaches and programs, then proponents of bilingualism will push for acceptance of languages other than English in other programs.

3. **The policy and process of bilingual education.** Recognizing some of the reasons behind the identification of a national language policy with bilingual education, one is tempted to hypothesize about the processes and outcomes of such a policy. Discussions of policy-making have traditionally emphasized the input stage (e.g. Schneider 1977). The approach suggested here places more emphasis on the expected outcome stage. Expected outcomes here refer to the future policy outputs anticipated by individuals to have an effect on their lives. Individuals pushing for a national language policy are

doing so in partial response to the manner in which they and others have been affected by particular issues in the past. Individuals promoting a national language policy of bilingual education for the United States may pattern their vision of the way it would be carried out according to the ways other policies which have affected their lives have been operationalized. Political science theorists propose four possible ways of achieving this (Smith 1969): distributive outcomes or policy types (3.1), regulative outcomes (3.2), redistributive function (3.3), and emotive symbolic outcomes (3.4).

3.1 **Distributive outcomes or policy types.** The orientation here is to expect the government to aid special interest groups in gaining their expectations. Interactions are primarily between government personnel and active individuals representing special interest groups. An example of this type of output is the cooperation between units of the Department of Health, Education and Welfare and social scientists, aided by minority language groups, in the preparation and distribution of curriculum materials. The training centers for bilingual education are another example of the distributive outcome of bilingual education policy--the provision of goods and services expected by recently politicized groups.

3.2 **Regulative outcomes.** These derive most often from sectors which want the government to intervene and give them preferential treatment by limiting certain activities of other groups or making available to them services formerly made available only to others. This regulative function is the source of the greatest conflict between the Office of Civil Rights (OCR) and bilingual education personnel. Homogeneous grouping frequently leads to conditions in violation of civil rights rulings, yet some degree of homogeneous grouping may, in some settings, be the most efficient and effective way of providing meaningful bilingual education. Bilingual education personnel often want their preferences for program goals to override the fact that the composition of their programs violates OCR rulings. Bilingual education proponents also point out that their program should have available the same considerations of time, money, and realistic expectations of outcome other education programs have had (Fishman 1978), even if such programs now have to be curtailed.

3.3 **Redistributive function.** This expected outcome is held by individuals who wish government decisions to benefit them as members of classes or broad social groupings at the expense of other classes or social groupings. The demands of Spanish speakers for bilingual services in the public arena are often so interpreted, and politicians are quick to point out that comprehensive provision of public schooling and services is not realistic for all minority language groups, and if these are distributed to one group, other groups will have to be denied the same privileges. Direct or indirect requests for retribution for past injustices in educational and economic opportunities fall in this category.

3.4 Emotive symbolic outcomes. Often issued only in public statements and not carried to fruition in specific policies are symbolic gestures or benefits from the government which will further specific causes at local levels. Largely ideological and affective, this benefit often helps local forces gather support for policies having one or more of the other types of outcome. A government official making a speech in the Southwest and mentioning the language rights of Mexican Americans provided for in the Treaty of Hidalgo fulfills such a function.

The respective impacts of each of these expectations will differ in terms of the intensity of debate and public response they engender. They are therefore likely to be fought out in different political arenas involving different political actors. Thus far, the major arena for a national language policy has been the Department of Health, Education and Welfare, but it is to be expected that if expectations of policy provisions in this area are met, other areas, such as law, social services, transportation, and public communication will become arenas for struggles similar to those which have surrounded bilingual education. Without a comprehensive national language policy which would provide federal support for the cultivation, study, and instruction of language(s), benefitting all sectors--the general, commercial, aesthetic, and diplomatic--the efforts applied to bilingual education will have to be applied to each of these areas separately, and differential responses and outcomes may be expected.

4. Planning for a language policy. Any language policy is, in effect, a cultural policy which calls for changes in the quality of life and cultural developments of specific groups in the nation. Both minority language groups and mainstream majority groups are affected. For example, for bilingual education in the United States, government representatives involved in regulating programs often attempt to speak Spanish in order to achieve credibility with personnel involved in local programs. Formerly monolingual majority language speakers are sometimes learning what they formerly considered a minority tongue in order to legitimate their political roles and to achieve communication in a larger network within their own nation. Such changes involve attitude shifts, as well as alterations in behavior patterns.

In some senses, to talk of planning a language/cultural policy is to contradict many definitions United States citizens have traditionally held of each of these terms. Language involves culture, one cannot be separated from the other, and their structures and functions are in the basic sense determined by their bearers. Policy, on the other hand, implies system and deliberation. Language and culture are processes that are organized and yet spontaneous, providing patterns within themselves. This is why any language policy must have at its center the notion that culture and language derive in large part from communities which bear them and cannot be planned to yield designated results which may not fit the needs and goals of communities. Therefore, any plans for a language policy must move cautiously, since they have the powerful potential of impinging on the sets of cultural choices open to citizens in their daily living. Within a democratic climate, there is something distasteful about the idea that language and culture should be subjected to the same kind of predictive planning used for economics, politics, and transportation. However, it may sometimes be prudent and efficient to plan aspects of language and culture, if such planning can be shown to benefit the majority of the population or to insure maintenance of constitutional rights to all groups. A national language policy, however, even in those circumstances where such proof is possible, may press together two disparate and often highly incompatible value systems. Individualism clashes with statism, as it did in civil rights issues. Freedom challenges constraint, and creativity resists being pitted against standardization.

Language policy cannot be equated with bilingual education; it must include literacy, the reform of public documents' legalese, renewal of interest and extension of expertise in foreign languages, and provision of rights for maintenance of minority languages. The latter does not necessarily mean government sponsorship for maintenance of the languages of those groups which can and have fostered their language in religious, aesthetic, and even sociocultural affairs. A national language policy would, however, make explicit the rights of these groups to continue to define the limits of uses of their languages within their own communities. A national language policy should also include what we may refer to as 'language building'--making available language resources in the arts, recreation, human services delivery, as well as education.

In the final analysis a national language policy must be an exercise in the orchestration of a new symphony of national language themes. Therefore, major planning for such a policy must include identification of the main themes and contradictions within the country. This has yet to be done in the United States. We cannot posit pluralism, democracy, decentralization, intergovernmental and international cooperation, and equality of educational opportunity as the basic currents of a national language policy, until we know more about how these have developed with relation to language in the United States.

REFERENCES

Albo, Xavier. 1977. El futuro de los idiomas oprimidos en los Andes. Lima: Universidad nacional mayor de San Marcos, Centro de investigación de lingüística aplicada.
Cymdeithas yr Iaith Gymraeg [Welsh must live]. 1974. n.p.
Dressler, Wolfgang, and Ruth Wodak-Leodolter. 1977. Language preservation and language death in Brittany. Internation Journal of Sociology of Language 12.33-44.
Fishman, Joshua. 1978. A gathering of vultures, the 'legion of decency' and bilingual education in the U.S.A. Review of: Language, ethnicity and the schools by Noel Epstein. National Association of Bilingual Education 2.13-16.
Geffert, H. M., et al. 1975. The current status of U.S. bilingual education legislation. Papers in applied linguistics, bilingual education series no. 4. Arlington, Va.: Center for Applied Linguistics.
Heath, Shirley Brice. 1976a. Colonial language status achievement: Mexico, Peru, and the United States. In: Language in sociology. Edited by Albert Verdoodt and Rolf Kjolseth. Louvain: Éditions Peeters. 49-92.
Heath, Shirley Brice. 1976b. A national language academy: Debate in the new nation. International Journal of the Sociology of Language 11.9-43.
Heath, Shirley Brice. (forthcoming) Standard English, biography of a symbol. To appear in: The English language: English in its social and historical context. Edited by Timothy Shopen and Peg Griffin. Arlington, Va.: Center for Applied Linguistics and Winthrop Publishers.
Kluwin, Bridget. (forthcoming) Coping with language and cultural diversity: A study of changing language instruction policy from 1860 to 1930 in three American cities. Stanford: Stanford University, School of Education.
Lewis, E. Glyn. 1972. Multilingualism in the Soviet Union: Language policy and its implementation. The Hague: Mouton.
Lieber, Francis. Manuscript collection. Caroliniana Library, Columbia, South Carolina.
La Nueva Crónica. 1974. Declaración de derechos humanos editan en 24 lenguas aborigenes. 13 July.
Peru. 1972a. Primer seminario nacional de educación bilingüe. Lima: Ministerio de Educación.
Peru. 1972b. Politica nacional de educación bilingüe. Lima: Ministerio de Educación.
Philadelphia. Annual report of superintendent of public schools. 1853, 1883, 1888, 1892, 1895, 1898-99, 1903.
Rubin, Joan, Björn H. Jernudd, Jyotirindra Das Gupta, Joshua A. Fishman, and Charles A. Ferguson. 1977. Language planning processes. The Hague: Mouton.
Stalin, Joseph. 1934. Marxism and the national and colonial question. New York: International Publishers.

Stalin, Joseph. 1942. Marxism and the national question. New York: International Publishers.
Schneider, Susan Gilbert. 1977. Revolution, reaction or reform. New York: Las Americas.
Smith, T. Alexander. 1969. Toward a comparative theory of the policy process. Comparative Politics 4.498-515.
Webster, Noah. Manuscript collection. New York Public Library.
Whiteley, W. H. 1969. Swahili, the rise of a national language. London: Methuen.
Wölck, Wolfgang. 1972. El reto del multilingüismo en el Peru. Lima: Instituto de estudios peruanos.

III. Bilingualism, Thought, and Cognition

BILINGUALISM AND THOUGHT

JOHN MACNAMARA

McGill University

Abstract. Recent studies conducted by linguists, anthropologists, and psycholinguists in the area of semantics make it possible to have a fresh look at the semantic processes of bilinguals. The new insights result in no small measure from the shedding of strict behavioristic constraints—without, however, abandoning the techniques developed in association with behaviorism. My paper will review with, hopefully, appropriate comments the work which has been done on the relationship between bilingualism and thought. The topics that arise include bilingualism and IQ, the coordinate-compound distinction, the Whorfian hypothesis, the problem-solving capacities of bilinguals and ethnosemantics.

If Whorf's hypothesis were true, if it were the case that differences among languages caused substantial differences in cognitive functioning, the bilingual person would be in a curious predicament. In his cognitive functioning, the bilingual would have to conform to one of three patterns, and each of the three would involve serious inconveniences. He might when using L_1 or L_2 always function cognitively in the manner appropriate to L_1 say; he would then have great difficulty in understanding speakers of L_2 or in being understood by them. Alternatively, he might always function cognitively in a manner appropriate to neither language and run the risk of understanding or being understood by nobody. Or he might have two cognitive systems, one for each language. He could then communicate with speakers of either language but he would have great difficulty in 'communicating' with himself. Whenever he switched languages he would have difficulty in explaining in L_2 what he had heard or said in L_1.

The implications which I am drawing from Whorf's hypothesis may seem preposterous, but I think that they follow logically. The differences in cognitive functioning which Whorf attributed to linguistic variables in syntax and vocabulary are far-reaching and profound. And though Whorf does not, to my knowledge, emphasize the effect which such differences might have on communication across language boundaries, the effects must surely be grave.

Our unwillingness to believe that the bilingual finds himself in the predicament I describe above is the measure of our unwillingness to accept the Whorfian hypothesis. But there are other grounds for caution. Psychologists, as Joshua Fishman (1960) points out, have been hard pressed to find any evidence in favor of the hypothesis. Only in its weakest form, only when it is taken as referring to the relationship between the suitability of vocabulary items to denote certain objects and some dependent cognitive functioning, is there support for Whorf in the psychological literature (see Lenneberg 1967, and Miller and McNeill 1969). Moreover, many of us instinctively join Church (1958) and Black (1959 and 1969) against Quine (1960) and numerous other philosophers in the view that one cannot establish a man's ontology from either his vocabulary or his grammar.

One is a little surprised, then, to hear Lounsbury (1969) say that in their thinking about limited areas of vocabulary and the related cognitive structures 'the leading social anthropologists of today incline ... in the direction of complete relativism' (Lounsbury 1969: 14). Lounsbury is referring specifically to kinship systems, but his remarks can presumably be extended to cover other folk taxonomies. The root reason for the prevailing opinion is the hope, perhaps even belief, that the componential analysis of folk taxonomies reveals psychological entities. Indeed several of the leading exponents of the art, Goodenough (1956), Frake (1962), Mathiot (1969), and Wallace (1962) have made statements which suggest that they are laying bare the bases used by people in classifying their environment. On the other hand, it is only fair to point out that this belief has been seriously questioned several times by social anthropologists themselves; see, for example, Burling (1969), Hymes (1969), Lounsbury (1969) and Wallace (1965). The claim that componential analysis reveals psychologically valid entities runs into Burling's (1969) objection that any set of terms can be analyzed, or systematically divided, in several different ways. Since each division demands a set of components somewhat different from any other division, and since the choice of one division rather than another is arbitrary, it follows that the psychological validity of the resultant components is highly questionable. Moreover, as Vermazen (1967) observes in discussing a similar problem connected with Katz and Fodor's (1963)

model of lexical structure, there is no principled way of selecting
components or bases of classification. We can effectively distinguish
men from women, for example, on the basis of skin texture, body outline, length of finger nails, hair ribbons and the like without ever
needing to carry the study further. The seemingly obvious candidate
for component status, then, need not be the one which people generally
employ. The truth is that we know very little about the bases which
people use for classifying the most familiar objects in their environment (see Polanyi 1968), and it is unlikely that language on its own
should provide the answer.

The point of all this is to emphasize once again the lesson which
psychologists drew from their studies of Whorf's hypothesis. Linguistic evidence on its own can be used to support linguistic conclusions only, never psychological ones. Since anthropologists have seldom gone beyond linguistic evidence in their analyses of folk taxonomies, it would be premature to make claims of psychological validity
for their componential systems. It follows, too, that one would be unwise to base claims for Whorfian relativism on such analyses.

Coordinate-compound distinction

The coordinate-compound distinction to which I now want to turn is
closely related to Whorfian relativism. Indeed I hope to show that in
some of its forms it is a veiled version of such relativism. It was
mainly Uriel Weinreich (1953) in his book, Languages in Contact, who
drew the attention of psychologists to the distinction. In that book he
tentatively suggests that on semantic grounds bilinguals seem to fall
into three types, which I shall call by the names which have subsequently become standard. 'Coordinate' bilinguals are those for whom
the corresponding pair of terms in two languages signify a single 'sementeme'. 'Compound' bilinguals are those for whom corresponding
terms signify a single sementeme. 'Subordinate' bilinguals are those
for whom a term in L_2 signifies first a term in L_1 and signifies a sementeme only indirectly. The three types may be illustrated by means
of Weinreich's own diagrams in which he uses the Russian word kniga
'book' together with the English word book.

(1) Coordinate   (2) Compound   (3) Subordinate

'book'   'kníga'   'book' ≡ 'kníga'   {'book'/'buk/'}
  | | | |
/buk/   /kn iga/   /buk/   /kn iga/ |
                                                /kn iga/

In Ervin and Osgood (1965) the subordinate type is subsumed into the compound one and criteria are given for judging to which of the two remaining types a bilingual belongs. Compounds are those who either learned one language through the medium of the other, as in old-fashioned language classes, or learned both languages in the same context, the home for instance. The coordinates or 'true' bilinguals are those who learned the two languages in different contexts, such as L_1 at home and L_2 at school (presumably by the direct method) and at work. Ervin and Osgood's illustration of the two types are shown in Figure 1 in which $\underline{S}$ and $\underline{R}$ stand for sign and response respectively,

FIGURE 1.

Coordinate	Compound
S_A ↗ $r_{\overline{m_1}}$ ------- s_{m_1} ↘ R_A S_B ↗ $r_{\overline{m_1}}$ ------- s_{m_1} ↘ R_B	S_A ↗ $r_{\overline{m}}$ ------- s_m ↘ R_A S_B ↗ ↘ R_B

$\underline{r}$ and $\underline{s}$ stand for 'mediating processes or meanings', and the subscripts $\underline{A}$ and $\underline{B}$ stand for different languages as do the sub-subscripts 1 and 2 in the diagram for coordinates. Not wishing to start old battles all over again, I will rest content with two observations about this theory. It falls heir to all the criticism that Chomsky (1959), Fodor (1965) and others have made of $\underline{S}$-$\underline{R}$ attempts to handle the phenomena of language. In addition, and here I am sure its authors would agree today, it is quite inadequate as a representation of the lexical structure which must be employed by anyone who speaks a natural language. Space permits me to do little more than refer to a number of sources: Chomsky (1965), Katz (1966), Katz and Fodor (1963), Katz and Postal (1964), Macnamara (in press), Macnamara and O'Clerigh (1969), Quillian (1967 and 1968) and Weinreich (1966). Among the principal weaknesses of the Ervin and Osgood model is the fact that it makes no provision for denotation as distinct from connotation or for emotive meaning as distinct from either. Moreover the model does not discuss the problem of selecting an appropriate meaning from among the many meanings of a polysemous term, although this is one of the major criteria which a satisfactory semantic theory must meet.

I fear that the man whose lead I have long followed in the study of bilingualism has added somewhat to the confusion which surrounds the coordinate-compound distinction. In some recent papers (Lambert

1966, Lambert and Rawlings 1969, Segalowitz and Lambert 1969) he shifts the distinction between coordinate and compound bilingualism to one between early and late bilingualism. Compound bilinguals are those who acquire both languages in their homes before they go to school; coordinate bilinguals are those who began to acquire their second language after school age. In this new way of classifying bilinguals he is joined by Stafford (1968) and by Stafford and Van Keuren (1968).

But to return to the point of departure! Through all the variations in the interpretation of the terms, 'coordinate' and 'compound', the distinction has always been a semantic one and for Ervin and Osgood, unless I am mistaken, it was a Whorfian one. Ervin and Osgood's compound bilinguals had a single set of 'representational mediation processes' for the two languages, whereas their coordinates had two sets of such processes, one for each language. Since mediation processes in their system are caused by signs or stimuli, it is fair to say that differences between languages cause different cognitive, nonlinguistic, mediating processes. For example, French uses the word couper in connection with the cutting of hair with a scissors and also the cutting up of a joint of meat with a knife; standard English divides the function of couper between cut and carve respectively. It follows that a coordinate French-English bilingual could well have different mediating processes associated with couper and cut. Admittedly, Ervin and Osgood seek to avoid the resultant inconveniences by suggesting that across languages the differences between translation equivalents are mostly slight. But as the above example shows this is not true. Ervin and Osgood also permit of elaborate connections between the coordinate's parallel mediating processes, in order to account for translation. Such connections might seem at first to preclude the plight of the Whorfian bilingual who cannot communicate with himself, who when he switches to L_2 can never make out what he has heard or said in L_1. But Ervin and Osgood's additional associations will not preclude this difficulty; they are not equivalent to an instruction 'compare and contrast', and make good any differences discovered by having recourse to other linguistic materials and other mediation processes. Yet only by means of such an instruction and a device to operate it could a person with something like 'coordinate systems' ever switch languages without becoming hopelessly lost.

Lest you think that I am being unfair to the Ervin and Osgood model, permit me to point out two other related difficulties. The model has no system which would permit of two sets of mediating processes associated with a single term and for permitting context to select between them. Yet the cutting of hair with a scissors and the carving of meat with a knife might well give rise to distinct mediation processes which might well compete for possession of a Frenchman's head when couper was encountered. Furthermore, Osgood's semantic system, like all the other ones which have since been proposed, does not handle grammar. Apart from anything else, this means the model is confined to pairs of lexical items; hence it cannot guard against the inconveniences I have outlined by systematically relating viande with couper in one expression and cheveux with couper in another expression so as to ensure that only the appropriate mediating processes are elicited.

On the subject of research into the coordinate-compound distinction I have little to add to what I wrote in the Journal of Social Issues in 1967. I then considered the evidence for the distinction to be exiguous, and I have seen no reason since to change my mind. I agree with Diller (1967) that the distinction as it stands is most likely a 'conceptual artifact', and I am fearful for the sturdiness of the tall cognitive and personality structures, which Diebold (1968) builds upon it. Perhaps my basic trouble is my belief that nothing like an adequate semantic system has been worked out for any language, let alone related semantic systems for two languages in bilingual harness.

This need not mean that we abandon work on the semantic systems of bilinguals; it is rather an invitation reculer pour mieux sauter. I suspect that the original inspiration for the coordinate-compound distinction owes more to instances of semantic interference than to Whorfian relativism. This sort of interference is well-known; it is beautifully illustrated for example by Professor Mackey (1962 and 1965). For instance, the Irish word lámh is the nearest equivalent to the English word hand in the sense of human member. However, unlike hand, lámh includes 'arm' in its denotation. If we start out not from words but from semantic fields we find numerous situations which I have previously illustrated with the French word couper serving the function of the English words cut and carve in at least some of their senses. It seems to me that such differences between the semantic systems of languages might well give rise to a whole range of bilinguals who vary in the extent to which they keep the semantic systems of their two languages distinct. Furthermore, I agree with Kolers (1963) and Fishman (1964) that the manner in which a person has learned his languages is unlikely to fix his semantic systems for life. Some may start out with fused semantic systems and gradually sort them out; others may start out with separate systems but gradually permit them to merge. Indeed, as John Gumperz (1964) has pointed out, it may be that distinct semantic systems can be maintained only by a person who makes a great conscious effort to do so, and much good language teaching is aimed precisely at achieving this effect.

At this point I want to forestall a possible source of confusion. The sort of distinction between semantic systems of which I have been speaking does not at all suggest a Whorfian relativism. It does not suggest that an Englishman either carves meat differently from a Frenchman, or perceives the carving of meat differently from a Frenchman, or is in the least different from a Frenchman in his approach to meat, simply because as an Englishman he has a special term for the action of slicing meat with a knife. Neither is there any suggestion that an Irishman's knowledge of anatomy is more confused than that of an Englishman. All I want to suggest is that when a well-educated Irish-English bilingual cashes the terms in the two languages, he may get different semantic values for the words lámh and hand; a bilingual who does not know the languages so thoroughly is likely to get the same value for both words, even when he should not. It follows that when the well-educated bilingual needs to denote precisely that which the word hand denotes, he has to go beyond the word lámh and either add a modifying expression or choose a different lexical item.

It may help to be more precise about the advantages of employing a distinction based on degree of semantic interference rather than the coordinate-compound distinction. The first is clarity. Any clarity which the coordinate-compound distinction seemed to have was deceptive. Weinreich said that kniga and book might denote different 'semantemes' for a coordinate bilingual, but he did not clarify what he meant by a 'semanteme' or how the two semantemes related to these words might differ. The differences between Ervin and Osgood's coordinates and compounds are securely locked inside the head where no one can see them. In contrast, I am tying semantic interference to denotation and more specifically what I might call 'denotational extent'. In the limited illustrative materials which I have used, lámh has a wider denotational extension than hand, and cut has a narrower denotational extension than couper. At a less concrete level, conscience (French) has a wider denotational extension that conscience (English).

Admittedly, I am not proposing any formal model of information processing or language processing, but then I do not believe that formalism in these areas is profitable at the present time. Formalism often results in hardening of the intellectual arteries; I for one feel freer when working from a nonformal base to explore the broad strategies of semantic functioning. One such strategy must call for an ability to relate the incoming linguistic message to stored information and to systems which process such information. Quillian (1968) points out that a highly likely sense for an ambiguous symbol can frequently be determined simply on the basis of frequency of association. For instance, frequency suggests the meaning 'down tools' for strike in (1) though other meanings are possible.

(1) The foreman called a strike.

The problem discussed by Bar-Hillel (1964: 174-179) is rather different. He noted that the meaning 'enclosure in which children play' is determined for pen in (2) on the basis of the relative sizes of boxes and pens in the sense of 'writing instruments'.

(2) The box is in the pen.

The successful interpretation of the word pen in (2), then, depends on access to stored information and also on the ability to carry out some computations on such information at the moment of recall. This follows from the fact that few will have readily available as a piece of information the fact that boxes are rarely small enough to fit inside even a large writing pen. Since we could presumably use the relative sizes of writing pens and any other physical objects with which we are familiar, it is more parsimonious to hypothesize a function which permits us to compare sizes, whenever such information is required, than to store the results of innumerable comparisons. On the assumption that this is correct, I would suggest further that such information is for the most part stored and processed nonlinguistically and probably unconsciously.

Ulric Neisser (1967) has recently made an excellent case for the theory of analysis by synthesis in perception. In essence, the theory proposes that on the basis of partial information one can usually form a correct hypothesis about that which one is perceiving. Applied to language this means that on the basis of partial information, linguistic, nonlinguistic, and stochastic, one can usually form a correct hypothesis about that which someone is trying to communicate. One of course tests the hypothesis against further information which comes one's way and if necessary modifies the hypothesis. My reason for mentioning the theory here is to suggest that if it is correct in broad outline—and it seems to be—we must visualize the human language user as a far more dynamic agent in his approach to speech than either Whorf or bilingual theory builders seem to imagine. Moreover, it seems likely that linguistic processes are only a small part of the cognitive functioning which is associated with either the production or the interpretation of speech. Furthermore, this very dynamism is surely the reason that the bilingual does not end up in any of the impasses to which Whorfian theorizing and the Ervin and Osgood model of coordinate and compound bilingualism seem inevitably to lead.

Bilingualism and IQ

The issues of which I have been speaking raise other more far-reaching issues which unfortunately I can do little more than allude to in this paper. The suggestion that linguistic functioning is to a great extent dependent on nonlinguistic functioning of many sorts is bound to disturb many philosophical spirits. However, it ties in nicely with the theory of Vygotsky (1962) and the oft-repeated theory of Piaget (see, for example, 1963 and 1965) that the origin of thought is distinct from that of language, and that insofar as the two are related in the early stages, language is the dependent partner. The investigations of Piaget's student, Sinclair-de-Zwart (1967 and 1969) support this theory and suggest that even in school children the development of basic cognitive schemata owe little to language, but rather that developments in language which occur at this time are dependent on prior nonlinguistic growth.

Essentially in the same tradition are recent papers by Bever (1970), Hebb, Lambert and Tucker (1970), and Macnamara (1970) all arguing for a much closer integration of nonlinguistic cognitive functioning with linguistic functioning than has been common in most of the recent discussions of language acquisition. In my paper, I attempt to establish the thesis that the majority of linguistic universals are due to certain essential features of human intelligence. These are the features which ensure that mathematics, logic and science are essentially the same the world over; these are the reason that every language is translatable into every other language; these are the basic reason for disbelieving Whorf.

Such communality in human intelligence has been obscured by the development of psychometrics and by the accompanying emphasis in psychology on individual differences. From their earliest beginnings intelligence tests have been designed to reveal individual differences in intelligence; they have never been designed for the purpose of revealing the essentials of intelligence. No analysis of IQs, then, however sophisticated or however comprehensive, could ever reveal what intelligence is; so it is little wonder that psychometric discussions on the topic have been barren. I suspect that the results of concentrating on IQs and on individual differences have been even more baneful than fruitless discussion of the nature of intelligence; I suspect that they have drawn attention away from factors which contribute to the development of intelligence. If I may be permitted to point a moral, one notices how interesting studies of child language became when in the early 1960s scholars abandoned the individual differences approach of earlier years and focussed instead upon the essentials of the process in which children differ very little. A similar moral can be drawn from the experimentally feeble and statistically naive investigations of Jean Piaget which have yielded results of such interest which have been replicable the world over.

This is the background against which I would like to pose the question so often posed by students of bilingualism, does bilingualism affect intelligence? Against such a background one wonders what the question might mean. I have never seen the question discussed in this context, but it seems unlikely that bilingualism should have any effect upon the development of the basic, common, cognitive structures. The question, however, has usually been translated into the form, does bilingualism affect IQ? In that form it is almost trivial. An indefinitely large number of factors can affect IQ without having any direct bearing on what we intuitively recognize as intelligence. Among such factors is command of language. Under certain circumstances bilingual children have frequently been found to have a poorer command of their school language than their unilingual counterparts—see Macnamara (1966). Under similar circumstances bilinguals have generally scored a lower mean verbal IQ than unilinguals, but not a lower mean nonverbal IQ—see Darcy (1953 and 1963). It seems then that grasp of the language variety in which an IQ test is couched can affect the outcome of the test—an honest but hardly a surprising discovery.

What does all this amount to? Instinctively I want to say that the results just mentioned do not mean that bilinguals are more stupid than unilinguals, they have only been made to appear so. I well realize, however, that deficiencies in the standard version of a school language can constitute added difficulty in schoolwork. Tom Kellaghan and John Macnamara (1967) have shown that such difficulties can arise from something other than ignorance of certain words, idioms and syntactic structures; they can arise from a fairly generalized unfamiliarity with and poor control of the standard language, at least in written form, so as to affect a student's problem-solving ability adversely. To conclude, then, bilinguals probably have need of some special help with language; poor control of the school language could well prevent a child from developing competence in several important areas of schoolwork. Granted that difficulties with the language are overcome, however, there is no reason to believe that bilingualism of itself should affect school progress in any way, adversely or beneficially. But of course a second language usually means access to a whole new world of people, literature and ideas, and so bilingualism can be an enormous advantage.

Before passing on to the last section, it is worth pausing for a moment to consider where the study of bilingualism and IQ fits in with Whorfian relativism and the coordinate-compound distinction. There is probably no direct connection between them; nevertheless they are all related to some more general view of the connection between language and thought. The fears, or hopes, which caused people to study the relationship between bilingualism and IQ seem to spring from the general view that language either constitutes or creates intelligence. It is not difficult to see how such a view is related to Whorfian relativism and to the Ervin and Osgood models for coordinates and compounds. It follows then, that the basic objections to both Whorfian relativism and the Ervin and Osgood semantic models can also be used against a direct causal connection which would make intelligence dependent upon bilingualism.

Bilingualism and creativity

The whole study of creativity which has waxed and waned over the past ten years seems to be bedevilled to an even greater degree than the study of intelligence. The enterprise to explain creativity in school children has had two main objectives: (1) to prove that something could be measured which was largely independent of IQ; (2) to purify measures of this 'something' and use them to establish a range of individual differences in it (see Dacey and Madaus 1969). Very little attention indeed has been paid to this 'something' or to the notion of creativity or to the relationship between creativity and intelligence. The fact that measures of creativity were designed almost entirely for the purpose of revealing individual differences in creativity meant that they were bound to miss the essentials of creativity, just as IQs miss the essentials of intelligence. The requirement that IQs and measures of creativity should as far as possible be orthogonal meant that the whole enterprise was committed from the outset to the trivial task of establishing that intelligence and creativity can differ in some peripheral ways. It is hardly unfair to say that the enterprise has been barren.

The whole thrust of Jean Piaget's life work has been to show that intelligence is essentially creative. If anything, he has attributed too much creativity to the mind and failed to stress the fact that the neonate must have a great deal of mental structure to explain intellectual creativity. Be that as it may, however, the main point is that the most important body of investigation into the nature of human intelligence results in the conclusion that the mind is essentially creative. Hardly a happy augury for studies of creativity which start from the assumption that the two are different in kind. To Piaget's work may be added the body of theoretical and empirical work on language which clusters around the writings of Noam Chomsky. Chomsky stresses the creativity involved in the use of natural language and others (see, for example, McNeill 1966) have found that the process of learning a language is a creative one. Perhaps the study of creativity would not have been so fruitless if it had been appreciated from the start that what its investigators were hunting for was not creativity at all, but rather unusual creations. That would not have given the investigators any greater guarantee of validity for their measures, but it would have set them free of the constraint that sought to justify the notion of creativity by showing that it could be distinguished from IQ.

Students of bilingualism have also wondered about the possibility that bilingualism should make people more creative. As I imagine Professor Lambert will discuss the evidence later in the conference, I will be brief. Both he and I are cautious about claims that bilingualism 'generates' creativity, though he tends to be more optimistic than I do. Apart altogether from the theoretical considerations which I mentioned, I am not impressed by the evidence that has been produced to indicate that bilinguals tend to be more creative than monolinguals. Taking the theoretical considerations into account, in particular the total absence of any indications of validity for measures of creativity in school children, I am of the opinion that the topic of bilingualism and creativity comes under Wittgenstein's rubric: <u>wovon man nicht reden kann, darüber muss man schweigen.</u>

Conclusion: Wanted: a theory of semantics

The saying that it is part of wisdom not to know (ignorare) certain things is attributed to Erasmus. I am not sure that I know what it means, but I would like it to include a counsel to realize and admit when we do not know something. Most of the topics which I have discussed have led me to make negative statements: I do not believe that there is any evidence to justify claims of Whorfian relativism; I do not believe that there is any evidence that there are two different sorts of bilinguals, coordinate and compound, at least as these have been described in the literature; I do not believe that bilingualism is directly related to intelligence; I do not believe that bilingualism is directly related to creativity. I want to add one other disclaimer to these: I am not even sure that the pair of concepts which are dissociated in each of these four statements are essentially unrelated. In other words, I am not even sure that any negativism is justified.

The reason is that each section of this paper is about the relationship between language and some aspect of thought and we have no semantic theory which even remotely approaches adequacy. Furthermore, I am not at all convinced that the empirical investigations to which I have alluded in this paper have contributed much to the building up of such a theory. Yet without an adequate theory of semantics, psychology and linguistics (and possibly philosophy) rapidly reach an impasse. One has the impression of one vogue succeeding another without any substantial progress. For what it is worth, my feeling is that valuable insights are going to come only through careful studies of infants, the development of their psychological functioning as a whole, of their classification of objects and the bases of such classification, of the assumptions which they make or do not make in their approaches to the world about them and in their approaches to language, of their ability to generalize, and the like. Furthermore, we need more careful studies of how language learning relates to other psychological developments. Among such studies, the analysis of bilingual language learning will have an honorable position. The road will be longer and more arduous, I imagine, than that which led to the major discoveries of modern physics, but the rewards will, I hope, be greater and less pregnant with destructive power.

REFERENCES

Bar-Hillel, Joshua. 1964. Language and information. Reading, Massachusetts, Addison-Wesley.
Bever, T. G. 1970. The cognitive basis for linguistic structures. In J. R. Hayes, ed., Cognition and language learning. New York, Wiley.
Black, Max. 1959. Linguistic relativity: the views of Benjamin Lee Whorf. Philosophical Review 68: 228-238.
_____. 1969. Some troubles with Whorfianism. In Sidney Hook, ed., Language and philosophy: a symposium. New York University Press, 30-35.
Burling, Robbins. 1969. Cognition and componential analysis: God's truth or hocus-pocus? In Stephen A. Tyler, ed., Cognitive anthropology. New York, Holt, Rinehart and Winston, 419-428.
Chomsky, Noam. 1959. Review of verbal behavior by B. F. Skinner. Language, 35: 26-58.
_____. 1965. Aspects of the theory of syntax. Cambridge, Massachusetts, M.I.T. Press.
Church, A. 1958. Ontological commitment. Journal of Philosophy, 55: 1008-1014.
Dacey, John S. and George F. Madaus. 1969. Creativity: definitions, explanations and facilitation. Irish Journal of Education, 3: 55-69.
Darcy, Natalie T. 1953. A review of the literature on the effects of bilingualism upon the measurement of intelligence. Journal of Genetic Psychology, 82: 21-58.
_____. 1963. Bilingualism and the measurement of intelligence: review of a decade of research. Journal of Genetic Psychology, 103: 259-282.
Diebold, Richard A. 1968. The consequences of early bilingualism in cognitive development and personality formation. In E. Norbeck, D. Price-Williams and W. M. McCord, eds., The study of personality: an interdisciplinary appraisal. New York, Holt, Rinehart and Winston, 218-245.
Diller, Karl C. 1967. 'Compound' and 'coordinate' bilingualism—a conceptual artifact. Paper presented to the Linguistic Society of America, Chicago, Illinois (mimeo).
Ervin, Susan and Charles E. Osgood. 1954. Second language learning and bilingualism. Journal of Abnormal and Social Psychology. (Supplement), 49: 139-146.
Fishman, Joshua A. 1960. A systematization of the Whorfian hypothesis. Behavioral Science. 5: 232-239.
_____. 1964. Language maintenance and language shift as a field of inquiry. Linguistics, 9: 32-70.

Fodor, Jerry A. 1965. Could meaning be an r_m? Journal of Verbal Learning and Verbal Behavior, 4: 73-81.
Frake, Charles O. 1962. The ethnographic study of cognitive systems. In Thomas Gladwin and William C. Sturtevant, eds., Anthropology and Human Behavior. Anthropological Society of Washington. Washington, D. C.
Goodenough, Ward H. 1956. Componential analysis and the study of meaning. Language, 32, 195-216.
Gumperz, John J. 1964. Linguistic and social interaction in two communities. In John J. Gumperz and Dell H. Hymes, eds., The Ethnography of Communication. American Anthropologist, Special Publication 3: 137-153.
Hebb, Donald O., Wallace E. Lambert, and G. Richard Tucker. 1970. Language, thought and experience. McGill University, Department of Psychology, (mimeo).
Hymes, Dell H. 1969. Discussion of Burling's paper. In Stephen A. Tyler, ed., Cognitive anthropology. New York, Holt, Rinehart and Winston, 428-431.
Katz, Jerrold J. 1966. The philosophy of language. New York, Harper and Row.
_____, and Jerry A. Fodor. 1963. The structure of semantic theory. Language 39: 170-210.
_____, and Paul M. Postal. 1964. An integrated theory of linguistic description. Cambridge, Massachusetts, M.I.T. Press.
Kellaghan, Thomas, and John Macnamara. 1967. Reading in a second language. In Marion D. Jenkinson, ed., Reading instruction: an international forum. Newark, Delaware, International Reading Association, 231-240.
Kolers, Paul A. 1963. Interlingual word associations. Journal of Verbal Learning and Verbal Behaviour, 2: 291-300.
Lambert, Wallace E. 1969. Psychological studies of the interdependencies of the bilinguals two languages. In Jaan Puhvel, ed., Substance and structure in language. University of California Press, 99-126.
_____, and Chris Rawlings. 1969. Bilingual processing of mixed-language associative networks. Journal of Verbal Learning and Verbal Behaviour, 8: 604-609.
Lenneberg, Eric H. 1967. Biological foundations of language. New York, Wiley.
Lounsbury, Floyd G. 1969. Language and culture. In Sidney Hook, ed., Language and Philosophy: A Symposium. New York University Press, 3-29.
Mackey, William F. 1962. The description of bilingualism. Canadian Journal of Linguistics, 7: 51-85.

_____. 1965. Bilingual interference: Its analysis and measurement. Journal of Communication, 15, 239-249.
Macnamara, John. 1966. Bilingualism and primary education. Edinburgh University Press.
_____. 1967. The bilingual's linguistic performance—a psychological overview. Journal of Social Issues, 23: 58-77.
_____. 1970. The cognitive basis of language learning in infants. Montreal: Department of Psychology. McGill University, (mimeo).
_____. In press. Parsimony and the lexicon. Language.
_____, and Anne O Cléirigh. 1969. Studies in the psychology of semantics: the projection rules. Dublin: Educational Research Center, St. Patrick's College, (mimeo).
Mathiot, Madelaine, 1969. The semantic and cognitive domain of language. University of California, Los Angeles, (mimeo).
McNeill, David. 1966. The creation of language by children. In John Lyons and Roger J. Wales, eds., Psycholinguistic papers: the proceedings of the 1966 Edinburgh Conference. Edinburgh University Press, 99-115.
Miller, George A., and David McNeill. 1969. Psycholinguistics. In G. Lindzey and E. Aronson, eds., Handbook of social psychology, vol. 3. Reading, Massachusetts, Addison-Westley, 666-794.
Neisser, Ulric. 1967. Cognitive psychology. New York, Appleton-Century-Crofts.
Piaget, Jean. 1963. Langage et operations intellectuelles. In Problèmes de psycholinguistique. Symposium de l'association de psychologie scientifique de langue française. Paris, Presses Universitaires de France.
_____. 1965. La formation du symbole chez l'enfant: Imitation, jeu et rêvs, image et représentation. (3rd edition). Neuchatel, Delachaux et Niestlé.
Polanyi, Michael. 1968. Logic and psychology. American Psychologist, 3, 27-43.
Quillian, M. Ross. 1967. Word concepts: a theory simulation of some basic semantic capabilities. Behavioral Science. 12: 410-430.
_____. 1968. Semantic memory. In Marvin Minsky, ed., Semantic information processing. M.I.T. Press, 216-270.
Quine, Willard Van Orman. 1960. Word and object. New York, Wiley.
Segalowitz, Norman, and Wallace E. Lambert. 1969. Semantic generalization in bilinguals. Journal of Verbal Learning and Verbal Behaviour. 8: 559-566.
Sinclair-de-Zwart, Hermina. 1967. Acquisition de langage et développement de la pensée. Paris, Dunad.

_____. 1969. Developmental psycholinguistics. In David Elkind and John H. Flavell, eds. Studies in cognitive development: Essays in honor of Jean Piaget. New York, Oxford University Press: 315-336.

Stafford, Kenneth R. 1968. Problem solving as a function of language. Language and Speech. 11: 104-112.

_____, and Stanley R. Van Kauren. 1968. Semantic differential profiles as related to monolingual-bilingual types. Language and Speech. 11: 167-170.

Vermazen, Bruce. 1967. Review of an integrated theory of linguistic descriptions by J. J. Katz and P. M. Postal, and the philosophy of language by J. J. Katz. Synthese, 17: 35-365.

Vygotsky, Lev S. 1962. Thought and Language. Cambridge, Massachusetts, M.I.T. Press.

Wallace, Anthony F. C. 1962. Culture and cognition. Science, 135: 351-357.

_____. 1965. The problem of the psychological validity of componential analysis. In E. A. Hammel, ed., Formal semantic analysis, Menasha, Wisconsin, American Anthropological Association. 229-248.

Weinreich, Uriel. 1953. Languages in contact. Publications of the Linguistic Circle. New York, no. 1.

_____. 1966. Explorations in semantic theory. In Thomas A. Sebeok, ed., Current trends in linguistics, vol. 3. The Hague, Mouton: 395-477.

COGNITIVE DEVELOPMENT IN THE BILINGUAL CHILD

VERA JOHN

Yeshiva University

Abstract. In most studies of bilingual children their intellectual development is assessed by means of intelligence tests. The facilitating or inhibiting role of their bilingual experience is evaluated in this fashion. Alternative approaches, based upon recent work on cognitive style, will be proposed in this paper. Views of intellectual development representing contemporary cognitive theory will also be discussed. Of particular interest is the role of visual conceptualization in the bilingual; some examples of instructional approaches with bilingual children will be discussed from the point of view of their possible effects upon broadening or narrowing the child's cognitive development. The recent research of Rohwer in elaborative learning will be considered in this context.

I am delighted, that after an excessively long period of preoccupation with the tested performance of bilingual children, even on the part of scholars, we are now asking questions concerning their thought processes. It is a sign of the times that two panelists have chosen independently the topic of Bilingualism and Thought.

My joy is a response to a concern born during my adolescence spent in a multilingual school. During our heated debates in Switzerland, we were concerned with the relative importance of images and words in the ideational processes of young people raised with several languages. Soon after starting the study of psychology I have learned that such a question had little scientific validity from an operational standpoint. But I was stubborn, and though I learned to ask more scientific questions, my curiosity persisted to this day. During the last decade interest in cognition revived dramatically; neobehaviorists, structuralists, and rationalists are again concerned with the magnificent, centuries-old inquiry into man's mind.

But interests in cognition, thinking, or the mind have had no substantive impact upon the schools in which children with two languages are struggling to learn and survive. The schools are under the influence of the better known approaches of psychologists. Of particular significance is the field of psychometrics, or the measurement of human skills and achievement, which endeavor is still of enormous importance in the planning of curricula, the placement of children, the evaluation of programs for minority children. Labov's powerful attack on educational psychologists, delivered at the Round Table last year, is of significance in this connection. He challenged the theoretical assumptions of the well-known 'deficiency' concepts, as well as the methodological soundness of testing ghetto children in isolation from each other, invoking topics and styles of communicative exchange alien to their world. But in spite of these criticisms the bilingual minority child is continually tested in the traditional way with standardized tools, though specialists will sadly admit that they have no appropriate tests in the childrens' native languages. The child's achievement is therefore assessed in English and is shown to lag behind other groups; witness the Coleman report.

Psychology has had an impact on another facet of the life of the bilingual child in this country. The currently popular TESOL programs show the influence of behaviorist learning theory as well as that of linguistics of the pretransformational era. The oral approach by means of which children are taught to repeat specific syntactical patterns is an illustration of an emphasis upon overt behavior stressed as basic by learning theorists. I have listened to Navajo children repeating in unison as well as individually, phrases such as <u>This is a pencil, These are pencils</u>. TESOL programs appeal to educators who have been seriously criticized for their failure to educate bilingual children successfully. Some of these TESOL programs are carefully thought out, attractively presented, and effectively organized in second-language instruction. But many contemporary linguists criticize these approaches. These linguists speak of language acquisition 'as primarily a cognitive enterprise rather than a behavioral one' (Scott, 1970, p. 81).

The emphasis on processes of thought generously laces the writings of Chomsky (1968), Jacobovits (1968), Troike (1970), and others. Their ideas offer stimulating reading to the cognitive psychologist. The field is not limited to speculations. The work of Bever at Rockefeller Institute lustrates one aspect of this emphasis. In studying speech perception he explores the role of attention in the processing of language input. He speaks of fluctuations between outward attention (social attention),

Cognitive Development in the Bilingual Child /109

and inward attention, the attention to, or thinking about a just heard message. His work, together with the cognitive implications of much contemporary research and theory, presents a challenge to behavioristic approaches to language.

Have we then decisively rejected all facets of behaviorism in approaches to learning, cognition, and language, and does our task consist only in convincing the practitioners among us that they are behind the times?

I do not think so. Great debates tend to strengthen the single factor features of theories, such as reinforcement in the case of learning theorists, or the innate features of the Language Acquisition Device, as in the case of the transformationalists. In distress over the intensity of the debates many research workers tend to a pragmatic position, picking and choosing from several theories. Educators often follow this course.

My own preference is hard to elaborate without a lengthy departure from the topic of this paper. Let me illustrate it, however, with some personal examples of multilingual education.

Peal and Lambert's findings (1962) concerning the cognitive flexibility of coordinate-bilingual children always struck me as highly important. Intuitively, it seems to me that their results may be of particular significance for children raised in instructional settings which afford an 'intellectualization' of their language experience. (Hence, the ensuing debate.) This type of experience characterized my own acquisition of French. My teachers attempted to acquaint me with that specialized use of language for thought which characterizes many French intellectuals, beyond a mastery of the spoken and written language. Their goal was to deepen my understanding, using a multilingual background as a basis for generalizations and contrast. The features of production of French was an end, not a means, of their tuition. I arrived in this country with such an approach to language learning. I was somewhat older than when I learned French; perhaps I lacked that easy mimicry of the young. I plunged into college work with little proficiency in English, and I neglected to pay much attention to the phonology of the English language. (A neglect that did not escape Charles Ferguson.) My primarily cognitive approach to language acquisition was of little assistance when I decided to improve my articulation. The instruction I then received was based on modeling, (for instance, I did not know how to produce the th sound). I was shown with the help of mirrors and drawings. Principles of learning, such as modeling and the use of corrective feedback, were relevant to this aspect of my struggle with the English language; while cognitive approaches, of great benefit to the acquisition of the semantic system, were of little use.

In short, different aspects of language acquisition may well be governed by widely different principles of learning and cognition. In this context, Courtney Cazden's conclusions, based on an experimental study, are of interest. She proposes that young children's acquisition of vocabulary profits from direct tuition, while syntactical growth is strengthened by the child's exposure to well-formed sentences. In the light of such findings, psycholinguists may wish to abandon single-factor theories; and in this way, follow the example of their colleagues, for instance the neurophysiologists, who no longer attempt to embrace with the same set of explanatory principles the knee-jerk and visual memory.

It is my hope, that from the current theoretical debates, multi-layered theories will emerge, taking into account man's propensities to display over-learned habits while also throwing some light on the agility of the human in grasping new knowledge by the well-practiced leaps of the mind. A fruitful arena for such theory is the developmental study of language and thought in various cultural and instructional settings.

One of the considerations, obvious to many of you, I am sure, which impels me to state this plea for a levels-of-analysis approach to theory building in the sciences of language and knowing, is the lack of such an approach to the education of the bilingual child. We observe either a well-intentioned laissez-faire approach in barrio and reservation classrooms, or a proliferation of pattern-drill techniques. As yet, little pedagogical attention has been paid to the applicability of cognitive approaches to second-language instruction. (An important beginning in this direction is Bernard Spolsky's (1970) paper presented at last year's Round Table.) What are some of the approaches to thought of relevance to the bilingual child?

Studies of Cognition. For students of behavior it is hard to deal with entities lodged inside the human mind, but such is the emphasis given to 'structure' in Jean Piaget's theory of intellectual development. Ideas are arranged in a particular body of knowledge or structure, according to the Swiss theorist, and it requires most of the years of growing into adulthood to achieve the necessary formal 'operations' to deal effectively with logically organized knowledge. Operations are a key concept in Piagetian theory; he describes them 'as the essence of knowledge: it is an interiorized action which modifies the object of knowledge. For instance, an operation would consist of joining objects in a class, to construct a classification' (Piaget 1964: 8). Can these operations be taught? Most followers of Jean Piaget would argue against direct tuition.

Professor Kohlberg, a Piagetian psychologist of development, has severely criticized compensatory programs for low-income children because of their highly content-oriented approaches (Kohlberg 1968). He argues in favor of an alternative approach, stressing multiple ex-

periences and activities. Such an approach to education is attempted
by the British Infant Schools. The free manner in which children move
from activity to activity is in stark contrast with the education of many
non-English speaking children in this country. I am referring particularly to those students who spend many hours in structured language
activities, stressing production skills. These children receive little,
if any, opportunity in conceptually enriching encounters, considered
important by the followers of the great Swiss psychologist.

Piaget and Chomsky confront the educationally-minded with the
same dilemma. While both emphasize an active organism, stressing
operations (Piaget) and hypothesis-testing (Chomsky) as crucial to the
development of the human mind and language, neither develops the
pedagogical implications of their conceptualizations. There are some
cognitive theorists, however, who have attempted to relate theory to
educational practice.

Jerome Bruner, whose approach to cognition has been deeply influenced by Piaget, deals with issues of learning and teaching in his book
Toward a Theory of Instruction (1966). He is particularly concerned
with the study of representations: 'how the child gets free of present
stimuli and conserves past experience in a model, and the rules that
govern storage and retrieval of information from this model' (p. 10).
Bruner postulates three methods of representation, starting with the
young child's reliance upon action. This 'enactive' mode bears some
resemblance to Piaget's emphasis upon internalized action. Next in
the developmental sequence is the 'ikonic' mode in which the child is
able to represent the world to himself by an image or a spatial schema
which is relatively independent of action.' Thirdly, he speaks of symbolic representation, and the role of language in the development of
models of reality. Of significance to the child growing toward this
mode of functioning are the dialogues he conducts with adults. To quote
Bruner again, he 'suggests that mental growth is in very considerable
measure dependent upon the growth from the outside in—a mastering of
techniques that are embodied in the culture and that are passed on in a
contingent dialogue by agents of the culture.'

Several aspects of Bruner's theory of cognition appear relevant to
the development and education of the bilingual child. The importance
of the ikonic mode of representation is one of these. Bruner and his
co-workers have shown in the research reported in Studies of Cognitive
Growth the importance of this mode of thought for children in their earliest years of schooling. Bilingual children often are caught between
two languages during those years, thus the instructional use of imagery
may be of great assistance to them. In addition, to help foster the development of the symbolic mode of representation as well, bilingual
children should have the opportunity to engage in cognitively rich dialogue with adults in their 'dominant' language.

A third area of interest in the recent studies of cognition is the focus on the 'processes' of learning and knowing. I have been particularly intrigued with the work of William Rohwer. The beginnings of his inquiry are rather typical for an experimental psychologist. He was working with paired-associate learning, and his subjects ranged broadly according to age, sex, ethnic membership, and social class. He demonstrated conclusively that when children were taught to 'elaborate' on a word-association pair by constructing a meaningful sentence, their performance increased dramatically.

The logic of this research propelled Professor Rohwer to move into an unusual next step for an experimental psychologist, namely theory-building. In studying self-generated images, sentences, or categories, Rohwer has developed a model of 'imaginative conceptual activity' in contrast with 'formal conceptual activity'. Low-income children profit greatly from instruction when they are encouraged to rely upon the former mode. Similarly, bilingual children could gain from such strategies for learning; these children are often the subject of ridicule for their unconventional use of words and metaphors. Where the child needs to rely upon language-for-the-self in the solution or recollection of tasks, his unique phrasing should not be considered an impediment, but as a creative use of words.

This research is but one example of the new trend in the study of active, individually developed, conceptual learning strategies. 'Learning by discovery' is another approach to open-ended instruction. The greatest benefits this latter method yields is in the development of children's comprehension of subject matter, particularly in mathematics. However, these primarily inductive methods of instruction have been lumped mistakenly with 'progressive education'. In the priorities of the post-Sputnik era, the failure of many school children in spelling and computation has been blamed on educational methods dating from a more permissive and relaxed atmosphere. Hence, the turn toward didactic instruction and programmed learning on the part of many school systems. It is ironic that the beleaguered school administrators have given up on inductive learning at the very time that psychologists are offering promising approaches to the schools.

I do not think that we have to face a similar impasse in the education of bilingual children. My optimism is based upon evidence such as the contribution of linguists to last year's Round Table: Labov, Scott, Troike, Spolsky, all of whom approached their subject matter from a fresh point of view. I am hopeful that these and other attempts at examining levels of language and concomitant processes of acquisition will yield a sophisticated theory of instruction.

Recommendations. As yet, the new insights of linguists and psychologists have had little impact upon the education of non-English speaking children. The classrooms we have observed in the barrios and on reservations reflect a new spirit of optimism; the promise of bilingual education is an exciting one. But in most instances the focus is upon the production skills of these children; their native language is considered a bridge, albeit a necessary one, to the acquisition of the English language.

A theoretical basis for second language instruction is still a hope for the future; lacking an integrated approach, I would like to make a few suggestions for the education of non-English speaking children, based upon ideas drawn from unrelated sources. My primary concern is the young child in pre-school and primary classes.

a. Comprehension: Dr. Troike (1970) made an important distinction in his Round Table presentation of last year between receptive and productive competence. According to his model, an instructional approach stressing receptive competence in individuals acquiring a second language or a second dialect may be a useful goal. This proposal is stressed more fully by Susan Ervin-Tripp (see paper in this symposium). In exploring the lessons of first language acquisition, it is suggested that children and adults should be given training in the development of comprehension skills before they are expected to improve their production skills.

The use of songs, stories, and short skits are effective in exposing young children to a new language. The great success of some television programs (such as Sesame Street) in creating motivation for new learning is of interest. While a primarily passive approach to language development is certainly not a plan I favor, some techniques can be adopted from the mass media to enliven the acquisition of English on the part of barrio and reservation children.

b. Cognitive development: Children convey their growing comprehension of a new language by gestures and pantomine. It is harder to judge whether school is helping them broaden their conceptual mastery of their environment while learning a new language. Teachers often neglect the cognitive aspects of growth. The use of language for purposes of problem-solving unfolds at an accelerated pace between the ages of four and seven, the very time when non-English speaking children are exposed to a second language. Caught between two languages, the young child needs special assistance in organizing his world. The use of ikonic representation, as described by Bruner, is seldom explored in these classrooms, where language and its acquisition dominate the curriculum. Nonverbal materials, as developed by Montessori schools, are also useful in dealing with concepts such as sequencing, size relationships, etc. in the bilingual classroom.

There are a number of programs which have a strong cognitive component, but they are aimed at ghetto children who speak an English dialect, (John and Moskovitz 1970). In addition, most of these efforts are

devoid of culturally appropriate content for children whose life differs
from that of the middle class child. But teachers can be helped to
adapt programs to their own community, and in learning how to use
local talents and materials. My experience with the Indian kindergarten programs (jointly sponsored by the National Association for the
Education of Young Children and the Bureau of Indian Affairs) was instructive in this regard. The Indian art students together with resource
personnel drawn from reservations, people not necessarily skilled in
linguistics, helped us to develop a curriculum related to the experiences of the rural Indian child.

c. Fluency: The non-English speaking child will, at one point in
his school life, in a bilingual program, show evidence that he is ready
for a more intensive learning experience in his second language. Once
his active and enthusiastic participation is insured, the young child is
willing to listen to and repeat choral language. The flexibility of the
young child, his willingness to imitate, playfully, songs, rhymes, dialogues, speaks in favor of a limited amount of experience that
strengthens fluency.

But the emphasis upon comprehension and cognitive development in
this set of informal recommendations is offered because I share with
many other speakers in this symposium the conviction that ultimately
the child becomes a successful learner of languages because he takes
an active part in the process of acquisition. He tests his notions about
grammar, he experiments with new sounds, he discovers the meaning
of words by direct tuition as well as by more indirect routes.

d. The use of language: Languages are acquired fast, and often
forgotten equally fast by young children. Unless instruction in English
is related to the life of the bilingual community in which the program
is placed, the child will have no reason to practice on his own that
which he is learning. Though this seems an obvious thought, its implementation requires more than common sense. Only with a knowledge of the sociolinguistic features of a community can a meaningful
language program be developed for the children of barrios and reservations.

REFERENCES

Bever, Thomas. 1967. Presentation to psycholinguistic circle of
New York.
Bruner, Jerome. 1966. Toward a theory of instruction. Cambridge,
Massachusetts, Harvard University Press.
_____, Rose Olver, Patricia M. Greenfield, et al. 1966. Studies
of cognitive growth. New York, Wiley and Sons, Inc.
Chomsky, Noam. 1968. Language and the mind. Psychology Today.
I, no. 9. 48-51, 66-68.

Jacobovitz, Leon A. 1968. Implications of recent psycholinguistic developments for the teaching of a second language. Paper delivered at San Antonio TESOL Convention.
John, Vera, and Sarah Moskovitz. 1970. Language acquisition and development in early childhood. National Society for the Study of Education. Chicago.
Kohlberg, Laurence. 1968. Early education: A cognitive developmental view. Child Development, XXIX. 1013-62.
Peal, Elizabeth, and William E. Lambert. The relation of bilingualism to intelligence. Psychological Monograph, General and Applied, vol. 76, no. 546.
Piaget, Jean. Cognitive Development in children: The Piaget papers. In R. E. Ripple and V. N. Rockcastle, eds., Piaget rediscovered: A report of the conference on cognitive studies and curriculum development. Ithaca, New York, School of Education, Cornell University. March 1964. 6-48.
Rohwer, William Jr. 1969. Learning, race and school success. Mimeographed paper. Berkeley, California, University of California.
Scott, Charles T. 1970. Transformational theory and English as a second language/dialect. In Alatis, James E., ed., MSLL no. 22. 75-92.
Spolsky, Bernard. 1970. Linguistics and language pedagogy—applications or implications? In Alatis, James E., ed., MSLL no. 22. 143-157.
Troike, Rudolph C. Receptive competence, productive competence, and performance. In Alatis, James E., ed., MSLL no. 22. 63-75.

SOME COGNITIVE AND SOCIOCULTURAL CONSEQUENCES OF BEING BILINGUAL

Wallace E. Lambert
McGill University

The technical literature on the consequences of becoming bilingual and/or bicultural stretches back to the turn of the century and is still growing. In the early literature (the 1920s and 1930s) one finds a generally pessimistic outlook on the effects of bilingualism, but since the 1960s a much more optimistic picture has been emerging. Bilingualism and biculturalism, as one might expect, generate much emotional and political steam and this often clouds whatever facts are available. Researchers in the early period generally expected to find all sorts of troubles, and they usually did: bilingual children, relative to monolinguals, were behind in school, retarded in measured intelligence, and socially adrift. One trouble with most of the early studies was that little care was taken to check out the essentials before comparing monolingual and bilingual subjects. Thus, such factors as social class background and educational opportunities were not controlled, nor was much attention given to determining how bilingual or monolingual the comparison groups actually were. But even though there were grounds for worrying about the adequacy of many of these studies, there was nonetheless an overwhelming trend in the outcomes: the largest proportion of these investigations concluded that bilingualism has a detrimental effect on intellectual functioning, a smaller number found little or no relation between bilingualism and intelligence, and only two suggested that bilingualism might have favorable consequence on cognition.

With this picture as background, Elizabeth Peal and I started an investigation on the bilingual-monolingual topic in the Canadian setting (Peal and Lambert 1962). We had, of course, strong expectations of finding a bilingual deficit, as the literature suggested, but we wanted to pinpoint what the intellectual

components of that deficit might be in order to develop compensatory strategies. We argued that a large proportion of the world's population is, by the exigencies of life, bound to be bilingual, and it seemed to us appropriate to help them, if possible. Thus we expected troubles, but did not find any.
We were able in our first investigation to improve on most of the shortcomings noted in the earlier research, and this made us feel relatively confident about the results (see Lambert and Anisfeld 1969). What surprised us, though, was that French-English bilingual children in the Montreal setting scored significantly ahead of carefully matched monolinguals on both verbal and nonverbal measures of intelligence. Furthermore, the patterns of test results suggested that the bilinguals had a more diversified structure of intelligence, as measured, and more flexibility in thought.
These results, suggesting the possibility that bilingualism might favorably affect the structure and flexibility of thought, came as a real surprise. But one investigation rarely has enough weight to change the course of events, even though an important follow-up study (Anisfeld 1964) confirmed the 1962 conclusions. What was needed was confirmation from other settings and from studies using different approaches. Fortunately, since then confirmations have started to emerge from carefully conducted research around the world, from Singapore (Torrance et al. 1970), Switzerland (Balkan 1970), South Africa (Ianco-Worrall 1972), Israel and New York (Ben-Zeev 1972), Western Canada (Cummins and Gulustan 1973), and, using a quite different approach, from Montreal (Scott 1973).
All of these studies (and we found no others in the recent literature to contradict them) indicate that bilingual children, relative to monolingual controls, show definite advantages on measures of 'cognitive flexibility', 'creativity', or 'divergent thought'. Ben-Zeev's study (1972), for example, involved Hebrew-English bilingual children in New York and Israel and the results strongly support the conclusion that bilinguals have greater 'cognitive flexibility'. In this case, the term means that bilinguals have greater 'skill at auditory reorganization' of verbal material, a much more 'flexible manipulation of the linguistic code', and greater advance in 'concrete operational thinking', as these were measured in her investigation. Ianco-Worrall's study (1972) involved Afrikaans-English bilingual children in Pretoria, South Africa, and it lends equally strong support for a somewhat different form of cognitive flexibility, an advantage over monolingual controls in separating word meaning from word sound. The conclusion is drawn that the bilinguals were between two and three years advanced in this feature of cognitive development, which Leopold (1949) felt to be so characteristic of the liberated thought of bilinguals. Worrall also found good support for a bilingual precocity in realizing the arbitrary assignment of names to referents, a

feature of thinking which Vygotsky (1962) believed reflected insight and sophistication.

The recent study by Scott (1973) of French-English bilinguals in Montreal is perhaps the most persuasive because it involved a comparison of young children, some of whom were given the chance to become bilingual over a period of years while others were not given the chance. She worked with data collected over a seven-year period from two groups of English-Canadian children; one group had become functionally bilingual in French during the time period because they had attended experimental classes where most of the instruction had been conducted in French, while the other group had followed a conventional English-language education program. At the first-grade level, the two groups had been equated for measured intelligence, socioeconomic background, and parental attitudes towards French people. In fact, had the opportunity been presented to them, it is likely that most of the parents in the control group would have enrolled their children in the experimental French program, but since it was decided in advance to start one experimental class per year only (see Lambert and Tucker 1972), no such opportunity was available.

Scott was interested in the possible effects that becoming bilingual might have on the cognitive development of children--in particular, what effect it would have on children's 'divergent thinking', a special type of cognitive flexibility (see Guilford 1950, 1956). In contrast, convergent thinking is measured by tests that provide a number of pieces of information which the subject must synthesize to arrive at a correct answer; thus, the information provided funnels in or converges on a correct solution. Measures of divergent thinking provide the subject with a starting point for thought--'think of a paper clip'--and ask the subject to generate a whole series of permissible solutions--'and tell me all the things one could do with it'. Some researchers have considered divergent thinking as an index of creativity (e.g. Getzels and Jackson 1962), while others suggest that until more is known, it is best viewed as a distinctive cognitive style reflecting a rich imagination and an ability to scan rapidly a host of possible solutions.

Scott was interested, among other things, in whether bilingualism promotes divergent thinking. Her results, based on a multivariate analysis, show that the group of youngsters who had become functionally bilingual through 'immersion' schooling were substantially higher scorers than the monolingual group with whom they had been equated for IQ and social class background at the first-grade level. Although the numbers of children in each group are small, this study gives strong support for the causal link between bilingualism and flexibility, the former apparently enhancing the latter.

There is, then, an impressive array of evidence accumulating that argues plainly against the common sense notion that becoming bilingual, i.e. having two strings to one's bow or two

Some Consequences of Being Bilingual /119

linguistic systems within one's brain, naturally divides a person's cognitive resources and reduces his efficiency of thought. Instead, one can now put forth a very persuasive argument that there is a definite cognitive advantage enjoyed by bilingual children in the domain of cognitive flexibility. However, only further research will tell us how this advantage, assuming it is a reliable phenomenon, actually works: whether it is based on a better storage of information by bilinguals, whether the separation of linguistic symbols from their referents or the ability to separate word meaning from word sound is the key factor, whether the bilingual contrasts of linguistic systems aid in the development of general conceptual thought, or whatever. In any case, this new trend in research should give second thoughts to those who have used the bilingual deficit notion as an argument for melting down ethnic groups. Hopefully, too, it will provide a new perspective for members of ethnolinguistic groups who may have been led to believe in the notion of a likely deficit attributable to bilingualism.

Because of its social significance, there is a great need for more research on this topic. An example of research to come is presented by Cummins (1976), who is intrigued by differences in findings of pre- and post-1960 studies. Cummins argues that perhaps because the more recent studies have all examined the degree of skill subjects actually have in the two languages (a neglected matter in the earlier work), there may therefore 'be a threshold level of linguistic competence which a bilingual child must attain both in order to avoid cognitive deficits and to allow the potentially beneficial aspects of becoming bilingual to influence his cognitive functioning'. This would suggest, among other things, that linguistic minority groups need assurance that the home language will be given a strong reading and writing base before or along with the introduction of the national language. It is a potentially productive hypothesis to test.

One feature of the studies just reviewed merits special attention: all the bases reported (those in Singapore, South Africa, Switzerland, Israel, New York, Montreal) dealt with bilinguals for whom the two languages involved have social value and respect in each of the settings. Thus, knowing Afrikaans and English in South Africa, Hebrew and English in New York and Israel, or French as well as English for English-speaking Canadian children, would in each case be adding a second, socially relevant language to one's repertory of skills. In no case would the learning of the second language portend the slow replacement of the first or 'home' language, as would typically be the case, for example, for French Canadians or Spanish Americans developing high-level skills in English. One might refer to the former instances as examples of an 'additive' form of bilingualism and contrast it with a more 'subtractive' form experienced by many ethnic minority groups who, because of national educational policies and social pressures of various sorts, are forced to put aside their ethnic language for a national language. Their degree of bilinguality at any point in time would likely reflect some stage in the subtraction of the ethnic language and its associated cultural accompaniments, and its replacement with another. The important educational task of the future, it seems to me, is to transform the pressures on ethnic groups so that they can profit from additive forms of bilingualism and biculturalism. I am going to examine an example of an attempt to make such a transformation in the last section of this paper.

Research on the thinking processes of the bilingual person has recently taken a new turn by focusing on the relation of language to brain functioning. Several of us at McGill have become interested in this area of research and we have used as a take-off point our earlier work on the contrasts between compound and coordinate types of bilingualism (see Lambert 1969). Currently, we are exploring the importance of the age of becoming bilingual, by contrasting 'early' versus 'late' bilinguals, that is, those who become bilingual in infancy versus those who become bilingual in the adolescent years.

Our earlier studies had suggested that those who develop their bilinguality early are more able and efficient at processing the meaning of linguistic information, in particular those general aspects of meaning that cut across the two languages. It is not that the two languages are less autonomous as linguistic systems for 'early' bilinguals, for they show no more signs of language mixing or interlanguage interplay than do 'late' bilinguals; but rather that early bilinguals seem to develop relatively more pervasive, superordinate meaning systems which subserve both languages. By way of contrast, the late bilinguals seem to have relatively more compartmentalized semantic systems for each of their languages, and in general their two language systems seem to be more functionally independent. Put in other terms, the early bilinguals have more compounded language systems and the late bilinguals have more coordinated systems.

This difference in degree of semantic distinctiveness that appears to be related to the age of becoming bilingual has been at the core of several of our more recent studies. Let me give two examples. The first was concerned with the 'language processing strategies' of bilinguals and toward this end we compared three groups of young adult bilinguals who had become bilingual in infancy, in childhood, or in adolescence (Genesee, Hamers, Lambert, Mononen, Seitz, and Starck 1978). At the time of testing, all were in their early twenties and all were perfectly balanced in their skills with English and French. The experimental procedure was a simple language recognition task in which the subject had merely to press a reaction-time button to indicate whether each word heard (presented monaurally through earphones) was French or English. At the same time, EEG activity in the left and right hemispheres of the brain was monitored, using the latest electronic equipment

and the wisdom about these brain matters that one can find in
abundance around McGill. Measures were taken of the latencies
of EEG reactions. Put technically, Averaged Evoked Reactions
were measured, and latencies to N_1, to P_2, and $N_1 - P_2$ peak
to peak amplitudes were calculated. These are commonly accepted indices of the neural activities that accompany the early
stages of perceptual processing of incoming information. They
are extremely rapid, occurring within 75 to 100 ms. after the
presentation of a stimulus, much in advance of the button push
which takes from 800-1000 ms.

Briefly, what we found was that these processing latencies
were much faster in the left than in the right hemisphere for
the 'early' bilinguals (the infant and childhood subgroups),
but faster in the right than in the left hemisphere for the
adolescent bilinguals. Statistically, this was a very clear difference, indicating a left hemisphere preference for early bilinguals and a right hemisphere preference for late bilinguals,
and it held up regardless of the ear of input of the stimulus
material and regardless of the language of input. It was also
true that the adolescent bilinguals were much faster in their
neurological processing than were the early bilinguals. We are
inclined to interpret these findings in terms of strategy differences: the early bilinguals seem to have a proclivity for a left-
hemisphere-based strategy, one that draws on what we believe
to be a more semantic or analytic form of processing, while
the adolescent subgroup seems to have a proclivity for a right-
hemisphere-based strategy, one relying more on a gestalt-like
or melodic form of processing.

To explore one implication of this interpretation, we recalled
our subjects and presented them with a somewhat more demanding task: to repeat aloud each word as it appeared monaurally
through the earphones. We reasoned that this task would require a deeper level of processing, one closer to a semantic
analysis, and thus more likely to involve the left hemisphere.
If this were true, the early bilinguals should react more
rapidly because of their left hemisphere proclivity, whereas
the adolescent subgroup should be at a disadvantage because,
for final processing, the stimulus information would have to be
transferred from the favored right hemisphere to the left.
Using a voice key to register reaction times, these expectations
were supported: the vocal reaction times were significantly
shorter for the early bilingual subgroups. In summary, then,
these findings help relate language learning experiences to
cerebral processing styles, and they fit well with other behavioral distinctions already found between early and late bilinguals.

This whole issue of age of becoming bilingual has been
carried an important step further in a fascinating recent study
conducted by Jyotsna Vaid, one of our graduate students
(Vaid 1977; Vaid and Lambert 1978). Put very briefly, the
processing strategies of two groups of French-English bilinguals

were studied in this case by means of an 'auditory Stroop test' designed to evaluate left and right cerebral hemisphere involvement. One group was made up of 'early' bilinguals, the other of 'late' bilinguals. In the procedure, information was directed alternately through left and right ears, and because the contralateral neural connections (e.g. those between left ear and right cerebral hemisphere) are stronger than the ipsilateral, one can make reliable inferences about the relative involvement of each cerebral hemisphere by analyzing how well the information presented to one ear or the other is finally processed.

In this version of the Stroop test, the stimuli presented were the simple words high, low, haute, and basse, but these were uttered one at a time in pitches that were related to word meanings either congruently (as in the word 'high' uttered in a high pitch) or incongruently (the word 'haute' uttered in a low pitch). In one condition, subjects were to differentiate low from high pitches, disregarding meaning, while in a second condition, they were to disregard pitch and respond to word meanings. Measures of field independence (Witkin 1976) were also taken.

Results indicate that both sex of subject and age of bilinguality affect the degree of right and left hemisphere involvement. For example, male early bilinguals tend to process meaning efficiently in both cerebral hemispheres whereas male late bilinguals and female bilinguals, both early and late, process meaning more efficiently in the right cerebral hemisphere. What these findings suggest is that, when comparisons are made with unilingual controls, bilingualism in general tends to engender a greater involvement of the right hemisphere in the encoding and decoding of meaning, with variations in extent of this involvement determined by sex and age of bilinguality. Thus, male unilinguals are more confined to the left hemisphere for the processing of meaning whereas male bilinguals involve both right and left hemispheres if their bilinguality starts in infancy, and mainly the right hemisphere if the bilinguality dates from adolescence. Female unilinguals start with a balanced involvement of both right and left hemispheres, and bilinguality, whether early or late in its origin, shifts the control of meaning mainly to the right hemisphere.

There is much more work to be done here to be sure of this shift-to-the-right with bilingualism and to clarify its significance. Might there be some connection between the symptoms of flexibility of thought among bilinguals, referred to earlier, and greater right hemisphere involvement? Why are there such marked early-late differences in degree of right hemisphere control of meaning among male subjects? And what is the significance of the very pronounced degrees of field independence (in Witkin's sense of the term) found among early bilinguals? These are some of the questions that have us presently thinking in a variety of directions.

Effects on identity. What about the notion that becoming bilingual and bicultural subtracts, through division, from one's sense of personal identity? Here, too, there are signs in the recent literature of interest in this topic, but there are still only a few studies to draw on. Three, however, do bear on the issue of the bilingual's sense of identity, and all three are encouraging in their outcomes.

The first is the study that Robert Gardner and I conducted with French-Americans in communities in New England and Louisiana (Gardner and Lambert 1972). We were interested in their ways of coping with a dual heritage, and we found that some oriented themselves definitely toward their French background and tried to ignore their American roots; others were tugged more toward the American pole at the expense of their Frenchness; and still others apparently tried not to think in ethnic terms, as though they did not consider themselves to be either French or American. These three types of reactions parallel closely those of Italian-American adolescents studied earlier by Child (1943). To me, these ways of coping characterize the anguish of members of ethnic groups when caught up in a subtractive form of biculturalism, that is, where social pressures (often from within their own group) are exerted on them to give up one aspect of their dual identity for the sake of blending into a national scene.

The important point here is that identities are fragile and they can, through social pressures, be easily tipped off balance. Thus, some of these young people were trying to be one thing or the other, while others were trying to be neither one thing nor the other. Most interesting was our finding of a fourth subgroup of French-American young people who were apparently successful at being both things, French and American. This subgroup was characterized by a realization of the social usefulness of knowing French, which was given strong parental support. The pattern suggested that this familywide orientation toward the value of French helped these young people become relatively more competent in both French and English.

Identities need not be so disturbed, though, as the study of Aellen and Lambert (1969) showed. In this case, we were interested in the adjustments made by adolescent children of English-French mixed marriages in the Montreal setting. We examined the degree and direction of the offsprings' ethnic identifications as well as a selected set of their attitudes, and personality characteristics.

The children of these mixed marriages come in contact with and are usually expected to learn the distinctive social and behavioral characteristics of the two cultures represented in their families. The question is whether the demands made on them necessarily generate conflicts, or whether the experience with two cultures possibly broadens and liberalizes the child, or whether some combination of both outcomes is typical. In addition to the cultural demands made on them, the children of mixed ethnic marriages may face other difficulties to the extent that their parents, as suggested by Gordon (1966) and Saucier (1965), may have married outside their ethnic group because of personal instability and immaturity. Much of the previous research suggests that persons who intermarry in this way often have relatively strong feelings of alienation, self-hatred, and worthlessness, and are disorganized and demoralized. Mixed ethnic children might well find it difficult to identify with their parents if these characteristics are typical or representative. Still, the offspring could develop understanding and sympathy for parents with such an outlook. On the other hand, people may intermarry in many instances because they have developed essenentially healthy attitudes and orientations which are nonetheless inappropriate within their own ethnic group, making intermarriage with a sympathetic outsider particularly attractive. They may have become, like Park's marginal man, 'the individual with the wider horizon, the keener intelligence, the more detached and rational viewpoint ... always relatively the more civilized human being' (Park 1964:376). In that case, their children might be particularly well trained in tolerance and openmindedness, especially since the children themselves are likely to feel that they, unlike their parents, are automatically members of both ethnic groups. The purpose of this investigation was to examine both these possibilities as objectively as possible by comparing groups of adolescent boys of mixed French-English parentage with others of homogeneous background, either French or English. All groups in the comparison were similar as to age, socioeconomic class, intelligence, and number of siblings.

It was found that the profile of characteristics of the boys with mixed ethnic parentage is a healthy one in every respect when comparisons are made with groups from homogeneous ethnic backgrounds; they identify with their parents, especially with their fathers, as well as the comparison groups do; they relate themselves to and identify with both ethnic reference groups, this being particularly so for those in a French academic environment; they show no signs of personality disturbances, social alienation, or anxiety; nor do their self-concepts deviate from those of the comparison subjects; they see their parents as giving them relatively more attention and personal interest, and their attitudes towards parents are as favorable as those of the comparison groups. They seek out distinctively affectionate relationships with peers; their general attitudinal orientations are similar to those of the comparison groups, while their specific attitudes towards both English and French Canadians are relatively unbiased; their values show the influence of both ethnic backgrounds as do their achievement orientations, which are less extreme than those of the comparison groups. Rather than developing a divided allegiance or repressing one or both aspects of their backgrounds, as has been noted among the offspring of certain immigrant groups

(Child 1943), they apparently have developed a dual allegiance that permits them to identify with both their parents, and to feel that they themselves are wanted as family members. One of the mixed ethnic boys summed up this finding by saying: 'I respect both my parents, and I respect their origins'. One might argue that the concern of the parents of mixed ethnic adolescents to 'include' their children is exaggerated, a symptom of tension and value conflict, but such an interpretation is negated by the apparent success these parents have had in passing on a sense of being wanted. There are, however, many features of this pattern of results that need further study.

This profile sketch is more characteristic of the mixed ethnic subjects who are part of the French-Canadian high school environment. These young people may be more susceptible to the English-Canadian culture than those attending English-Canadian schools would be to French-Canadian culture because of the Canadian cultural tug of war which seems, at least until recently, to be controlled by the more powerful and prestigious English-Canadian communities (see Lambert 1967).

Two general modes of adjustment to a mixed ethnic background became apparent. In one case, these young men incorporate both ethnic streams of influence, which are either modified by the parents before they are passed on to their children, or are tempered by the adolescents themselves, so that they are less extreme than those represented by either of the major reference groups. A tendency to amalgamate both cultural streams of influence is suggested by the contrasts noted between the ethnically mixed groups and the homogeneous groups, e.g. the unbiased ethnic identifications of the former, their perceptions of parents as being inclusive, their favorable attitudes towards both English and French Canadians, and their less extreme achievement values. In the other case, they tend to adapt their views to the predominant features of the academic-cultural environment in which they find themselves. This form of adjustment is suggested by the tendency of the mixed ethnic groups to line up with the respective homogeneous groups with whom they attend high school, e.g. their choices of the values they hope to pass on to their own children, the personality traits they see as desirable, and their judgments of the relative attractiveness of English-Canadian or French-Canadian girls.

This illustration provides hope for biculturality in the sense that offspring of mixed-ethnic marriages appear to profit from the dual cultural influences found in their families. Rather than cultural conflicts, we find well-adjusted young people with broad perspectives who are comfortable in the role of representing both of their cultural backgrounds. We also have here an illustration of the additive form of biculturalism; the boys studied were caught in the flow of two cultural streams and were apparently happy to be part of both streams.

There is a similar type outcome in the investigation conducted by Richard Tucker and myself (Lambert and Tucker 1972) concerning the English-Canadian children who took the majority of their elementary schooling via French, and who after grades 5 and 6 had become functionally bilingual. Here we were able to measure on a yearly basis their self-conceptions and their attitudes towards English-Canadian, French-Canadian, and French-French ways of life. The attitude profiles of the children in the experimental French program indicate that by the fifth grade important affective changes have occurred during the course of the project. The children state that they enjoy the form of education they are receiving and want to stay with it; their feelings toward French people have become decidedly more favorable; and they now think of themselves as being both French- and English-Canadian in personal makeup.

It is this apparent identification with French people--those from Canada and those from Europe--that raises the question of biculturalism. Has the program made the children more bicultural? It is difficult to answer this question because the meaning of bicultural is so vague. It is certain that the children now feel they can be at ease in both French- and English-Canadian social settings, and that they are becoming both French and English in certain regards; but they are not becoming less English as a consequence. It is certain, too, that they have learned that in classes with European-French teachers they should stand when a visitor enters, while they need not stand in classes that are conducted by English-Canadian or French-Canadian teachers. We wonder how much more there is to being bicultural beyond knowing thoroughly the languages involved, feeling personally aligned with both groups, and knowing how to behave in the two atmospheres. Are there any deeper personal aspects to cultural differences? That is, does culture actually affect personality all that much or is it perhaps a thinner and more superficial wrapping than many social scientists have suggested?

The attitudes of the parents at the start of the project were basically friendly and favorable, although marked with very little knowledge about the French-Canadian people around them. These parents wanted their children to learn French for what appear to be integrative reasons--getting to know the other ethnic group and their distinctive ways--but they did not want them to go so far as to think and feel as French Canadians do. In other words, they were guarded and did not want their children to lose their English-Canadian identity. How will they interpret the attitudes of their children who by grade 5 come to think of themselves as being both English- and French-Canadian in disposition and outlook? Some may see this as a worrisome sign of identity loss, and although we are not optimistic we believe they would, if patient, come to view their children's enjoyment in having both Englsh- and French-Canadian friends and both types of outlooks as a valuable addition, not a subtraction or cancellation of identities. As we see it, the children are acquiring a second social overcoat which seems to increase their interest in dressing up and reduces the monotony of either coat used alone. Our hope is that the children can convince worried parents that the experience is, in fact, enriching and worthwhile, but the pressures against the children doing so are powerful.

These studies suggest to us that there is no basis in reality for the belief that becoming bilingual or bicultural necessarily means a loss or dissolution of identity. We are aware of the possible pressures that can surround members of ethnolinguistic minority groups and make them hesitant to become full-fledged members of two cultural communities. At the same time, though, we see how easy and rewarding it can be for those who are able to capitalize on a nation's dual heritage. The question of most interest, then, is how in modern societies these possibilities can be extended to ethnolinguistic minority groups.

Actually, very little has been done in North America over the years to help ethnolinguistic minority groups maintain respect in their linguistic and cultural heritage so that they could become full-fledged bicultural members of their national societies. Still, there are several recent developments in the American society that hold out a new and exciting type of hope. These developments, in fact, constitute another instance where the United States has an opportunity to set an outstanding example of what can be done for ethnic minority groups. The first development is a new perspective, generated, it seems, by the critical self-analysis of collegiate activists in the sixties, on what it means to be American. It was American collegiates who demanded national respect for minority groups of every variety, including Afro-Americans and American Indians. As a nation, these young people argued, we have no right to wash out distinctive traditions of any minority group since their ways of life, relative to the so-called American way of life, are in many respects admirable.

The second development, which may have stemmed from the first, takes the form of a national willingness to help minority groups. One way this willingness to help manifests itself is in new educational laws that provide extensive schooling in Spanish for Spanish-Americans in America's large centers, in the passage of the Bilingual Education Act, and in new laws passed in states such as Massachusetts which provide schooling in any number of home languages whenever a group of parents request it.

The third development is a new direction in psycholinguistic research which, although only now getting underway, indicates that the hyphenated American can perhaps most easily become fully and comfortably American if the Spanish, the Polish, the Navajo, or the French prefix is given unlimited opportunity to flourish. For example, the research of Padilla and Long

(1969; see also Long and Padilla 1970) indicates that Spanish-American children and adolescents can learn English better and adjust more comfortably to America if their linguistic and cultural ties with the Spanish-speaking world are kept alive and active from infancy on. Peal and Lambert (1962) came to a similar conclusion when they found that FC young people who are given opportunities to become bilingual (through education in French language schools and through social contacts in English language settings) are more likely than monolinguals to be advanced in their schooling in French schools, to develop a diversified and flexible intelligence, and to develop attitudes that are as charitable towards the other major Canadian cultural group as towards their own. A similar conclusion is drawn from the recent work of Lambert and Tucker (1972), where EC youngsters--whose home and community environments give them a solid and sure base of English language competence --are given most of their elementary training via French. These children too, seem to be advanced, relatively, in their cognitive development, their appreciation for French people and French ways of life, and their own sense of breadth and depth as Canadians.

In view of these sympathetic and supportive new developments, is it now possible to assist the hyphenated American to become fully and comfortably bilingual and bicultural? Is it now possible to counteract and change the reactions of ethnically different children in America so that they will no longer feel different, peculiar, and inferior whenever they take on their Spanish, Portuguese, Polish, Navajo, or French styles of life as temporary replacements for the American style?

My own thinking on this matter is based on the following working hypotheses: that in bilingual communities where differential prestige is accorded to the languages and to the ethnolinguistic groups involved, then attention should be placed by both linguistic groups on the development of skills in the language more likely to be overlooked. Thus, for FCs in Canada, rather than exploring early immersion-in-English programs, the FC community should consolidate and deepen its control of French, and branch into English language training as early as possible, but only as signs appear that full competence in the potentially neglected home language is assured. In this way trends toward subtractive forms of bilingualism or biculturalism can be transformed into additive ones.

An American example of this sort of transformation is the case of French-Americans in northern New England, who have recently been given a chance to be schooled partly in their home language (Dubé and Herbert 1975a and 1975b; Lambert, Giles, and Picard 1975; Lambert, Giles, and Albert 1976). In the northern regions of Maine, some 85% of families have kept French alive as the home language or one of the two home languages, even though traditionally all schooling has been conducted in English. We participated in an experiment wherein a random selection of schools in the area were permitted to offer about a third of the elementary curriculum in French and where a second sample of schools with children of comparable intelligence scores and socioeconomic backgrounds served as a control or comparison in that all their instruction was in English. After a five-year run, the children in the 'partial French' classes clearly outperformed those in the control classes on various aspects of English language skills and on academic content, such as math, learned partly via French; at the same time French had become for them a much more literate language (in contrast to mainly audio-lingual) because of the reading and writing requirements of the French schooling. In fact, recent reports show that the French-trained children are consistently ahead of the control children in English language achievement test scores as well as in grade placement levels. This means that they may now have a better chance to compete with other American children in enterprises that call for educational abilities; they apparently have been lifted from the typical low standing on scholastic achievement measures that characterizes many ethnolinguistic groups in North America.

An important element in this transformation appears to be a change in the self views of the French-trained youngsters who, our research has shown, begin to reflect a deep pride in being French, and a realization that their language is as important a medium for education as is English (Lambert, Giles, and Picard 1975). Similar community-based studies are underway in the American Southwest, and these, too, are based on the belief that ethnolinguistic minorities need a strong educational experience in their own languages and traditions before they can cope in an 'all-American' society or before they will want to cope in such a society.

NOTE

An earlier version of this paper, entitled 'The effects of bilingualism on the individual: Cognitive and socio-cultural consequences', was published (1977) in: Bilingualism: Psychological, social and educational implications. Edited by P. A. Hornby. New York: Academic Press.

REFERENCES

Aellen, C., and W. E. Lambert. 1969. Ethnic identification and personality adjustments of Canadian adolescents of mixed English-French parentage. Canadian Journal of Behavioral Science 1.69-86.
Anisfeld, E. 1964. A comparison of the cognitive functioning of monolinguals and bilinguals. Unpublished Ph.D. dissertation. McGill University.

Balkan, L. 1970. Les effets du bilinguisme français-anglais sur les aptitudes intellectuelles. Bruxelles: Aimav.
Ben-Zeev, S. 1972. The influence of bilingualism on cognitive development and cognitive strategy. Unpublished Ph.D. dissertation. University of Chicago.
Child, I. L. 1943. Italian or American? The second generation in conflict. New Haven: Yale University Press.
Cummins, J., and M. Gulutsan. 1973. Some effects of bilingualism on cognitive functioning. University of Alberta, Edmonton, Alberta. Mimeo.
Cummins, J. 1976. The influence of bilingualism on cognitive growth: A synthesis of research findings and explanatory hypotheses. St. Patrick's College, Dublin. Mimeo.
Dubé, N. C., and G. Herbert. 1975a. St. John Valley Bilingual Education Project. Prepared for the U.S. Department of Health, Education and Welfare under contract No. OEC-0-74-9331, August. Mimeo.
Dubé, N. C., and G. Herbert. 1975b. Evaluation of the St. John Valley Title VII Bilingual Education Program, 1970-1975, Madawaska, Maine. Mimeo.
Gardner, R. C., and W. E. Lambert. 1972. Attitudes and motivation in second-language learning. Rowley, Mass.: Newbury House.
Genesee, F., J. Hamers, W. E. Lambert, L. Mononen, M. Seitz, and R. Starck. 1978. Language processing in bilinguals. Brain and Language 5.1-12.
Getzels, J. W., and P. W. Jackson. 1962. Creativity and intelligence. New York: Wiley.
Gordon, A. I. 1966. Intermarriage. Boston: Beacon Press.
Guilford, J. P. 1950. Creativity. American Psychologist 5.444-454.
Guilford, J. P. 1956. The structure of intellect. Psychological Bulletin 53.267-293.
Ianco-Worrall, A. D. 1972. Bilingualism and cognitive development. Child Development 43.1390-1400.
Lambert, W. E. 1967. A social psychology of bilingualism. Journal of Social Issues 23.91-109.
Lambert, W. E. 1969. Psychological studies of the interdependencies of the bilingual's two languages. In: Substance and structure of language. Edited by J. Puhvel. Los Angeles: University of California Press. 99-126.
Lambert, W. E., and E. Anisfeld. 1969. A note on the relationship of bilingualism and intelligence. Canadian Journal of Behavioral Science 1.123-128.
Lambert, W. E., H. Giles, and A. Albert. 1976. Language attitudes in a rural city in northern Maine. McGill University. Mimeo.
Lambert, W. E., H. Giles, and O. Picard. 1975. Language attitudes in a French-American community. International Journal of the Sociology of Language 4.127-152.

Lambert, W. E., and G. R. Tucker. 1972. Bilingual education of children: The St. Lambert experiment. Rowley, Mass.: Newbury House.

Leopold, W. F. 1949. Speech development of a bilingual child. 4 vols. Evanston, Ill.: Northwestern University Press, 1939-1949.

Long, K. K., and A. M. Padilla. 1970. Evidence for bilingual antecedents of academic success in a group of Spanish-American college students. Unpublished research report. Western Washington State College.

Padilla, A. M., and K. K. Long. 1969. An assessment of successful Spanish-American students at the University of New Mexico. Paper presented to the annual meeting of the AAAS, Rocky Mountain Division, Colorado Springs.

Park, R. E. 1964. Personality and cultural conflict. Publication of the American Sociological Society, 1931, 25.95-110. Republished in: R. E. Park, Race and culture. Glencoe, Ill.: The Free Press.

Peal, E., and W. E. Lambert. 1962. The relation of bilingualism to intelligence. Psychological Monographs 76.1-23.

Saucier, J. F. 1965. Psychiatric aspects of interethnic marriages. Montreal: McGill University. Mimeo.

Scott, S. 1973. The relation of divergent thinking to bilingualism: Cause or effect? Unpublished research report. McGill University.

Torrance, E. P., J. C. Gowan, J. M. Wu, and N. C. Aliotti. 1970. Creative functioning of monolingual and bilingual children in Singapore. Journal of Educational Psychology 61.72-75.

Vaid, J. 1977. Hemispheric involvement in the language processing of bilinguals. M.A. thesis. McGill University.

Vaid, J., and W. E. Lambert. 1978. Cerebral involvement in the cognitive functioning of bilinguals. McGill University. Mimeo.

Vygotsky, L. S. 1962. Thought and language. Cambridge, Mass.: MIT Press.

Witkin, H. A. 1976. Socialization and ecology in the development of cross cultural and sex differences in cognitive style. Paper presented at the 21st International Congress of Psychology, Paris.

IV. Ethnicity and Multilingualism

PATTERNS OF LITERACY
IN MULTILINGUAL SITUATIONS

Charles A. Ferguson
Stanford University

The issue of literacy is often an important component in the analysis of multilingual situations, and this is true whether the analysis is purely descriptive or policy oriented and whether the multilingualism is individual or societal. Yet the patterns of literacy in multilingual settings are rarely analyzed as such except to discuss the extent of illiteracy or the choice of languages for literacy education, and even at this Georgetown University Round Table on international aspects of bilingual education almost no attention is paid to literacy as such. The purpose of this paper is to highlight some of the features of patterns of literacy which may be important in the analysis of language situations. The examples are largely taken from other countries, but the patterns of literacy discussed are relevant also for bilingual situations in the United States.

Some of the important issues in literacy, such as methods of teaching adult literacy and the relation of literacy to development, have received extensive study, and the research literature on the reading process and the teaching of reading is enormous and still growing. In this paper no attempt is made to review or evaluate these large bodies of research. Instead, four issues are explored which have received much less study but seem important in the relation of literacy to multilingualism.

Functions of literacy. One such issue concerns the functions of literacy in individuals and societies. Social scientists and language specialists of various kinds are now trying to understand how the uses of writing may vary from one society to another and how the introduction of literacy into different communities may have very different effects. This field has been a traditional area for anthropologists, but their accounts

have generally focused only on the invention and diffusion of
writing systems (cf. Kroeber 1948), including the so-called
'stimulus diffusion' of cases like Vai and Cherokee, in which
a new writing system is invented on the basis of the inventor's
familiarity with the idea of writing rather than knowledge of a
particular writing system which serves as a model or source.
These studies hardly touch on the range of functions of
literacy and the quite different values associated with it in
different societies.

We have, however, a small stream of anthropologically oriented
studies on literacy which provide a good starting place for
future research on functions. These include Andree Sjoberg's
papers (Sjoberg 1964, 1966), the succession of studies associated with the name of Jack Goody (Goody and Watt 1963; Goody
1968, 1977), and the recent work on the ethnography of writing by Keith Basso (Basso and Anderson 1973, Basso 1974).
(It is interesting to note that the Sjoberg, Goody, and Basso
studies are relatively independent and refer hardly at all to
one another.) This body of research is, however, totally inadequate for our understanding of the functions of literacy in
multilingual contexts. In spite of efforts to be truly crosscultural and general, the research has emphasized only a few
major cases--notably, the spread of the Semitic alphabets and
the experience of ancient Greece and modern Europe. Information on traditions in South Asia and East Asia has provided
some corrective, and a few studies of 'exotic' Native American
and West African cases have helped, but the roles of literacy
in multilingual developing nations, in language minorities of
highly literate nations, and in international communication have
hardly been examined at all from this perspective.

Historical studies of the extent and functions of literacy in
society typically do not pay attention to minority languages
(e.g. Cipolla 1969; Schofield 1968; Furet and Sachs 1974;
Alleton 1977; Heath 1977). International studies, including
UNESCO publications on literacy, also focus on one language
at a time even in multilingual nations where literacy in different languages often has quite different functions in the same
populations (cf. UNESCO 1973; Gorman 1977).

In Ferguson (1971), I sketched some of the different functions of literacy in different languages and different writing
systems in Ethiopia, but that article devoted a great deal of
space to the nature of the writing systems themselves and the
different ways they were acquired; relatively little space was
left for functional analysis.

Let me give just two examples of different ranges of functions of literacy in particular speech communities, in order to
illustrate the notion of differing patterns of literacy. The
Tuareg are a society of some thousands of people, many of
them nomadic, who live in a large section of the Sahara and
neighboring areas. They have had a writing system for centuries, the tifinagh, which provides an adequate representation

of their language, one of the Berber languages of North Africa. Many of the Tuareg today are literate in their traditional writing system. The occasions of its use, however, have remained severely limited. In this speech community, writing is used for scratching graffiti of the 'Kilroy was here' variety on rocks in the desert; it is used for brief love notes, and for various kinds of talismans and charms. There seems to have been no tendency to extend the function of literacy beyond these limits, and the present-day uses may even represent reduction from an earlier range of uses (Cohen 1958 II:334-335). The Cherokee nation in 1820 was a society of some thousands of Native Americans living chiefly in North Carolina and Arkansas, without a traditional writing system. One Cherokee man, Sequoyah, invented a syllabary to write the language and within a few years most of the Cherokee were literate in the syllabary. They supported a newspaper and the publication of books, and they used the writing system to send letters and keep records. In this second case, the use of writing served important communicative functions as well as being an important symbol of social integration and group identification (Walker forthcoming[1]). The two societies, mid-twentieth century Tuareg and mid-nineteenth century Cherokee can be characterized as 'literate', but the functions of literacy are strikingly different in them. Put in other terms, the outcome of the introduction of writing in these societies was different and the resulting patterns of literacy differed in important and not well understood ways.

As an example of different functions of literacy in different languages within the same overall pattern of literacy use, we may cite the literacy of Ethiopian Muslims. Educated Muslims in Ethiopia typically are literate in three languages--Amharic, Arabic, and English--none of which is their mother tongue. Each of the three has its own writing system and the three systems are very different. Literacy in Amharic is the basic literacy of the national education system and is used in signs, newspapers, and a variety of communicative settings. Literacy in Arabic provides religious identification and at some levels of competence makes works written in Arabic accessible (they may be traditional Islamic texts or they may be modern publications of Arab countries). Literacy in English is the basis of higher education and is the symbol of membership in the modernizing elite (Ferguson 1970, 1971).

Nature of writing systems. Our first issue dealt with patterns of literacy use; our second issue is the other side of that coin--patterns of the structure of writing systems themselves. There is a significant body of literature on the creation and modification of writing systems. A few years ago someone made the observation that the most active field of applied linguistics throughout the world was not foreign language teaching or research in machine translation, but orthography creation and reform. Whether this is true or not, it is clear

that many nations and language communities are struggling with
orthographic problems, and in some cases they are focal points
of considerable tension. China has recently announced hundreds
of newly simplified characters and new orthographies for several
minority languages (cf. Ferguson 1977); Norway has had four
spelling changes in the last 75 years (Gundersen 1977); Zambia
is trying to unify the orthographies of its seven major languages
(Kashoki 1978); writing systems for a number of Indian languages in North America are currently being devised or promul-
gated (Walker forthcoming).

Beginning with earlier literature on the history of writing
(e.g. Jensen 1969, Cohen 1958, Gelb 1952) and a generation's
worth of articles and books on linguistic factors in the structure and use of writing systems (e.g. Pike 1947, Berry 1958,
Smalley 1964, Haas 1976), we are now seeing studies which
emphasize the social factors of attitudes, processes of diffusion,
and patterns of acceptance. This new trend is typified by
Joshua Fishman's fine recent book on the applied sociolinguistics of writing systems (Fishman 1977; cf. also Garvin 1954,
Ferguson 1968) and we are about to see movement from speculative discussions and the comparison of disparate case studies
toward careful, systematic experimental and correlational investigations. Even this promising line of research, however,
has only lightly touched the issues of writing systems in multilingual settings and the symbolic value of orthographic changes
in a variety of sociopolitical contexts.

As an example of 'multigraphism', let us note some literacy
aspects of the Panjabi-Hindi-Urdu language complex in Northern
India. For several centuries the literate minority among the
millions of native speakers of Panjabi have typically been literate either in Hindi or Urdu, which served as the public and
formal languages of the Panjabi speech community. Hindi is
written in Devanagari script which runs from left to right,
with noninitial vowels represented by attachments to the consonant letters; Urdu is written in Arabic script which runs from
right to left and omits many of the vowels. In general, Hindus
were literate in Hindi and Muslims in Urdu; very few Panjabis
learned both scripts. In recent years three factors led to a
change in this situation: expansion of education, expanded
roles of regional languages in education and public life, and
reluctance of Sikhs to be identified with either Hindus or Muslims. Now many Panjabis are becoming literate in their mother
tongue, making use of a third script, Gurmukhi, which had
traditionally been used in very limited functions for writing the
language. This change in the pattern of literacy alters the access of Panjabis to written materials and affects the group
identification of millions of people. Any serious study of the
acquisition of literacy in Panjabi would have to include discussion of the characteristics of the respective writing systems
and their significance in the community.

Acquisition of literacy in non-Roman systems. A third issue is the analysis of learning to read in scripts other than the Roman alphabet and the acquisition of literacy by methods other than the use of primers and classrooms. The one very limited study of my own in this area, already referred to (Ferguson 1971), examined several traditional paths to literacy in multilingual Ethiopia; it convinced me of the value such research would have for our understanding of the reading process and educational problems related to reading.

Many people in Ethiopia learn to read Amharic, the national language, by a traditional method which does almost everything that all schools of reading instruction in the United States would agree does not work. They learn by rote memorization of unintelligible texts in a dead language, reading being learned separately from writing, and their literacy in Amharic is in effect an incidental by-product of the process. This method may have little to commend it for general adoption, but it has a lot to teach us about the processes involved in learning to read. I have no ready way of measuring the actual amount of research, but I believe I am on safe ground if I say that probably 99 percent of the research on the reading process is on the Roman alphabet and is related to contemporary educational settings in the United States and parts of Europe. It is a pleasure to note a small surge of research on the reading of Chinese and Japanese characters which has taken place in the last few years (e.g. Rozin et al. 1971, Tzeng et al. 1977), but this research is just beginning and its unexpected and sometimes contradictory findings are only a tantalizing indication of its potential importance.

On the one hand, our smug confidence that an alphabetic system is the easiest to learn is shattered by evidence that under some conditions morphemic writing of the Chinese type or syllabic writing of the Japanese kana type may be easier for English-speaking children than either standard English orthography or more consistent phonetic orthographies of the i.t.a. type. On the other hand, evidence is accumulating that speakers of Chinese in their mental processing of the characters make use of phonetic aspects of the morphemes represented. Again, there is much to be learned here.

Reading specialists in the Middle East or South Asia are, to a considerable extent, applying ideas based on European and American research in situations where many aspects of the writing systems--and hence the reading process--are very different from the left-to-right, consonant and vowel letters, capital and lower case systems used for almost all the languages of Europe and the United States. Basic research on learning to read systems of the Hebrew and Arabic type and the Devanagari type is needed.

To address this question more directly in the context of multilingualism, let us note that in Asian countries there are many millions of people acquiring literacy in two languages with

different writing systems (e.g. Bengali and English) or in one
language in two writing systems (e.g. Hindi-Urdu), or in two
languages in the same writing system (e.g. Marathi and Hindi).
It seems undeniable that there are many areas of research here
which are relevant for understanding education problems in
multilingual settings.

Language variation and literacy. The last few years, a number of linguists have turned their attention to the analysis of linguistic variation within speech communities, especially variation which correlates with social variables; and indeed, Georgetown University is the site of an annual conference on linguistic variation. It is somewhat surprising that there is so little research on reading in relation to variation in language. In many languages there is extensive dialect variation but a single standard written language. Linguists and literacy specialists have for a long time discussed the fit between phonologies and writing systems, and there are sometimes rich discussions of dialect variation in connection with the creation of new orthographies, but there is very little experimental research exploring the differences in reading processes as related to dialect differences in phonology (or for that matter, syntax, lexicon, or patterns of discourse). Most of the research in this field is devoted to the investigation of the general effects of so-called 'Black English' on reading skills, but such research is hard to interpret without a larger body of research on regional and social dialect variation in respect to the reading process.

The research area which I am indicating is simply that of literacy in multidialectal settings, as an area related to that of literacy in multilingual settings. In fact, it may sometimes be difficult to draw a boundary line between the two. One particular language situation, diglossia, is receiving some research attention with respect to literacy. In diglossic situations, the form of the written language is strikingly different from the ordinary spoken language, and it seems likely that reading problems have a special flavor in such situations. Recently, one sociologist, De Silva of York University in England, wrote a book, <u>Diglossia and Literacy</u>, in which he examined a number of cases of diglossia in South Asia such as Tamil and Singhalese where the situation is a pure diglossic one, with a high variety and a low variety which are very different. He sees severe educational problems in the diglossia, severe problems in national development and in the development of individuals. His study is based largely on naturalistic observation rather than experimental techniques, but it marks a direction in which literacy research is needed.

Conclusions. In this paper I have listed four issues in the relation between literacy and multilingualism, explored them briefly, and then declared them important as research topics.

Patterns of Literacy in Multilingual Situations /141

Further, I have tended to suggest that research on one topic should take account of research on other topics and that experimental studies are needed in addition to observation and analysis. It is a pleasure in my concluding remarks to point to beginnings of the kind of literacy research I would like to see, in which there is focus on the functions of literacy in the society, the nature of the writing systems used, the acquisition of non-Roman systems, and linguistic variation. I am referring to several of the papers presented at the NIE Conference on Writing held at the Southwest Regional Laboratory in June, 1977--in particular, those by Szwed, Heath, and Scribner and Cole. The last one, which is based on patterns of literacy among the Vai in Liberia, actually examines every one of the four topics listed in this paper; also, it combines anthropological field work with the methods of experimental psychology, and it raises general questions relevant to educational problems on the American scene. It is this kind of research which demonstrates, more convincingly than my exhortations to virtue, the significance of studying literacy in connection with multilingual situations.

NOTE

1. Subsequently, Cherokee literacy declined dramatically, as a result of a number of factors, including the authorities' insistence on literacy in English and the Cherokee view of schools as a white man's institution. At present, the literacy in either Cherokee or English is relatively low, and knowledge of the traditional syllabary is required only for certain Christian religious activities and for the practice of traditional Cherokee medicine. For discussion, see Walker (forthcoming).

REFERENCES

Alleton, Viviane. 1977. Usages of Chinese writing. Diogenes 99.37-59.
Basso, Keith. 1974. The ethnography of writing. In: Explorations in the ethnography of speaking. Edited by R. Bauman and J. Sherzer. London: CUP. 425-432.
Basso, Keith H., and Ned Anderson. 1973. A Western Apache writing system: The symbols of Silas John. Science 180. 1013-1022.
Berry, Jack. 1958. The making of alphabets. In: Proceedings of the 8th International Congress of Linguists. Oslo: Oslo University Press. 752-764.
Cipolla, Carlo M. 1969. Literacy and development in the West. Baltimore: Penguin Books.
Cohen, Marcel. 1958. La grande invention de l'ecriture et son evolution. Paris: Imprimerie Nationale.
De Silva, M. W. Sugathapala. 1976. Diglossia and literacy. [= CIIL Adult Literacy Series 2]. Manasagangotri, Mysore, India: Central Institute of Indian Languages.

Ferguson, Charles A. 1968. St. Stefan of Perm and applied linguistics. In: Language problems of developing nations. Edited by J. A. Fishman et al. New York: Wiley.
Ferguson, Charles A. 1970. The role of Arabic in Ethiopia: A sociolinguistic perspective. In: Georgetown University Round Table on Languages and Linguistics 1970. Edited by James E. Alatis. Washington, D.C.: Georgetown University Press. 355-370.
Ferguson, Charles A. 1971. Contrasting patterns of literacy in a multilingual nation. In: Language use and social change. Edited by W. H. Whitely. London: Oxford University Press. 234-253.
Ferguson, Charles A. Aspects of literacy teaching in the People's Republic of China. In: Language and literacy: Current issues and research. Edited by T. P. Gorman. Tehran: International Institute for Adult Literacy Methods. 227-234.
Fishman, Joshua A. 1977. Advances in the creation and revision of writing systems. [= Contributions to the Sociology of Language 8]. The Hague: Mouton.
Furet, François, and Vladimir Sachs. 1974. La croissance de l'alphabétisation en France (XVIIIe-XIIe siècles). Annales: Economies, Sociétés, Civilisations 29.714-737.
Garvin, Paul L. 1954. Literacy as a problem in language and culture. In: Georgetown University Round Table on Languages and Linguistics 1954. Edited by Hugo J. Mueller. Washington, D.C.: Georgetown University Press. 117-129.
Gelb, Ignace J. 1952. A study of writing: The foundations of grammatology. Chicago: University of Chicago Press.
Goody, Jack, ed. 1968. Literacy in traditional societies. Cambridge: Cambridge University Press.
Goody, Jack. 1977. The domestication of the savage mind. Cambridge: Cambridge University Press.
Goody, Jack, and Ian Watt. 1963. The consequences of literacy. Comparative Studies in Society and History 5.304-345. Reprinted in: Literacy in traditional societies. Edited by J. Goody. Cambridge: Cambridge University Press. 1968. 27-68.
Gorman, T. P., ed. 1977. Language and literacy: Current issues and research. Tehran: International Institute for Adult Literacy Methods.
Gundersen, Dag. 1977. Successes and failures in the reformation of Norwegian orthography. In: Advances in the creation and revision of writing systems. Edited by J. A. Fishman. The Hague: Mouton. 247-265.
Haas, W., ed. 1976. Writing without letters. Manchester: Manchester University Press.
Heath, Shirley Brice. (to appear) The ethnohistory of writing in America. Paper presented at the NIE Conference on Writing. To appear in the published proceedings.

Jensen, Hans. 1969. Sign, symbol, and script: An account of man's efforts to write. [English translation of Die Schrift in Vergangenheit und Gegenwart.] New York: Putnam.
Kashoki, Mubanga E. 1978. Harmonization of African languages: Standardization of orthography in Zambia. Paper prepared for UNESCO. Mimeo.
Kroeber, Alfred. 1948. Anthropology. (Chapter 13, Story of the alphabet, 504-537.) New York: Harcourt, Brace.
Pike, Kenneth L. 1947. Phonemics: A technique for reducing languages to writing. Ann Arbor: University of Michigan Press.
Rozin, P., S. Poritsky, and R. Sotsky. 1971. American children with reading problems can easily learn to read English represented by Chinese characters. Science 171.1264-1267.
Schofield, R. S. 1968. The measurement of literacy in preindustrial England. In: Literacy in traditional societies. Edited by J. Goody. Cambridge: Cambridge University Press. 311-325.
Scribner, Sylvia, and Michael Cole. (to appear) Unpackaging literacy. Paper prepared for the NIE Conference on Writing. To appear in the published proceedings.
Sjoberg, Andree. 1964. Writing, speech, and society: Some changing interrelationships. In: Proceedings of the 9th International Congress of Linguists. The Hague: Mouton. 892-897.
Sjoberg, A. 1966. Socio-cultural and linguistic factors in the development of writing systems for preliterate peoples. In: Sociolinguistics. Edited by W. Bright. The Hague: Mouton. 260-276.
Smalley, William A., et al. 1964. Orthography studies: Articles on new writing systems. London: United Bible Societies.
Szwed, John F. (to appear) The ethnography of writing. Paper prepared for the NIE Conference on Writing. To appear in the published proceedings.
Tzeng, Ovid J. L., Daisy L. Hung, and William S-Y. Wang. 1977. Speech recoding in Chinese characters. Journal of Experimental Psychology 6.621-630.
UNESCO. 1973. The Experimental World Literacy Programme: A critical assessment. Paris: The UNESCO Press and UNDP.
Walker, Willard. (to appear) Native American writing systems. To appear in: Language in the USA. Edited by C. A. Ferguson and S. B. Heath.

CULTURE AND ETHNICITY
IN THE BILINGUAL CLASSROOM

Robert J. Di Pietro
University of Delaware

Abstract. As programs in bilingual education reach new
levels of maturity, more is said about the need to make them
responsive to the cultures of the students involved. Ethnicity,
however, remains a neglected dimension. A survey of the
literature dealing with bilingual curricula and the training of
bilingual teachers reveals a lack of differentiation between the
terms 'culture' and 'ethnicity'. A major part of the problem
stems from the fact that we have no intellectual tradition built
around ethnicity. Yet, the interaction of ethnicity with language is no less significant than that of culture with language.
Ethnicity plays a major part in shaping the identity of people,
especially when they are children. Due to the linguistic and
cultural alternatives provided by bilingual education, the problem in developing an ethnic self-awareness may be increased.
It can be shown that ethnicity plays a major part in the expectations that teachers have for their students. The cognitive
flexibility that is a supposed benefit of bilingual education may
be negated by an unwanted sense of disorientation in the affectual domain unless attention is paid to the ethnic component.
The paper makes a strong plea for bilingual educators to join
ranks with the sponsors of ethnic heritage studies in America
for the purpose of creating a multifaceted form of bilingual-
bicultural-multiethnic education.

'In San Francisco, preschool teachers are examining their
feelings about persons of other ethnic backgrounds as they
study the causes of racial and cultural stereotyping and their
effect on children'. So began the HEW News bulletin of
November 28, 1977, as it announced the funding of 64 new
Ethnic Heritage Studies grants under the provisions of Title IX

of the Elementary and Secondary Education Act. Other ethnic projects financially supported by HEW in the current fiscal year include a study of the multiethnic heritage of Oakland, California, a program for school librarians in Boulder, Colorado, a multimedia presentation of the history of the Jews of Michigan, a curriculum materials development project for the Polish heritage of St. Louis, Missouri, and a program for training adults to be peer teachers in ethnic courses in New York City. Obviously, ethnicity has come of age as a factor in American education. Or has it? Not one of the 64 grants listed in the bulletin amounts to more than $50,000 and the total expenditure is $2.3 million, a figure which pales considerably when compared to federal support of bilingual education, now over $100 million.

Why this uneven treatment of bilingualism and multiethnicity by our national legislators? Part of the answer lies in the different ways legislation on the two issues came about. Bilingual education was seen by many of its political supporters in the U.S. Congress as an antipoverty measure, i.e. as a way of bringing equal economic opportunities to those Americans cut off from the mainstream because of language. The federal requirement that potential benefactors of bilingual education be not only non-English-speaking but also poor has kept funds from going to those school districts with bilingual children from middle-income families. As a result, bilingual education was stigmatized and kept from becoming a viable alternative to the usual type of monolingual, mainstream public education found in American schools. The Ethnic Heritage Studies Act, on the other hand, was typified as 'enrichment' right from the start. In the view of many of its supporters, this act represents an effort to provide new generations of American children with information about the diversity of culture and ethnicity in their backgrounds. Where the bilingual education act focused primarily on language and was considered to be needed for certain segments of the American population, the ethnic heritage act is inclined to 'nonvital' issues such as immigrant history and the social institutions of ethnic groups.

No matter how our elected representatives on Capitol Hill may wish to structure reality, it is inevitable that we come to talk about the interconnections of ethnicity, language, and culture in bilingual education. Both linguistics and anthropology have a long tradition of associating language with culture. The link of language with ethnicity or culture with ethnicity, however, is not so clear. Whereas we can use the term 'cultural system' and include language in it when we describe aspects of a society, we have yet to establish a theoretical niche for ethnicity which would satisfy all investigators. Certainly, one cannot discuss ethnicity without mentioning the cultural behavior that marks the phenomenon. Ethnicity without its cultural specification would be as meaningless as language removed from culture. It will be difficult to extricate these concepts

but even if we do not progress beyond recognizing that
ethnicity, culture, and language are interconnected, we will
have made at least a start toward articulating bilingual curricula to reflect all three.
    The first order of the day is to find a clear definition of
ethnicity. The task is so great, however, that we must proceed in short, deliberate steps. We might begin with observing that the term 'ethnic' demarcates groups of people who
share one or more of a number of characteristics: race,
religion, historical origin, family relationship, marriage patterns, life styles, and language. But before we discuss how
these characteristics operate to define ethnic groups in the
United States, we must point out, as did Fishman (1977) at
last year's Georgetown University Round Table, that the term
'ethnic' often carries with it a derogatory or demeaning sense.
Ethnicity, especially when it refers to membership in a minority group, is perceived sometimes as a threat to the stability
of a society. The term 'nativism' has been coined by political
scientists and historians to describe a national phenomenon
which emerges in times of crisis such as war and depression,
and takes the form of hostility toward some ethnically marked
group (see Vecoli 1973:90). Nativism leads to the formation of
a social 'establishment' which enacts exclusionary practices
against those groups perceived to be outside the establishment.
Some ethnic groups who have been victims of nativism in the
United States are the Jews, the blacks, the Italians, the Irish,
and Hispanic peoples.
    In an interview with the journalist Noel Epstein (see Epstein
1977:46-47), Professor Higham of Johns Hopkins University
describes ethnic groups as 'likely to be suspicious, narrow-
minded [and] riddled with prejudices'. Ethnic politics in the
United States is often restricted by the media to neighborhood
affairs. A recent editorial in the Washington Star ('Mr. Biaggi
and the Irish', February 22, 1978) labeled it '... a harmless
ritual of honoring old-country traditions and heroes beloved by
some of a politician's constituents--laying wreaths on Columbus
Day and marching on St. Patrick's.' As sometimes happens
with the term 'dialect', 'ethnic' can be thrown as an insult at
those who have it by those who perceive themselves as not
having it. The expression, 'I speak the language but you
speak a dialect' has its counterpart in 'I am an American but
you are an ethnic American'. In this way, Americans who
hyphenate their nationality run the risk of being stereotyped
by other Americans who do not. Sometimes, ethnic Americans
reverse the stereotyping process by qualifying 'mainstream'
Americans. For example, a Chinese American told me that
Americans in general eat more, drink more, and are more
boastful than Chinese Americans.
    For some groups in the United States, ethnicity comes in
phases. In the first phase it embodies a struggle to preserve
a home-country identity. The second stage begins when the

children and grandchildren of the foreign-born seek to
legitimize an identity of their own. This search for an
identity may involve a whole-scale rejection of the parents'
ethnic affiliation or possibly some compromise of ethnic traits
or even the development of completely novel characteristics.
A final stage is marked by nostalgia for the old ways and a
quest for one's roots.

Perhaps the most important trait of ethnicity is that it
represents an attachment of some sort to a group. In a publication of the National Project on Ethnic America of the American Jewish Committee, Joseph Giordano (1973:11) writes that,
'... ethnicity ... is more than a distinctiveness defined by
race, religion, national origin or geography. It involves conscious and unconscious processes that fulfill a deep psychological need for security, identity, and a sense of historical
continuity'. We should hasten to add that these conscious and
unconscious processes do not make uniform and predictable use
of cultural patterns in achieving ethnic distinctiveness. Considerable variation occurs within each marking feature.

For example, it is not equally important to all Hispanic
Americans to know how to speak Spanish, nor to all American
Indians to know their ancestral tongues. Moreover, when
Spanish or some other 'ethnically' marked language is spoken
by a group, that language can display considerable variation
in form. In some cases, an ethnic group can decide that a
particular marking feature should be intensified in use. Thus
we find a dramatic rise in enrollments in the study of Italian
and Hebrew in recent years among Jewish and Italian Americans. In neither case is the language being studied the one
which is most closely associated with earlier generations. For
most Italian Americans, standard Italian is almost as foreign as
French or Spanish might be and for Jewish Americans, Yiddish,
not Hebrew, was the predominant functional language of their
families. Yet, standard Italian and Hebrew have become the
ethnically desired languages in this country--and not the
various Italian dialects or Yiddish.

To give another illustration of how ethnic Americans may
vary in their use of language as a marker of their identity,
Hispanic peoples living in the Southwestern states have come
to realize that the area has a special variety of Spanish. This
realization easily leads to a debate concerning the use of the
regional Spanish in bilingual programs. Some people accept it
and others do not. Arguments mustered against the regional
variety in education are usually cultural ones. When evaluated
in terms of accessibility to a body of written literature and
communication with other people, regional varieties can never
compete with the standard form of any language. However,
bilingual educators must come to realize that the choice of language may be one of the defining characteristics of the local
Chicano or other ethnicity. In such cases, alienation from
regional speech can be interpreted as an assault on ethnic

identity. Steps to avoid the potential for assault must be
taken in the preparation of bilingual programs built around
the standard varieties of the languages.
Culture in educational programs involves not only subject
matter but also the style of presentation. In the ideal bilingual
program subject matter, presentation in the classroom, and language choice all work together to expand the child's sense of
being. The need to harmonize all three components is perhaps
more critical in some sources than in others. For example,
history, as taught in traditional American schools, has been
used by curriculum programmers more to instill a national
identity in the students than to inform them about the past.
History does not report, it interprets. It presents civilization as a spotlight casting various peoples in its brilliance.
Some inventors are extolled while others are ignored. Past
events, such as the Battle of the Alamo or Custer's Stand, are
given values which are sometimes diametrically opposed to the
ethnic self-image of the students. According to an eighteenth
century philosopher named Giambattista Vico (see Bergin and
Fisch 1968), the sense of nationhood brings with it a conceit,
a feeling that one's country is superior to all others in all
ways. In multiethnic nations, the conceit is often concentrated
within the cultural system of one or a few establishment groups.
Even those social scientists of a nation who study the cultural
ways of other peoples are not always imbued with a sense of
altruism. Here are the words of anthropologist Margaret Mead
on this point (as cited in Epstein 1977:70):

How often has our Western attempt to preserve native
dress, old customs, different styles of architecture, to
respect native laws and customs, been only a thin disguise over an unwillingness to admit a people, newly
entering into our way of life, to full participation in
the culture which we claim to value so highly?

Some educators resent the inroads made by various ethnic
groups into the subject matter of schools in much the same way
they object to making bilingualism a significant part of the
curriculum. Ethnic awareness can be as much a threat to the
monolingual, mainstream establishment as is the fear that multilingualism will become a new requirement for advancement to
positions of national power and economic well-being. Public
education in my own childhood left me with the impression that
people from eastern and southern Europe were the least desirable elements of their countries of origin, certainly not as
strong, beautiful, or bright as their northwestern brothers
and sisters. The inscription on the Statue of Liberty in New
York Harbor describes such people as the 'wretched refuse' of
other shores. In a survey of over 500 American executives,
Reed M. Powell (1970) concluded that ethnicity enters very
much into the hiring and promoting of people in the business

Culture and Ethnicity in the Bilingual Classroom /149

world. When asked whether their ethnicity helped or hindered them in their careers, 31.6 percent of the executives of northwest European extraction answered that it had helped them and only 5.3 percent answered that it was a hindrance. For executives of Asiatic backgrounds, only 5.1 percent felt that their ethnicity was a help, and 71.8 percent thought that it worked against them.

Distrust of ethnics by the establishment reached ignoble heights in the Second World War. During that war over 100,000 Japanese Americans were placed in concentration camps. Just before the Allied invasion of Sicily in July, 1943, General George Patton exhorted his troops with the following speech (from Gorer 1948):

When we land, we will meet German and Italian soldiers whom it is our honor and privilege to attack and destroy. Many of you have in your veins German and Italian blood, but remember that these ancestors of yours so loved freedom that they gave up home and country to cross the ocean in search of liberty. The ancestors of the people we shall kill lacked the courage to make such a sacrifice and continued as slaves.

Fishman (1966) pointed out that a million German Americans stopped speaking German as a result of the First World War. We have yet to assess the psychological damage done to Americans of German and Italian heritage as a result of the Second World War.

American education is founded on the principle that the school experience of learning must extend from the family and the home. In practice however, the gap between home and school is evident. The large numbers of immigrants from various countries that entered the United States from 1880 on changed forever the home life-styles of this country. As a result, the school changed its function from that of extending home experiences to a process of alienation from home values. The founding of the Parent-Teachers' Association in a very important way was an effort to stop this estrangement from continuing. But the PTA does not make school policy or write educational programs. Home and school remain separate, and bilingual programs have inherited the problems engendered by this separation. Hopefully, the information about differences in learning styles among ethnic groups contained in such books as Functions of Language in the Classroom by Cazden, John, and Hymes (1972) eventually will have an influence on American education and help bring home and school together.

The lack of responsiveness to language and culture in mainstream American education has led to unilateral action by several ethnic groups. For example, in Cleveland, a city with an especially large and diversified ethnic population, an Association of Ethnic Heritage and Language Schools has been

organized. Popularly called 'Saturday Schools', they offer
afterhours or weekend instruction in 22 different languages.
At present, over 300 teachers have been employed to teach
7,000 students 22 different languages. According to the
December 1977 issue of the Newsletter of the National Ethnic
Studies Assembly (volume 4, no. 1, p. 12), the Association
also conducts workshops for teachers and is publishing a useful handbook for teachers and administrators.

Italian American clubs have become especially active in
sponsoring language instruction in recent years. From a survey of the activities of 19 Italian cultural organizations located
throughout the United States and Canada, I learned (Di Pietro
1977) that classes in Italian are being set up in many locations.
As of December, 1977, these organizations reported 845 students, children and adults alike, enrolled and 42 teachers employed. Since my sampling was very restricted, these figures
must represent only the tip of an immense iceberg of instructional activity unseen or ignored by our educational establishment. At least professional educators in the well-endowed bilingual programs should make an effort to close ranks with
these ethnic programs to advance the cause of multilingual/
multicultural education in the United States. The alternative
they would provide to monolingual, monocultural education
would help legitimize ethnic and cultural pluralism in this
country. Since this pluralism grows from the communities
themselves, it cannot be ignored by school authorities who
defend their programs on the basis of community support.

We have already progressed considerably from the time when
American Indian children were made to stand in dark closets
for speaking their tribal languages in school and when Spanish
American children were fined for using their home language on
school playgrounds. From personal visits to public schools in
nearby Virginia, I have been able to gather evidence of increased sensitivity by teachers and principals to their students'
ethnicity. In addition to the long-established ethnic groups of
the area, northern Virginia has recently attracted numbers of
Hispanic people, Koreans, and Vietnamese.

The following episode is an illustration of the kinds of problems that occur with regard to ethnic diversity and the solutions which can be found. The principal of an elementary
school in Fairfax County, Virginia, with a sizable enrollment of
Korean children, designated a day when children were to bring
food representative of their home cultures. Some of the Korean
children brought food which the other children refused to eat.
These refusals were accompanied by several remarks made directly to the Koreans about the food's lack of appeal. A plate
of the food was then taken to the principal's office. The
principal's immediate response was to express gratitude for
the food and to eat it with apparent relish in front of the
Korean children who brought it to her. This action seemed to
make the Korean children very happy. Later on, one of them

told the principal that her mother had stayed up until three
a.m. preparing the food. By recognizing the importance the
Korean children placed on acceptance of their food by a school
authority, the principal was able to repair the psychological
damage inflicted by the children's classmates.

This episode suggests several broader issues to consider with
regard to ethnic marking. Will food always be a marker of
ethnic identity in such situations? How does its markedness
compare to that of dress, skin color, name, and language? In
another episode, an East Indian child refused to bring any
samples of food from home because he claimed not to like
Indian cooking himself. In fact, he said that he did not like
any 'foreign' food. The only meal of the week which he enjoyed
was the one on Friday evening. On that occasion, the family
eats a typically American dish: pizza!

To pursue the question of ethnic marking among recently
arrived groups, interviews were conducted with several teachers who work in the bilingual program at Key Elementary
School in Arlington, Virginia. The Key School has one of the
most ethnically diversified student populations in the state.
Under the sponsorship of the Arlington County Teacher Corps,
instruction is offered in Spanish, Korean, and Vietnamese.
Separate classes have been established for native and nonnative
speakers of these languages. ESL is also offered and all children spend a part of the day being taught in traditional
English-only courses. Although the curriculum is not fully
multilingual, the school has much support from the community
for the efforts it is making toward this goal.

In the interview, the teachers spoke at length about the effects that names had on the self-image of the children in their
classes and on their own children. One Vietnamese teacher
reported that she named her son 'Bang'. At home, he goes by
the nickname of 'Bee'. Schoolmates, however, started to call
him 'Bang-Bang', as in the expression, 'Bang! Bang! You're
dead!'. This development led the boy to select a new name for
himself: 'Bing', which was based on his home nickname 'Bee'.
'Bing' sounds like a Vietnamese name while also resembling an
American nickname (as in 'Bing' Crosby). Besides, one of the
maintenance men at the school is nicknamed 'Bing'.

Another way to preserve the ethnic status of a name while
averting its potential for derision by outsiders was offered by
a second Vietnamese teacher. Her child, born in the United
States, has an English first name, 'William', by which he is
known in school. At home, the name is changed to 'Liem'
which is phonetically close to 'William' but is a typical Vietnamese name.

A Korean teacher said that one of the native Korean children
in her class was named 'Sophie' by her parents. After being
allowed to study Korean in school, the child took it upon herself to change her name to 'Soh Fi' by which she wishes to be
known to all. After learning how to write her name in the

Korean alphabet, another little girl now uses that spelling on
all her assignment papers, including the ones she writes for
the English-speaking teachers.

A native Spanish-speaking teacher, when asked if she ever
hispanicized the names of her non-Latino students, responded
with the following vignette:

> I once had a little girl in my class named 'Tam'. Since
> this name is close to 'Tamara'--a name which I happen to
> like very much--I began to call her that. But the little
> girl would not accept this version of her name and in-
> sisted that I call her by her 'real' name.

A girl in the sixth grade followed an opposite course. Not
only did she hispanicize her own name, but she also identified
closely with Paraguayan ethnicity. Although born in North
America, she attended school for a few years in Paraguay.
Apparently, those years spent in South America were critical
ones in establishing her sense of self. She knows how to play
the Paraguayan harp and can perform many dances of Paraguay.

Since some of the teachers of Spanish were nonnative speakers of the language, I asked them if they ever hispanicized
their own surnames in the classroom. One teacher responded
that, while he often hispanicized the names of his students,
he always used an English pronunciation of his own name because to do otherwise would sound 'forced' to him.

When asked about the effect of ethnicity on teaching style,
several teachers observed a change in their techniques when
they moved from classes with mainstream children to those with
Vietnamese, Korean, and Spanish children. They agreed that
they became more 'demanding' with the ethnically marked children. For example, an Argentine-born teacher told me that
she made her Latino children take more pains with their hand-
writing. She also made them copy passages from books. One
of the Vietnamese teachers required her Vietnamese children
to stand up when she entered the classroom. Also, when they
handed things to her, she expected them to extend the object
with both hands as children do in Vietnam as a sign of respect
to an elder. Neither the Argentine teacher nor the Vietnamese
teacher felt that they could ever use the same techniques with
mainstream children.

In discussing their experiences with ethnic labeling, a
Vietnamese teacher said that her Vietnamese students become
very upset if someone takes them for Chinese. A similar reaction was observed among Korean children who do not like
being called Japanese. The teachers all agreed that incorrect
ethnic labeling was one of the chief causes of serious fights
among the children.

The teachers also concurred that it was important to build
up the children's self-image. When asked if this end was
achieved through teaching about the history of the various

countries, some teachers expressed a preference for other methods. One used the device of giving each child the flag of the country from which his or her parents came and requiring him or her to do reports on contemporary aspects of the country. Children with mixed ethnic backgrounds were given flags representing the country of origin of both parents. Such children were free to choose one over the other, or keep both, or even make some sort of adjustment in the emphasis they gave each country. This flagging device not only gives the children a base around which to organize their school activities but it also provides a point of reference for the ethnic alignments they will have to make later on in life.

There is much that needs to be done in bilingual education in order to assure that the children's sense of ethnic identity will emerge unscathed from it. Paralleling the articulation of the many points of language and culture which comprise the substance of the curriculum, we need to uncover those 'stress' points where ethnicity becomes an issue. Tastes in food, pronunciation and choice of names, and shifts in teaching style are only a few of the areas where such stress points may occur. Teachers being prepared for bilingual education should be put through a training period where they are encouraged to do some self-analysis about their own ethnicity. A regular series of inservice workshops should be established for those teachers already at work. In such workshops, discussions could center on the problems that have come up in the classroom with regard to the building of self-esteem in the students. Some readings that are useful in this respect are the recent articles by Krug (1977) on the origin of cultural pluralism and by Driedger (1976) on in-group evaluations of ethnic self-identity.

As Fishman (1977) has already pointed out, we lack an intellectual tradition in connection with the study of ethnicity. The Center for Applied Linguistics, an organization which, for some time, has considered itself a champion of bilingual-bicultural education in the United States, recently published a position paper on the subject (see Linguistic Reporter, vol. 20, no. 3, December, 1977, pp. 1, 6-7). In this position paper, eight points are set forth as 'integral parts' of every 'effective bilingual program'. One of these parts is the development of a positive 'self-image' in the students. However, no further detail is given about how this 'positive self-image' is to be achieved, or about how it interacts with the other seven parts (e.g. fluency and literacy in both languages and cross-cultural 'understanding'). Lambert (1977) gives a review of some of the literature dealing with the ethnic factor in education. Like many other specialists in bilingual education, he does not sharply distinguish between 'culture' and 'ethnicity'.

While cultural differences between groups may be great or small, ethnic identity cannot be quantified in the same way.

To use a personal example, as an American of Italian extraction, I find much that is similar to my home culture in the ways of Hispanic Americans. Finding these cultural similarities, however, does not make me any less of an Italian American. Perhaps this is because culture is practiced while ethnicity is believed. Unlike culture which admits adjustments, ethnicity does not appear to be malleable. To educators who take the position that all children should be led eventually into the mainstream of our school programs, I offer the following point for reflection. If you succeed, as well you might, in altering the cultural patterns of such groups as the Vietnamese so that they no longer stand up for the teacher, so that they no longer show respect for older persons, so that they become more assertive and individualistic in their classroom behavior, you will not have loosened the ties of their ethnic affiliation. But you will have created stress points and you will have to decide whether your efforts at cultural and linguistic assimilation were worth the trouble after all. The individual examples of reaction to intercultural stress as presented in this paper suggest the need for an approach that does more than survey group behavior and create test instruments to be administered to all children of a particular ethnic group. We must develop a bilingual methodology that is humane and cognizant of the uniqueness of each child's psyche.

A major portion of the answer to the question of why attention should be paid to ethnicity in a bilingual program lies in understanding that ethnicity conveys a sense of belonging to someone or to some group in a world of strangers. Without this psychological anchor, the many cognitive advantages gained through the use of a bilingual-bicultural curriculum may be eclipsed by a feeling of rootlessness in the affectual domain. While it might be argued that ethical values such as honesty and love are universal and independent of one's ethnicity, these values cannot easily guide a person who is rootless. To disenfranchise children of their ethnicity through education is to make no real progress over former demonstrations of open hostility to the life and language of the home.

APPENDIX

There has been a recent blossoming of works dealing with various aspects of ethnicity in America. The items listed in this appendix will serve as useful references to those teachers who wish to render their school programs sensitive to the ethnic component.

(1) Gambino (1975) describes the contents of several ethnic studies programs already in operation. The author also supplies a list of ethnic studies resource centers and a bibliography which covers works of a general and specific nature on ethnicity. The specific groups covered are: Blacks, Germans,

Irish, Italians, Jews, Mexican-Americans, Asiatics, Puerto Ricans, and Slavs.

(2) Scarpaci (1975) is a collection of the papers originally presented at a conference cosponsored by the American Italian Historical Association and the American Jewish Historical Society at Towson State College in Baltimore. These papers deal with the interaction of Jews and Italians in America, focusing on the various roles played by women. Several of the papers concentrate on the school experiences of the two groups.

(3) Kolm (1973) is the most extensive bibliography to date on all aspects of ethnicity in the United States. Its 1,694 entries cover a wide range of studies on specific ethnic groups, bilingualism, culture, and education. Four hundred fifty-one of the entries are annotated.

(4) Inglehart and Mangione (1974) is a selective bibliography of works on white ethnics, the literature of European ethnic groups in America, history, autobiography and criticism. Teachers of literature should find this collection especially useful.

(5) Herman (1974) is a practical guide to how to integrate ethnicity into the school system. It includes remarks on textbook selection, bilingual-bicultural programs, teacher certification, and experimental curriculum development.

(6) Elazar and Friedman (1976) discuss ethnic pluralism and its impact on the school system of Philadelphia, Pennsylvania.

(7) The Immigration History Research Center of the University of Minnesota (826 Berry Street, St. Paul, Minnesota 55114) has published a guide (dated April, 1975) to its extensive manuscript holdings (over 2,000,000 items) of records generated by the ethnic groups themselves. The Center welcomes inquiries about its collections and offers scholarships for research projects to interested parties. The person to contact is Professor Rudolph J. Vecoli, Director of the Center.

(8) The Center for Migration Studies (209 Flagg Place, Staten Island, N.Y. 10304) publishes the International Migration Review which appears quarterly and contains a wide range of studies on the sociological aspects of ethnicity in America. Among other books published by the Center is Tomasi (1977), dealing with the political, cultural, psychological, and linguistic facets of Italian American ethnicity.

REFERENCES

Bergin, T. G., and M. H. Fisch. 1968. The new science of Giambattista Vico. Ithaca, N.Y.: Cornell University Press.
Cazden, C. B., V. P. John, and D. Hymes. 1972. Functions of language in the classroom. New York: Teachers College Press.
Di Pietro, R. J. 1977. Report of a survey taken of Italian cultural organizations in North America. Available from the author.

Driedger, Leo. 1976. Ethnic self-identity: A comparison of ingroup evaluations. Sociometry 39.131-141.
Elazar, Daniel, and Murray Friedman. 1976. Moving up: Ethnic succession in America. New York: Institute on Pluralism and Group Identity of the American Jewish Committee (165 East 56th Street, New York, N.Y. 10022).
Epstein, Noel. 1977. Language, ethnicity, and the schools. Washington, D.C.: George Washington University Institute for Educational Leadership.
Fishman, Joshua. 1966. Language loyalty in the United States. The Hague: Mouton.
Fishman, Joshua. 1977. Language, ethnicity, and racism. In: Georgetown University Round Table on Languages and Linguistics 1977. Edited by Muriel Saville-Troike. Washington, D.C.: Georgetown University Press. 297-309.
Gambino, Richard. 1975. A guide to ethnic studies programs in American colleges, universities and schools. Working papers. New York: The Rockefeller Foundation.
Giordano, Joseph. 1973. Ethnicity and mental health. New York: National Project on Ethnic America of the American Jewish Committee.
Gorer, Geoffrey. 1948. The American people: A study in national character. New York: W. W. Norton.
Herman, Judith, ed. 1974. The schools and group identity. New York: Institute on Pluralism and Group Identity.
Inglehart, Babette, and Anthony R. Mangione. 1974. The image of pluralism in American literature. New York: Institute on Pluralism and Group Identity.
Kolm, Richard. 1973. Bibliography on ethnicity and ethnic groups. Washington, D.C.: National Institute of Mental Health (available through the U.S. Government Printing Office, Washington, D.C. 20402).
Krug, Mark M. 1977. Cultural pluralism: Its origin and aftermath. Journal of Teacher Education 27.3-4.
Lambert, Wallace. 1977. Culture and language as factors in learning and education. In: Current themes in linguistics. Edited by Fred Eckman. Washington, D.C.: Hemisphere Press.
Powell, Reed M. 1970. Race, religion and the promotion of the American executive. Columbus: Ohio State University.
Scarpaci, Jean A., ed. 1975. The interaction of Italians and Jews in America. New York: The American Italian Historical Association (209 Flagg Place, Staten Island, N.Y. 10304).
Tomasi, S. M. 1977. Perspectives in Italian immigration and ethnicity. New York: Center for Migration Studies.
Vecoli, Rudolph J. 1973. European Americans: From immigrants to ethnics. In: The reinterpretation of American history and culture. Edited by W. H. Cartwright and R. L. Watson, Jr. Washington, D.C.: National Council for the Social Studies.

THE CONTRIBUTION OF ETHNOGRAPHIC RESEARCH TO BICULTURAL BILINGUAL EDUCATION

Courtney B. Cazden
Robert Carrasco
Abdil Abel Maldonado-Guzman
Harvard University

Frederick Erickson
Michigan State University

There is special meaning in talking about the contribution of ethnographic research to bilingual education at a Georgetown University Round Table on Languages and Linguistics. One of the first, and still one of the most widely cited, ethnographic studies focusing on language and cultural issues in education was first reported here at Georgetown exactly 10 years ago. At the 1970 Georgetown University Round Table on 'Bilingualism and Language Contact: Anthropological, Linguistic, Psychological, and Sociological Aspects', Susan Philips reported her research on the 'acquisition of rules for appropriate speech usage' on the Warm Springs Indian reservation in Central Oregon. From a comparison of interaction patterns, which she called participant structures, in Indian and non-Indian classrooms and in the Indian community, she was able to explain the Indian students' silence and nonparticipation in traditional classroom lessons. In her words,

Indian children fail to participate verbally in classroom interaction because the social conditions for participation to which they have become accustomed in the Indian community are lacking ... In reviewing the comparison of Indian and non-Indian students' verbal participation under different social conditions, two features of the Warm Spring children's behavior stand out. First of all, they show relatively less willingness to perform or participate verbally when they must speak alone in front of other students. Second, they are relatively less eager to speak when the point at

which speech occurs is dictated by the teacher, as it is
during sessions when the teacher is working with the
whole class or in a small group. They also show considerable reluctance to be placed in the 'leadership' play
roles that require them to assume the same type of dictation of the acts of their peers.
  Parallel to these negative responses are the positive ones
of a relatively greater willingness to participate in group
activities which do not create a distinction between individual performer and audience, and a relatively greater
use of opportunities in which the point at which the student speaks or acts is determined by himself, rather than
by the teacher or a 'leader' (1970: 95, 85-86).

Philips (1974) later called these rules for appropriate language use the 'invisible culture'. Dell Hymes, who introduced Philips at Georgetown University, wrote about work such as hers in a more recent paper entitled 'Ethnographic Monitoring' (in press):

  Schools have long been aware of cultural differences, and
  in recent years have attempted to address them, rather
  than punish them. Too often the differences of which the
  school is aware, of which even the community is aware, are
  only the most visible, 'high' culture symbols and the most
  stereotyped conventions. What may be slighted is the 'invisible' culture (to use Philips' title), the culture of everyday etiquette and interaction, and its expression of rights
  and duties, values and aspirations, through norms of communication. Classrooms may respect religious beliefs and
  national custom, yet profane an implicit ceremonial order
  having to do with relations between persons. One can
  honor cultural pride on the walls of a room yet inhibit
  learning within them.[1]

In the 10 years since the 1970 Georgetown University Round Table on Languages and Linguistics, ethnographic research in education has grown into a strong alternative to the previous hegemony of educational psychology, to use McDermott's (in press) phrase, in the educational research field. (It has grown so fast, in fact, that in the February, 1980 newsletter of the American Educational Research Association, ethnographer Ray Rist [1980] even worries about the growth in an article entitled 'Blitzkrieg ethnography: On the transformation of a method into a movement'.) But probably because of the lack of appropriate personnel, very little of this ethnographic research has been done in bilingual education settings. Except for a few studies of classroom code-switching (see, for example, articles in Duran, in press), it is still true, as Fishman wrote a few years ago (1977: 32), that

There is as yet no data [on classroom dynamics] even though the consensus of expert opinion is definitely that the school environment is of overriding importance with respect to bilingual education outcomes ... social dimensionality must be recognized *within* the bilingual education classroom, rather than merely *outside* of it in 'the community' and 'in society'. Societal factors dictate much of *what* is taught and *to whom*; as well as *how* it is taught and by whom; and finally how all of those involved in the teaching-learning process interact with each other ... Unfortunately, none of these topics has been well documented to date and the ethnography, the sociology, the social-psychology and the educational psychology of the bilingual education classroom are all little more than gleams in the eyes of a few researchers (emphasis in the original).

In a footnote to that statement, Fishman mentions the now well known Mexican-American education study by the United States Civil Rights Commission (1972): an observational study of teacher-student interaction in 494 elementary and secondary classrooms in the Southwest. Fishman relegates that study to a footnote because none of the classrooms were bilingual. We mention it, but also only in passing, in order to explain why this observational study is not properly considered ethnographic.

Socially, the Commission study is very significant. As Fishman says (1977:32), it 'clearly documents intra-classroom stratification in the treatment of Anglos and Chicanos', and that in classrooms that had been selected from only those schools with no previous civil rights violations or investigations, and in which teachers were aware that an observer from a Federal civil rights agency was present. But its usefulness is limited because the data consist only of frequencies of coded categories of teacher and student talk. Such quantitative evidence can be sufficient for legislative action or legal decisions, but it is not sufficient to guide attempts at change. When one tries to move from summary findings to search for the classroom dynamics that produce them, one must change to more qualitative sociolinguistic and ethnographic methodology. In the conclusion of her own study, Philips comments (1974:311-312) on the Commission Report:

> The orientation of the Commission Report is such that cultural differences of the sort considered [here] are not dealt with in attempting to account for the disparities discussed. The impression is given that the disparities are due to what is typically referred to as discrimination. But even where teachers are well-intentioned, the results are similar, because the minority students' efforts to communicate are often incomprehensible to the teacher and cannot be assimilated into the framework within which she operates.

The teacher, then, must be seen as uncomprehending, just as the students are. And it is primarily by virtue of her position and her authority that the students and not the teacher come to be defined as the ones who do not understand.

The ethnographers' hypothesis is that problems in cross-cultural communication contribute to the patterns of interaction in those Southwestern classrooms as they do in Warm Springs.
Several ethnographic studies in bilingual education settings are currently in progress. We report on our Bilingual Classroom Interaction Project being conducted in Chicago, then describe three other bicultural--though not bilingual--programs, and end with questions for educational policy raised by this work and by the draft revision of the *Lau* Guidelines.

The Bilingual Classroom Interaction Project. In Chicago, we have been observing and videotaping in two first grade classrooms where the teachers and all their children are Mexican-American. Our purpose is to describe the social and cultural organization of interaction, especially as it can be shown to differ from interaction in more mainstream Anglo classrooms. In some ways, our two classrooms differ noticeably--one more structured, the other more open. But in other ways, in qualitative aspects of the teacher-student relationships, these two teachers both express a personalized style, a style characterized by 'cariño'--a close and caring relationship. To members of Hispanic communities, the concept of cariño is nothing new. One contribution of ethnographic description is to make explicit for more widespread awareness what members of that (or any other) community tacitly know and do.
For this discussion, we are going to talk only about the more structured classroom, which is conducted wholly in Spanish except for 30 minutes a day of ESL. To give a flavor of life in this room, we quote from the comments in Cazden's field notes, written immediately after her first visit to the classroom in November, 1978. These comments express the admiration of a former first-grade teacher:

> I have never seen as well-functioning a first grade society. By this I mean the extent to which the children know where and when and what to do; there is a minimum of time spent giving directions (cues so reduced that often Robert Carrasco and I never were aware of them); little if any need for negative sanctions; maximum task focus on part of children. And yet all this without any sense of strong military-type discipline. The children can take 'time out' to chat or dance and never get out of control ... Aside from making the room a pleasure to spend time in, such a smooth system should have tremendous educational advantages: minimum time spent

on discipline and maximum available for learning (Cazden, field notes, Chicago, November 27, 1978).

Our research task can be described as an attempt to determine whether cultural congruence between the teacher and her children contributes to this remarkable social organization.
Consider just the first event in each school day. We have eight examples of this event on videotape, of which one focal instance from a day in December, 1978 has been examined in some detail. Briefly, before school begins, a few children arrive and put the chairs down. Without any noticeable signal from the teacher, they gradually move quietly but not silently into a circle on the floor in the open space in front of the blackboard; girls on the left and boys on the right, bringing their homework papers with them. Several children wait and accompany the teacher as she walks over, morning coffee in hand, to join the children on the floor. During the next 12 minutes, two instrumental tasks are accomplished: collecting *tarea* 'homework' and calling the roll. What is obvious to even the first-time observer is their flawless execution; what we realized only in more careful videotape analysis are the culturally responsive expressive functions that are accomplished as well.
The homework is collected in a participant structure that conforms to descriptions of mainstream classroom discourse (e.g. Mehan 1979). The basic lesson sequence, addressed to each child in alphabetical order, has the usual three parts. In this case, the teacher calls each child's name; the child quietly hands her the homework; and the teacher acknowledges by recording a mark in her grade book. More extended conversations, which Mehan calls 'conditional' sequences, are sometimes interpolated into this basic structure: when the teacher asks whether the child knows the work (to which some nod 'no' with surprising honesty); or elicits a reason for the homework's absence; or praises with words and applause.
But during these 12 minutes of mainstream classroom discourse structure, there are frequent expressions of cariño: in-group forms of address; frequent use of diminutives; a reminder to the children of norms of interpersonal respect; and expressions of the teacher's knowledge of her children's family life. A few words about each.
Except when actually calling the children's names during both homework collection and roll call, the teacher speaks to each child with terms of endearment such as *papi* or *mami*, sometimes shortened to *pa* and *ma*. For instance:

T. Carlos López   Carlos López.
   Los estudiaste, papi?   Did you study them, papi?
   Sí? OK.   Yes? OK.
   Ya los sabes todos? Sí?   You know them all? Yes?

Of the 20 children present and called on during homework collection, the teacher calls the name only initially to 10 children; adds an affectionate term of address to another 10 children; and repeats the child's name only in 3 of the 15 extended sequences.[2]

The teacher's diminutives on this particular day are as follows:

    Le tengo que poner su estrell*ita*.
    'I have to put down a star for you.'

    Lo sabes tú? Sí? Tod*itos*?
    'You know them? Yes? All of them?'

    Yo quiero que tú me digas con tu boqu*ita*, papi.
    'I want you to tell me with your mouth, papi.'

    Quiero que estén callad*itos*, eh?
    'I want everybody to be quiet, OK?'

    Gracias a Dios*ito* por esas abuel*itas*.
    'Thank God for those grandmothers.'

No translation carries the correct connotation of these diminutive endings. They do not change the meaning of the term to which they are attached (*star*, etc.), but rather function here --like *tú* vs. *usted*--to express closeness in the speaker-listener relationship. Evidence that the children and teacher share this stylistic feature apart from its literal meaning comes when one child refers that day to Frederick Erickson, a more than six-foot-tall observer, as *un profesorcito!* The teacher had explained that Erickson had been her teacher, 'like you have me as your teacher', when she had been at Harvard. Introduction of the visitor ended with this interchange:

    T. Él is mi maestro.
         'He is my teacher.'
    C. Maestro como un profesorcito.
         'Teacher like a professorcito.'
    T. Como un professorcito de verdad que sí. OK.
         'Like a professorcito, that's right. OK.'

The children were reminded of the importance of *respeto* when the teacher asked Vincente to say *Con permiso di pa* 'Say "Excuse me", pa' when he stepped in front of another child to hand in his homework, even though the seating arrangement on the floor makes that unavoidable. The teacher is expected by parents to continue and reinforce the teaching of manners started in the home.

Evidence of the teacher's knowledge of the children's families appears in sequences of noninstrumental talk at the end of

both the homework collection and the roll call. When Edith--
the classroom *comadre-informadora* 'gossip know-it-all' reports
at the end of homework collection that Juan got upset in the
lunchroom the day before, the teacher asks 'Were you mad,
papi? at your mother?', knowing that his mother is a cafeteria
volunteer. Again, at the end of roll call, the teacher accounts
to the children for the absence of Anibal's mother, a classroom
aide, with a long description of her illness, and then asks
questions about Juanito's mother, whom she knew had also
been sick. When Juan explains that he stayed with his grandmother while his mother was sick, the teacher expresses, in
her thanks to God, her shared understanding of the extended
family in Hispanic communities, and of the important role of
grandparents in children's lives.

Gracias a Diosito por esas abuelitas que nos cuidan, por
que si no, estamos muy tristes sin las mamis.

'Thank God for those grandmothers who take care of us,
because otherwise we are very sad without mommies.'

In addition to the specific stylistic features of address terms,
diminutives and other expressions of respect, and personalized
knowledge, we believe that in time slot, topic, and style, this
talk about health and families at the beginning of the school
day is an aspect of invisible Latino culture. In Hispanic communities, when people come together to transact any business,
it is inappropriate--even rude--to begin the 'agenda' immediately. Hall (1959) describes the problems encountered by an
Anglo businessman who expects to open an appointment with an
immediate focus on business affairs. To be effective, he must
learn to use that beginning slot in the conversation as this
teacher has so effectively done.[3]

Three studies of bicultural education. Our argument that
the effectiveness of the social organization in the Chicago classroom is in part due to its culturally appropriate features will
be stronger when we have a comparison with an equally bilingual but not equally bicultural teacher. In three other
studies, the argument for cultural appropriateness can be made
more strongly. These describe two classrooms on the Odawa
reservation in Ontario, the Kamehameha program in Hawaii,
and a Catholic boarding school for Eskimo students in Alaska.

The Odawa Indian Reservation. On the Odawa Indian Reservation in northern Ontario, Erickson and Mohatt (in press)
wanted to see whether Philips' findings could be generalized
to other reservation settings, and whether they could be used
to improve education for other Indian children. Their work included first-hand observation; videotaping in two first grade
classrooms and in some of the children's homes; and interviews

and collaborative research with the school staff in summer courses that involved Indian staff members in field observation and reflections on their own lives. Videotaping was done in the classrooms of two teachers, both considered very effective by their colleagues. One was an experienced Indian teacher who was a member of the local reserve community and had taught there for 21 years. The other was non-Indian, an experienced teacher who was teaching Indian children for the first time.

The Indian teacher taught in ways that those Warm Spring children would have felt comfortable with. She taught children in small groups; her comments to individual children were what Erickson and Mohatt called 'privatized': face-to-face, soft in volume, and very individual. Her pace was slower and smoother in ways they document in precise quantitative terms. What one sees in this Indian teacher's classroom, and in other classrooms taught by Native American teachers, is not an ideal cultural type of 'purely Indian' interactional etiquette, but a 'mixed form' typical of contemporary Native American communities. The Indian teacher had intuitively found ways of accommodating the culturally 'mainstream' English-Canadian curriculum to Odawa principles of communicative etiquette. Her class was truly bicultural.

The Anglo teacher, at least in the beginning of the year, was much more the typical mainstream teacher, contrasting with his Indian colleagues in important ways. But mixed forms also appeared in his teaching as the year went on. In the beginning, the children were arranged in rows of individual seats and spent much of each day in whole group lessons, in which the teacher addressed questions to individual children by name. But as the year progressed, the non-Indian teacher adopted some of the ways of his Indian colleague next door. These adaptations did not derive from any explicit theory of Odawa communicative etiquette. Instead, they seem to have come partly from the supervisory suggestions made by the principal of the school, who was a member of the reserve community and who seems intuitively to have understood the underlying value of the Indian first-grade teacher's style. They may also have come partly from the teacher's own 'radar' that told him what kinds of changes worked. For whatever reason, as the year progressed, the children were seated in table groups instead of rows during whole group lessons; the teacher began to call on table groups rather than individual children; he decreased the total amount of time spent each day in whole group lessons and increased the amount of time spent with children in small groups. In the public arena of large group instruction he still tended to 'spotlight' individual children. But by changing overall patterns of classroom organization, 'privatized' arenas for contact with students were introduced, and these became the predominant settings for academic skill instruction as the year went on. This teacher had also developed culturally mixed forms of classroom participation structures.

The Kamehameha program in Hawaii. The Kamehameha Early Education Project (KEEP) is a private experimental school dedicated to finding ways to improve the academic performance of Polynesian Hawaiian children in the early grades (Au and Jordan in press). When a phonics-based method of teaching reading was used for the first two years of the program, the children's reading performance was in the bottom quartile on standardized tests. In the program's third year a new approach to reading instruction was tried, in which a greater emphasis was placed on reading comprehension. The new program, selected because its pedagogical model was the opposite of the previously unsuccessful one, had unanticipated consequences.

In the new approach, comprehension was stressed in small group discussions of the stories to be read. These discussions gradually took on an overlapping turn structure similar to the overlapping speech that is common in ordinary Polynesian conversations, and especially in the stylized speech event termed 'talk story' (Watson-Gegeo and Boggs 1977). In talk story, a story is co-narrated by more than one person, and the speech of the narrators is also overlapped by audience responses. The Kamehameha children were familiar with this structure in their lives outside of school, and gradually introduced it into the story discussions at school when the structure of the reading groups made that possible.

After this change, the children's reading achievement increased dramatically. Researchers Au and Jordan attribute this dramatic growth in reading to the children's fluent use of the talk story discourse structure as an aid to reading comprehension, although the researchers only recognized the similarity after the fact. The Kamehameha reading lessons still looked like school talk; they only partially resembled the ways of speaking of the talk story speech event as it is found in more pure forms in everyday life in the community. The reading lesson thus became a culturally mixed form; a small change in participant structures which seems to have brought large improvements in academic achievement.

St. Mary's Boarding School in Alaska. The last example is Klienfeld's (1979) study of effective bicultural education at St. Mary's Catholic Boarding School for 200 Eskimo high school students in southwestern Alaska. This is a book-length study, the first to be published in Rist's *Ethnographic Perspectives on American Education*. St. Mary's had been singled out by Collier (1973) in his earlier film study of Alaskan education, and Klienfeld set out to find out what makes St. Mary's work.

St. Mary's graduates have had exceptionally high rates of college entrance and success, as far back as the 1960s, before special college programs for Native Americans were instituted. As a group the students and graduates are exceptionally self-confident and verbal. For example, Collier (1973:102-103) describes an evening when St. Mary's seniors stopped at a public high school in Bethel on their way home from a trip:

> One by one, speaking through a mike, the St. Mary's students address the whole assembly in clear, spirited English with accounts that send the Bethel Eskimos into roars of laughter and bring mystified looks to many of the Bethel teachers. As one teacher was heard to say, 'These kids have had an education! We can't get our boys to speak like that!' Both boys and girls from St. Mary's spoke out fluently with beaming and confident faces. The miracle of education had come to Bethel.

As impressive as the students' college success and their verbal ease is what Collier calls their 'psychic well-being', and their ease in adjusting back into village life, often in leadership positions.

These results seemed all the more surprising because, in Klienfeld's words (1979:12),

> St. Mary's seemed a most unlikely institution to have impressive effects on Eskimo students caught in the maelstrom of cultural change. A run-down boarding school in southeast Alaska, it is the last of a dying breed, a mission school established by the Jesuits to bring Catholicism to the Eskimo along the Bering Sea Coast.

To find out what made St. Mary's work, Klienfeld did extensive participant observation; interviews with students, graduates, and staff; and analyses of videotapes of 'school situations that particularly revealed the school's ideology and structure of interpersonal relationships'.

She found that St. Mary's is staffed by young spiritually committed volunteers without spouses or children who are 'free to devote all of their passionate energies to the students' (p. 50). To sum up their mode of working in one sentence: school was constantly in session. 'A volunteer and a young man at St. Mary's might be teacher and student, coach and basketball player, co-members of a school repair crew, and buddies in late night bull sessions' (p. 131). 'Coming from small villages where everyone knew everyone else across many situations, students sought a similar structure of social relationships' (p. 30). 'Most classes taught by volunteers were a mixture of factual information, personal experiences of the teacher, references to Eskimo village life, delightful in-jokes, and broad humor' (p. 34). And the goals of responsibility to others and inner emotional stability were achieved 'by transforming the small stuff of life into tests of character, into dramas of moral choice' (p. 64).

In a provocative conclusion, Klienfeld suggests that the hyphenated term 'bilingual-bicultural' may be unfortunate, because the formal paralellism of the two terms may mask important differences between the phenomena themselves. Between two languages (or two dialects), the appropriate relationship in education and in life is separation, with codeswitching from one to another in appropriate contexts. But biculturalism may require not separation and switching, but a fusion of elements from both cultures; not dualism but synthesis. At St. Mary's, as in the classrooms in Chicago, Ontario, and Hawaii, the school fuses elements from both cultures, whatever the language of instruction. (See also Paulston 1978.)

In all these situations, the bicultural fusion happened without explicit ethnographic knowledge or guidance. But ethnographic research has, after the fact, documented the elements of that fusion as an aid toward its more widespread application. Microethnographic analysis of videotaped scenes reveals the specific features of the cultural organization of social relationships. And the findings of general (and more macro) ethnography help place that microethnographic analysis in the broader context of school and community life. We believe these studies have important implications for the education of minority children and their teachers in complex multi-ethnic societies.[4]

Implications for educational policy. The Office of Civil Rights document known as the *Lau* Guidelines (OCR 1975) includes in its second requirement a direction to school systems to consider cognitive and affective aspects of how children learn so that appropriate teaching styles can be provided that will maximize their educational achievement. Although the word 'culture' is not used, that document did raise the important question about what, in addition to language, must be changed. In this sense, the Guidelines directed our efforts toward culturally, as well as linguistically, appropriate education. That guideline, as it is now worded, is not without its problems, especially because of the inconclusive research on cognitive styles. (See De Avila's paper in this volume.) But as Cazden and Legett (in press) argue in a review of research relevant to the implementation of this guideline, cultural differences exist not only in cognitive information processing styles, but also in the interactional contexts in which people prefer to learn and to demonstrate what they have learned in some kind of performance. Classroom participation is both an indicator of children's learning and a valuable learning activity in itself, especially in bilingual programs. Therefore, the diagnosis of classroom environments, and the development of the kinds of bicultural environments described in this paper, are extremely important.

The revised *Lau* Guidelines, in draft form in May, 1980, are strengthened in many ways but not with respect to biculturalism. In one version, a section entitled 'Culture' says only, 'A recipient's education programs and activities shall be operated with respect for the culture and cultural heritage of the students enrolled in them' (Section 80.40). And the definition of 'qualified bilingual education teachers' says about language only that teachers must be 'able to converse in the appropriate primary or home language with considerable proficiency' (Section 80.32). More generally, ESL and foreign language instruction is increasingly being broadened beyond patterns of language structure to cultural patterns of language use, as Muriel Saville-Troike argues so persuasively in this volume (see also Taylor and Wolfson 1978). It is all the more striking, therefore, that the revised *Lau* Guidelines draft reverts to a narrower conception of language in bilingual education.

Interestingly, a parallel narrow interpretation of the domain of governmental decree occurred in the 1979 Ann Arbor decision on Black English (Ann Arbor ... n.d.; Perry 1980). Originally, the plaintiffs in that case demanded help in overcoming academic problems that resulted from social, cultural, and economic--as well as linguistic--differences. But the court dismissed all of the claims relating to the cultural, social, and economic deprivations, and ruled in favor of the children only on the barrier of language, where language is defined by its structural features alone. As Dell Hymes and others argued at a conference on the case (Detroit, February, 1980), cultural and social factors will have to be reintroduced in actual implementation of the decree, via a broader conception of language that includes differences in language use and interactional style.

With respect to bicultural/bilingual education, perhaps only its bilingualism can be required by law. When the Court of Appeals rejected the Cardenas Plan in Denver, it explicitly said just that:

> The clear implication of arguments in support of the court's adoption of the Cardenas Plan is that minority students are entitled under the fourteenth amendment to an educational experience tailored to their unique cultural and developmental needs. Although enlightened educational theory may well demand as much, the Constitution does not (Center for Law and Education 1975:55).

The authors of the revised *Lau* Remedies seem to agree with Judge Joiner in Detroit and the Court of Appeals in Denver about the limits of what the Constitution demands. But if, as part of 'enlightened educational theory', we want to go beyond that legal minimum toward education that is bicultural as well as bilingual, ethnographic research has an essential role.

Contribution of Ethnographic Research /169

A joint committee of two affiliates of the American Anthropological Association--the Council on Anthropology and Education and the Society for Applied Anthropology--has issued a strong statement on 'Culture and bilingual education' (Council ... 1979). Their resolution states in part that 'culture is an important part of the dynamics of the teaching-learning process in all classrooms, both bilingual and monolingual'. We agree, and urge continued ethnographic research to document all that statement means.

NOTES

The research reported here was supported by NIE grant 78-0099 to Frederick Erickson and Courtney B. Cazden. A version of this paper, 'What the bilingual teacher needs to know in addition to language', was presented by Cazden at Ohio State University, April 25, 1980, co-sponsored by the Faculties of Foreign Language Education and Early and Middle Childhood Education.

1. Although it is not evident from the title, Hymes' paper is entirely about bilingual education and the many potential contributions of ethnographic research to the planning, conduct, evaluation, and justification of bilingual education programs. We see our focus on classroom interaction as exemplifying one part of his broader view.
2. An analysis of the distribution of basic and extended sequences during homework collection raises an important issue that is beyond the focus of this paper.

Basic sequence: T calls 'Edith Roldan'; receives paper from Edith, who is at her right side, without speaking or looking at her; and marks in her record book.

Extended sequence: See T's talk to Carlos Lopez, on p. 68 of this text.

Although on this particular morning 7 girls and 13 boys are present and called on for their homework, 3 of the 5 basic sequences are with girls. That is, the boys are receiving proportionately more comments on their work than the girls. It would be easy to jump to a hypothesis about differentiated behavior of boys and girls as another aspect of Hispanic culture. Whether or not such differentiation is evident in a fuller analysis of life in this classroom, we know that such differentiation has been documented in Anglo classrooms as well (e.g. Dweck et al 1978). In the distribution of address terms during the extended sequences, girls receive proportionately more affectionate terms than the boys; 4 utterances of *mami* to the 4 girls vs. 7 utterances of *papi* to the 11 boys.

3. See Cazden (1979) for a complementary discussion of this same teacher's interactional style within the framework of Brown and Levinson's (1978) comprehensive model of contrasting styles of politeness. And see Yanguas (1980) for an example of

research methodology appropriate to this same Hispanic culture. Yanguas interviewed 25 working-class Puerto Rican adults as part of a larger study of the acquisition of English as a second language (directed by K. Hakuta and H. Cansino, Huron Institute, Cambridge). She is herself of Spanish background, and her mother works as a seamstress in the Boston area. Some of the informants were co-workers of her mother's, or co-members of the same Catholic parish. Because her first interview was with a woman her mother knew well, the mother offered to come along. The mother's presence helped so much to create an informal speech setting, a culturally appropriate combination of social talk and interview, that her mother--or sometimes her father--accompanied Yanguas on almost all her interviews, even with strangers. Because such a research procedure would seem so strange--even bizarre--within the mainstream Anglo culture, this example may highlight the importance of cultural differences even more vividly than the classroom examples.

4. For an international view, see LeVine (1979). From Navajo, Japanese, and Gusii (Western Kenya) examples, LeVine discusses the demands of Western schools--such as competitiveness and public assertions of self--and the ways in which different non-Western societies respond to the 'institutionally induced noncongruence' between these schools and their own indigenous culture. Outside the domain of education altogether, religious observances can also be bicultural, sometimes controversially so, as in Zaire, where Catholicism (43 percent of the population) 'is overlaid with African meaning'. The *New York Times* (May 3, 1980) reports the Vatican's views on preparations for Pope John Paul II's visit: 'The Vatican declined a proposal by the Zairian clergy that this Sunday's mass, with the Pope the principal celebrant, be said in Lingala, the language of the capital. The mass will be in Latin and in French, the official language of this former Belgian colony. The length of the Lingala rite was one of the major reasons given for its refusal, but several bishops in Kinshasa said that they felt the Pope turned it down largely to avoid the impression that the Vatican approved the African liturgy.

'"It is still an experiment", a Jesuit priest said. "For seven years the Vatican has not said no to us, but we have not been given formal approval either."

'The liturgy widespread in Zaire and adapted to many tribal languages, makes a place for dancing and features drums, spears, and knives. Ancestors are honored along with saints, for ancestor worship is an ancient part of the culture. The congregation is allowed to shout back at the priest in the pulpit and to challenge him with questions. Throughout, though, the priest is given the respect that a village chief commands, and the clergy here anticipate criticism from the Pope for this change in the ancient rite, among others.' As with the research methodology example cited, this religious example may

lend added weight to classroom work. If a bicultural context
adds to the power of worship, should it not add to the power
of education as well?

REFERENCES

Ann Arbor decision: Memorandum opinion and order and The
 educational plan. (n.d.) Arlington, Va.: Center for
 Applied Linguistics.
Au, K. H., and C. Jordan. (in press) Teaching reading to
 Hawaiian children: Finding a culturally appropriate solution.
 In: Culture in the bilingual classroom. Edited by H. Treuba,
 G. P. Guthrie, and K. H. Au. Rowley, Mass.: Newbury
 House.
Brown, P., and S. Levinson. 1978. Universals in language
 usage: Politeness phenomena. In: Questions and polite-
 ness: Strategies in social interaction. Edited by E. N.
 Goody. Cambridge: Cambridge University Press. 56-310.
Cazden, C. B. 1979. Language in education: Variation in
 the teacher-talk register. In: Georgetown University Round
 Table on Languages and Linguistics 1979. Edited by J. E.
 Alatis and R. Tucker. Washington, D.C.: Georgetown Uni-
 versity Press. 144-162.
Cazden, C. B., and E. L. Leggett. (in press) Culturally
 responsive education: A discussion of Lau Remedies II.
 In: Culture in the bilingual classroom. Edited by H. T.
 Treuba, G. P. Guthrie, and K. H. Au. Rowley, Mass.:
 Newbury House. [earlier version ED 135-241]
Center for Law and Education. 1975. Bilingual-bicultural edu-
 cation: A handbook for attorneys and community workers.
 Cambridge, Mass.: Center for Law and Education.
Collier, J., Jr. 1973. Alaskan Eskimo education: A film
 analysis of cultural confrontation in the schools. New York:
 Holt, Rinehart and Winston.
Council on Anthropology and Education and the Society for
 Applied Anthropology. 1979. Report from Joint CAE/SFAA
 Policy Committee on Culture and Bilingual Education.
 Anthropology and Education Quarterly 10.196-200.
Duran, R. P., ed. (in press) Latino language and communi-
 cative behavior. Advances in discourse processes. Vol. VI.
 Norwood, N.J.: Ablex.
Dweck, C. S., W. Davidson, S. Nelson, and B. Enna. 1978.
 Sex differences in learned helplessness: II: The contin-
 gencies of evaluative feedback in the classroom, and III:
 An experimental analysis. Developmental Psychology 14.268-
 276.
Erickson, F., and G. Mohatt. (in preparation) Cultural
 organization of participant structures in two classrooms of
 Indian students. In: Doing the ethnography of schooling.
 Edited by G. D. Spindler.

Fishman, J. 1977. The social science perspective. In: Bilingual education: Current perspectives: Social science. Arlington, Va.: Center for Applied Linguistics. 1-49.
Hall, E. T. 1961. The silent language. Greenwich, Conn.: Premier Books. [original, 1959]
Hymes, D. (in press) Ethnographic monitoring. In: Culture in the bilingual classroom. Edited by H. T. Treuba, G. P. Guthrie, and K. H. Au. Rowley, Mass.: Newbury House.
Klienfeld, J. S. 1979. Eskimo school on the Andreafsky. New York: Praeger.
LeVine, R. A. 1979. Western schools in non-Western societies: Psychosocial impact and cultural response. In: Families and communities as educators. Edited by H. J. Leichter. New York: Teachers College Press. 185-191. [Also in Teachers College Record 1978-1979: 749-755.]
McDermott, R. P. (in press) Educational psychology: An uninvited guest to a discussion on ethnography and education. In: Ethnography and education: Children in and out of school. Edited by P. Gilmore and A. Glatthorn. Philadelphia: University of Pennsylvania Press.
Mehan, H. 1979. Learning lessons. Cambridge: Harvard University Press.
Office of Civil Rights. 1975. Findings specifying remedies for eliminating past educational practices ruled unlawful under *Lau vs. Nichols*. Washington, D.C.: Department of Health, Education and Welfare. [Also reprinted in The Linguistic Reporter 18(2).]
Paulston, C. B. 1978. Biculturalism: Some reflections and speculations. TESOL Quarterly 12.369-380.
Perry, T. 1980. Toward an interpretive analysis of the *Martin Luther King, Jr. v. Ann Arbor School District Board* case. Unpublished qualifying paper, Harvard Graduate School of Education.
Philips, S. U. 1970. Acquisition of rules for appropriate speech usage. In: Georgetown University Round Table on Languages and Linguistics 1970. Edited by James E. Alatis. Washington, D.C.: Georgetown University Press. 77-101.
Philips, S. 1974. The invisible culture: Communication in the classroom and community on the Warm Springs Indian Reservation. Unpublished doctoral dissertation. University of Pennsylvania.
Rist, R. C. 1980. Blitzkreig ethnography: On the transformation of a method into a movement. Educational Researcher 9.8-10.
Taylor, B. P., and N. Wolfson. 1978. Breaking down the free conversation myth. TESOL Quarterly 12.31-39.
United States Commission on Civil Rights. 1972. Mexican American educational study, Report V. Washington, D.C.: Superintendent of Documents.

Watson-Gegeo, K. A., and S. T. Boggs. 1977. From verbal play to talk story: The role of routines in speech events among Hawaiian children: In: Child discourse. Edited by S. Ervin-Tripp and Mitchell-Kernan. New York: Academic Press. 67-90.

Yanguas, M. J. 1980. The social parameters involved in language choice and preference among working-class Puerto Ricans in the Cambridge area. Unpublished honors thesis. Harvard/Radcliffe College.

BILINGUAL EDUCATION IN THE UNITED STATES UNDER ETHNIC COMMUNITY AUSPICES

Joshua A. Fishman
Yeshiva University

Notwithstanding the long-term capitalist establishment, old line Marxist, and mainstream sociological deprecation of ethnicity (reviewed in Fishman 1978), and notwithstanding the more recent recrudescence of pseudo-intellectual anti-ethnicity alarms (see, for example, Epstein 1977, Patterson 1977), there may very well be more ethnic community sponsored mother tongue schooling in the United States today than there was 20 years ago. In the early 1960s, when last I attempted to estimate the magnitude and distribution of this universe, my best estimate pointed to 2,000 units that I had identified with certainty and roughly a thousand more that I 'sensed' were there but that I could not definitively locate (Fishman 1966). Now, 20 years later, I have fully identified nearly 5,000 units and still have a 'sense' of another 1,000 or more whose exact locations and languages have not yet been fully established.[1] Although it may not be justified to conclude that ethnic community mother tongue schooling has tripled in these two decades under the impact of the 'ethnicity boom' of the late 1960s and the 1970s (trend studies for little studied phenomena are not overly reliable since they are unduly influenced by such inter-investigator or inter-study factors as 'auspices' and 'reputation'), there should be no doubt in anyone's mind that we are dealing with a quantitatively huge and much understudied (and underappreciated) universe of substantial significance for the total non-English language enterprise in this country. Such schools are to be found in every section of our country and, indeed, in every state of the Union, with even the 'least ethnic' parts of our country (the 'deep South' and the 'corn-belt') maintaining hundreds upon hundreds of such schools (Fishman 1980a).

How wasteful we are, in our rich America, and how uninformed are our language professions and disciplines, if we blithely overlook some 6,000 schools and some 600,000 children who, together, constitute a resource of talent, dedication, and experience that we might all profit from in various ways. Our collective, self-imposed ignorance and self-denial (or should we call it repression?) merit even more amazement and regret when one realizes that these schools represent an old and proud American tradition, that they are now primarily maintained by English-speaking (and often English-dominant) parents, that by all signs they are well established and unlikely to disappear, and that they obviously contribute to important aspects of total identity for millions upon millions of our citizens. The following remarks constitute no more than a minor attempt to provide an overview of this colorful and revealing universe of language life in the United States, a universe that fully merits the most serious consideration.

Some ideological and pedagogic assumptions. A number of articles of faith characterize the activists, teachers, and parents most fully involved in operating, supporting, and fostering ethnic community non-English mother tongue schooling in the United States (Fishman 1979). The most fundamental assumption is that there is an eternal relationship between their ethnicity and its associated language. Indeed, this assumption posits a crucial causal relationship such that the ethnic mother tongue is viewed as a truly Herderian (and Whorfian) dynamo. If ethnic continuity is at all conceivable without the ethnic mother tongue--and for many it is not--it is nonetheless viewed as emaciated, lifeless, joyless, and peculiarly unauthentic under such circumstances. Thus, use--even if traditionalized and ritualized--of the ethnic mother tongue is more than merely desirable; it is morally necessary, that is, it is an imperative that has ramifications and implications far above and beyond empirical verification or practical consequences. It is not so much interpersonal communication that such schools aim at-- they do that, too--but a transcendental, intuitive, and infinitely subtle sensitivity, appreciation, and awareness of self, community, destiny, history, and the rarest of rare uniqueness and mysteries.

No wonder, then, given the depth of devotion lavished upon the language and ethnicity link, that stable bilingualism and biculturalism in the United States are viewed as attainable objectives rather than as impossible dreams. This is not to say that they are viewed as simple goals or inevitable attainments by any means. Nevertheless, given intense planning, devotion, and a constant search for better methods, materials, and implementational opportunities at a truly communal level, it is firmly believed that the ethnic community mother tongue school can and will make a significant and independent contribution to the total language maintenance and ethnic maintenance outcome.

Are these ideas irrational? contra-empirical? I would prefer to call them supra-rational convictions. Obviously, these schools are loci of community viability, creativity, and identity. Obviously, without them social alienation and dislocation would be even greater than they currently are in the United States. I reject the 'irrational' designation because there is ample evidence that effective ethnic mother tongue schools are operating on more than emotion alone. Indeed, there seems to be a mutually reinforcing feedback system between beliefs, practices, and attainments in many of the schools and communities involved, so that the more the foregoing assumptions are subscribed to, the greater the curricular innovativeness and the academic success of the schools involved. There is a very definite rapport and reward cycle in operation, so that parental time, effort, funds, love, concern, and reinforcement, on the one hand, and student-teacher attainment, on the other hand, are mutually and maximally reinforcing, at least insofar as esprit de corps is concerned. This is of no little moment in the life of a school and community, although it is, of course, not the same as language learning or language maintenance per se.

Actually, no miracles are to be reported along these latter lines. Generally speaking, these schools and their communities are far too weak to stem the tide of Americanization and anglification that has progressively engulfed our public life as well as encroached upon our more private intimacy. With the exception of the Old Order Amish-Mennonites-Hutterites, the Hasidim and the Navajos, our ethnolinguistic minorities are more fond of their languages than they are fluent or frequent users of these languages. Viewed dispassionately from the outside, the ethnic community non-English mother tongue schools are distinctly secondary forces when confronted by the overall massive dislocation, de-traditionalization and secularization of modern American urbanization, industrialization, geographic mobility, destruction of inner city ethnic primary settlement neighborhoods, and growing intermarriage rates across religious and ethnic lines.

These schools have no magic wands to wave. If they pursue their goals somewhat more conscientiously than do most other schools, they accomplish them--like most schools--only moderately and modestly, at best. The parents (and often the teachers) maintaining and conducting the schools are generally English speakers (indeed, they are usually English dominant individuals); so are their children and pupils and so they will remain, by and large. Why then are these schools maintained at such great price in time and effort? Clearly, because the pursuits of biculturism--indifferently successful though it may be--is integratively functional and meaningful. These schools are now part of a pattern of ethnicity-in-America. They represent an American way of being ethnic and an ethnic way of being American: a particularistic, relatively stable, more comfortably meaningful way of combining the mainstream with one's own unique side stream in a 'manageable way'. Rather than being reflections of foreignness, these schools now represent the indigenization of ethnicity as an American way of life.

Ethnicity as an American way of life. The National Council for Education Statistics has provided us with a means of testing for foregoing ethnographic conclusions, based upon visiting dozens of schools during the past few years. Its 1976 study of language use provides state-by-state data on the 'non-English language background' population of the United States (NCES 1976).[2] The correlation between the number of foreign-born non-English language background children aged 6-18 in the various states and the total number of ethnic community mother tongue schools, state by state, is no more than .07. On the other hand, the correlation between the number of native-born non-English language background children aged 6-18 in the various states and the total number of ethnic community mother tongue schools, state by state, is .63. Obviously, then, we are dealing with a community pattern that is aimed primarily at American-born children. However, it is not only a child-centered community pattern. The correlation between the total number of non-English language background persons (adults and children) and the total number of ethnic community mother tongue schools, state by state, is fully .80.

Thus, we are dealing with an intergenerational phenomenon in addition to an inter-nativity one. Ethnic community mother tongue schools typically serve second, third, and even fourth generation American-born children. They are most common among those groups which have had ample experience in 'working out' the American system. Such schools are now just beginning to grow among our Portuguese, Spanish, Filipino, Indochinese, and Native American populations, which have only recently begun to interact significantly with the American mainstream. Thus, the number of persons of Spanish language background in each state correlates only .58 with the number of Hispanic ethnic community mother tongue schools, state by state. On the other hand, the number of persons of German language background in each state correlates .74 with the number of German ethnic community mother tongue schools, state by state.[3] Once again we see that the ethnic community mother tongue school is an accommodation to American interactive reality. In a sense, and particularly so in recent years, Americans with ethnic mother tongue backgrounds are exactly that, i.e. both of those things simultaneously, and their ethnic community mother tongue schools enable them all the more to express and to integrate these two aspects of their identity.

Biculturism under local community auspices. Ethnic community mother tongue schools in the United States are reflections not of foreignness nor of hostility to the American Anglo

'mainstream', but of a wish and need to enrich that stream with
a more personally meaningful perspective, with a more communally authentic dimension. While the actual accomplishments
of these schools are often far from dazzling or dramatic (as is
the case too for most of the far better funded public schools of
our country), these schools are maintained for extra-academic
reasons as much as, if not more than, for academic ones. A
great deal of community effort, emotion, dedication, and intergenerational heightened experience goes into the organization
and maintenance of these schools. They are authentic channels of biculturism, of voluntary Americanism, and of American
voluntarism rather that of diethnia or dinomia (Saville-Troike
1978, Fishman 1980b) under local neighborhood or community
control. They represent contributions to cultural growth and
creativity, and to controlled translinguification and transethnification of considerable vintage and of no mean value on the
American scene. They are eminently worthy of study, respect,
and assistance.

NOTES

The research reported here was initiated under NIE grant
G-78-0133 and is being continued--and expanded with respect
to yet other non-English language ethnic community institutions
and processes--under the following grants: OE #G007901816,
NSF #BNS-7906055, and NIE #NIE-G-79-0122.
  1. My greatest gaps are currently with respect to ethnic
community schools employing Arabic, Russian, Polish, Chinese
(other than on the West Coast), and the various languages involved in Buddhist traditions. I would welcome assistance
from academics and laymen knowledgeable about the community
schools of these language groups and willing to help me enumerate them more fully.
  2. The designation 'non-English language background' is a
technical one and definitely does not imply non-English or
limited English-speaking, or even non-English mother tongue.
Its technical definition is as follows: 'Persons of any age
whose usual or second household language is not English, or
if 14 years of age, whose mother tongue is other than English,
whether or not they usually speak English.'
  3. Obviously, these two groups are not equally well reported (counted, located) by NCES or other census studies.
Nevertheless, underreporting is primarily a phenonenon involving foreign-born Hispanics so that, all in all, the point
I am making probably holds valid even for Hispanics. Their
ethnic community mother tongue schools will increase as their
mainstream-experience increases. The same can be expected
in connection with Native Americans.

REFERENCES

Epstein, Noel. 1977. Language, ethnicity and the schools. Washington, D.C.: George Washington Institute for Educational Leadership.

Fishman, Joshua A. 1980a. The ethnic community mother tongue school in the USA: Dynamics and distributions. International Migration Review 14(2).235-247.

Fishman, Joshua A. 1980b. Bilingualism and biculturism as individual and as societal phenomena. Journal of Multilingual and Multicultural Development 1.3-16.

Fishman, Joshua A. 1979. The significance of the ethnic community mother tongue school: Introduction to a study. NABE Journal 3.39-48.

Fishman, Joshua A., et al. 1966. Language loyalty in the United States. The Hague: Mouton. [Reissued 1979, New York: Arno Press.]

National Center for Education Statistics. 1978. Geographic distribution, nativity and age distribution of language minorities in the United States. Washington, D.C.: NCES.

Patterson, Orlando. 1977. Ethnic chauvinism: The reactionary impulse. New York: Stein and Day.

Saville-Troike, Muriel. 1978. A guide to culture in the classroom. Rosslyn, Va.: National Clearinghouse for Bilingual Education.

V. Language Proficiency

INTERNATIONAL COMPARISONS OF FOREIGN LANGUAGE LEARNING IN THE IEA PROJECT

John B. Carroll
University of North Carolina at Chapel Hill

In the short time that I have been allotted, I can do little more than draw your attention to two massive studies of foreign language learning that were conducted in the so-called IEA project. Perhaps because these studies[1] were published in Sweden (though available also through a United States distributor), they have received little notice in this country. I was the author of the first of these and the chairman of the committee that supervised the study of French as a foreign language. The companion volume is by E. Glyn Lewis and Carolyn Massad, concerning the teaching of English as a foreign language. Unfortunately, I understand, the latter volume is at present out of print, though I can conceive circumstances wherein it might be reprinted.

Many here may be curious about what the IEA project was. IEA is an abbreviated acronym for International Association for the Evaluation of Educational Achievement. Headquartered in Europe, but with branches or correspondents in some 21 countries, it has conducted studies of comparative achievements of primary and secondary school students in a number of subjects, including mathematics, science, civic education, reading comprehension, and literature. There are now published volumes reporting each of these subjects, with several summary and technical volumes.[2] The data of all these studies are now available in a data bank on magnetic tape that contains literally millions of data points.[3]

English as a Foreign Language and French as a Foreign Language were two of the subjects included in this mammoth effort. These subjects were chosen as representative of two types of foreign language subjects, and as being rather commonly taught in the curricula of the various countries

participating in the IEA project. I have to emphasize the
word 'foreign' in the phrase 'foreign language'. These studies
were not designed as studies of bilingual education, however
that may be defined. The directors of the IEA projects in
English and French did not even make much of a distinction
between 'foreign language' and 'second language'. In every
case, we looked at the results of instruction in English or
French as a school subject, although in some cases, e.g.
English as studied in Sweden or the Netherlands, one might
indeed say that English was being studied as a kind of 'second
language' that is prominent in the cultural life of the country.
Obviously, the goals and conditions of instruction in foreign
language varied somewhat over the ten countries in which we
looked at instruction in English, and in the eight countries in
which we looked at instruction in French, but it turned out
that they did not really differ very much. In most countries
in which English was taught as a second or foreign language,
it was being studied more for utilitarian and practical aims than
for literary or cultural objectives, while the reverse was generally the case for French. Also, the studies concerned achievement at the 14-year-old level and at the 'preuniversity' level,
i.e. anywhere from grade 11 to grade 14, depending on the
educational system of the country.

In view of all these considerations, you may ask how relevant
these IEA studies are to bilingual education, which I gather
has focused not so much on learning a second or foreign language as on learning to handle two languages simultaneously--
building up certain skills in the mother tongue while also acquiring skills in a second language, along with relevant cultural content in the two languages. Further, it would seem
that bilingual education has been devoted more to instruction
in the very early school years, with the hope that a considerable degree of true bilingualism will develop in the later years.
For various reasons, the IEA studies were not able to examine
any kind of second or foreign language instruction in the early
school grades. Further, most of the studies in English and
French instruction were conducted in the more developed countries, whereas bilingual education has been of greatest interest
in some of the less developed countries, or at least only in
certain subpopulations in the more developed countries.

Nevertheless, I believe the IEA studies can be instructive to
students of bilingual education in several ways.

First, they offer models of research designs that might be
useful in any efforts to assess the results of bilingual education. The IEA studies were based on quite careful procedures
of sampling. To the greatest extent feasible, an attempt was
made, in each country, to define the population of potentially
testable students (e.g. all 14-year-old students who had had
at least two years of French instruction), and then to draw
representative samples from that population. The populations
were defined in generally comparable ways across all the

countries, in such a way that the studies could yield conclusions generalizable across countries. The studies developed a large number of instruments that can be used as models for similar devices in studies of bilingual education. These instruments included tests of language proficiency at various levels of advancement, that is, tests of reading, writing, speaking, and listening. Some of the instruments developed for the French study have, in fact, been extensively used in the Canadian studies of 'French immersion' in the province of Ontario and elsewhere; I think we can agree that these studies of 'French immersion' are highly relevant to bilingual education. The IEA instruments also included questionnaires for getting at types of instruction, qualifications of teachers, student interest and motivation, etc. Also, the methods of data collection in the IEA studies could be adapted to studies of bilingual education. I would draw your attention to the procedures of statistical analysis employed in my study of French as a foreign language.

There are, however, broader and more substantive implications of the IEA studies for bilingual education. I should point out that the title given for this address is in some ways misleading. The IEA studies, that is, were not 'comparative' in the sense of asking which countries came out ahead, and which fell behind. We did not regard the IEA project as a kind of international intellectual Olympics, although some reports of it in the press have tended to give that impression. I cannot tell you which countries had the best instruction in English as a foreign language, or in French, because the IEA studies did not yield that kind of information. To be sure, the average level of achievement varied widely over countries, and it was our task to try to explain the reasons for these variations.

So, what were some of the reasons that we found for variations in levels of achievement across and within countries? (I draw attention to the fact that there was probably as much variation within countries as between countries.) I think you will agree that many of the reasons we identified will apply as much in bilingual education as in more conventional foreign language instruction.

The results in the two studies--the English and the French studies--were highly similar. Since I know the French study better than the English one, I will refer to the results from the French study. I found ways of pooling my data over countries and even over different subpopulations to boil my results down to something more readily comprehensible and digestible than the voluminous results for particular countries and populations. The final product, then, concerned what I like to think of as an 'international French class'. To be sure, it is a very large class, situated in different countries, taught by different teachers, and composed of different kinds of students at different educational levels, but it is a 'class' in the

sense that all the goals and even the methods are very much
the same over the different countries and the different kinds
of students. All the students are studying French, and as
far as school instruction is concerned, French is French, the
world around. The special analysis to which I refer here has
to do with nearly 8,000 students learning French in English-
speaking countries--England, Scotland, New Zealand, and the
United States. (We also studied groups of students in non-
English-speaking countries, Chile, the Netherlands, Sweden,
and Rumania, and the results were not appreciably different,
with some exceptions.) In the group of 8,000 students studying French in English-speaking countries, I was able to identify
seven variables that together accounted for about 50 percent of
the variance in achievement in either reading or listening skill;
for this type of predictive study, that is a very large amount
of variance.

The most important variable was the number of years of instruction that the student had been exposed to, i.e. a measure
of the time devoted to foreign language study. In all my work
on learning, time has consistently appeared as an extremely important variable. In the present case, over the 8,000 students,
the number of years of study ranged from less than two years
to more than eight or nine years; the average number of years
of instruction varied considerably over the countries. The
number of years of instruction was the best predictor of final
level of achievement, having correlations of .63 with both reading and listening proficiency tests. Time of exposure to study
is not, of course, the only determinant of achievement; some
students need and take less time than others, while other students require and take much more time than the average.

Among the other variables that determine achievement are the
student's motivations and aspirations, the degree to which the
student finds foreign language study easy or hard as compared
to other subjects, and the actual amount of effort the student
devotes to homework. The role of motivation in our data is
interesting. We asked students, in a questionnaire, to indicate how much they aspired (a) to read the foreign language,
and (b) to understand the language when it is spoken. These
two types of aspiration are not perfectly correlated; some students are more interested in reading the language, while others
are more interested in competence in the spoken language. We
found that aspiration to read French predicted reading proficiency much better than it did listening proficiency, and
aspiration or interest in understanding French predicted proficiency in listening to spoken French better than it did reading proficiency. There were also suggestions in our data that
students do better in instruction that is adapted to their particular types of aspirations with respect to emphasis on reading
and writing vs. listening and speaking.

We had no direct measures of 'foreign language aptitude' as
I have defined and measured it in some of my other studies,

but the questionnaire item that asked students whether they found foreign languages easier or harder than other subjects may indeed reflect variations in student foreign language aptitudes. This one questionnaire item had a significant correlation with levels of proficiency finally reached, and made a highly significant contribution to the prediction of the criterion variables after other effects were controlled for. Whatever the reason for this variation, we have to say that individuals appear to differ in their facility in learning a foreign language. Currently, I am studying this variation, working on the assumption that it has something to do with properties of a person's short-term memory capacity, either for visual or auditory materials.

In all, five variables out of the seven had to do with characteristics of the students, or with the amount of instruction they had received. The two other variables that made a significant contribution to the prediction of learning success had to do with characteristics of teachers and with modes of instruction. Teachers do make a difference, according to our results, although we have been able to identify only one major source of this difference, namely, the teacher's self-rated competence in the language being taught, either in the written or the spoken aspects of the language.

The instructional variable that shows up most clearly in our results is a measure of the extent to which students are encouraged to use French in the classroom more than they do their native language. This variable is based on students' reports of the relative amount of time that they spend speaking their mother tongue as compared to the target language. This finding should not be interpreted to mean that students and teachers should necessarily speak the target language all the time in class, but it points to the fact that a generous use of the foreign language in the classroom is one of the most important factors in getting students to achieve high levels of proficiency in the spoken language.

I could go on to mention many other findings in these IEA studies, but time does not permit. I will, however, mention that we found that the age of starting study of a foreign language makes very little difference in the eventual level of proficiency attained, once account is taken of the number of years of instruction. If anything, it appears that students who start relatively late, rather than earlier, learn somewhat faster. I recognize that this finding seems to contradict the widely held belief that an early start is important, but I am compelled to report what we found. Perhaps there is really no contradiction when it is realized that our findings pertain not to 'natural' foreign language acquisition in a bilingual environment, but to acquisition of a foreign language in a school setting.

I must leave it to my audience to make whatever inferences may be made from these findings with regard to bilingual education. Since children are children, whether they are studying a foreign language as a school subject, or as a skill in the context of bilingual education, it would seem that somewhat the same factors would affect their success. In any event, I encourage you to consider the results of the IEA studies for what they may suggest about bilingual education. I would hate to think that I spent a good portion of my time, over a period of about eight years, working on the IEA study without generating any results that could be applied to the important social problem that is represented by bilingual education.

NOTES

1. John B. Carroll, *The teaching of French as a foreign language in eight countries*. Stockholm: Almqvist and Wiksell International, and New York: John Wiley (Halsted Press), 1975. (International Studies in Evaluation, V.)

E. Glyn Lewis and Carolyn E. Massad, *The teaching of English as a foreign language in ten countries*. Stockholm: Almqvist and Wiksell International, and New York: John Wiley (Halsted Press), 1975. (International Studies in Evaluation, IV.)

2. L. C. Comber and J. P. Keeves, *Science education in nineteen countries: An empirical study*. Stockholm: Almqvist and Wiksell, 1973. (International Studies in Evaluation, I.)

A. C. Purves, *Literature education in ten countries: An empirical study*. Stockholm: Almqvist and Wiksell, 1973. (International Studies in Evaluation, II.)

R. L. Thorndike, *Reading comprehension education in fifteen countries: An empirical study*. Stockholm: Almqvist and Wiksell, 1973. (International Studies in Evaluation, III.)

J. V. Torney et al., *Civic education in ten countries*. Stockholm: Almqvist and Wiksell, 1974. (International Studies in Evaluation, VI.)

A. H. Passow et al., *The national case study: An empirical comparative study of twenty-one educational systems*. Stockholm: Almqvist and Wiksell, 1976. (International Studies in Evaluation, VII.)

G. F. Peaker, *An empirical study of education in twenty-one countries: A technical report*. Stockholm: Almqvist and Wiksell, 1975. (International Studies in Evaluation, VIII.)

D. A. Walker, *The IEA six subject survey: An empirical study of education in twenty-one countries*. Stockholm: Almqvist and Wiksell, 1976. (International Studies in Evaluation, IX.)

3. Information on the IEA Six-Subject Data Bank can be obtained from the Office of Educational Research and Development, University of Kentucky, Lexington, Kentucky 40506.

THE RELATIVE PROFICIENCY
OF LIMITED ENGLISH PROFICIENT STUDENTS

Heidi Dulay and Marina Burt
Bloomsbury West, San Francisco

It has been generally assumed that most children of limited English proficiency are more fluent in their native language than in English. Our research investigations suggest that this assumption is not correct. In a Southern California school district, for example, where about 800 Hispanic limited English proficient (LEP) children have been identified, less than half speak Spanish better than English. The district found, in fact, that almost 40 percent of their LEP children spoke no Spanish at all. As will be seen shortly, this situation is not unique to this school district, nor is it unique to California.

This subpopulation of children, like other LEP children, has English language skills that are not quite on a par with those of nonminority English speakers their own age. Unlike other LEP children, however, their level of Spanish skills is equally low or substantially lower. Most of these children can communicate in English; they simply have not scored at norm levels in English language skills--a problem many underachieving monolingual native English speakers also have.

The existence of children who are underachieving in two languages does not detract from the merits of being bilingual (any more than the existence of underachieving monolingual English-speaking school children reflects upon the language skills of the rest of the monolingual population). In fact, there is a growing literature indicating that knowing more than one language is cognitively enriching.

Psycholinguistic studies indicate that people who control more than one language are verbally more skillful than monolinguals, and they mature earlier with respect to linguistic abstraction skills. Lerea and Laporta (1971) and Palmer (1972) report, for example, that bilinguals have better auditory memory than monolinguals,[1] and Slobin (1968) found that bilinguals are

better at intuiting meaning from unknown words. Feldman and
Shen (1971) discovered that low income bilingual children were
better at learning new labels than low income monolinguals, and
Peale and Lambert (1962) concluded that ten-year-olds who
spoke both French and English demonstrated higher skill in
linguistic abstraction than their monolingual counterparts.

Similarly, neurolinguistic research is beginning to suggest
that people who know more than one language make use of more
of the brain than monolinguals do. Though the evidence is
scant, it seems that the part of the brain that is used in
second language functioning remains underdeveloped in monolingual brains. Albert and Obler (1978) reviewed a series of
post-mortem studies on polyglot brains--brains of people who
spoke from 3 to 26 languages--and found that certain parts of
these brains were especially well developed and markedly fur-
rowed.

During the last decade, we and many others have spent much
time emphasizing the enriching aspects of bilingualism and pointing out evidence for the educational advantages of instruction
via the child's stronger language (Dulay and Burt 1980, 1979a,
1979b, 1979c, 1976; Troike 1978; Plante 1977; Rosier and Farella 1976; Modiano 1973; Balasubramonian et al. 1973; Treviño
1968; Ramos et al. 1967). Many have been persuaded that instruction through the child's mother tongue is useful in helping
immigrant children hold their own in school. To wit, the
federal government alone spends over $250 million a year on
bilingual education (González 1980), a phenomenal increase from
the $7 million with which the Elementary and Secondary Educa-
tion Act (ESEA) Title VII started in 1968.

During the last two years, we have turned our attention to
previously overlooked subpopulations of LEP children--those
for whom new educational approaches must be developed because their proficiency in the 'home' language is not as high
as had been assumed.

The purpose of this paper is to bring these students to the
attention of educators, scholars, students, and policymakers.
We also clarify terms and procedures used in 'relative proficiency' assessment, summarize available data pertaining to
the size and home language characteristics of the various LEP
subpopulations, and suggest the outlines of programmatic
recommendations.

Data on the size of LEP subpopulations. When the English
and home (or primary) language[2] proficiency of LEP students
are compared, three distinct subgroups within the population
of limited English proficient students emerge: (1) students
who are more proficient in their primary language; (2) students who, though limited in English, are more proficient in
English than in their primary language; and (3) students whose
proficiency in their primary language and in English is limited

The Relative Proficiency of LEP Students /191

to an equal extent. We refer to these students as 'primary-language-superior', 'English-superior', and 'comparably limited', respectively. Each group has unique linguistic characteristics and correspondingly different educational needs. As Table 1 shows, each comprises a substantial portion of the total limited English proficient population, depending on the district.

Table 1. Proportion of LEP students in three relative proficiency categories (California, Fall 1978).

Grade span of district & county	% Spanish superior	% Equally limited	% English superior	No. of children	Instrument used*
D1: K-8, Santa Clara	6	16	78	166	BSM
D2: K-6, Monterey	26	57	17	208	BINL
D3: 7-12, Santa Barbara	12	65	23	284	BINL
D4: K-8, Riverside	40	22	38	784	LAS
D5: K-8, Ventura	51	35	14	675	LAS
D6: K-6, Los Angeles	81	9	10	206	LAS
D7: K-2, San Diego	90	7	3	576	BSM
Total				2,899	

*Instruments: BSM = Bilingual Syntax Measure; LAS = Language Assessment Scale; BINL = Bilingual Inventory of Natural Language.

The data displayed in Table 1 were compiled from assessment data made available to us by school districts in California. We collected the data as part of a project sponsored by the California Department of Education to help refine the conceptual framework for bilingual education in California (Dulay and Burt in press, 1979d, 1979e). Although time and fiscal constraints did not permit us to use statistical sampling techniques to select the sample, the data represent almost 3,000 students drawn from seven counties spanning the geography of California. We used data from all the LEP students in each district to arrive at the percentages in the table. Thus, the percentages indicated for each subgroup are true proportions, not estimates.

The districts used a three-step process to assess the students. First, a home survey (described later in this paper) of all students in the district was conducted to identify all students from a language background other than English. The identified 'national origin minority' (language minority) students were then tested to determine whether they were proficient English speakers. All students who were proficient in English were eliminated from further testing, while those who scored in the limited range were classified as 'limited English proficient'.[3] The LEP students were then tested to determine their home language proficiency. A comparison of Hispanic students' English and Spanish proficiency scores yielded their relative proficiency classification. (See the next section for a detailed description of these procedures.)

The districts used three instruments that are among the four recommended by the State of California for proficiency testing for purposes of identifying children for bilingual programs:

Bilingual Syntax Measure (BSM), *Bilingual Inventory of Natural Language* (BINL), and *Language Assessment Scale* (LAS). All three have comparable English and Spanish versions, enabling districts to obtain relative proficiency classifications as well as independent Spanish and English proficiency scores. All three measure oral proficiency only.

Procedures and criteria to determine relative proficiency.
The key to relative proficiency assessment is testing the students in each language independently. Proficiency scores obtained in each language may be used to prescribe instruction in each language and may be compared to determine the student's stronger language. (See Burt and Dulay 1978 for discussion of the uses of assessment data.)

To illustrate relative proficiency assessment, let us take a district that uses a test with five proficiency levels. (The three tests used by the districts have either four, five, or six proficiency levels.) The English version is usually given first to determine whether the student is limited in English. English-speaking majority students usually score in the top level of these tests; thus, students scoring in the top level are considered proficient while those who score in the lower levels are usually considered limited to varying degrees. Figure 1 illustrates this concept.

Figure 1. Limited English proficiency classification.

English proficiency levels	Classification
5: Proficient	= Proficient or fluent in English
4: Intermediate	
3: Survival	
2: Comprehension only	= Limited English Proficient (LEP)
1: Beginning	

If the Spanish, Pilipino, Chinese, or other language version of the test is also given, the same proficiency levels are generated for that language and are matched with the student's English level. In this study, a student was considered superior in one of the languages tested if he or she scored one full level higher in one language than the other.

Figure 2 illustrates all the Spanish-English level combinations that yield a Spanish-superior classification, while Figure 3 illustrates the same for English-superior classification. Ten different Spanish-English level combinations yield a Spanish-superior classification, while only six combinations yield an English-superior classification. This is unavoidable because students who score at Level 5 in English are proficient and therefore not included in the count, whereas students who score at level 5 in Spanish are included if they score at a level lower in English.

Figure 2. Spanish-superior classification.

English levels	Spanish levels	Classification
5	5	
4	4	
3	3	= Spanish superior
2	2	
1	1	

Figure 3. English-superior classification.

English levels	Spanish levels	Classification
5	5	
4	4	
3	3	= English superior
2	2	
1	1	

As Figure 4 illustrates, students who score in the same level in both languages and are within the range of limited proficiency are 'equally limited'.

Figure 4. Equally limited classification.

English levels	Spanish levels	Classification
5	5	
4	4	
3	3	= Equally limited
2	2	
1	1	

We use the less common term 'superior' because the more popular term 'dominant' has caused confusion. Dominance may be defined in several ways. To some it means relative proficiency as defined earlier in this paper. To others it means relative comfort in using two languages; if a student is more comfortable using language X, the student may be said to be X-dominant (cf. San Diego City School District 1977). Other indirect measures of language dominance that were first used in basic research on bilingualism have also been associated with dominance. Word association tests, for example, which Lambert, Havelka, and Gardner (1959) used in their theoretical studies of bilingualism, also yield information on dominance, but such information does not directly measure proficiency in either language. (A more comprehensive discussion of these concepts is beyond the scope of this paper; see Hernandez, Burt, and Dulay 1978 for an overview of language dominance concepts.)

In brief, dominance can mean relative proficiency, but it also has other meanings that fall quite short of relative proficiency. Fortunately, the term 'superiority' has not been used in other fields or other research efforts, only in recent bilingual policy work. We can thus be relatively sure that it means-- or will mean--relative proficiency to our readers.

Discussion of findings. The proportion of LEP students who are actually Spanish-superior (the first column of numbers in Table 1) ranges from a high of 90 percent in a border district in San Diego County to a low of 6 percent in a northern California district. These are the students who conform to the characteristics that most of us usually think about when we speak of limited English-speaking students.

The next two columns represent students who are also LEP but do not have the Spanish skills that the Spanish-superior students have. The proportion of English-superior students also spans a wide range: from a high of 78 percent in the northernmost district to a low of 3 percent in the border district. Districts that are geographically in between show percentages of English- and Spanish-superior students that are within the range set by the first two.

Although no formal empirical study has yet been conducted to probe the factors underlying district differences, it appears that the farther away the district is from the Mexican border, the more English-superior students there are. It is also usually the case that the closer a district is to the border, the more recent immigrants there are in the community, while districts farther away have more second and later generation families who use English as a matter of course. Studies of Spanish language maintenance in the United States have documented the loss of Spanish by Hispanic communities over time (Hernandez-Chavez 1978, Merino 1976). Such findings are consistent with the decline in the percentage of Spanish-superior children as one moves northward from the California-Mexico border.

The existence of large numbers of LEP students who are English-superior or equally limited in both languages is not unique to California. According to Professor Bernard Spolsky of New Mexico, the problem is just as severe in the public schools of New Mexico. Many Hispanic children who are underachieving in English language skills speak little or no Spanish. Spolsky reports that four doctoral dissertations done at the

University of New Mexico, in addition to his own observations, document this phenomenon (Teitelbaum 1976, Ortiz 1975, Brisk 1972, Timmins 1971).

Similarly, the Federal District Court of Colorado found that Chicano students in the Mesa County Valley School District who were limited in English were also limited in Spanish (*Otero v. Mesa*). And the consent decree in *Aspira of New York, Inc. v. Board of Education of the City of New York* states that transitional bilingual education should be offered at least to students whose proficiency in English was lower than their proficiency in the native language. (Cf. Esptein 1977:29.)

The data reported in Table 1 are based only on oral proficiency assessments, not reading and writing. The proportion of English-superior LEP children would increase dramatically if we included students who are classified as LEP based on their underachievement in English reading or writing. We refer to children who are fluent English speakers but limited English readers or writers. Preliminary data from a national bilingual assessment project[4] indicate that most Hispanic students reading below grade level in English read substantially less well in Spanish.

A comparison of two different counts of California LEP students--one using only oral proficiency assessment, the other using reading and writing criteria as well--indicates that the addition of children who are limited only in English reading or writing skills (they are orally proficient) doubles the LEP population. According to the State of California, there were 275,000 LEP students in California in 1978. This count was based largely on oral English proficiency assessments. On the other hand, the National Institute of Education's Children's English and Services Study reports that there were 584,000 LEP students in California in 1978 (*Forum* 1979);[5] this figure was based on the assessment of reading and writing, as well as oral English skills. Although one could question the comparability of the oral assessment in the two counts, the comparison suggests that the data reported in Table 1 probably underestimate the percentages of LEP students who are English-superior or comparably limited.

Home language data: Corroboration of the relative proficiency findings. The finding that large numbers of limited English proficient students are actually English-superior or comparably limited in their home language and English has great educational significance. No instructional approaches have been developed for such students and their development will entail some change from the approaches currently used for limited English proficient students. Changes in instructional approach invariably entail different requirements for teachers which, in turn, set the wheels of politics in motion.

A recognition of the potential impact of our findings on the education and politics of LEP students led us to search for independent evidence that would confirm--or disconfirm--our relative proficiency findings. We turned to data on the language LEP students speak at home. If a LEP student were English superior, his or her home language proficiency would, at best, be at the 'survival' level; probably more commonly, the student would be able to understand some of the language but would not be able to speak much of it. Consequently, most of the English-superior students would have to speak English at home, even if their parents or other adults spoke another language.

If our relative proficiency criteria and assessments were sound, we should find that the majority of Hispanic students classified as English-superior speak English at home, while the majority of students classified as Spanish superior speak Spanish at home.

Obtaining home language information is radically different from obtaining language proficiency information. The procedure involves survey questionnaires or interviews rather than testing. And parents, rather than students, are the sources of the information. The inherent differences between home language data collection methodology and relative proficiency assessment techniques make home language data maximally useful as an independent check against the accuracy of relative proficiency results.

The *Home Language Survey*, a four-item questionnaire used by California school districts to survey parents, includes a question that asks what language the child speaks at home. The *Home Language Survey* is the first step in the identification of LEP students. It determines which students are 'national origin minority' and who should, therefore, be tested to determine English proficiency.

We analyzed the *Survey* data that had been collected by two of the districts from which we had obtained relative proficiency assessment data. One district was in Northern California, the other in Southern California; one used the *Bilingual Syntax Measure*, the other used the *Language Assessment Scale* to measure students' proficiency in English and Spanish.

The results are striking. According to the *Survey*, 84 percent of the English-superior students spoke English at home; 90 percent of the Spanish-superior students spoke Spanish at home; approximately half of the comparably limited students spoke English and approximately half spoke Spanish at home.

These findings, displayed in Table 2, corroborate the relative proficiency data presented in Table 1. They add persuasive evidence for the existence of a large subpopulation of LEP children who are English-superior.

'Home language': A misnomer? Some readers may ask, as we did, how it is possible that students who do not fluently speak a language other than English can be classified as having a home or primary language other than English.

Table 2. Number and percentage of LEP students by relative proficiency and language student speaks at home.

Languages students speak at home	Relative proficiency of LEP students		
	Spanish superior	English superior	Equally limited
English	38 (10)	280 (84)	121 (49)	429 (47)
Spanish	324 (90)	55 (16)	126 (51)	505 (53)
	362	335	247	994

The answer turns out to be quite simple. The *Lau* Remedies (Office for Civil Rights 1975) define 'primary' or 'home language' so that the definition need not refer to the language the *student* speaks at home. According to the Remedies, a student's primary or home language is other than English if it meets any one of the following descriptions: the student's first acquired language is other than English; the language most often spoken by the student is other than English; the language most often spoken in the student's home is other than English, *regardless of the language spoken by the student* (Office for Civil Rights 1975:Section I; emphasis added). These definitions have been used as the basis for developing ESEA Title VII regulations as well as state bilingual education policies throughout the country.

California's *Home Language Survey* is a typical outgrowth of the *Lau* Remedies. It includes four questions:

1. Which language did your son or daughter learn when he or she first began to talk?
2. What language does your son or daughter most frequently use at home?
3. What language do you use most frequently to speak to your son or daughter?
4. Name the languages in the order most often spoken by the adults at home.

A response of a non-English language to any of the four questions classifies the student as having a home language other than English. This includes a response of 'English and X'. Thus, if a parent answered 'English' to the first three questions and 'Pilipino' or 'Pilipino and English' to the fourth, the child would be classified as having Pilipino as his or her home language.

Such a response profile is not uncommon. Nor is it uncommon for the response to Question 2 to be 'English' and to Questions 3 and 4 to be 'Spanish'. Adults often continue speaking their native language in a new country long after their children start using the new language as their preferred language. Often children will answer parents in English even though the parents speak to them in another language.

This type of exchange was common in both our homes. Burt's parents spoke Dutch to each other and to their children, but her younger sister and brother would answer their parents in English. Burt, the oldest girl, spoke Dutch to her parents and English to her younger sister and brother.

Dulay's home language situation illustrates yet another common occurrence in bilingual families. While her first languages were Spanish and Tagalog, these languages became her weaker languages shortly after she started school (conducted in English), although the adults in the family continued speaking three languages in her home.

In a study of bilingual education practices in California, Development Associates (under contract to the State of California) found that if Question 4 of the *Home Language Survey* is the only item where parents indicated that a language other than English was spoken, the child is generally a fluent English speaker. Development Associates (1979) thus recommended that Question 4 be dropped from the *Home Language Survey*.

The concept of home language is multifaceted. Because the criteria used to determine home language may vary significantly, one cannot assume that students themselves speak the language designated as their primary or home language. It becomes necessary, therefore, to assess the student's actual proficiency in the home language to determine whether the student speaks it fluently.

Program suggestions. Relative proficiency assessments yield three groups of LEP students: primary-language-superior, English-superior, and comparably limited students. There is general consensus, at least in educational policies throughout the country, that two major educational goals should govern instructional approaches for all three groups. Programs should at least aim to enhance the student's academic achievement and should improve their English language skills.[6] The programmatic suggestions outlined here address these goals.

While the program goals for all three groups are the same, the shape of the program for each varies; each group has different linguistic characteristics and correspondingly different instructional needs.

1. **Program suggestions for primary-language-superior LEP students.** This group of students is the one that most people think of when they think of programs for LEP students.

Students whose English skills are limited and whose skills in the home language are stronger should be given the opportunity to learn the basic academic subjects in their home language in addition to special English (second language) instruction. Such an instructional approach removes the handicap under which non-English-superior students would be working if they were to receive academic instruction through English.

This approach assumes that the program is implemented with qualified teachers, adequate curriculum, and sufficient instructional materials, so that instructional quality is assured. If staffing, curriculum, or materials are inadequate, the advantages of instruction through the student's stronger language may not be realized; they would be outweighed by the disadvantages of inadequate program implementation.

This approach is consistent with the transitional bilingual education program defined in the *Lau* Remedies, although it need not be transitional to work. If students are permitted to continue developing their home language after they have become proficient in English, the approach recommended earlier would no longer be transitional. Such a choice should be made jointly by the students, their parents, and school personnel.

In our work for the California State Board of Education and the California legislature, we called the type of program suggested here a 'core bilingual' program because it can be implemented within either a transitional or a maintenance context, and because the academic core of the curriculum is taught in the student's home language. Nonacademic subjects such as music, art, and physical education should be taught in English to provide the students opportunities to attend classes with native English speakers and thereby promote their acquisition of English and bicultural skills.

Although it is possible to conduct successful academic classes using both English and the home language as mediums of instruction, such an approach is extremely difficult. We would recommend instead using only the home language as the instructional medium in basic academic classes for non-English-superior students, until the students are ready to begin the transfer into English medium instruction. Thus, students would spend about half a day in English-medium classes and half a day in classes taught through their native language. This would entail student grouping by language superiority for basic academic classes.

We have presented detailed rationales for this recommendation elsewhere (Dulay and Burt 1978, 1980; see also Nadeau 1979). In brief, teaching academic subjects through the stronger language maximizes the probability that classes will hold the students' attention; it prevents dilution of the time spent on conceptual learning; and it is easier on teachers who would not have to deal with teaching both concepts and English at the

same time, a practice that often results in inadvertently giving students conflicting feedback on their performance.
If the home language is used as the medium of academic instruction, English second language classes become the vehicle for teaching technical vocabulary. ESL classes, therefore, should be articulated with the subject matter curriculum so that technical vocabulary in English is taught. A short transition period where English is the medium of academic instruction may also be useful before the student is transferred to a regular English-medium subject matter class.

In sum, the general program features we would recommend for non-English-superior LEP students are: (1) basic academic instruction through the home language; (2) English second language instruction which is articulated with the subject matter curriculum; (3) nonacademic subjects such as art, music, and physical education taught through English and taken with native English-speaking students; and (4) a transition period in which academic subjects are taught through English before the student transfers to the regular school curriculum.

2. **Program suggestions for English-superior LEP students.** This group of students has been largely overlooked by educational policymakers, researchers, and curriculum developers. There is no research to assist in program development for these students, nor is there much discussion of the problem by educational practitioners. Following the same general rationale used for non-English-superior students, however, broad outlines of a program can be recommended.

Since these LEP students' stronger language is English, it follows that they would suffer less of an academic handicap if the academic curriculum were taught in English rather than in their home language. Their underachievement in English, however, would necessitate special instruction to promote English language development. Such instruction would be different from the regular English language arts curriculum. Techniques would be drawn from a variety of methodologies, including English second language instruction, English as a second dialect, and remedial English.

Since English-superior students are underachieving in English language skills, subject matter teachers of these students should be aware of the special English needs of their students so that problems in English do not get confused with problems in conceptual learning. If teachers knew of their students' language problems, they might make a special effort to use more visual teaching techniques than they otherwise might have.

Part of a program for English-superior LEP students might also be a class designed to develop their home language skills. Such a class would not be using the home language to facilitate conceptual learning (as is done in programs for non-English-superior students). Its aim would be that the students learn the home language. Pedagogical techniques that teach second language through teaching content may, of course, be used in such a class. The ultimate goal of the class, however, would be primary language acquisition rather than content learning.

The decision to include such a component should rest with the students, their parents, and the teacher. The resources of the school would also play an important role. If a bilingual program for primary-language-superior students were operating, it would be fairly easy to extend the resources of that program to implement the primary language component for English-superior LEP students. The existence in the school of a foreign language program that included the target language would also facilitate the inclusion of this component in the program.

As mentioned earlier, little is known about the specific learning needs of this LEP subpopulation. While we await researchers' findings, it seems that we should at least make sure that the students' stronger language--English--is used as the medium of academic instruction and that they receive special English instruction. Further, if the community and the children's parents are oriented toward bilingualism, schools should make an effort to provide opportunities for children to revitalize their native language.

3. **Program suggestions for comparably limited students.** The students for whom it is most difficult to develop even the broadest outlines of programmatic recommendations are the comparably limited students. They do not demonstrate superiority in either language, and they underachieve in both.

Some educators feel that comparably limited students should be taught academic subjects in the home language because it would allow home support for the students' school work and may provide a boost for the students' self-esteem. Others recommend English-medium instruction because English is the language the students will ultimately have to master to succeed in the United States job market.

Educators have not generally recommended a dual language approach to academic instruction for these students for several reasons. Some children who are limited in both languages exhibit difficulty in using language in general. Thus, it is thought that they should not be made to deal with two languages when learning concepts.

Other children in this group speak a language variety resulting from a combination of the primary language grammar and a slice of the English lexicon (see, for example, Acosta-Belen 1975). Many of these children are not proficient in either English or Spanish, but may be proficient in a third language system. Although such a system is cognitively as valid and logical as either of the two source languages, most educators prefer to use standard varieties of English or the primary language, for social reasons. Looking ahead to the child's future, most parents and educators also feel that children should become proficient in at least one standard language, and the school is the place to learn it.[7]

Still other children in this LEP subgroup--probably a very small minority--may have 'code-switched' during the testing, giving some answers in English and some in the home language, or they may have switched languages within a single response. Code-switching typically occurs when the speaker perceives his or her interlocutor to be bilingual, thus capable of understanding both languages (for a discussion of code-switching, see Haugen 1953; Gumperz and Hernández 1972; Dulay, Hernández, and Burt 1978; Dulay and Burt 1972; Dulay, Burt, and Krashen in press). Students who perceived that the tester was bilingual would feel free to code-switch in order to better communicate nuances of meaning. Such students are typically proficient in both languages; they have simply not demonstrated their abilities due to their misperception of the testing task. This problem is basically one involving testing procedures. It can be avoided by training testers to use verbal and nonverbal cues to make it clear to the student that during the testing procedure only one language should be used. Or school districts can use testers who are monolingual or superior speakers of the language being tested.

All in all, we are left with the decision regarding whether to use the home language or English as the medium of basic academic instruction for comparably limited children. (The language in which other components of the curriculum should be taught is not at issue here.)

Some, including ourselves, have recommended further testing to see whether tests other than the one initially used might yield a superior classification in one language (see Assembly Bill 690/1979 and California State Board of Education 1979). Such a procedure is costly, however, and may still yield inconclusive results.

In examining home language data, we discovered an alternative--or a supplement--to further testing in this situation: using the language the *child* speaks at home. This approach would be cost effective since schools already have that information by virtue of having conducted a home survey. It also enjoys some (though scant) empirical support.

As Table 2 indicates, students who demonstrate superiority in one language speak the language in which they are superior at home. In analyzing our home language data for Question 2 (the language the child speaks at home), we find that parents of about one-half of the equally limited children report that the children speak English at home, and one-half report that they speak Spanish.

Given the importance of continuity between home and school, it might be best to choose the language of instruction for comparably limited bilinguals on the basis of the language the child speaks at home (Question 2). Thus we would recommend that comparably limited bilinguals who speak English at home would best be instructed in English, while those who speak another language at home might benefit more from instruction through that language. In either case, the students would additionally receive special English language instruction appropriate to their needs. Further, if parental choice, community orientation, and school resources permit it, students should be given opportunities to revitalize their home language.

As with the other groups, these recommendations assume that the type of program selected can be implemented properly. For with inadequate resources, the advantages of program design are eliminated and the program may even become detrimental to the student.

Some warnings. There will always be special circumstances that dictate program features other than the ones recommended here. Although each of the three special circumstances we are going to mention deserves much lengthier discussion, space constraints permit only brief comment.

1. **Parental input.** Parental dissatisfaction or disagreement with recommended program features should be taken into consideration. Education becomes much easier if schools respond to parents' goals and instructional preferences for their children. For example, many Korean, Vietnamese, and Filipino parents prefer English-medium instruction for their children, even if they are superior in their home language.

States have become responsive to the need for parental satisfaction with school bilingual programs and have included withdrawal, notification, information, and consultation rights of parents in their statutes (see California Reorganized Code, Chapter 7, 1977; Illinois Transitional Bilingual Education, Chapter 122, 1973; Texas Education Code Sub-chapter L, among others), proposed rules, or pending legislation.

2. **School resources.** School resources, too, must be considered before attempting to install new programs. It is often better to wait until teachers are properly trained, curriculum designed, and necessary materials procured before a program is implemented. Otherwise, its full benefits may not be realized and critical innovations may be scrapped before they can be implemented properly. Often it is better to settle, in the interim, for a less than ideal program design that can be implemented well rather than to attempt the ideal and be crushed by problems of implementation.

3. **Children with exceptional needs.** There are some LEP children who score at very low proficiency levels in both languages. If, for example, on a five-level proficiency test a student scores at Level 2 in one language and Level 1 in another, or at Level 2 in both, one may assign the student to a

relative proficiency category, but such assignment is programmatically meaningless. Such students have demonstrated performance below the normal range and cannot be treated as normal English-superior, primary-language-superior or equally limited students are treated. Using the Bilingual Syntax Measure I (1975), for example, children who score at Level 3 or lower in both languages, regardless of relative proficiency, are not counted under any of the relative proficiency categories but are identified as needing 'special diagnosis'.

Even if such students are placed in the best designed and implemented programs, they may fail without more specialized help. Further assessments to probe speech, hearing, or language disorders, mental retardation, or emotional disturbance must be made in both languages to determine the students' needs.

At the other end of the performance scale are primary-language-superior LEP students who have recently immigrated to the United States and who have enjoyed a good education in their home countries. Often these students have surpassed their Anglo-American grademates and do not benefit much from grade-level academic instruction in their own languages. Acquiring English skills is their major need. Thus, intensive English second language instruction, combined with selected subject matter and/or nonacademic classes taught through English may be most appropriate. Such students may also benefit from an advanced language arts class in their native language, appropriate to their level.

Summary. The recommendations made in this paper comprise an appeal for greater variety in designing bilingual programs, less legal rigidity in mandating home language instruction, better matching of program features to student characteristics, the inclusion of parental input, and serious consideration of implementation factors when planning programs.

We have found that limited English proficient students are not a linguistically homogeneous population; they comprise at least three relative proficiency groups and two groups with exceptional needs. LEP student diversity was the basis of the bilingual education conceptual framework passed by the California Board of Education in April, 1979; it was the basis of California Assemblyman Richard Alatorre's attempt to improve the state's bilingual legislation (Assembly Bill 690/1979), and it is central to the proposed *Lau* regulations pursuant to Title VI of the Civil Rights Act (U.S. Department of Education, 1980). If we care about the academic needs of language minority students, we cannot but channel our energies toward creating a selection of program options that are sensitive to their various needs and goals.

NOTES

This research was supported in part by a contract to Bloomsbury West from the California State Department of Education in 1979. We are grateful to Starrett Dalton, Administrator, Department of Research and Evaluation, Riverside Unified School District, for his assistance in aggregating the data.
1. Although Lerea and Laporta also report that their monolingual subjects learned *visual* stimuli in fewer trials.
2. The terms 'home language' and 'primary language' have been used synonymously in much of the contemporary bilingual education literature. For example, 'primary language' is defined in California law as the language the student first acquired or the language spoken in the home (California Education Code, Section 52163(g)). Similarly, 'primary-language-superior' is synonymous with 'non-English-superior'; and 'comparably limited' is synonymous with 'equally limited'.
3. In this paper, the term 'limited English proficient' includes children who are 'non-English speaking' (NES) as well as those who are 'limited English speaking' (LES). It can also include those who are limited in English reading and writing skills if tests measure those skills.
4. Not yet released.
5. This study estimated that there were 3.6 million LEP children in the United States in 1978.
6. Programs for LEP students may, of course, have other goals, such as the maintenance or revitalization of the student's home language. These are also important, but they enjoy less general public consensus.
7. This approach does not preclude the teacher's accepting the student's use of a nonstandard or mixed language variety. The teacher simply uses the standard variety herself.

REFERENCES

Acosta-Belen, E. 1975. On the nature of Spanglish. Journal of Contemporary Puerto Rican Thought 2.2.
Albert, M. L., and L. K. Obler. 1978. The bilingual brain. New York: Academic Press.
Aspira of New York, Inc. v. Board of Education of the City of New York. 1974. Civ. 4002, S.D.N.Y.
Assembly Bill 690. 1979. Introduced by Assemblyman Richard Alatorre, April 16. Final version in Senate Finance Committee August 22, 1979. California Legislature, 1979-1980 Regular Session.
Balasubramonian, K., H. N. Seelye, and R. E. De Weffer. 1973. Do bilingual education programs inhibit English language achievement? A report on an Illinois experiment. ERIC ED 118703.
Bilingual Syntax Measure I. 1975. New York: The Psychological Corporation (Harcourt Brace Jovanovich).

Brisk, M. 1972. Spanish syntax of the pre-school Spanish American: The case of New Mexican five-year-old children.
Burt, M., and H. Dulay. 1978. Some guidelines for the assessment of oral language proficiency and dominance. TESOL Quarterly 12.177-192.
California Education Code, Sec. 52163(g). 1978. In: West's Annotated California Codes. St. Paul, Minn.: West Publishing Co.
California State Board of Education. 1979. Legislative language presented by the California State Department of Education, H. Dulay and M. Burt to the Committee on Specially Funded Programs, at the March and April Board Meetings.
Development Associates, Inc. 1979. Evaluation of California's educational services to limited and non-English speaking students. Interim Report No. 3. Prepared for the Office of the Legislative Analyst, California Legislature, Sacramento, December 26.
Dulay, H., and M. Burt. 1972. Goofing: An indicator of children's second language learning strategies. Language Learning 22(2).235-252.
Dulay, H., and M. Burt. 1976. Why bilingual education: A summary of research findings. San Francisco: Bloomsbury West. (2nd ed. 1978.)
Dulay, H., and M. Burt. 1978. From research to method in bilingual education. In: Georgetown University Round Table on Languages and Linguistics 1978. Edited by James E. Alatis. Washington, D.C.: Georgetown University Press. 551-575.
Dulay, H., and M. Burt. 1979a. Research priorities in bilingual education. Educational Evaluation and Policy Analysis 1.39-53.
Dulay, H., and M. Burt. 1979b. The efficacy of bilingual education. Educational Evaluation and Policy Analysis 1.72-73.
Dulay, H., and M. Burt. 1979c. Bilingual education: A close look at its effects. Focus, No. 1. Rosslyn, Va.: National Clearinghouse for Bilingual Education.
Dulay, H., and M. Burt. 1979d. Curriculum options in bilingual education. Presentation to the California State Board of Education, Committee on Specially Funded Projects, March.
Dulay, H., and M. Burt. 1979e. Testimony before the Senate Education Committee of the California State Legislature, August.
Dulay, H., and M. Burt. 1980. Aspects of bilingual education for LES/NES students. In: Bilingual program, policy, and assessment issues. Edited by California State Department of Education. Sacramento: California State Department of Education.

Dulay, H., and M. Burt. 1980. A misdiagnosed population. Educational Researcher 9.29.
Dulay, H., M. Burt, and S. Krashen. (in press) The second language. New York: Oxford University Press.
Dulay, H., E. Hernandez-Chavez, and M. Burt. 1978. The process of becoming bilingual. In: Diagnostic procedures in hearing, speech, and language. Edited by S. Singh and J. Lynch. Baltimore: University Park Press.
Epstein, N. 1977. Language, ethnicity and the schools. Washington, D.C.: Institute of Educational Leadership, George Washington University.
Feldman, C., and M. Shen. 1971. Some language related cognitive advantages of bilingual five-year-olds. Journal of Genetic Psychology 118.235-244.
Forum. 1979. Study finds 3.6 million school-age children are limited English proficient. Forum 2:6. Rosslyn, Va.: National Clearinghouse for Bilingual Education.
Gonzalez, J. 1980. TESOL and bilingual education. Paper presented at the 14th Annual International TESOL Conference, March 4-9, San Francisco.
Gumperz, J. J., and E. Hernandez-Chavez. 1972. Bilingualism, bidialectalism and classroom interaction. In: Functions of language in the classroom. Edited by C. B. Cazden, V. P. John, and D. Hymes. New York: Teachers College Press.
Haugen, E. 1953. The Norwegian language in America. Philadelphia: University of Pennsylvania Press.
Hernández-Chávez, E. 1978. Language maintenance, bilingual education, and philosophies of bilingualism in the United States. In: Georgetown University Round Table on Languages and Linguistics 1978. Edited by James E. Alatis. Washington, D.C.: Georgetown University Press. 527-550.
Hernández-Chávez, E., M. Burt, and H. Dulay. 1978. Language dominance and proficiency testing: Some general considerations. NABE Journal 3.41-54. Also published in: Proceedings of the Second International Conference on Frontiers in Language Proficiency and Dominance Testing 3. Edited by J. E. Redden. Carbondale, Ill.: Department of Linguistics, Southern Illinois University.
Lambert, W., J. Havelka, and R. Gardner. 1959. Linguistic manifestations of bilingualism. American Journal of Psychology 72.77-82.
Lerea, L., and R. Laporta. 1971. Vocabulary and pronunciation acquisition among bilinguals and monolinguals. Language and Speech 14.193-300.
Merino, B. 1976. Language acquisition in bilingual children: Aspects of syntactic development in English and Spanish by Chicano children in grades K-4. Ph.D. dissertation. Stanford University.
Modiano, N. 1973. Indian education in the Chiapas Highlands. New York: Holt, Rinehart and Winston.

Nadeau, A. 1979. Why aren't bilingual programs working? Reach 1(3).22-32.
Office for Civil Rights. 1975. Task force findings specifying remedies available for eliminating past educational practices ruled unlawful under *Lau v. Nichols*.
Ortiz, L. 1975. A sociolinguistic study of language maintenance in the northern New Mexico community of Arroyo Seco. Doctoral dissertation. University of New Mexico.
Otero v. Mesa County Valley School District, No. 51. 1975. Civil Action No. 74-W-279 (D. Colorado December 31).
Palmer, M. 1972. Effects of categorization, degree of bilingualism and language recall of select monolinguals and bilinguals. Journal of Educational Psychology 63.163-164.
Peal, E., and W. Lambert. 1962. The relation of bilingualism to intelligence. Psychological Monographs 76(27).1-23.
Plante, A. J. 1977. Connecticut pairing model proves effective in bilingual bicultural education. Phi Delta Kappan 58.427.
Ramos, M., J. Aguilar, and B. P. Sibayan. 1967. The determination and implementation of language policy. Philippine Center for Language Study Monograph Series No. 2. Quezon City, Philippines: Alemar/Phoenix.
Rosier, P., and M. Farella. 1976. Bilingual education at Rock Point: Some early results. TESOL Quarterly 10.379-388.
San Diego City School District. 1977. San Diego observation assessment instrument. Los Angeles: Center for the Study of Evaluation, University of California at Los Angeles.
Slobin, D. 1968. Antonymic phonetic symbolism in three natural languages. Journal of Personality and Social Psychology 10.301-305.
Teitelbaum, H. 1976. Assessing bilingualism in elementary school children. Doctoral dissertation. University of New Mexico.
Timmins, K. M. 1971. An investigation of the relative bilingualism of Spanish surnamed children in an elementary school in Albuquerque. Doctoral dissertation. University of New Mexico.
Trevino, B. 1968. An analysis of the effectiveness of a bilingual program in the teaching of mathematics in the primary grades. Doctoral dissertation. University of Texas.
Troike, R. 1978. Research evidence for the effectiveness of bilingual education. NABE Journal 3.13-24.
U.S. Department of Education. 1980. Nondiscrimination under programs receiving federal assistance through the Department of Education, effectuation of Title VI of the Civil Rights Act of 1964. Proposed Rules. Federal Register 45, August 5. 52052-52076.
Weinreich, U. 1953. Languages in contact: Findings and problems. The Hague: Mouton.

THE CONSTRUCT OF LANGUAGE PROFICIENCY IN BILINGUAL EDUCATION

James Cummins
The Ontario Institute for Studies in Education

It is frequently claimed (e.g. Troike 1978) that bilingual education in the United States is in critical need of research in order to document the validity (or otherwise) of its basic psychoeducational assumptions. The urgency for such documentation is highlighted by the growing sociopolitical backlash against bilingual education which can be illustrated by the following quotation from an article by Tom Bethell (1979:30) entitled 'Against bilingual education: Why Johnny can't speak English':

> Bilingual education is an idea that appeals to teachers of Spanish and other tongues, but also to those who never did think that another idea, the United States of America, was a particularly good one to begin with, and that the sooner it is restored to its component 'ethnic' parts the better off we shall all be. Such people have been welcomed with open arms into the upper reaches of the federal government in recent years, giving rise to the suspicion of a death wish.

Teachers of minority language children who are committed to bilingual education are frequently confronted with similar negative views from fellow teachers and school administrators who may feel threatened by the expansion of bilingual education. Fears of bilingual education tend to be rationalized in both sociopolitical and psychoeducational terms; the sociopolitical argument, articulated by Bethell as well as in many articles in the popular press (e.g. *New York Times* editorial, November 22, 1976) is that bilingual education will promote social fragmentation and Quebec-style separatist movements. The psychoeducational argument is that if minority children are deficient

in English, then they need instruction in English, not their
first language (L1). The alternative argument, for bilingual
education, rests on the counter-intuitive assumption that instruction in L1 will promote English skills more effectively than
instruction in English. It is not surprising that this 'Less
equals more' rationale would be difficult both for proponents
to articulate and for opponents to swallow.

The apparent counter-intuitive nature of the psychoeducational argument makes it all the more imperative to supply unequivocal empirical evidence for its validity. Bilingual education is tolerated in the United States only on psychoeducational grounds. If evidence for the validity of the psychoeducational assumptions underlying bilingual education is not
forthcoming, it is likely that policy decisions will be taken
solely on the basis of sociopolitical considerations. Given the
present climate, the sociopolitical argument for bilingual education, i.e. the desirability of a culturally pluralistic society
(see, for example, Fishman 1976, Kjolseth 1972), would carry
very little weight compared to the fear of social fragmentation.

The fact that evidence from the few program evaluations
that were reasonably well controlled does appear to support bilingual education (see, for example, Troike 1978) is counter-
balanced by the fact that there is as yet no clear evidence
that bilingual education is reducing inequality of educational
opportunity on the large scale that was originally envisaged.
Despite the shortcomings of the AIR study (Danoff 1978) in
design (see, for example, O'Malley 1978, Swain 1979), there is
no doubt that the negative tone of its findings contributed to
the widespread confusion about the goals and methods of bilingual education at all levels of the educational hierarchy,
from policy-makers to classroom teachers.

However, the roots of the confusion regarding the psychoeducational rationale for bilingual education lie not so much in
the lack of research documenting the effects of bilingual education, as in the real conceptual confusion which underlies the
rationale for transitional programs. In fact, there is an
enormous amount of well-controlled research documentation
about bilingual education both in the United States and elsewhere (see Engle 1975). However, the invalid a priori assumptions with which the research is approached often make the
findings look contradictory. For example, much of the impetus
for the development of bilingual education in the United States
derived from the 'linguistic mismatch' hypothesis that mismatch
between the language of the home and the language of the
school leads to retardation in the acquisition of reading and
other academic skills (Downing 1978, UNESCO 1953). The fact
that this assumption is contradicted by the findings of immersion programs in Canada and elsewhere (see Cummins 1979a,
Swain 1979, for reviews) casts doubt on the entire psychoeducational rationale for bilingual education (see Epstein 1977).

This paper is an attempt to clarify the theoretical underpinnings of bilingual education. I argue that there is a very good reason why educators should be confused about the rationale for bilingual education as it is currently implemented in the United States; the reason is that the psychoeducational assumptions underlying transitional programs are largely invalid. This assertion is based on three considerations: first, the assumptions of transitional bilingual education suffer from internal logical inconsistencies; second, the 'linguistic mismatch' hypothesis which supplies the rationale for providing initial instruction in L1 is contradicted by considerable research evidence; third, research findings suggest that the educational benefits of bilingual education may be cumulative, and thus, aborting the program at an early stage is unlikely to realize these benefits.

These logical and empirical problems in the psychoeducational assumptions underlying transitional bilingual education all stem from a failure to conceptualize adequately the construct of language proficiency and its cross-lingual dimensions. In other words, there has been relatively little inquiry into what forms of language proficiency are related to the development of literacy skills in school contexts and how the development of academic proficiency in L1 relates to the development of academic proficiency in L2. The invalidity of the assumptions underlying transitional bilingual programs can be illustrated by a consideration of these two issues.

Cognitive/academic language proficiency. Oller (see Oller 1978, 1979; Oller and Perkins 1978) has argued on the basis of a large number of studies that 'there exists a global language proficiency factor which accounts for the bulk of the reliable variance in a wide variety of language proficiency measures' (1978: 413). This factor is strongly related to IQ and to other aspects of academic achievement. Most of the data reported by Oller and Perkins involved performance on discrete-point measures of literacy-related skills (for example, vocabulary and reading comprehension tests) or on integrative tests such as oral and written cloze and dictation. Farhady (1979) has shown that there is no difference between discrete-point and integrative tests in terms of their loadings on a global proficiency factor.

Oller's general position is supported by a large body of research showing high correlations between literacy skills and general intellectual skills. Verbal intellectual skills are more strongly related to reading than are nonverbal skills. For example, Strang (1945) reported correlations of .41-.46 between nonverbal abilities and reading, and of .80-.84 between verbal abilities and reading. Consistent with these empirical findings, several theorists have emphasized the importance of reasoning in the reading process (Downing 1979, Singer 1977, Vernon 1971), while others (for example, Goodman, Goodman, and

Flores 1979; Smith 1971) have pointed out that fluent reading skills require that readers make use of their total knowledge of language and of the world to make predictions about information in the text.

However, it is clear that not all aspects of language proficiency are related to cognitive and literacy skills. For example, with the exception of severely retarded and autistic children, everybody acquires basic interpersonal communicative skills (BICS) in a first language, regardless of IQ or academic aptitude. As Chomsky (1965) has pointed out, the phonological, syntactical, and lexical skills necessary to function in everyday interpersonal contexts are universal across native speakers. There are individual differences in the ways in which native speakers manifest these linguistic skills in interpersonal communicative contexts, e.g. oral fluency, but for the most part these differences are not strongly related to cognitive or academic performance. Thus, I prefer to use the term 'cognitive/academic language proficiency' (CALP) in place of Oller's 'global language proficiency' to refer to the dimension of language proficiency that is strongly related to literacy skills.

It is possible to present diagrammatically the distinction between CALP and BICS by adapting Roger Shuy's (1976) 'iceberg' metaphor.[1] In Figure 1, the 'visible' language proficiencies of pronunciation, vocabulary, grammar, which are manifested in everyday interpersonal communicative situations, are above the surface, but the cognitive/academic language proficiency required to manipulate or reflect upon these surface features outside of immediate interpersonal contexts is below the surface, and, I argue, has usually been ignored in policy decisions regarding language of instruction.

Figure 1. The 'iceberg' representation of language proficiency.

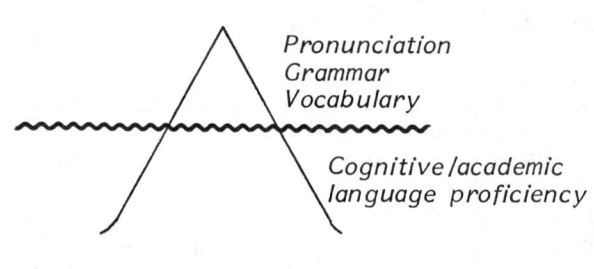

Pronunciation
Grammar
Vocabulary

Cognitive/academic
language proficiency

Manifestation of
language in
interpersonal
communicative
contexts

Manipulation of
language in
decontextualized
academic situations

Distinctions similar to that between CALP and BICS have
been made by several investigators. Hernández-Chávez,
Burt, and Dulay (1978), and Burt and Dulay (1978), for
example, distinguish between 'natural communication' tasks
and 'linguistic manipulation' tasks which, they report, 'give
quite different results in terms of the quality of the language
produced' (Hernández-Chávez et al. 1978:52). Burt and Dulay
(1978:184) define this distinction as follows:

> A natural communication task is one where the focus of the
> student is on communicating something to someone else--an
> idea, some information, or an opinion in a natural manner
> ... On the other hand, a linguistic manipulation task is one
> where the focus of the student is on performing the con-
> scious linguistic manipulation required by the task.

Burt and Dulay regard linguistic manipulation tasks as primarily assessing metalinguistic awareness, although the decontextualized noncommunicative tasks such as oral and written
cloze, sentence repetition, dictation, etc., that they include
in this category would not usually be regarded as measures of
metalinguistic awareness. In terms of the present framework,
metalinguistic awareness is regarded as one specialized aspect
of CALP. Several studies have reported that development of
metalinguistic skills is significantly related to overall cognitive
development (see Ryan and Ledger 1979 for a review).
A similar distinction to that proposed by Burt and Dulay
(1978) has been noted by Krashen (1978) in discussing the
'Words in sentences' subtest of the *Modern Language Aptitude
Test* (Carroll and Sapon 1959). Krashen notes (1978:9) that
this subtest involves 'a conscious awareness of language and
grammar, quite different from the tacit knowledge or "competence" Chomsky (1965) claims all native speakers have of their
language'. Further evidence for the distinction comes from the
finding that the oral language production skills of preschoolers
are only weakly related to the later acquisition of reading skills
in school (Wells 1979). The CALP-BICS distinction is also
parallel to the distinction which Olson (1977) makes between
the social and ideational functions of language and Halliday's
(1975) distinction between pragmatic and mathetic functions of
speech.
There is also clear evidence for the CALP-BICS distinction
in L2 contexts (see Cummins 1980a, 1980b), although it may
not be apparent in the initial stages of L2 acquisition. For
example, Skutnabb-Kangas and Toukomaa (1976) report that
although parents, teachers, and the children themselves considered Finnish immigrant children's Swedish to be quite fluent,
tests in Swedish which required cognitive operations to be
carried out showed that this surface fluency was not reflected
in the cognitive/academic aspects of Swedish proficiency.

Another illustration comes from Fillmore's (1979) one-year longitudinal study of five Spanish-speaking kindergarten children learning English. There was considerable variation in the extent to which the children sought out the company of English speakers and desired to identify with them. After three months of exposure to English, the most social and outgoing child, Nora, had learned more English than two of the others would learn by the end of the year. Fillmore (1979:221) argues that 'the secret of Nora's spectacular success as a language learner can be found in the special combination of interests, inclinations, skills, temperament, needs, and motivations that comprised her personality'. She suggests (1979:227) that the differences between the five children in rate of English communicative skills acquisition 'presumably had nothing to do with intellectual or cognitive capacity'. Thus, we would not necessarily expect Nora to surpass the other children to the same extent in development of English literacy skills, since overall cognitive abilities appear to underlie these to a greater extent than personality variables. In a similar way, IQ has been found to be largely unrelated to the acquisition of L2 communicative skills in French immersion programs (see Genesee 1976).

In summary, there exists a reliable dimension of language proficiency which is strongly related to literacy and to other decontextualized verbal-academic tasks. This dimension of cognitive/academic language proficiency appears to be largely independent of these language proficiencies which manifest themselves in everyday interpersonal communicative contexts. These latter forms of language proficiency are either near universal across native speakers or unrelated to cognitive/academic skills.

Interdependence of CALP across languages. Oller does not consider in detail the question of whether his global language proficiency factor underlies an individual's performance in different languages. In fact, the entire question of how the development of L1 proficiency relates to the development of L2 proficiency has received little attention until recently in the context of bilingual education. However, it has been hypothesized that the cognitive/academic aspects of L1 and L2 are interdependent and that the development of proficiency in L2 is partially a function of the level of L1 proficiency at the time when intensive exposure to L2 begins (Cummins 1979a; Skutnabb-Kangas and Toukomaa 1976). In other words, previous learning of literacy-related functions of language (in L1) will predict future learning of these functions (in L2). This interdependence hypothesis is illustrated in Figure 2.

Figure 2 expresses the point that despite the obvious differences between L1 and L2 in terms of the surface features of phonology, syntax, and lexicon, there is a common underlying proficiency that determines an individual's performance on cognitive/academic tasks (e.g. reading) in both L1 and L2. The dual-iceberg diagram also allows for the possibility that there may be nonsurface aspects of proficiency in each language that are not interdependent and that may not be related to CALP.

Figure 2. The 'dual-iceberg' representation of bilingual proficiency.

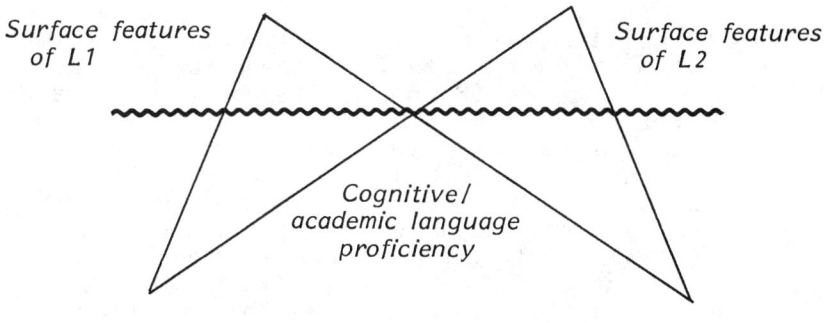

In this respect it is useful to distinguish, as Genesee (1979) does, between language-specific skills and more general aspects of language proficiency. Genesee (1979:74-75) suggests that

> One might expect the language-specific skills (those which are not easily transferable from language to language) to include the more technical aspects of language, such as spelling patterns or syntactic rules, whereas the transferable skills may be more in the nature of cognitive processes, such as the use of one's knowledge of the syntactic transitional probabilities of a language in reading.

Genesee's (1979) discussion is related only to transfer of reading skills but some sociolinguistic rules may also be language-specific.

It is important to note that although language-specific skills may not be easily transferable across languages, there may be high correlations between language-specific skills (e.g. L1 spelling and L2 spelling) if CALP underlies an individual's acquisition of these skills in each language. In general, also, one would expect proficiency in languages that are similar to be more highly correlated than proficiency in languages that are dissimilar.

Also, the hypothesized interdependence between L1 and L2 does not exist in an affective or experiential vacuum and there are several factors which might reduce the relationship between L1 and L2 measures of CALP in comparison to those between intralanguage (L1-L1, L2-L2) measures. For example, when motivation to learn L2 (or maintain L1) is low, CALP will not be applied to the task of learning L2 (or maintaining L1). The interdependence hypothesis also presupposes adequate exposure to both languages.

Empirical support for the interdependence hypothesis comes from correlational studies, studies on the 'optimal age' question in L2 acquisition, and evaluations of bilingual education programs for both minority and majority language students.

Correlational studies. If L1 and L2 CALP are manifestations of a common underlying proficiency, it would be predicted that L2 CALP will be significantly related to measures of L1 CALP and each will show a similar pattern of correlations with other variables such as verbal and nonverbal ability. Evidence supporting this prediction from nine recent studies is presented in Cummins (1979b). In these studies the correlations between L1 and L2 CALP ranged from .77 to .42, with the majority in the range .6 to .7. In addition, L1 and L2 showed a very similar pattern of correlations with language aptitude and IQ variables. For example, the relationships between both L1 and L2 and verbal IQ or language aptitude measures were, for the most part, in the .6 to .7 range, while those between L1 and L2 and nonverbal IQ tended to be in the .4 to .5 range.

Age and L2 acquisition. The interdependence hypothesis would predict that older L2 learners, whose L1 CALP is better developed, will acquire cognitive/academic L2 skills more rapidly than younger learners. Recent reviews of research on the age issue confirm this prediction (Cummins 1980c, 1980d; Ekstrand 1978; Genesee 1978; Krashen, Long, and Scarcella 1979). In no study did younger learners acquire L2 CALP more rapidly than older learners. No advantage for older learners in acquiring L2 BICS would be predicted on the basis of the interdependence hypothesis. The research shows no clear trend in aspects of L2 proficiency directly related to communicative skills, such as oral fluency, phonology, and listening comprehension. In some studies older learners display an advantage, whereas in others younger learners perform better. A variety of factors might affect rate of acquisition of L2 communicative skills (see Cummins 1980c; Genesee 1978; Krashen et al. 1979). However, the consistency of the findings in relation to L2 CALP acquisition strongly suggests that level of L1 CALP is a major determinant.

Bilingual program evaluations. The success of French immersion programs for majority language anglophone children in Canada and elsewhere is well documented (see Cummins 1979a, Swain 1978) and need not be considered in detail. Briefly, evaluations have consistently shown that children instructed mainly through French (L2) in the early grades suffer no adverse academic or cognitive consequences and catch up with regular program comparison groups in English language skills shortly after formal English language arts is introduced (usually about grade 2 or 3). Many investigators have remarked on the rapid transfer of reading skills from French to English (for example, Genesee 1979, Lambert and Tucker 1972).

Immersion programs in other contexts show very similar results (see Cohen and Swain 1976, Cummins 1977a). For example, Macnamara's (1966) study of bilingualism in Irish primary education shows that using Irish as a major medium of instruction for children whose L1 is English results in higher achievement in Irish at no cost to achievement in English (see Macnamara 1966:101, Table 11.1). Macnamara's findings have been frequently misinterpreted as support for the linguistic mismatch hypothesis (see Downing 1978; see Cummins 1977b, 1978 for discussion of Macnamara's results).[2]

The findings from immersion programs are sometimes regarded as inconsistent with findings that, for many groups of minority language children, instruction through L1 is more effective in promoting literacy skills in both L1 and L2 than instruction through L2 (see Cummins 1979a). However, the inconsistency disappears when the data are viewed within the context of the interdependence hypothesis, rather than in terms of home-school language switching, or linguistic mismatch.

Many evaluations of L1-medium or bilingual education programs for minority language children demonstrate a very similar transfer of language skills across languages to that observed in immersion programs. For example, several studies involving minority francophone students in Canada show that instruction through French (L1) is just as effective in promoting English proficiency as instruction through English. Carey and Cummins (1979) reported that grade 5 children from French-speaking home backgrounds in the Edmonton Catholic school system bilingual program (80 percent French, 20 percent English, from K-12) performed at an equivalent level in English skills to anglophone children of the same IQ in either the bilingual or regular English programs. A similar finding is reported in a large-scale study carried out by Hébert et al. (1976) among grades 3, 6, and 9 francophone students in Manitoba. At all grade levels there was a significant positive relationship between percentage of instruction in French and French achievement, but no relationship between percentage of instruction in French and English achievement. In other words, francophone students receiving 80 percent instruction in French and

20 percent instruction in English did just as well in English as students receiving 80 percent instruction in English and 20 percent in French. The findings of a longitudinal evaluation of the bilingual program for Navajo students at Rock Point (Rosier and Farella 1976), in which all initial literacy skills were taught in Navajo, showed that by grades 5 and 6, students were performing at the national U.S. norm in English reading. Prior to the institution of the bilingual program, students at Rock Point were two years below the norm in English reading despite intensive ESL instruction in the school. Troike (1978) has reviewed findings from other bilingual programs in the United States which showed that minority students performed as well or better in English skills as compared to students in English-only programs, and examples continue to multiply (for example, Legaretta 1979).

The evaluation of a recent 'language shelter' program for Finnish immigrant children in Sodertalje, Sweden, reports findings very similar to those of the Rock Point Navajo evaluation. The extremely poor academic performance of Finnish L1 children in Swedish-only schools has been documented by Skutnabb-Kangas and Toukomaa (1976). The Sodertalje program, however, used Finnish as the exclusive language of instruction in the first two years of school and Swedish was gradually introduced in the third year. In subsequent years Swedish became the main language of instruction but teaching of Finnish was continued throughout the school. By grade 6, children's performance in this program in both Finnish and Swedish was almost at the same level as that of equivalent Swedish-speaking children in Finland, which was a considerable improvement in both languages compared to their performance in Swedish-only programs (Hanson 1979).

In these programs for minority language children, as well as in immersion programs for majority children, instruction through the minority language has been effective in promoting proficiency in both languages. These findings support the following formulation of the interdependence hypothesis:

To the extent that instruction in L_x is effective in promoting cognitive/academic proficiency in L_x, transfer of this proficiency to L_y will occur provided there is adequate exposure to L_y (either in school or environment) and adequate motivation to learn L_y.

In summary, two main points have been made: (1) CALP is a reliable dimension of individual differences in decontextualized literacy-related functions of language which appears to be distinct from interpersonal communicative skills in L1 and L2; (2) L1 and L2 CALP are interdependent, i.e. manifestations of a common underlying proficiency. The immediate psychoeducational implication of these hypotheses for bilingual education is that, for either minority or majority language students, instruction through a minority language will be just as effective as, or more effective than, instruction through the majority language in promoting literacy skills in the majority language. Much of the current confusion about the rationale for bilingual education (among supporters and opponents alike) stems from a failure to grasp this point.

Misconceptions underlying English-only and transitional bilingual programs. The psychoeducational assumptions underlying arguments both for English-only and transitional bilingual programs for minority children reveal a failure to consider the cognitive/academic proficiency underlying the acquisition of literacy in L1 and L2. Naturally, the cross-lingual dimensions of this proficiency are also ignored.

The Separate Underlying Proficiency model of bilingualism. Those who argue for English-only programs on psychoeducational grounds implicitly assume the validity of a Separate Underlying Proficiency (SUP) model of bilingual proficiency. They usually assume a direct link between amount of exposure to English in school (and home) and achievement in English literacy. It follows that instruction in L1 will result in lower levels of L2 proficiency than instruction in L2. The SUP model is illustrated in Figure 3.

Figure 3. The Separate Underlying Proficiency (SUP) model of bilingualism.

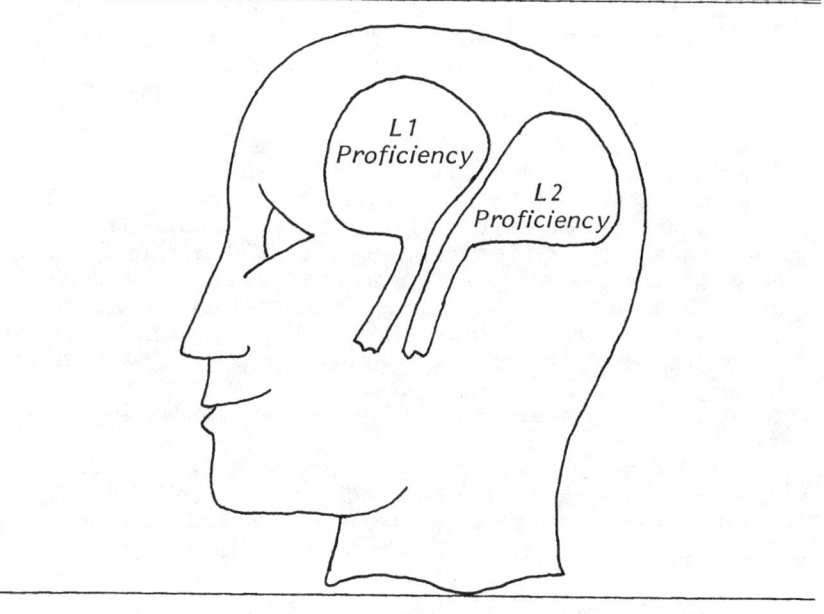

Two interrelated misconceptions about bilingualism can be illustrated with reference to Figure 3. First is the 'balance effect' hypothesis (Macnamara 1966), which assumed that there was only so much linguistic capacity available and therefore sharing it between two languages would lead to lower levels of proficiency in each compared to unilingual speakers. It can be seen in Figure 3 that as one of the bilingual's 'linguistic balloons' gets inflated, less room is left for the other. The second misconception is that the two 'balloons' or sets of linguistic abilities are separate. Therefore, stimulation of one implies that the other is not being stimulated and will consequently decline in relation to the language ability of unilingual speakers of that language.

Two examples illustrate how the 'common sense' assumptions of the SUP model get expressed at both a policy and classroom level. The first example is taken from Bethell's article (1979: 32-33), where he approvingly quotes Congressman John Ashbrook's opposition to bilingual education:

> The program is actually preventing children from learning English. Someday somebody is going to have to teach those young people to speak English or else they are going to become public charges. Our educational system is finding it increasingly difficult today to teach English-speaking children to read their own language. When children come out of the Spanish-language schools or Choctaw-language schools which call themselves bilingual, how is our educational system going to make them literate in what will still be a completely alien tongue ...?

The second example illustrates the way the SUP assumptions often operate subtly in school contexts. It is drawn from an ongoing study in which the psychological assessments of over 400 minority language children from a large urban school system in Canada are being analyzed (Cummins 1980b).

The case of Maria. Maria (not child's real name) was referred for psychological assessment by her first grade teacher, who noted that she has difficulty in all aspects of learning. Maria was given both speech and hearing and psychological assessments. The former assessment found that all structures and functions pertaining to speech were within normal limits and hearing was also normal. The findings were summarized as follows: 'Maria comes from an Italian home where Italian is spoken mainly. However, language skills appeared to be within normal limits for English.'

The psychologist's conclusions, however, were very different. On the Wechsler Preschool and Primary Scale of Intelligence (WPPSI), Maria obtained a verbal IQ of 89 (23rd percentile) and a performance IQ of 99 (47th percentile). The full-scale IQ was 93 (32nd percentile). The report to Maria's teacher read as follows:

Maria tended to be very slow to respond to questions, particularly if she were unsure of the answers. Her spoken English was a little hard to understand, which is probably due to poor English models at home (speech is within normal limits). Itialian is spoken almost exclusively at home, and *this will be further complicated* [emphasis added] by the coming arrival of an aunt and grandmother from Italy.

There is little doubt that Maria is a child of low average ability whose school progress is impeded by lack of practice in English. Encourage Maria's oral participation as much as possible, and try to involve Maria in extra-curricular activities where she will be with her English-speaking peers.

The implicit message to the teacher is clear: Maria's communication in L1 with parents and relatives detracts from her school performance, and the aim of the school program should be to expose Maria to as much L2 as possible in order to compensate for these deficient linguistic and cultural background experiences. There is absolutely no evidence either in the psychological assessment or in the literature (see, for example, Yee and LaForge 1974, Ramirez and Politzer 1976) to support these assumptions, yet they are communicated to the teacher as though they were 'scientifically' proven (e.g. 'There is little doubt ...').

In summary, the 'common sense' assumptions of the SUP model are widely believed at all levels of the educational hierarchy, despite the fact that they are patently false. Among the hundreds of evaluations of bilingual programs for both minority and majority language children carried out all over the world during the past 20 years, I know of none which provides any support for such a model. The pattern of results revealed in a large majority of these evaluations is one where there is a significant relationship between amount of instructional time through the minority language and achievement in the minority language, but no relationship between amount of instructional time through the majority language and achievement in that language. The main problem in the SUP model is that it focuses on the obvious differences between L1 and L2 in surface forms (phonology, syntax, lexicon) and ignores the more critical cognitive/academic language proficiency that underlies successful literacy development, whether instruction is in L1 or L2. Failure to take account of the common proficiency underlying literacy development in both L1 and L2 is also evident in the linguistic mismatch hypothesis which provides much of the rationale for transitional bilingual education.

The logic of transitional bilingual education. The failure of L2-only programs to promote L2 literacy skills effectively among some groups of minority language children was interpreted by many academics as support for the hypothesis that mismatch between the language of the home and the language of the school is a major cause of academic retardation among minority children (see Downing 1978, John and Horner 1971, UNESCO 1953, United States Commission on Civil Rights 1975). This 'linguistic mismatch' hypothesis is exemplified in the well-known UNESCO statement that 'it is axiomatic that the best medium for teaching a child is his mother tongue' (UNESCO 1953:11).

Linguistic mismatch. The linguistic mismatch hypothesis implies that in order to reverse minority children's school failure, initial instruction should be in the child's dominant language. The focus on initial mismatch gives rise to a transitional form of bilingual education in which children are switched to an L2-only program when they are assumed to have acquired sufficient L2 proficiency to benefit from instruction through that language.

As pointed out previously and by other investigators (Bowen 1977, Tucker 1977), the success of immersion programs suggests that the linguistic mismatch hypothesis provides a very insecure psychoeducational foundation upon which to construct the edifice of bilingual education. In terms of the dual-iceberg model (Figure 2), the mismatch hypothesis focuses on L1-L2 mismatch in terms of the 'visible' surface forms and either ignores the underlying conceptual proficiencies which are critical for learning to read (see, for example, Downing 1979), or else implicitly assumes that they are separate for each language. The immersion findings suggest that 'surface' linguistic mismatch becomes an important factor only when it is accompanied by mismatch between children's input CALP and the school program.[3] In summary, one of the basic psychoeducational assumptions of transitional bilingual education appears to have little validity as a general theoretical principle and shows an inadequate conceptualization both of the construct of 'language proficiency' and its cross-lingual dimensions.

Internal logic. The inconsistent internal logic of transitional bilingual education similarly points towards a poorly conceived program. On the one hand, it is assumed that bilingual instruction in the early grades will be more effective in raising the level of English proficiency of limited- or non-English proficient (LEP and NEP) students than instruction through the medium of English only. In other words, less time through the medium of English will result in greater development of the English language skills underlying literacy. In terms of Figure 3, the assumption is that inflating the L1 balloon will simultaneously succeed in inflating the L2 balloon to a greater extent than if attempts were made to inflate only the L2 balloon. In other words, in the initial grades the SUP model is rejected in favor of a Common Underlying Proficiency (CUP) model such as that illustrated in Figure 4.[4] In the CUP model, experience with either language can, theoretically, promote the development of the proficiency underlying both languages, given adequate motivation and exposure to both, either in school or wider environment.

Figure 4. The Common Underlying Proficiency (CUP) model of bilingualism.

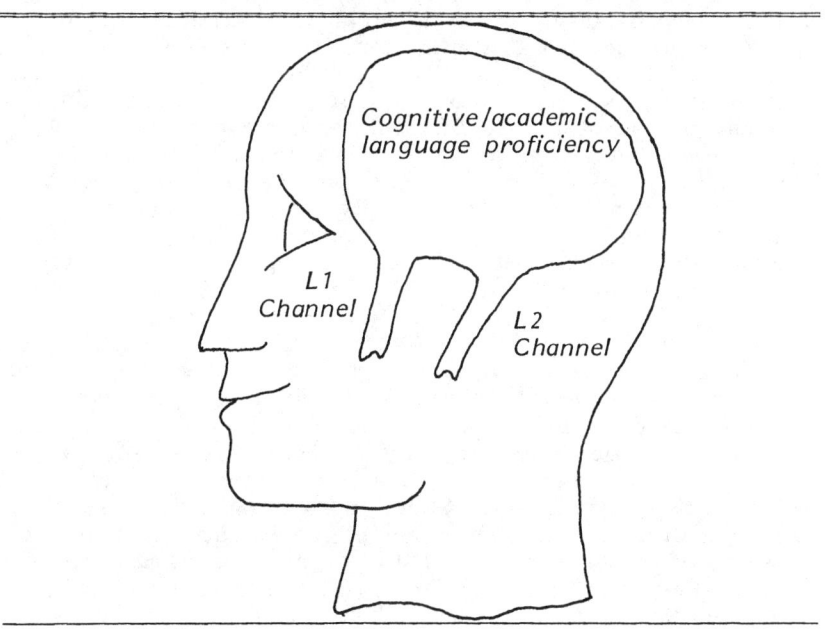

Within the context of the CUP model, transitional programs assume that because the L2 channel is initially restricted, instruction in the early grades should be through the L1 channel. However, as soon as the L2 channel has expanded sufficiently, all instruction should be given in English in order to promote fully the development of English proficiency by maximizing exposure to English instruction. In other words, despite the implicit endorsement of a CUP model in the early grades, transitional programs revert to a SUP model by assuming (without any evidence) that children's English skills will not develop adequately unless they are mainstreamed to an English-only program. If it were assumed that English skills would continue to develop adequately in a bilingual program, then there would be no psychoeducational justification for aborting the promotion of L1, especially in view of the considerable funds currently being expended in the United States on foreign language teaching (President's Commission 1979).[5]

The extent of the logical contradiction involved in the mainstreaming process can be seen in the fact that minority students in the early grades of transitional programs are expected to make so much progress in the cognitive/academic skills underlying English literacy that after two or three years they should be at a level where they can compete on an equal footing with their unilingual English-speaking peers who have had all their instruction in English. The findings reviewed in the present paper suggest that this basic 'less equals more' expectation is realistic; what is not realistic, however, is the time frame. The data suggest that 'equality' of academic potential and performance is not attained until the later grades of elementary school. Many minority students will be fluent in English prior to that time and may qualify to exit from a bilingual program on the basis of a 'natural communication' task such as the Bilingual Syntax Measure or the Basic Inventory of Natural Language. However, as emphasized earlier, fluency in English BICS does not necessarily imply commensurate proficiency in English CALP. The evidence reviewed in the next section suggests that rate of growth in English CALP in bilingual programs accelerates in the later grades of elementary school.

Cumulative benefits. A considerable body of recent evidence, again from both minority and majority situations, suggests that in its effort to avoid the taint of cultural pluralism, transitional bilingual education may also deny minority children the opportunity to reap the educational benefits of their bilingualism. As outlined earlier in this paper, there is no logical psychoeducational reason to assume that bilingual instruction will be any less effective in promoting the cognitive/academic proficiency underlying English literacy in the later grades of elementary school than it is assumed by transitional programs to be in the early grades. In fact, as Troike (1979) points out, several longitudinal evaluations (Gonzalez 1977, Leyba 1978, Rosier and Farella 1976) suggest that the full benefit of bilingual instruction may not become apparent until the fifth or sixth year of instruction. In these evaluations, students in the bilingual program reached national grade-level norms in English reading only in the fifth grade. As outlined earlier, the Sodertalje program for Finnish immigrant children in Sweden (Hanson 1979) showed a similar pattern of cumulative growth in L2 proficiency.

Several 'enrichment' bilingual programs for majority language children also show a trend for achievement gains in majority language literacy skills to become apparent in the later grades of elementary school. For example, students in French immersion programs in Ontario have consistently performed significantly better than comparison groups in aspects of English language skills in grades 5 and 6 (see Swain 1978). Recent findings from the longitudinal evaluation of a Ukrainian-English bilingual program[6] in Edmonton, Alberta, also show that the bilingual students in grade 5 perform significantly better than the comparison groups, despite 50 percent less instructional time through the medium of English. In previous grades no significant group differences were observed in English language skills (Edmonton Public School Board 1979).

These findings of cumulative advantages as a result of bilingual education are consistent with the 'threshold' hypothesis (Cummins 1979a) that there may be threshold levels of bilingual proficiency which bilingual children must attain both in order to avoid cognitive/academic deficits and to allow the potentially beneficial aspects of becoming bilingual to influence their cognitive/academic growth. The research findings reviewed in Cummins (1979a) suggest that cognitive/academic benefits accrue to students who reach a 'higher threshold' level of bilingual proficiency, i.e. high levels of proficiency in both languages. The fact that students in bilingual programs begin to pull ahead of comparison groups in the later grades of elementary school, when literary skills in both languages have become well established, is clearly consistent with the threshold hypothesis.

Conclusion. The failure of the Separate Underlying Proficiency model and of the linguistic mismatch hypothesis to account for the research findings, as well as the logical confusion in the rationale for transitional bilingual programs, derive from a failure to conceptualize adequately the nature of language proficiency underlying literacy skills. These theoretical approaches focus on obvious differences between languages in surface forms, while ignoring the common conceptual basis for the development of literacy skills in L1 and L2. The Common Underlying Proficiency model, on the other hand, is capable of accounting for the research findings from both majority and minority language bilingual situations because of its emphasis on the interdependence between the cognitive/academic language proficiencies underlying L1 and L2 literacy skills.

An immediate educational implication is that the entire mainstreaming endeavor in transitional bilingual programs is based on an a priori assumption that is not only inconsistent with the initial assumptions of transitional programs but is also contradicted by a mass of research evidence. Evaluations of bilingual programs involving both majority and minority language groups from many parts of the world show clearly that there is no educational support for the assumption that children should be switched to a majority language program in order to develop adequate literacy skills in the majority language. In fact, many longitudinal evaluations of bilingual programs show that the rate of growth in majority language literacy skills increases substantially in the later grades of elementary school, with the result that children in the bilingual program often perform better in majority language literacy skills than comparison groups of children in unilingual programs, despite considerably less instructional time through that language.

What should be the role of research in the present United States bilingual education context? The implication of the analysis in the present paper is that research should be directed towards clarifying the development of bilingual cognitive/academic proficiency rather than towards facilitating the implementation of a program which represents a compromise between faulty psychoeducational considerations (the linguistic mismatch hypothesis), on the one hand, and faulty sociopolitical considerations (the social fragmentation hypothesis) on the other. This compromise has given rise to the requirement that minority children be mainstreamed to English-only programs as soon as possible, a requirement that is not only subject to enormous practical difficulties, but is also logically inconsistent and directly contrary to the research evidence. Researchers engaged in developing entry and exit criteria for transitional programs should consider the fact that their findings may be used to ensure mediocrity of educational opportunity for minority children. The educational difficulties of minority children will be alleviated only when educators stop thinking in terms of the minimum adaptations of school systems required to provide equal educational opportunity and start thinking instead of optimizing educational opportunity by continuing to promote literacy skills in both L1 and L2. The psychoeducational basis for this type of program can be found in the Common Underlying Proficiency model of bilingualism, while resourceful administrators may be able to find both the necessary sociopolitical and financial support in the recommendations of the President's Commission on Foreign Language and International Studies (1979).

NOTES

Preparation of this paper was made possible by the financial support of the Multiculturalism Directorate of the Department of the Secretary of State, Ottawa.

1. Shuy's use of the iceberg metaphor is principally to illustrate the fact that the visible features of language which are assessed by most tests are not necessarily those that are most critical. He suggests that the less visible dimensions of semantic and functional meaning are critical for language functioning but are seldom assessed. The emphasis in the present paper is clearly different from Shuy's, but the two approaches are not necessarily contrary if CALP is viewed as one aspect of semantic and functional meaning.

2. My discussions of Macnamara's findings regarding the achievement in Irish (L2) of children in Irish immersion programs (Cummins 1977b, 1978) erred in accepting Macnamara's interpretation that differences in favor of the immersion group

were not educationally significant. In fact, the immersion group performs as well in Irish as native Irish speakers and significantly better than comparison groups of children in less intensive Irish programs. Macnamara's dismissal of these significant differences is based on the fact that supplementary analyses showed that instruction through Irish is not significantly related to achievement in Irish in areas where there is a greater amount of Irish used in the environment (the west of Ireland), although the relationship between Irish achievement and amount of instruction through Irish remains significant in areas where English is used almost exclusively outside school. This pattern of results is precisely what would be predicted on the basis of the present analysis of bilingual program evaluations.

3. It is beyond the scope of the present paper to consider the student input by educational treatment interactions that result in varying academic outcomes for minority language children. These have been considered in Cummins (1979a, 1980a). There appear to be complex interactions between sociocultural, psychoeducational, and school program variables in determining outcomes. However, there is no evidence, as assumed in the linguistic mismatch hypothesis, that minority children who are dominant in L2 should be educated through L2. This strategy ignores the 'cultural mismatch' variable and denies children the opportunity to develop a cognitively and academically beneficial form of bilingualism (see Cummins 1979a).

4. The CUP model illustrated in Figure 4 embodies the same assumptions as the 'dual-iceberg' model in Figure 2. The two illustrations, however, permit different aspects to be highlighted. Specifically, the dual-iceberg model illustrates the distinction between surface and underlying dimensions of language proficiency, whereas the CUP model allows the instructional component to be illustrated by means of the 'balloon inflation' metaphor.

5. Obviously, the main reasons for mainstreaming children out of bilingual programs are sociopolitical, but it is important to expose the psychoeducational contradictions in this policy since mainstreaming is often rationalized in psychoeducational terms.

REFERENCES

Bethell, T. 1979. Against bilingual education. Harper's, February.
Bowen, J. D. 1977. Linguistic perspectives on bilingual education. In: Frontiers of bilingual education. Edited by B. Spolsky and R. Cooper. Rowley, Mass.: Newbury House.
Burt, M., and H. Dulay. 1978. Some guidelines for the assessment of oral language proficiency and dominance. TESOL Quarterly 12.177-192.

Carey, S. T., and J. Cummins. 1979. English and French achievement of grade 5 children from English, French and mixed French-English home backgrounds attending the Edmonton Separate School System English-French immersion program. Report submitted to the Edmonton Separate School System, April.

Carroll, J. B., and S. M. Sapon. 1959. Modern language aptitude test. New York: Psychological Corporation.

Chomsky, N. 1965. Aspects of the theory of syntax. Cambridge, Mass.: The MIT Press.

Cohen, A. D., and M. Swain. 1976. Bilingual education: The immersion model in the North American context. TESOL Quarterly 10.45-53.

Cummins, J. 1977a. Immersion education in Ireland: A critical review of Macnamara's findings. Working Papers in Bilingualism, No. 13.

Cummins, J. 1977b. A comparison of reading achievement in Irish and English medium schools. In: Studies in reading. Edited by V. Greaney. Dublin: Educational Company of Ireland.

Cummins, J. 1978. Immersion programs: The Irish experience. International Review of Education 24.273-282.

Cummins, J. 1979a. Linguistic interdependence and the educational development of bilingual children. Review of Educational Research 49.222-251.

Cummins, J. 1979b. Cognitive/academic language proficiency, linguistic interdependence, the optimal age question and some other matters. Working Papers in Bilingualism, No. 19.

Cummins, J. 1980a. The language and culture issue in the education of minority language children. Interchange 10.72-88.

Cummins, J. 1980b. Psychological assessment of immigrant children: Logic or intuition? Journal of Multilingual and Multicultural Development, Vol. 1.

Cummins, J. 1980c. Age on arrival and immigrant second language learning: A reanalysis of the Ramsey and Wright data. Unpublished manuscript. Ontario Institute for Studies in Education.

Cummins, J. 1980d. The cross-lingual dimensions of language proficiency: Implications for bilingual education and the optimal age question. TESOL Quarterly 14.

Danoff, M. N. 1978. Evaluation of the impact of ESEA Title VII Spanish/English bilingual education program: Overview of study and findings. Palo Alto: American Institutes for Research.

Downing, J. 1978. Strategies of bilingual teaching. International Review of Education 24.329-346.

Downing, J. 1979. Cognitive clarity and linguistic awareness. Paper presented at the International Seminar on Linguistic Awareness and Learning to Read, Victoria, Canada.

Edmonton Public School Board. 1979. Evaluation of the bilingual (English-Ukrainian) program, fifth year. Research report.
Ekstrand, L. H. 1978. Bilingual and bicultural adaptation. Doctoral dissertation. University of Stockholm.
Engle, P. L. 1975. Language medium in early school years for minority language groups. Review of Educational Research 65.283-325.
Epstein, N. 1977. Language, ethnicity and the schools. Washington, D.C.: Institute for Educational Leadership.
Farhady, H. 1979. The disjuctive fallacy between discrete-point and integrative tests. TESOL Quarterly 13.347-358.
Fillmore, Lily Wong. 1979. Individual differences in second language acquisition. In: Individual differences in language behavior. Edited by C. J. Fillmore, D. Kempler, and W. S.-Y. Yang. New York: Academic Press.
Fishman, J. 1976. Bilingual education: What and why. In: English as a second language in bilingual education. Edited by J. E. Alatis and K. Twaddell. Washington, D.C.: TESOL.
Genesee, F. 1976. The role of intelligence in second language learning. Language Learning 26.267-280.
Genesee, F. 1978. Is there an optimal age for starting second language instruction? McGill Journal of Education 13.145-154.
Genesee, F. 1979. Acquisition of reading skills in immersion programs. Foreign Language Annals, February.
Gonzalez, G. A. 1977. Brownsville Independent School District Bilingual Education Program Title VII--Final Report for 1976-1977. Brownsville, Texas.
Goodman, K., Y. Goodman, and B. Flores. 1979. Reading in the bilingual classroom: Literacy and biliteracy. Rosslyn, Va.: National Clearinghouse for Bilingual Education.
Halliday, M. A. K. 1975. Learning how to mean. London: Edward Arnold.
Hanson, G. 1979. The position of the second generation of Finnish immigrants in Sweden: The importance of education in the home language to the welfare of second generation immigrants. Paper presented at symposium on the position of the second generation of Yugoslav immigrants in Sweden, Split, October.
Hébert, R., et al. 1976. Rendement académique et langue d'enseignement chez les éléves franco-manitobains. Saint-Boniface, Manitoba: Centre de recherches du College Universitaire de Saint-Boniface.
Hernández-Chávez, E., M. Burt, and H. Dulay. Language dominance and proficiency testing: Some general considerations. NABE Journal 3.41-54.
John, V. P., and V. M. Horner. 1971. Early childhood bilingual education project. Modern Language Association.

Kjolseth, R. 1972. Bilingual education in the United States: For assimilation or pluralism? In: The language education of minority children. Edited by B. Spolsky. Rowley, Mass.: Newbury House.

Krashen, S. 1978. The monitor model for second-language acquisition. In: Second-language acquisition and foreign language teaching. Edited by R. C. Gingras. Arlington, Va.: Center for Applied Linguistics.

Krashen, S. D., M. A. Long, and R. C. Scarcella. 1979. Age, rate and eventual attainment in second language acquisition. TESOL Quarterly 13.573-582.

Lambert, W. E., and G. R. Tucker. 1972. Bilingual education of children: The St. Lambert experiment. Rowley, Mass.: Newbury House.

Legaretta, D. 1979. The effects of program models on language acquisition by Spanish speaking children. TESOL Quarterly 13.521-534.

Leyba, C. F. 1978. Longitudinal Study Title VII Bilingual Program, Santa Fe Public Schools, Santa Fe, New Mexico. Los Angeles: National Dissemination and Assessment Center, California State University.

Macnamara, J. 1966. Bilingualism and primary education. Edinburgh: Edinburgh University Press.

Oller, J. W. 1978. The language factor in the evaluation of bilingual education. In: Georgetown University Round Table on Languages and Linguistics 1978. Edited by J. E. Alatis. Washington, D.C.: Georgetown University Press.

Oller, J. W. 1979. Language tests at school: A pragmatic approach. New York: Longmans.

Oller, J. W., and K. Perkins. 1978. Language in education: Testing the tests. Rowley, Mass.: Newbury House.

Olson, D. R. 1977. The formalization of linguistic rules. In: Language learning and thought. Edited by J. Macnamara. New York: Academic Press.

O'Malley, J. M. 1978. Review of the evaluation of the impact of ESEA Title VII Spanish/English bilingual education program. Bilingual Resources 1.6-10.

President's Commission on Foreign Language and International Studies. 1979. Strength through wisdom: A critique of U.S. capability. Washington, D.C.: U.S. Government Printing Office.

Ramirez, A. G., and R. L. Politzer. 1976. The acquisition of English and the maintenance of Spanish in a bilingual education program. In: English as a second language in bilingual education. Edited by J. E. Alatis and K. Twaddell. Washington, D.C.: TESOL.

Rosier, P., and M. Farella. 1976. Bilingual education at Rock Point--Some early results. TESOL Quarterly 10.379-388.

Ryan, E. B., and G. W. Ledger. 1979. Children's awareness of sentence grammaticality. Paper presented to the Annual Meeting of the Psychonomic Society, Phoenix, Arizona.
Shuy, R. W. 1976. Problems in assessing language ability in bilingual education programs. Mimeo.
Singer, H. 1977. IQ is and is not related to reading. In: Issues in evaluating reading. Edited by S. F. Wanat. Arlington, Va.: Center for Applied Linguistics.
Skutnabb-Kangas, T., and P. Toukomaa. 1976. Teaching migrant children's mother tongue and learning the language of the host country in the context of the sociocultural situation of the migrant family. Helsinki: Finnish National Commission for UNESCO.
Smith, F. 1971. Understanding reading. New York: Holt, Rinehart and Winston.
Spolsky, B., and R. L. Cooper. 1978. Case studies in bilingual education. Rowley, Mass.: Newbury House.
Strang, R. 1945. Variability in reading scores on a given level of intelligence test scores. Journal of Educational Research 38.440-446.
Swain, M. 1978. French immersion: Early, late or partial? The Canadian Modern Language Review 34.577-586.
Swain, M. 1979. Bilingual education: Research and its implications. In: On TESOL '79: The learner in focus. Washington, D.C.: TESOL.
Troike, R. 1978. Research evidence for the effectiveness of bilingual education. NABE Journal 3.13-24.
Troike, R. 1979. Research findings demonstrate the effectiveness of bilingual education. Institute for Cultural Pluralism Newsletter 1.6-7.
Tucker, G. R. 1977. The linguistic perspective. In: Bilingual education: Current perspectives, Vol. 2, Linguistics. Arlington, Va.: Center for Applied Linguistics.
UNESCO. 1953. The use of vernacular languages in education. Monographs on fundamental education.
United States Commission on Civil Rights. 1975. A better chance to learn: Bilingual-bicultural education. Clearinghouse Publication 51, May.
Vernon, M. D. 1971. Reading and its difficulties. London: Cambridge University Press.
Wells, C. G. 1979. Influences of the home on language development. Bristol Working Papers on Language.
Yee, L. Y., and R. La Forge. 1974. Relationship between mental abilities, social class, and exposure to English in Chinese fourth graders. Journal of Educational Psychology 66.826-834.

A LANGUAGE FACTOR DEEPER THAN SPEECH: MORE DATA AND THEORY FOR BILINGUAL ASSESSMENT

John W. Oller, Jr.
University of New Mexico

Imagine walking into a classroom and overhearing students reciting lists of numbers. Other students are busy copying numbers, and still others are transforming lists--e.g. reciting them in reverse order--and so forth. Suppose then that someone resembling a teacher approaches and you ask, 'What are these students doing?' The person in authority responds, 'They are studying arithmetic. Some of them are preparing for an arithmetic test, and others are being tested.' Would you believe the teacher? Would you agree that reciting numbers is the same as studying arithmetic? Would you accept such practices as tests of arithmetic?

Now imagine a different scene. This time the students in the classroom are reciting phrases, sentences, requests, denials, apologies, and the like. In the first case we heard students saying things like, 'eight eight three one five seven three, five six two six three one seven two one', and so on. In this instance we hear, 'Is the secretary busy? Is the alphabet important? Is the doctor available?' There are also, of course, variations on these items. For instance, we also hear, 'The secretary is not busy. The alphabet is not important. The doctor is not available.' Another student is saying, 'The secretary is busy. The secretary was busy. The secretary used to be busy.' Of course, there are many other variations, and some of the students--apparently those who are more advanced--are also reading and writing the various utterance forms. Again you ask the teacher what the students are doing. He responds that they are studying language. Because the utterances are in English, he says it is English they are studying. But he is quick to point out that some of them are taking tests in English. The others are preparing themselves for the same tests.

Isn't it interesting that we are apt to regard the recitation of numbers as an extraordinarily ridiculous way to practice, or teach, or test arithmetic, while many language teachers regard the recitation of lists of utterances as a valid method of practicing, teaching, and testing language skill? Hardly anyone would agree that a detailed analysis of the sounds associated with numbers, or the syllable strings that constitute a given exemplar (consider the syllables of *seven* and *eleven*, for instance), are a very important part of the theory of numbers, yet many linguisticians and testing specialists give the very strong impression that the sounds and syllables of words are somehow a faithful reflection of the heart and soul of language. Most of us would be singularly unimpressed if the arithmetic teacher in the example given were to defend the recitation of a number like *eight eight three one five seven three* by pointing out that it is the sum of 'two two two one four five zero and six six one zero one two three'. We would probably remain unconvinced if the teacher pointed out that this number could be used to illustrate the null transformation by subtracting it from itself, or the unity transformation by dividing it by itself, or the identity transformation by multiplying it by one, and so forth. The mere fact that a great deal of arithmetic can be done with any number does not make repeated recitation of the number into an arithmetic curriculum or test. We see arithmetic as requiring something deeper than the mouthing of the surface forms of numbers--regardless of whether they are short or long.

Oddly, however, language educators are apt to defend the recitation or other manipulations of the surface forms of language more vigorously. They are apt to argue that merely mouthing words of a language is much closer to language use than the recitation of numbers is to arithmetic. Such mouthings are apt to be defended as the foundational method for practicing, teaching, or testing language skill. Nowadays, for instance, it is popular to teach students to apologize in many different ways. One is apt to hear students saying such things as, 'I'm sorry', 'I'm very sorry', 'Oh how stupid of me. I'm so very sorry'. And so on. The list of possible apologies is being explored these days with much the same fervor that linguists once had for phonemes, morphemes, and syntactic patterns. Although the latter have not completely lost their appeal to language curriculum writers and test specialists, they have in part given way to lists of larger units of speech-- so-called 'speech acts' and the like. Where students used to learn to discriminate phonemes, they are now engaged in large measure in discriminating between degrees of politeness in refusing an invitation, denying an assertion, and so on. The level of analysis in the theories has been shifted to encompass broader stretches of speech, but the taxonomic listing approach still remains.

Creative pedagogues and theoreticians will defend the listing method by pointing out that you have to have building blocks before you can erect the imposing edifices of discourse. An old bromide still common is the statement that 'mechanical manipulation must precede communicative use', and many a classroom teacher will still insist that 'you have to know the elements before you can put them together in meaningful ways'. While the linguisticians and their proselytes are defending various lists, sublists, and inventories, the reading specialists are similarly defending a taxonomic approach to reading.
Early on, readers are supposed to acquire a list of graphophonemic correspondences which is thinly camouflaged in such nonsensical discourse as, 'The man ran. Dan can fan the man. The ram ran.'[1] Or, the reading curriculum writer may appeal to a more transformational approach by using all possible permutations of a greeting or some other speech form in order to illustrate certain syntactic patterns while sticking with a limited repertoire of lexical items. In one primer, for instance, one encounters such forms as, 'Good morning, Bing. Good morning, Sandy. Good morning, Sun. Bing runs. Sandy runs. Bing and Sandy run. Bing chases Sandy. Sandy chases Bing.'[2] In the series in question there would be no reason for surprise over forms like, 'Bing and Sandy chase the sun. The sun chases Bing and Sandy.' Since Bing is a dog and Sandy is a cat, and since both of them behave in remarkably peculiar ways, there is no reason for the sun to behave normally.

Of course, the reading specialists and the linguisticians, most of whom consider themselves ever so much better than any number of speech therapists, will be quick to defend their methods of language instruction by pointing out that the apparently meaningless strings of disconnected phrases, sentences, or nonsensical discourses can all be used in meaningful ways. If, for example, Bing and Sandy were pilots in a supersonic aircraft, they might indeed chase the sun if they started out at dusk and travelled west. Or, they might be chased by the sun if they started at dawn and travelled in the same direction. There are even potential occasions when a silly question like, 'Is the alphabet important?' might be construed in a sensible way. It may require a severe exercise of the imagination to supply meaning to a very long list of unrelated words, phrases, sentences, or speech acts, but it can be done in much the same manner that we are able to associate arithmetic operations with any number or list of numbers. Unfortunately, by similar logic it would be possible to defend a list of articles of clothing and diet as a theory of culture. It would be possible to argue that exterior paint is equivalent to architecture and that everything worth knowing about truth and justice can be learned from a study of hair styles.

We might refer to the speech oriented approach to language learning, teaching and testing as the 'superficial theory', or the 'listing method'. It implies and presupposes that language

A Language Factor Deeper than Speech

use is little more than the mouthing of utterances. It suggests that practice in mouthing utterances will produce skill in language use, and further, that this skill can be broken down into multiple lists or inventories of elements. The curriculum can then teach the lists of elements (phonemes, morphemes, words, phrases, syntactic patterns, speech acts, functions, notions, etc.) in various modalities (listening, speaking, reading, and writing, or receptive versus productive, or oral versus written) and the tests can assess the elements on the various lists in similarly differentiated modalities. If phoneme discrimination is really different from morpheme use (or 'functor' use, as some might prefer to call it), then this should presumably be reflected in the curriculum and testing. If word knowledge is really different from knowledge of grammar, then this should similarly be reflected in the curriculum and in the tests. If reading and writing are really different in some fundamental sense from listening and speaking, then this too should be reflected in curriculum and tests. In fact, every valid distinction between the various inventories of elements, skills, and whatever else the grand inventory of inventories requires, should be embodied in some manner in the curriculum and in the tests. From the vantage point of the analytically inclined, especially those who fit into the category of what I have been calling 'linguisticians', all of this should be sounding more and more reasonable. (For a paradigm example of this approach in action, see the remarkable paper by Rosenbaum in this volume.) If we can make hundreds of distinctions, why settle for only a few dozen? If it is possible to make thousands, why settle for only hundreds? Why not be as explicit in our analysis as possible? Why not get right down to the very finest grained sort of analytical diagnostic teaching and testing that can possibly be done?

Indeed, what other approach is there? We certainly must teach the phonemes, the morphemes, the lexical items, the syntactic patterns, the speech acts, and no doubt many other inventories of elements as well. How can this be accomplished? All of these inventories of elements must be tested too. How can this be done? How can we be certain that we are covering the necessary elements and representing them in reasonable proportions on our tests and in our curricula? I believe that what we require is an approach that is radically at odds with the traditional analytical method--what we called above the 'superficial method'. I believe that sound theoretical consideration would lead us to conclude that language is deeper than speech. The essence of language is deeper than the modality of processing. The heart and soul of language are not to be found in its surface form or its outward manifestations any more than the true personality of an individual can be gauged by an examination of skin, hair color, or clothing. The identity of a person is not to be found in the clothing that he wears. Neither is the essence of language to be found in the

surface form of utterances. A person may change clothes and
remain the same individual--in fact, a person who refused to
ever change clothes might be considered to have lost his senses
and the most important part of his identity in the process. In
the same way surface manifestation may change and the essence
of language use may remain the same. We may speak of an
event, or listen to talk about it, or read about or write about
it without altering the content of the discourse. We may speak
briefly or extensively without changing the nature of what is
talked about or the essence of the message communicated. Surface form is important only as a slave to meaning. Otherwise,
it is quite insignificant--literally without significance. It matters
very little whether a message is received over the telephone,
while sitting at home in one's living room, at the office, riding
on a bus, or in a letter, by telegram, orally, or written; what
matters is the meaning of the message as it relates to the stream
of experience. What is it about? Who is it from? Why was it
sent? What were the antecedent conversations or previous
interactions to which it relates? What consequences are likely
to follow from it? In short, what does it mean?

The mind naturally recoils at the suggestion that recitation
of numbers is a valid method of learning, teaching, or testing
arithmetic. Our reaction to the recitation of lists of disjointed,
unrelated, meaningless drivel in language classrooms should be
no less intense. As Piaget (1947) pointed out concerning
arithmetic, in his excellent treatise on human intelligence, reciting correct answers is not the same as solving the problems.
In the same way, acts such as mouthing utterances, or putting
them down on paper, or converting marks on paper into utterance forms, do not constitute language use. Even if long lists
of phonemic contrasts, morphemic manipulations, syntactic patterns, and speech acts could be efficiently internalized, they
would no more resemble normal language use than long lists of
numbers would resemble common uses of arithmetic. Lists
simply do not have the precedents, presuppositions, implications, consequences, truth-value, and meanings that are characteristic of the fabric of normal communication. Normal language
use is deeper, wider, richer, and more meaningful in every
sense of the term than lists of surface elements, no matter how
broad their scope. We can see immediately that lists of phonemes, morphemes, words, phrases, and sentences are less
meaningful than typical discourse, but it takes a little more
insight to see that the same must be said of lists of multiple
ways to apologize, or take one's leave, or make a request,
etc. Therefore, wouldn't it make good theoretical sense to
concentrate on meaningful language use in all aspects of testing
and assessment as well as curriculum design and instruction?
Why use meaningless disconnected lists of any sort of surface
structures?

It appears that a very strong argument can be offered from
a purely theoretical point of view in favor of meaningful

discourse and against meaningless lists of surface forms. However, some will want to argue that careful research into first and second language acquisition will not support the use of meaningful discourse from the first stages of language learning and teaching. They will contend that it is necessary to begin with meaningless elements and later make a transition to discourse. After all, isn't this the way children operate in learning their first language? Surprisingly, as far as the surface oriented theories are concerned, children even in the earliest stages of babbling do not apparently attend exclusively to surface form. Even the cry of the neonate is filled with presuppositional meaning and implication. For one thing, there is the presupposition that mother will respond. There is the moral implication of an obligation to do so. Some adults deny this implication, but that does not erase the fact that such an implication exists and demands attention on the part of adult society. The point here, however, is not to make a case for any particular presupposition or implication, but to argue that the earliest communications of infants have propositional significances and values.

Unlike the meaningless sentences of so many educational exercises in language classrooms and elsewhere, the utterances of infants have pragmatic connections to the events of experience. They are not like the meaningless transformations of so many language classrooms these days, where students say things like, 'John is a boy. Is John a boy? John is not a boy? John is a boy, isn't he? John isn't a boy, is he?'; where it makes no difference whether John even exists and if he does exist, he cannot meet all of the requirements of the utterances about him.[3] Contrast the typical curricular nonsense with the sorts of things that young children actually say or with the sorts of things that constitute normal discourse, and an enormous difference is soon apparent. Walker (of Hart, Walker, and Gray 1977, and other publications) has observed that the actual speech of children before five years of age bears a closer resemblance to the prose found in newspapers and periodicals for the home than it does to the language used in readers for the primary grades. Similar criticisms could be levelled at much of the material used for second language instruction worldwide, but especially in so-called foreign language classrooms. A great deal of what the student is exposed to simply lacks any pragmatic motivation. Compare sentences like, 'The alphabet is important. The doctor is available. The soup is ready.' with the sort of things a three-year-old is apt to say.

Take a couple of homey examples. One of my little nieces recently astounded her Uncle Rico with the following remarks. It seems she was quarrelling with her seven-year-old brother and had passed well beyond the bounds of reason. When the hulk--otherwise known as Rico--intervened, she defended herself with the remark, 'I wad jus' twying to assewt my wiw,

Unca Wico.' On another occasion, in a similar discussion with her eight-year-old sister, Cori, the same three-year-old asserted, 'But Cowi, my heawt is in the wight pwace.' Or consider one further example from seven-year-old Evan. First, it is necessary to understand that he is the sort of kid who wears glasses, is small for his age, and enjoys reading more than football. He told his grandmother after a romp in the cow pasture one day, 'You know, Grandma, it sure makes ya feel good to be able to scare something as powerful as a cow!'

Perhaps the most important aspect of real utterances generated in normal discourse is that they are temporally related to experience. They presuppose certain meaningful antecedents and imply certain meaningful consequences. In a question like, 'Is the alphabet important?', we haven't a ghost of a notion what alphabet is being discussed because the existence of any particular alphabet was quite irrelevant to the author of the widely used English series from which this example comes. On the other hand, when Evan says it made him feel good to scare a cow, he has a particular experience in mind. He is fully cognizant of the fact that his own forty-odd pounds is hardly a match for the ponderous weight of a Hereford heifer. There is a big difference between saying something that has some true connection to experience and merely mouthing words that are not relatable to experience in any determinate way (especially if you are not already a native speaker of the language in question). Even the presuppositions and implications of the utterances of genuine discourse can be said to have truth value. This sort of meaning not only does not, but cannot exist when the utterances in question are not and never have been associated with any particular meaningful experience. For instance, what presuppositions and implications can be drawn from a list of statements which are immediately followed by their negative transforms? Or by questions to which the answers have already been given? Under what sort of conceivable circumstances can alphabets be important, doctors available, secretaries busy, soup ready, John correct, and so forth? Before you arrive at page two, the curriculum becomes impossible to visualize in a meaningful frame of experience.

There are remarkable properties in discourse that are not to be found in surface forms cut loose from their moorings in experience. Consider another example. This one comes from a talk at the University of New Mexico given by William Labov some time ago. Probably the details of the story have been changed somewhat, but this is itself instructive of the structure and nature of discourse. It seems that Labov asked a certain longshoreman up in Maine to tell him about some incident where the fellow had nearly been shaded out of the picture. The man proceeded to relate an incident in a bar. He and his friends were seated at a table when another man and a woman entered. As well as I can remember, the story told in the words of the longshoreman went roughly as follows.

'So this woman, she was comin' on to me. She smiles at me
and I smile back. But this fella she was with, he didn't like
it, and he comes over to me kinda threatin' like. Me, I wasn't
worried. My friends was all there. So I reached out and give
him a little shove. Next thing I know, I'm lookin' up at the
ceiling, and this friend, he's bendin' over me sayin', "Don't
move your head. Your throat's been cut"'. Labov said that
he had video-taped audiences where he told this story and
when he gets to the part about the throat, nary a head moves.
It seems that people get into the story to the point that they
can practically feel the warm red liquid running down their
own necks.

Perhaps the most salient feature of the discourse in question
is its progressive movement. There is a meaningful sequence
from one point to the next. Because of this connectedness, it
is possible to make inferences regarding things that are not
stated overtly in the discourse. For instance, we know that
the man who cut the longshoreman's throat was the same one
he reached out to push away. Further, we may have some
very vivid impressions about the look and smell of the bar-
room, even though no description of it was offered. We may
assume that the man whose throat was cut was shortly taken
to a hospital and patched up. We know in any case that he
lived to tell the tale. Because of what we know about the work
of longshoremen, we may infer a great deal about the look and
manner of the man who was injured and the friend who told
him not to move his head. We may also infer that the man who
was handy with the blade probably didn't look too imposing,
and a great deal else. In fact, a vast depth of knowledge can
be brought to bear on the interpretation of a discourse that
relates to genuine experience--a repertoire that is utterly useless when it comes to lists of disconnected, unrelated strings
of sentences, apologies, or whatever.

We can also do certain things with discourse that it is impossible to do with nonsense. For instance, we can summarize
it, e.g. a longshoreman told Labov about an occasion where he
was nearly killed. We can expand it, as we were doing above.
We can understand talk about it, participate in talk about it,
read about it, or write about it. We can answer questions
about it, and dramatize the events of the discourse. And, of
course, we have not yet begun to exhaust the possibilities--we
have scarcely scratched the surface. Yet in all of this we have
already gone far beyond what could be done with nonsense.
Consider the fact that there is no logical answer to a question
out of the blue such as, 'Is the alphabet important?' or 'Is the
doctor available?', while questions like, 'Why wasn't the longshoreman worried?' suggest a host of genuine possibilities.
The difference is that the utterances of real discourse are related to experience in meaningful ways, whereas nonsense is
not. To cut utterances loose from experience is to destroy
the better part of the linguistic enterprise. It is similar to

cutting the answers to arithmetic problems loose from the
problems. A list of answers is relatively meaningless apart
from the problems and the computations that led to them.
Similarly, a list of sentences is by itself meaningless. On the
other hand, if the sentences are meaningfully related to experience in known ways, they acquire properties that speech
alone does not have. Understanding discourse must be viewed
as a process of relating utterances to experience. There is
no such thing as understanding utterances in isolation from
experience. What little meaning can be associated with inanities like, 'Is the alphabet important?' has to do with what we
know about alphabets and what it is for something to be important. Producing discourse, or participating in it, is also
a process of relating utterances or surrogates of them to experience. The principal thing in all of the mental activity is
not the surface form of speech, but the propositional logic,
the meaning that motivates speech (or signing or whatever
other manifestation language assumes) and endows it with
significance.

The die-hard discrete point teacher and tester will assert at
this point that we still must attend to features, phonemes, morphemes, lexicon, surface syntax, and all the rest. This is
true, but does it not make a great deal of sense to do so within
the context of meaningful discourse rather than lists of meaningless utterances? Instead of having learners (or examinees)
merely mouth or write down representations of mouthings of
utterances, would it not make good theoretical sense to have
them work with texts where every utterance is tied to a meaningful experience in a discoverable way? For instance, consider the difference between the assertion, *The man got his
throat cut*, versus *The secretary is not busy*. In the first
case, there is an event or a factual state of affairs which is
referred to; in the other, there is neither secretary nor business, nor the lack of it. What I am saying is that it makes
no sense to practice using nonsensical utterance forms when
the possible connections to experience are only obscured by
the nature of the exercise. All of the elements of speech have
their being and their true significance in genuine acts of communication, whether it be mere phatic communion or content
oriented interaction. All of them can be taught and tested
within the context of discourse. Further, there are excellent
reasons to suppose that this can be done far more efficiently
if discourse is used, and there is no reason to suppose that it
can be accomplished at all with the surface oriented methods of
discrete point practitioners.

What I am leading up to is the inferential conclusion that
there are good reasons to suppose that the ability to comprehend and produce discourse in a language may be a relatively
indivisible faculty. Consider in this regard where the ability
to discriminate phonemes comes into play in interpreting the
text about the longshoreman. What about the ability to use

functors? morpheme knowledge in general? syntactic skill? sociolinguistic competence? pragmatic competence? intelligence? What about listening comprehension? speaking ability? reading ability? writing ability? Isn't it at least possible that the mental operations necessary to the interpretation of discourse or its production may be relatively unitary in nature and far deeper and more important than the superficial modality of processing or the analytical categories associated with the surface forms of speech? On this score, we know that certain meanings which surface in one language in word order or in morphology, may appear in another in the lexicon or in the paralinguistic domain. It seems plausible at least to suggest that we might expect to find a powerful language factor that is deeper than speech and which is largely impervious to changes in processing modality. This proposal is not new (see Oller 1977; Oller and Perkins 1978, 1980; and Oller 1979), but it has not been received everywhere with unbridled enthusiasm.

Many theorists (see Cummins, this volume, and his references) expect to find multiple factors of language proficiency. For years it was supposed that there would be clearly distinct variances associated with the traditionally posited components of phonology, lexicon, and grammar (to name only three), and the traditionally recognized skills of listening, speaking, reading, and writing. More recently, Cummins, for one, has proposed a distinction between what he sees as a general factor of ability to comprehend and participate in academic discourse and another general factor of communicative competence which would extend beyond the academic context. The latter he believes to be common to all normal human beings, whereas the former is cultivated and learned. Swain and Canale, on the other hand, see communicative competence as divisible into multiple subcomponents. Their model is too elaborate to go into in any detail, but it calls for separable components of sociolinguistic and pragmatic competence, each of which is also distinct (in the model) from linguistic competence.[4] Many other theories could be mentioned in this regard, but ultimately we must get beyond the hunches, opinions, and theories, and attempt to determine by appropriate empirical methods what the facts are. It seems to me rather appalling that so many people in our field are willing to decide the nature of language proficiency by a poll of the experts instead of by appeal to empirical findings. Altogether too many papers on this and related topics simply end up by offering a kind of smorgasbord of opinions which are about as relevant to the issues as opinions on the value of pi are to mathematics.

What then does the research show? At present there seem to be two live options. Either a single general factor of language proficiency exists which exhausts all of the reliable variance in all sorts of language processing tasks, or a general factor exists which exhausts most of the reliable variance in all of the tests that have been studied. The claim that multiple unrelated components exist has long since been ruled out. The important remaining question is whether there is any specific variance (i.e. variance that is unique and reliable) which is associated with particular modalities of processing or with particular components of proficiency. The empirical problem can be viewed as one of correlation. If tests aimed at a certain construct (e.g. skill or component) are correlated with each other and with tests aimed at some distinct construct (or constructs), the correlations of tests aimed at the same construct should exceed the correlations of tests aimed at different constructs. That is, arithmetic tests should correlate more strongly with each other than with reading tests, and so forth for all possible constructs. On the other hand, if the reading tests and the arithmetic tests correlate as strongly across categories as within, we must assume that there is something wrong either with the tests or with the theories of the constructs the tests are supposed to be measuring. There are many complications of this theme of test validation, but all of them rely ultimately on the basic statistical method of correlation. Methods of multiple regression, principal components analysis, classical factoring, and many other complications may be employed, but ultimately the requirement is still the same: tests aimed at the same construct should correlate more strongly with each other than tests aimed at different constructs (other things being equal).

Are there multiple factors of language proficiency? Is language proficiency clearly distinct from what has been called nonverbal proficiency? Educators and language testers have almost universally assumed positive answers to both of these questions and to many similar questions. Unfortunately, the research has not universally borne out these assumptions. In fact, it has nearly universally disputed them. Regarding the possibility of multiple factors of language proficiency, we might expect to find some variance in listening and speaking tasks that will not be present in reading and writing tasks. The research shows to the contrary that the major part of the variance in listening and speaking tasks is also present in reading and writing tasks and vice versa. For instance, see the papers by Oller and Hinofotis, Scholz et al., Hisama, Hendricks et al., and Kaczmarek in Oller and Perkins (1980). The empirical findings consistently support the argument for a rather unitary general factor which exhausts all or nearly all of the reliable variance in all of the tasks so far investigated. Regarding the possibility of distinguishing language proficiency from 'nonverbal' intelligence, see the paper with Chesarek in Streiff and Oller (in press). Also see the paper by Flahive in Oller and Perkins (1980). Again the results show rather clearly that nonverbal intelligence tasks generate variances that are largely coincident with the variances generated by so-called 'verbal' tasks. One of the types of tests often associated with a 'nonverbal' factor, at least in theory, is the sort of arithmetic test found in the California Achievement Test battery. However, Streiff showed recently in a replication of an earlier study in northern Arizona that even the computation score on the CAT battery was nearly perfectly correlated (within the limits of its reliability) with a general factor of language proficiency. A cloze test in a written format correlated with that factor at .95, while the computation subscore from the CAT correlated with the same factor at .90 (see Streiff and Oller in press).

Examples already available in the testing literature could be cited much more extensively. However, rather than refer to a much longer list of previously published studies, it may be useful to turn to a consideration of research recently completed at Resource Development Institute in Austin, Texas. An extensive description of the testing done and the motivation for it is available from RDI (Scott 1979), so the tests and populations sampled are described only briefly here. In the third field trial, a sample of 573 subjects were tested. All were adults who were potential recipients of social services provided in one form or another by the United States Department of Health, Education, and Welfare. More than four-fifths of the examinees tested were from a minority background where the primary language was Spanish, Vietnamese, Chinese, or a Native American language. The rest were native speakers of English, but from socioeconomic levels roughly comparable to those of the subjects from non-English, minority backgrounds. The purpose of the RDI project was to devise an English language test that would discriminate well between natives and nonnatives and that would serve to help calibrate the various points on the scale of responses to the language question on the 1980 U.S. Census. More specifically, the government wanted to know the meaning of points on the language scale in relation to social services provided by DHEW. For instance, if a person says he does not speak English very well (i.e. answers 'not very well' to the Census question, 'How well do you speak English?'), what is the likelihood that such a person would be denied benefits normally provided by DHEW agencies?

By the time the third field trial came around, RDI staff had narrowed their battery of tests to a total of 80 items. Early in the discussions they had decided to opt for pragmatic tests rather than discrete point tests, but an attempt was made nonetheless to differentiate four categories of language processing tasks. First, there were two tests where the difficulty was focused almost entirely in listening comprehension. One of these was a task that required examinees to respond to certain imperatives, and the other required them to indicate whether two statements had the same or different meanings. Second, there were two tasks that required listening and speaking--a repetition task and a question-answer task. Third, there were two tasks requiring reading comprehension--a multiple choice reading test and a multiple choice cloze test. Fourth, there were two tasks which required both reading and writing--a questionnaire in a written format, and a standard cloze test. In each case items were related to a sequential text wherever possible and in all cases there were multiple instances of cross-clause discourse level constraints which limited the range of possible responses. As a validity check, four additional scores were obtained. A trained linguist interviewed each subject and assigned a rating of speaking ability on a Likert-type scale. Subjects were also asked to rate their own abilities in speaking, reading, and writing on similar scales. Since there were multiple measures aimed at a plurality of possible constructs, one might expect the various scores to sort out into several factors. For example, there might be separate factors of oracy and literacy, or of receptive versus productive skills, and the like.

To test the possibility that a single general factor might explain the lion's share of variance in all 12 scores, a principal components analysis was run with unities on the diagonal of the 12 x 12 correlation matrix. The results of this analysis are given in Table 1.

Table 1. A principal components analysis over 12 English language proficiency tests (N = 573).

Tests	Loading on g	h^2
Imperatives	.89	.79
Paraphrase recognition	.87	.76
Repetition	.89	.80
Oral question and answer	.79	.62
Multiple choice reading	.92	.85
Multiple choice cloze	.93	.87
Written questionnaire	.86	.74
Standard cloze	.90	.81
Expert rating of speaking	.90	.80
Self rating of speaking	.83	.68
Self rating of reading	.81	.66
Self rating of writing	.79	.63

A single general factor accounts for the vast majority of reliable variance in every single test. There can be little doubt that there exists a large and powerful language factor underlying performance on all of the diverse tasks employed. There is no evidence that the constructs of receptive versus productive skill, or oracy versus literacy, can be distinguished. To a very great extent we may say that all of the tests are measuring the same thing. It is doubtful, in fact, that any subset is measuring anything that some other subset cannot measure. On the average, 75 percent of the total variance generated by each test is attributable to a single general factor. The smallest amount of variance shared with that factor by any test was 62 percent and the largest was 85 percent.

Critics might argue that the results just reported are due to the rather wide range of variability in skills of the tested subjects. They might very well contend that if the range of variability were restricted, the general factor would dissipate and multiple uncorrelated factors would remain. Because of the fact that the original raw data was not available for further analysis, it was not possible to refute the just mentioned criticism directly with the RDI data. However, many studies with multiple measures of language proficiency have been done with more restricted ranges of proficiency in the subjects tested. (See the studies I have cited from Oller and Perkins 1980, for instance.) Nevertheless, to show that the hypothetical criticism just posed is, in fact, not generally correct, I consider here one further study by Caulfield and Smith (in press). They used a highly restricted range of proficiencies by taking a sample of Spanish students at the secondary level. Since all 28 of their subjects were drawn from a single class at the advanced intermediate level, there is no reason to suppose that the variability of the sample was in any way artificially inflated. To the contrary, one might well argue that it was, in fact, artificially depressed.

Caufield and Smith used seven tests: a standard cloze test, a Spolsky type noise test, the four subscores in listening, speaking, reading, and writing from the Modern Language Association tests, and an oral interview. A principal components analysis of their 7 x 7 correlation matrix with unities on the diagonal is given in Table 2.

Table 2. A principal components analysis over seven foreign language proficiency tests for a sample of subjects with a restricted range of proficiencies (N = 28).

Tests	Loadings on g	h^2
Cloze test	.92	.85
Noise test	.94	.89
MLA listening	.81	.66
MLA speaking	.90	.80
MLA reading	.90	.80
MLA writing	.95	.90
Oral interview	.86	.75

Again the results clearly sustain the hypothesis that there is indeed a very large and powerful factor of language proficiency which underlies all of the tests. On the average, 81 percent of the total variance in the input test scores is attributable to a single factor. The smallest amount of variance that any test shared with that factor was 66 percent and the largest amount was 90 percent. The picture is not very different here from the case of the more varied population of ESL/EFL subjects. There is again no evidence of separable factors associable with distinct constructs.

Allowing the possibility that it may still be possible later on to show small amounts of reliable variance attributable to separable constructs, is there anything now that can be recommended to practitioners in language education, especially bilingual education? Laying aside the controversies concerning the small amounts of reliable variance in language tests and in other educational and psychological tests still to be accounted for, some practical recommendations can be made based on present findings. For one, we should be generally aware of the fact that there is a language factor deeper than speech which pervades every kind of educational or psychological test that has been investigated so far (and this includes a surprisingly large and diverse array of tests). We should steadfastly resist the authoritarian or democratic elitist approaches to test design that appeal to the opinions of well-known personages in the profession. We must insist on the application of appropriate empirical tests to the tests themselves. No amount of expert eye-balling and no magic number of meetings with advisory committees (no matter how impressive their credentials nor how fluent they may be in multiculturalism and test jargon) will supplant the need for careful empirical research. At the moment, the following recommendations seem to be well supported by the requisite type of research: (1) Tests should be based as much as possible on meaningful language processing tasks under normal temporal constraints. (2) Discourse appears to be a better basis for test material, in general, than are lists of utterance elements (including those at the level of speech acts). (3) Deep language proficiency appears to pervade all sorts of educational and psychological tasks to such an extent that it is doubtful whether traditional psychological tests should be employed for the types of diagnosis often implicit in their labels. (4) Educators should recognize that all sorts of tests aimed at a tremendous diversity of constructs may be measures of language proficiency more than anything else and should interpret scores accordingly. (5) Finally, educators in all areas should recognize that normative language proficiency may be about all that we can measure with the degree of accuracy that curricular efforts demand. Therefore, we should probably do everything possible to improve deep level language competence across the entire curriculum and we should evaluate our success with appropriate language tests.

NOTES

1. These examples come from a reader by Rasmussen and Goldberg (1970), published by Science Research Associates.

The book begins with a list of isolated words and follows them by a nonsense story. There are colorful pictures, but they are not pictures of anything--merely meaningless patterns. Presumably, this keeps them in perfect harmony with the nonsense sequences of sentences which are just about as meaningful throughout as the ones cited here.

2. These sample sentences are a rough similitude of the Sun Up materials by Early, Cooper, Santeusanio, and Adell (1974) published by Harcourt, Brace, and Jovanovich. They are supposed to represent the sort of thing that will 'delight young readers' (p. xv). The book is filled with other examples which present the world of children as so different from that of adults as to be nearly unrecognizable as genuine. Of course, the authors maintain that it is a world that children understand and greatly enjoy. The talk of children, on the other hand, belies this (Hart, Walker, and Gray 1977).

3. This particular example comes from a talk by Stephen Krashen at SPEAQ in Quebec City, Canada, 1978.

4. This model was discussed at sessions on language testing organized by Adrian Palmer, Lyle Bachman, and Peter Groot at the 1979 and 1980 TESOL Conventions in Boston and San Francisco, respectively. It is one of the most elaborate and eclectic models yet to be offered. At present, efforts are underway primarily by Palmer and Bachman (and no doubt the OISE researchers as well) to put it to the test.

REFERENCES

Canale, M., and M. Swain. 1979. Theoretical bases of communicative approaches to second language teaching and testing. Mimeo. Ontario Institute for Studies in Education, Toronto, Canada.

Caulfield, Joan, and William C. Smith. (in press) The reduced redundancy test and the cloze procedure as measures of global language proficiency. Modern Language Journal.

Chesarek, S., and J. Oller. 1979. Cognitive and language performance of a bilingual population on standardized tests. Paper presented at the Research Colloquium on Bias in Standardized Testing at the 13th Annual TESOL Convention, Boston, Massachusetts, February 28. Revised version in Streiff and Oller (in press).

Cummins, James. 1980. Construct of language proficiency and bilingual education. [This volume, 81-103.]

Early, M., E. K. Cooper, N. Santeusanio, and M. Y. Adell. 1974. Teacher's edition: Sun Up reading skills 1. New York: Harcourt, Brace, and Jovanovich.

Flahive, D. 1980. Separating the g factor from reading comprehension. In: Oller and Perkins, eds. (1980:34-47).

Hart, N. W. M. S., R. Walker, and B. Gray. 1977. The language of children: A key to literacy. Reading, Mass.: Addison-Wesley.

Hendricks, D., G. Scholz, R. Spurling, M. Johnson, and L. Vandenburg. 1980. Oral proficiency testing in an intensive English language program. In: Oller and Perkins, eds. (1980:77-90).
Hisama, K. K. 1980. An analysis of various ESL proficiency tests. In: Oller and Perkins, eds. (1980:47-53).
Kaczmarek, C. M. 1980. Scoring and rating essay tasks. In: Oller and Perkins, eds. (1980:151-159).
Krashen, S. 1978. Language acquisition and second language teaching. Paper presented at SPEAQ, Sixth Annual Convention, Quebec City, Canada, June.
Oller, J. 1977. How important is language proficiency to IQ and other educational tests? Paper presented at the First International Conference on Frontiers in Language Dominance and Proficiency Testing, Southern Illinois University, Carbondale, April. [Also in: Oller and Perkins, eds. (1978:1-6).]
Oller, J. 1979. Language tests at school. A pragmatic approach. London: Longman.
Oller, J., and F. B. Hinofotis. 1980. Two mutually exclusive hypotheses about second language ability: Indivisible or partially divisible competence? In: Oller and Perkins, eds. (1980:13-23).
Oller, J., and K. Perkins, eds. 1978. Language in education: Testing the tests. Rowley, Mass.: Newbury House.
Oller, J., and K. Perkins, eds. 1980. Research in language testing. Rowley, Mass.: Newbury House.
Piaget, J. 1947. The psychology of intelligence. Totowa, N.J.: Littlefield.
Rasmussen, D., and L. Goldberg. 1970. A pig can jig. Chicago: Science Research Associates.
Rosenbaum, Harvey. 1980. The Entry/Exit Project: A status report. [This volume, 00-000.]
Scholz, G., D. Hendricks, R. Spurling, M. Johnson, and L. Vandenburg. 1980. Is language ability divisible or unitary? A factor analysis of 22 English language proficiency tests. In: Oller and Perkins, eds. (1980:24-33).
Scott, Robert. 1979. The measure of adult English language proficiency: Final report. Austin, Texas: Resource Development Institute.
Streiff, Virginia. 1979. Another look at the English language factor in educational tests for bilinguals. Paper presented at the 13th Annual TESOL Convention, Boston, Mass., March.
Streiff, V., and J. Oller. The language factor: More tests of tests. MS. University of New Mexico.

VI. *Curriculum, Materials, and the Profession*

BILINGUAL EDUCATION AS A PROFESSION

María Medina Swanson
Bilingual Education Service Center
Arlington Heights, Illinois

In his article 'Profession Anyone?', Thelen (1973:178) recalls the story about the two bricklayers. When asked what they were doing, one said, 'I'm laying bricks', and the other replied 'I'm building a cathedral'. One is described as a tradesman; the other, as having the soul of an artist or professional. One stresses the activity itself; the other, the meaning of the activity.

It is not how expertly or skillfully they daub mortar on to each brick, nor the hours of supervised practice they've had, nor how much they know about their job, nor how loyal they are to their boss, nor how much they know about other constructions. It is how they savor and feel about what they are doing, in their sensing relationships between their work and that of others, in their appreciation of potentialities, in their sense of form, in their need for and enjoyment of significance, in their identification of self with civilized aspirations, in their whole outlook on life.

Thelen then draws similar distinctions between teachers who teach school and teachers who educate children, between training programs that produce manpower and those that turn out professionals. The tradesman teacher can follow all sorts of precise instructions and can recall specific examples to emulate. The professional teacher has an 'internalized sense of education' and can spontaneously create appropriate structure in response to specific situations. The one looks for a particular tool to use--the other mobilizes his entire self providing a 'holistic' response to the total situation.

In his description of the 'professional', Thelen has captured the very essence of the bilingual educator. During the past ten years, a growing number of teachers, paraprofessionals, administrators, coordinators, curriculum specialists, psychologists, evaluators, counselors, trainers, professors, and parents have become involved in the implementation of bilingual education. Unlike other professionals, the vast majority of these individuals had very little specialized training designed to prepare them for this work. What they did have was a vision, an understanding of the need to provide a meaningful education to the millions of children in this country who come from homes in which a language other than English is spoken. And so, with an 'internalized sense of bilingual education', they rolled up their sleeves and started building a program, with no experience, no curriculum, no materials, but a great deal of enthusiasm and a sense that they were making a significant contribution towards a final outcome: an educational system that not only would be responsive to the educational needs of children of diverse linguistic and cultural backgrounds, but would view these differences as important reflections of the cultural and linguistic mosaic that characterizes our country, and thus would incorporate the instruction of these languages and the understanding of these cultures into the entire school curriculum-- our 'cathedral'.

The steps to the building of our cathedral were many. First, the need had to be established in the community and the building site selected. Second, a detailed plan had to be developed with input and approval of all concerned parties. Third, a permit had to be secured from the school board. Fourth, adequate financing needed to be sought. Fifth, upon funding, a good contractor or project coordinator had to be retained to manage all project activities, purchase necessary materials, and hire appropriate personnel.

As these preliminary steps were taken, bilingual education progressed from a vague concept to a 'semi-concrete' program specifying goals, objectives, curriculum and classroom schedules, in much the same manner as an architect's design develops into a multiplicity of technical diagrams setting forth the foundation, the walls, the wiring, the plumbing, etc. But, however exemplary, well planned, and meticulously outlined, the real challenge was in transposing the plan from the paper to the classroom, the school, and the community.

The first obstacle we encountered was the plan itself. Although there was consensus as to the philosophy of bilingual education, the design and implementation of the program were left up to each district. As a result, many of these local plans set forth unrealistic goals and inadequate provisions to carry them out. Second, there was a tremendous scarcity of bilingual personnel available to carry out these programs. But even the few bilingual teachers and aides that were available had little or no previous experience or training in bilingual education. Third, the lack of adequate curriculum materials in the target language imposed not only a serious obstacle to pupil progress but a very taxing additional burden on the teacher.

Imagine trying to construct an impressive, majestic brick cathedral without bricks or mortar, with inexperienced workers or skilled carpenters instead of bricklayers, and with non-existent or very limited resources for training them. Yet, that is how most bilingual programs got off the ground in the late sixties. Our pioneer teachers and aides relied on their instinct and ingenuity, and on extremely hard work to implement meaningful programs for students of limited English proficiency.

Through their efforts, a variety of curriculum designs and program models were developed. In addition, curriculum materials from other countries were collected, examined, and reviewed by teachers and curriculum specialists at the Materials Acquisition Project in order to determine their applicability in our schools. Listings and annotated bibliographies were disseminated throughout the country. Although most of the initial efforts on the part of teachers to create materials resulted in mediocre products of the 'cut-and-paste and mimeograph' variety, some of the more experienced programs, Miami for instance, developed curriculum materials worthy of national dissemination. By the early seventies, these materials and others were being edited, duplicated, and distributed to all programs requesting them by the National Consortium for Bilingual Education and later by the Dissemination Center for Bilingual-Bilcultural Education.

The learn-as-you-go approach that most teachers and aides had to espouse as they began bilingual instruction was gradually enhanced by pre- and in-service training at the local level, especially in those districts with university resources. New teachers received practical training from the more experienced, for example, on how to teach reading and other content matter in the native language of the students, how to individualize instruction in order to meet the needs of children of varying language abilities, how to adapt curriculum materials, and how to teach cultural content. These efforts at the local level eventually expanded to the regional, state and, as of the spring of 1972, to the national level when the first National Bilingual Bicultural Education Conference was held in Austin, Texas.

That single event had a considerable impact on bilingual education. For the first time, bilingual educators from all over the United States came together as a professional group to share knowledge, resources, and experiences. For the first time, the few commercial publishers that had ventured to put together materials for bilingual programs became aware of a real and expanding market in bilingual education. The overall spirit of that conference was excitement at the discovery that our individual efforts to change the traditional educational system were not really isolated but part of a nationwide movement. Furthermore, the federal effort was beginning to have impact at the state level, with a handful of states already implementing bilingual programs on state monies and a growing number following the Massachusetts leadership in establishing mandated programs. The following year in San Diego a second such gathering drew over 5,000 participants, including some representatives from other countries. It was here that the initial steps were taken to form a national professional organization. At the third annual conference in New York, over 4,000 bilingual educators formally adopted the constitution and bylaws of the National Association for Bilingual Education; and in 1975 the first officers of that organization were installed during the Fourth International Bilingual Bilcultural Education Conference in Chicago. In subsequent years the NABE assumed complete responsibility for sponsoring and conducting the annual conference which continues to be a major professional event, attracting an average of 3,000 to 4,000 bilingual educators.

One of the reasons why bilingual programs placed such emphasis on in-service training and professional development via workshops and conferences was the scarcity of programs at the college level. Although a small number of institutions of higher education had begun graduate-level programs in bilingual education, and although some of the strongest supporters and experts we relied upon in the bilingual education movement were college professors, as late as 1973-74 there were virtually no programs to prepare teachers. About that time, things began to change. As states requiring bilingual instruction increased and, consequently, the demands for bilingual teaching certificates, pressure was put on state departments of education, universities, and teacher-training institutions to do something about it. It was easier said than done. The universities encountered practically the same problems that public school bilingual programs had confronted--lack of program models, lack of trained personnel, and lack of materials. But they too rolled up their sleeves, and began a systematic attack on all fronts.

By 1974, task forces and conferences to develop guidelines for teacher preparation and certification had been formed in a few states. During the same year, under a Title V EPDA grant, the Center for Applied Linguistics brought together 15 bilingual education specialists from nine states to develop a document designed to assist teacher certification agencies and educational institutions not only to establish certification standards for bilingual teachers, but also to design and evaluate bilingual teacher education programs. The resulting <u>Guidelines for the Preparation and Certification of Teachers of Bilingual-Bilcultural Education</u> were disseminated throughout the country and served as models or points of departure for many state agencies and institutions of higher education.

The Educational Amendments of 1974 which reauthorized bilingual education and amended the Bilingual Education Act of 1968 (Title VII ESEA) provided much needed 'capacity building' assistance to bilingual education. Specifically, the new provisions emphasized the need to prepare bilingual teachers; to develop bilingual teacher-education programs in universities; to prepare and train bilingual counselors, administrators, and paraprofessionals; to provide for inservice training for teachers and paraprofessionals; and to provide fellowships for individuals seeking advanced degrees in bilingual education. Furthermore, the 1974 Act provided additional support to bilingual programs by establishing a National Network composed of Materials Development Centers to develop instructional and testing materials, Dissemination and Assessment Centers to publish and disseminate these materials; as well as to conduct needs assessments for materials and support services; and Training Resource Centers to provide intensive training to classroom personnel. The new law also authorized a substantial increase in appropriations to fund local education programs and set aside funds for state education agencies to provide technical assistance.

At last, the resources so desperately needed to implement bilingual programs were finally going to be provided. The bricks, the mortar, the bricklayers, the foremen, the engineers, and the architects were on the way! At last, we would be given the skills and tools needed to upgrade our adobe mission.

Although it is probably too soon to realize the full impact of these new resources--especially the much needed bilingual teachers who are now students, the curriculum materials that are still in the development and pilot-testing stage, and the core of bilingual education experts and researchers who are now fellows in graduate programs across the country--bilingual education has made impressive advances.

One of the most obvious is its growth. Since 1974, the number of federally funded projects has more than doubled, the number of state and locally supported programs has increased dramatically, and the number of colleges and universities now offering courses and teacher preparation programs, graduate degrees, and post-doctorate studies in bilingual education is now well into the hundreds.

Another is the increased knowledge, expertise, and level of sophistication of these bilingual professionals. Whereas in the early seventies we were asking how to do it, now we're concerned about how to do it well. Whereas a few years ago we were desperately trying to develop a curriculum, now we are concerned that this curriculum be coordinated with the overall school program. Whereas then we were developing our own materials, now we are more concerned about adapting existing materials to meet the individual needs of our students. Then, we assessed students to determine language dominance, now we are concerned about determining language proficiency and diagnosing learning problems. From a program designed for students of limited English proficiency, we are now saying that bilingual education should be available to all students.

There is no doubt that, as a profession, we have grown wiser. But, we have also grown a little sadder. Our shining optimism is showing a few tarnished spots here and there. Our soaring enthusiasm has gone through some treacherous air pockets. On more than one occasion we have had to resort to Geritol to help us keep our youthful energy.

The first and last of all our problems is the basic underlying fact that the vast majority of our colleagues, supervisors, school board members, government representatives, friends, relatives, and neighbors do not understand bilingual education. They either feel threatened by it, feel that it just is not necessary, or feel nothing at all. This is further complicated by the present economic difficulties facing federal, state, and local governments. Why should they worry about bilingual education when there are so many 'real' problems to worry about-- energy, oil, unemployment, the dollar, inflation, taxes. So we worry about bilingual education! As a result, the bilingual professional must spend unmeasured amounts of time and energy explaining and defending what it is all about.

Bilingual teachers also must cope with job instability. In the majority of cases, districts will not issue a contract to the bilingual staff until the program has been funded. Since invariably they are the last hired, they are first in line to be dismissed, laid off, or not re-hired in times of financial crises. Some districts will hire teachers on a permanent 'temporary' basis thereby avoiding the whole issue of tenure. In far too many cases, bilingual teachers are viewed as 'add-ons' rather than regular members of the school faculty. In some cases efforts by bilingual teachers to remedy this have been defeated by teacher unions.

Finally, the bilingual education profession has been expected to prove that bilingual education works, or else face extinction. This is not an easy threat to live with since so little was known about how to implement a program when we began. In fact, even today there is no body of research to substantiate what program models and approaches work best in given circumstances. Federal bilingual programs were designed to demonstrate effective ways of teaching children of limited English-speaking ability, not to prove that children could get high marks on regular standardized tests. Yet, children in bilingual programs have too often been evaluated by insensitive evaluators with inadequate instruments and improper designs, and these results have been nationally disseminated to show that bilingual education is not doing too well.

But under the circumstances, how could it be expected to do better? There were no resources, no trained personnel, no materials, and no provision for them until the Amendments of 1974. Without bricks, or tools, or experience, we did our best; we built an adobe mission--not too elegant--but it was full of life, energy, and love. And let us not apologize for our mission--that is how many great cathedrals began.

We have come a long way, but we have longer to go. New challenges are always surfacing--institutionalization of bilingual education, increased research and evaluation, development of adequate diagnostic instruments, among others. Notre Dame took centuries to build. I hope bilingual education, the greatest undertaking in American education during our lifetime, will not take quite so long.

REFERENCES

Acosta, Robert Kelly, and George M. Blanco. 1978. Competencies for university programs in bilingual education. U.S. Department of Health, Education and Welfare. (No. [OE] 78-079031).

Andersson, Theodore, and Mildred Boyer. 1978. Bilingual schooling in the United States. Second edition. Austin, Texas: National Educational Laboratory Publishers, Inc.

Bilingual Teacher Preparation Conference Report. 1974. Springfield, Ill.: State of Illinois Board of Higher Education.

Evaluation study executive summary. 1978. Final report: Impact of ESEA Title VII Spanish-English bilingual education program. U.S. Department of Health, Education and Welfare, Office of Planning, Budgeting, and Evaluation. [March, 1978].

Fishman, Joshua. 1978. A gathering of the vultures: The 'legion of decency' and bilingual education in the USA. NABE Journal 2.2 (March, 1978).

Future that's twice as bright, a: Bilingual education in Illinois. 1978. Arlington Heights, Ill.: Illinois Resource Center; Bilingual Education Service Center.

Goldsmith, Ross P., and Sheila R. Reifle. 1978. Summary report on the National Assessment Survey of Title VII ESEA Basic Project Directors' and Teachers' Needs for the Products and Services of the National Network of Centers for Bilingual Education. Austin, Texas: Dissemination and Assessment Center for Bilingual Education.

González, Josué. 1978. The state of bilingual education today: Un vistazo y un repaso. NABE Journal 2.1 (January 1978). New York: Anaya Las Americas.

Guidelines for the preparation and certification of teachers of bilingual/bicultural education. 1974. Arlington, Va.: Center for Applied Linguistics.

La Fontaine, Hernan et al., eds. 1978. Bilingual education. Wayne, N.J.: Avery Publishing Group.

National Advisory Council on Bilingual Education. 1978.
Third Annual Report. Washington, D.C.: Department of
Health, Education and Welfare, Office of Bilingual Education.
Navarro, Billie, and H. Ned Seelye. 1977. Bilingual program
designs. Arlington Heights, Ill.: Bilingual Education Service Center.
Politzer, Robert L. 1978. Some reflections on the role of
linguistics in the preparation of bilingual cross-cultural
teachers. In: Bilingual education paper series. Los
Angeles: National Dissemination and Assessment Center,
California State University, July, 1978.
Saville-Troike, Muriel. 1978. A guide to culture in the
classroom. Arlington, Va.: National Clearing House for
Bilingual Education.
Schneider, Susan Gilbert. 1976. Revolution, reaction or
reform: The 1974 Bilingual Education Act. New York:
L. A. Publishing Company.
Swanson, María Medina. 1974. Bilingual education: The
national perspective. In: Responding to new realities.
Edited by Gilbert A. Jarvis. ACTFL Review of Foreign
Language Education, Vol. V.
Thelen, Herbert. 1973. Profession anyone? In: New perspective on teacher education. Edited by Donald J.
McCarty. Jossely-Bass. 178-193.

LINGUISTICS AND PREPARATION OF BILINGUAL MATERIALS

Robert Lado
Georgetown University

1. **Definitions.** Bilingual materials are designed to contribute toward bilingualism on the part of students who are not fully bilingual but are in the process of becoming so. Materials printed in two languages, such as product labels and instructions for markets extending beyond one language area, are excluded because they are not designed to contribute toward achieving bilingualism but are intended for communication in whatever language is most accessible to the users.

We must admit at the outset that teaching-learning materials alone do not produce bilinguals. There must be a comprehensive bilingual/bicultural program with trained teachers and broad support from parents and the community. Bilingual materials can contribute significantly to such a program, however, and it is difficult to imagine a good bilingual program without them.

Such materials can be divided into those that are intended for bilingual mastery and those that contribute primarily to other studies in the educational development of bilinguals.

2. **Natural bilingualism versus bilingual programs.** Since language is acquired naturally by children through participation in meaningful situations involving the native language, and bilingualism is acquired naturally also by participating in meaningful situations involving two languages, one could hypothetically assume that bilingual materials should simply expose children to situations in both languages as in natural bilingualism, without any special order, selection, organization, or emphasis.

Such a view, however, would lead to the use of monolingual materials in both languages without regard to the special learning capabilities, cognitive mapping, and linguistic and cultural needs of bilinguals. This creates problems since that part of the dominant language that has already been internalized need not be taught for that purpose, and what has not been internalized in the second language requires special exposure which is usually absent or deemphasized in native language materials. The result is bound to be frustration and failure in what is not known, boredom with what is already known, and wasted time and effort in the haphazard occurrence of what needs to be learned.

Furthermore, since mental maturity and second language competence are not usually at the same level, the use of separate monolingual native language materials for both languages keeps the bilingual student either below his level of maturity in order that the language be accessible to him linguistically, or at his level of maturity but beyond his linguistic competence. Either solution presents problems.

3. **Role of linguistics.** Linguistics helps to understand what must be included in materials for bilingual mastery and to check the appropriateness of the language in those that contribute primarily to other educational objectives.

Linguistics describes, explains, and relates the elements, units, patterns, and rules that constitute a language and arrives at explicit understandings of the nature of language. And central to that nature is its power to govern the production and comprehension of an unlimited number of new sentences from a limited number of rules, patterns, and elements.

Because of the practically limitless number of sentences that can be produced and understood by the speakers of a language, it would be hopeless to try to learn all the sentences needed for even ordinary communication as discrete items. It is imperative that the student internalize by whatever means the system of rules, patterns, and elements of a second language to become bilingual.

Linguistic studies of language acquisition among bilinguals can help us select and order the language component of bilingual situations, and if the materials are to be more economically organized than the haphazard, hit-or-miss stance of anything that happens to be said spontaneously in each situation, we need to plan the sequence and grading of the materials with the aid of linguistics.

Much is being made nowadays of letting the students do what they spontaneously want to do. This is evident when we are urged to let them begin by creating their own dialogues, or talk only about themselves. That is like having an airline pilot ask the passengers which way to point the plane after takeoff for the sake of their motivation and interest. It would certainly be downright exciting to be on such a flight. The pilot would surely have the undivided attention of the passengers, and they would never forget that adventure--their own

exploration into the unknown. But would they get to their
destination at all, let alone get there on time? I prefer to
have the pilot decide which way to head the plane. Perhaps
we have forgotten the famous question posed by a progressive
education pupil some decades ago: 'Teacher, do we have to
do what we want to do today?' As I recall, that question
helped to dismantle progressive education.

Linguistics can help us go beyond a mere replication of the
natural acquisition of two languages by (1) organizing the
materials cumulatively in strategically selected situations, (2)
planning reentry as needed for mastery, (3) providing accurate and economically worded explanations, (4) providing the
most complete, best organized inventory of the elements, patterns, and rules that constitute the system of the language,
and (5) grading.

Grading is a dimension of good materials that can be achieved
more effectively through the aid of linguistics. The difficulty
of added layers of embeddedness, for example, can be sensed
in part by experienced teachers, but it can be understood
more precisely by those same teachers if laid bare by linguistic analysis. And motivation depends to a considerable degree
on whether the progression in difficulty is suited to the developing capacity of the students: if the complexity is beyond
their power of comprehension, they will be discouraged. If,
on the other hand, the materials are too simple, the students
will be bored and will not maintain their learning drive.

4. How does linguistics contribute to the foregoing?

4.1 Internal structure of the system.

Linguistics makes a
unique contribution in describing and explaining the internal
structure of the language system. Bilingual materials must
contribute to the internalization of the structure of at least
one of the languages, assuming that the structure of the first
or dominant one has already been internalized. There is no
better source than linguistics to find the explicit description
of the internal structure of the languages.

The native speaker has mastered the great bulk of the system
of his language by the time he enters school at the age of six.
He still has to develop further some complex rules and to learn
to discriminate with greater precision many differences in construction which he has acquired superficially. But the corps
of the language has been internalized, while in the second language, the internalization of that central corps still remains to
be accomplished.

Bilingual materials writers must turn to linguistics for the
description of that internal corps of the system. How does the
language express questions in contrast to statements, requests,
and exclamations? How does it express various types of questions such as those that elicit yes or no answers; those that
inquire as to the place, time, and manner of an occurrence by

means of interrogative pronouns; questions that are intended to
elicit the subject of an action which is otherwise known to the
inquirer; those that elicit a complete report because presumably
the questioner knows nothing of the event or has doubts as to
the veracity of a previous account and wishes a full report;
questions that merely require assent to the statement to which
they are appended; questions that seek a cause; those that
elicit an indirect object as reply; those that are conditional,
contrary to fact, hypothetical, rhetorical, indirect, or are used
as polite invitations, etc.?

How does the language express number, tense, gender,
mood? How does it avoid excessive repetition, that is, what
elements do speakers normally delete as they carry on communication? How does the speaker expand sentences and parts of
sentences to give greater detail to what is being communicated?

Even educated native speakers are unable to express the rules
or describe the patterns by which they construct and understand sentences unless they have made a special study of them
in grammar or linguistics courses or in independent reading.

Linguistics develops a metalanguage to describe those rules,
patterns, units, and elements that native speakers have internalized and use largely out of conscious awareness. And those
descriptions help the developer of bilingual materials to make
certain that the bilingual student will be exposed to the structural corps of the language in teaching-learning strategies.
The linguistic descriptions do not state how the structures
are to be internalized; that is the responsibility of the bilingual
materials writer and teacher. Good linguistic descriptions
merely present them in neat, compact, comprehensive statements.

Fries' (1952) description of the question patterns of modern
English made it possible to prepare more effective materials to
teach questions to foreign students, as Chomsky's auxiliary
transformations make it possible to plan the teaching-learning
of that major rule in modern English more effectively for speakers of other languages. In that sense, English as a Second
Language (ESL) materials are part of the bilingual materials
in which English is one of the languages to be mastered. In
the same sense, Jespersen's description of mass nouns and
count nouns makes it possible to develop better lessons for
bilingual materials.

Without linguistic grammars, bilingual materials will be haphazard in their preparation and difficult to evaluate with regard to imparting the central corps of the language.

4.2 **Conflicting points of view versus bad advice.** Problems
that seem to plague linguistic study are the frequent revolutions in its philosophy and point of view. In my experience we
have seen the rejection of traditional grammar by the structuralists, the repudiation of structuralism by Chomsky and the
transformationalists, the attack on transformationalism by the

generative semanticists and sociolinguists, and the internal disagreements within each of those views and movements. How is the bilingual teacher and the developer of bilingual materials to turn confidently to linguistics, and when, since linguists may do a 180-degree about-face without warning, and sometimes twice in succession? How can we discern which linguistics to apply, and which advice is good and which is bad?

There is one characteristic of linguistic and grammatical studies that distinguishes what we may be able to use and what we may not. It is simply whether or not the study describes or explains some comprehensive part of a particular language. The studies we cannot use are those that tell us how linguistic studies should be carried out or how bad previous studies have been, but which do not describe or explain any substantial part of any language. Given the complexity of language, we can expect that when the authors of such papers get down to the business of describing or explaining a language, they will change their model. On the other hand, any study that describes or explains any substantial part of a language can be reinterpreted with relative ease in a form that is suitable for bilingual materials, whereas papers that merely tell us how the study should be conducted cannot easily be implemented even if their suggestions are sound. In any event, the applied linguist who works on bilingual materials is not the one responsible for the basic linguistic studies; the applied linguist is responsible for the pedagogical organization and presentation of the two languages in their cultural frames of reference, and that is a major responsibility in itself.

On the basis of that characteristic, we find useful Jespersen's Essentials of English Grammar (1933) and the larger A Modern English Grammar (1909), published before structuralism had come on the scene. We find useful Fries' The Structure of English (1952) in a structural key. Because it explains a substantial part of English, we find useful Chomsky and Halle's The Sound Pattern of English (1968), but we still consult Kenyon and Knott's A Pronouncing Dictionary of American English (1944), of prestructural vintage. And we find indispensable the standard dictionaries that lexicographers compile in monolingual and bilingual formats. The usefulness of the sources just cited and similar works is enhanced by clarity of presentation, accuracy of description, and comprehensiveness or completeness, regardless of the model or philosophy of the authors.

On the basis of that characteristic, we must reject the advice of a recent article which first boasts that in the nascent field of the analysis of the meaning of sentences in utterances there are already three approaches: the performative, the prescriptive, and the pragmatic, and that only the pragmatic approach meets all the objections of that author to the first two. The article then advises us that since learners are going to make mistakes anyway, 'Why not encourage the students to

learn effective though incorrect forms such as "Why do you
there?"' I asked a number of persons what they would understand if asked such a question by a foreign student and their
interpretation varied from 'Why did you do that there?' to 'What
are you doing there?' To my query as to their reaction to
such a question, they said things like, 'He has a problem with
his English. The words put together do not mean anything.
He does not know much English. What does he mean? Does
he mean what are you doing or why are you doing that?'

In addition to not describing or explaining any comprehensive
part of the English language, the advice violates sociolinguistic
realities, since listeners do react to markedness of various
types. From a structural linguistic point of view, it is not
English. From a transformational point of view, it is not a
well-formed sentence. From the point of view of linguistic
geography, it does not represent any recognizable geographic
variety of the language. From the point of view of communication, it is confusing. The professionally committed ESL teacher,
whether in a bilingual program or in a regular ESL class, should
simply refuse to teach it.

4.3 Sociolinguistics, variation, and secondary reactions. A
major decision to be made in the preparation of bilingual
materials concerns the particular variety or varieties of the
language to be presented. This decision has been the source
of much discussion and controversy with regard to Black English in reading materials.

More recent studies of variation point to the gradience of
registers normally used by the speakers of a language. Sociolinguistic studies are useful in the preparation of bilingual
materials by providing both the descriptions and secondary reactions to various standards and registers. Making use of such
data can prevent alienation and at least some of the failures
and injustices that result from ignoring the language varieties
used by the pupils and forcing some inflexible artificial standard on them, or at the other extreme, ignoring any standard
variety altogether and limiting the materials exclusively to the
local variety of the language at a particular time.

The decision as to what varieties to present is not up to the
sociolinguist but, as Fishman (1977) points out, to the parents,
the community, and the school, taking into account the realities
involved and the educational and societal objectives adopted.
The training of bilingual teachers becomes crucial in view of
the finding by Shuy et al. (1969) that listeners react negatively
more than favorably to accented speech.

4.4 Psycholinguistics. Psycholinguistics studies the processes involved in using a language, the limits of immediate
memory in those processes, and the acquisition of language by
children, although the latter need not be the exclusive domain
of psycholinguistics nor is psycholinguistics limited to child

language acquisition studies. Psycholinguistic studies, including those on child language acquisition, however, are still in a very tentative discovery stage and cannot be expected to give us sufficiently detailed and comprehensive descriptions and explanations of substantial portions of the language for bilingual materials preparation. Psycholinguistic studies are a good source of research problems in bilingual studies and of possible explanations of observations in performance among bilinguals.

4.5 **Discourse analysis.** This recent development in linguistics shows good initial studies of extended discourse in conversation or in the separate skills of speaking and listening, reading and writing. It is clear that the analysis of isolated sentences cannot give a full description of a language simply because language is used typically in suprasentential utterances.

The developing analysis of conversational rules, including gradience and turn-taking, will obviously be useful in the preparation of bilingual materials. This takes us into the ethnography of speaking (Gumperz and Hymes 1972; Gumperz and Hernandez-Chavez 1971; McDermott 1977, among others), which goes beyond language to account for linguistic interaction. Again, the particular approach of the analyst is of less interest than the actual descriptions produced, since a few examples are of little practical value in the preparation of bilingual materials.

4.6 **Early bilingual reading.** Another potential contribution to bilingual materials can come from the emerging field of early bilingual reading. Although early reading is not restricted to linguistics in origin, it is a linguistic process bearing strong resemblance to language acquisition. Two recent doctoral dissertations, Past (1976) and Lee (1977), describe case studies of children who were taught to read in two languages before first grade as an aid to bilingual and bicultural development.

4.7 **Contrastive linguistics and error analysis.** The learning strategies of a bilingual differ from those of monolinguals who are extending their knowledge of their only language. Bilinguals may apply the rules of their dominant language when they process new utterances in the other; and as they master the second language they may transfer rules from it to the first. These transfers go unnoticed when the two languages coincide, but they become apparent when the two languages differ. Thus, we notice differences in the English spoken by bilinguals when their dominant language is Spanish, French, Arabic, and Vietnamese, for example. We even notice differences in the English spoken by Spanish speakers from different parts of the Spanish-speaking world, e.g. Argentina and Mexico, Puerto Rico and Peru, and Spaniards from different regions of Spain.

Contrastive linguistics applies linguistic techniques to the analysis of the similarities and differences between two languages. Where the two systems differ, a potential learning problem is identified, and provision can then be made to cope with it. When they coincide, no problem is anticipated; we actually expect facilitation because the system already internalized by the student will also function in the second language and need not be made the object of conscious verbalization and practice.

Contrastive linguistics does not predict that every speaker will make every possible mistake shown by differences between the two languages (Lado 1957), any more than medical science can predict which individuals will be affected by an epidemic developing in a particular area. It would be reckless, however, to ignore the threat posed by a serious epidemic simply because the doctor cannot say that you personally will be affected; you take your chances at your own peril. And so it is with all the social sciences, where 100 percent predictions are the exception, and factors that account for as little as 5 percent of variance may be considered important.[1]

Error analysis identifies learning problems on the basis of performance. In addition to errors attributable to native language transfer, there are problems that result from the complexities of the second language itself. These may involve overextension of a rule to utterances where it does not apply, or underextension where it does apply. There are also errors which, although not directly traceable to the native language, appear more often when the bilingual is translating from one language to the other than when he/she is speaking or writing from thought. The avoidance phenomenon, the fact that bilinguals avoid the use of potentially troublesome constructions and words, is not explained by error analysis, but it is by contrastive analysis (Schachter 1977).

In all, both contrastive linguistics and error analysis can contribute to the preparation of better BL materials. They both depend on good linguistic analysis and they both help in determining which parts of the language systems will require special attention and which will not, and what linguistic explanations will most clearly and economically point out the specific learning tasks facing the students.

4.8 Applied linguistics. Although all good linguists are able to interpret linguistic studies for their possible application to bilingual materials, it is the main responsibility of applied linguistics to work out pedagogical sequences, practical explanations, grading, and adaptations to age, educational level, and setting. Here too, unless the applied linguist has the specific expertise for a particular bilingual adaptation, he/she will have to collaborate with bilingual teachers and others who can supply that expertise. And again, it will not be satisfactory that the applied linguist simply suggest how to adapt the description to the particular bilingual group involved. The applied linguist should prepare the sequencing and explanations and let the bilingual teacher prepare the actual lessons. Even this, of course, does not guarantee successful materials.

5. **Limitations of linguistics.** Once the materials and their sequencing have been chosen and set, linguistics has less to contribute to them. We must turn to pedagogics and the psychology of learning. Yet theories of learning are too vague and somewhat simplistic to account for bilingual acquisition and provide adequate models for the complexities and specifics of achieving bilingualism. The state of the art takes us back to gifted bilingual teachers and developers of bilingual materials, who will do well to look into what linguistics can contribute to the success of their work, and who must try out and improve their materials in the field before publishing them.

6. **Conclusion.** BL materials developers need descriptive, structural, transformational, and/or generative semantic linguistics to determine what is meant by English and Spanish or whatever the two languages may be. This determination is necessary for the selection, progression, and explanation of the language component of BL materials.

BL materials writers need sociolinguistics for the social implications of variations in the language, including information on the effects of dialect markedness, accentedness, and acceptability.

BL materials writers need psycholinguistics to understand better the processes of speaking and listening, reading and writing, and the limits of the utterances that can be processed as language.

Within this need for linguistics, BL materials developers need the result of the work, the descriptions of English and of markedness of variations and of the processes and dimensions of memory, rather than polemics as to what sect of linguistics has the whole truth, or how the description is to be done or should have been done, usually by others. The BL materials writer may legitimately be expected to fill in some details of information which may not be mentioned in larger descriptions, but it is the responsibility of the linguist to provide the larger description with considerable detail, not simply stating the way it ought to be done.

We have had too much of showing with a few selected examples that all previous linguistic studies were wrong, and not enough serious studies showing the results of better descriptions. We need works like Jespersen's, Kenyon and Knott's, Fries', Chomsky and Halle's, Shuy's, etc. which give us material to work with. The particular theoretical basis fades into the background as we examine the actual descriptions and explanations provided.

BL materials do not need off-the-cuff dicta based on speculative if legitimate linguistic views. If linguistics provides only polemics as to what theory is best, or advises the use of language that is meaningful only in some highly restricted view of language, BL materials writers and teachers will do well to ignore linguistics and apply whatever common sense in language they can muster on their own. If, however, linguistics provides comprehensive descriptions of specific languages, factual and insightful studies of social variation and reactions to markedness and accentedness, factual and revealing studies of the processes of speaking and listening, reading and writing, and error and contrastive analyses showing the areas of stress and difficulty, BL materials writers and publishers cannot afford to ignore them.

NOTE

1. Einar Haugen, author of The Norwegian Language in America, A Study in Bilingual Behavior, suggested in the discussion at this Round Table that in addition to leaning on his native language competence to construct utterances in the second language, the bilingual speaker may be particularly concerned about errors that are sharply marked as resulting from his particular language base.

REFERENCES

Andersson, Theodore. 1978. Preschool biliteracy. [This volume, pp. 461-472.]
Chomsky, Noam, and Morris Halle. 1968. The sound pattern of English. New York: Harper and Row.
Corder, S. P. 1967. The significance of learners' errors. International Review of Applied Linguistics 5.161-170.
Di Pietro, Robert. 1971. Language structure in contrast. Rowley, Mass.: Newbury House.
Ferguson, Charles A. 1962. Contrastive structure series. Chicago: University of Chicago Press. English and German, Kufner and Moulton. 1962. English and Italian, Agard and Di Pietro. 1965. English and Spanish, Stockwell and Bowen. 1965.
Fishman, Joshua A. 1977. 'Standard' versus 'dialect' in bilingual education: An old problem in a new context. The Modern Language Journal 61.7.315-325.
Fries, Charles C. 1952. The structure of English. New York: Harcourt, Brace.
Gumperz, J. J., and D. Hymes, eds. 1972. Directions in sociolinguistics: The ethnography of communication. New York: Holt, Rinehart and Winston.
Gumperz, J. J., and Eduardo Hernandez-Chavez. 1971. Bilingualism, bidialectalism, and classroom interaction. In:

Language in social groups. Edited by J. J. Gumperz. Stanford University Press.
Haugen, Einar. 1953. The Norwegian language in America, A study in bilingual behavior. Philadelphia: University of Pennsylvania Press.
Jespersen, Otto. 1909. A modern English grammar. Heidelberg.
Jespersen, Otto. 1933. Essentials of English grammar. New York: Henry Holt.
Kenyon, John S., and Thomas A. Knott. 1944. A pronouncing dictionary of American English. Springfield, Mass.: G. and C. Merriam.
Lado, Robert. 1957. Linguistics across cultures. Ann Arbor: University of Michigan Press.
Lee, Ok Ro. 1977. Early reading as an aid to bilingual and bicultural adjustment for a second generation Korean child in the U.S. Unpublished doctoral dissertation. Georgetown University.
McDermott, Ray P. 1977. The ethnography of speaking and reading. In: Linguistic theory: What can it say about reading? Edited by Roger W. Shuy. Newark, Del.: International Reading Association. 153-185.
Past, Alvin W. 1976. Preschool reading in two languages as a factor in bilingualism. Unpublished doctoral dissertation. The University of Texas at Austin.
Past, Kay E. C. 1976. A case study of preschool reading and speaking in two languages. In: Georgetown University Papers on Languages and Linguistics, Number 13: Early Reading. Edited by Robert Lado and Theodore Andersson.
Schachter, Jacquelyn. 1974. An error in error analysis. Language Learning 24.2.205-214.
Schachter, Jacquelyn. 1977. Some reservations concerning error analysis. TESOL Quarterly 11.441-450.
Shuy, Roger W., ed. 1977. Linguistic theory: What can it say about reading? Newark, Del.: International Reading Association.
Shuy, Roger W., J. C. Baratz, and W. A. Wolfram. 1969. Sociolinguistic factors in speech identification. National Institute of Mental Health Research Project Number MH-15048-01.
Stockwell, Robert P., J. Donald Bowen, and John W. Martin. 1965a. The grammatical structures of English and Spanish. Chicago: University of Chicago Press.
Stockwell, Robert P., and J. Donald Bowen. 1965b. The sounds of English and Spanish. Chicago: University of Chicago Press.
Weinreich, Uriel. 1953. Languages in contact. The Hague: Mouton.

CLASSROOM PRACTICES IN BILINGUAL EDUCATION

Mary Finocchiaro
City University of New York

Any attempt on my part to make generalizations about classroom practices in bilingual education which would be valid within any one country or across countries could lead only to my embarrassment and to your confusion. There can be no serious question of setting forth a list of definitive practices which would serve, even reasonably well, in the United States, Great Britain, Holland, Yugoslavia, Tunisia, or any other country we might wish to name. Professor Mackey's comprehensive typology of possible bilingual programs published a few years ago, and Professor Glyn Lewis' speech on types of bilingual communities provide ample evidence to account for some of the sociolinguistic difficulties involved in preparing such a list.

But in an international conference devoted to bilingualism, we cannot ignore other crucial factors in addition to the sociolinguistic setting; for example, the vexing question of the attitude and motivation of language learners resulting from special circumstances which may have made bilingual programs hated but imperative or, on the other hand, eminently desirable. Attitude would naturally vary depending on whether imposed migration or political, social, or technological changes have forced people to accept bilingual programs or whether, on the other hand, the people themselves are eager to learn the language of persons living just across the border with whom they may wish to engage in trade, or more important still, to live in friendship.

I feel compelled to add to the complex array of types and attitudes a longer list of over 300 variables with which every school administrator and classroom teacher is all too familiar. Nor am I taking into account the individual differences which will coexist after even a few days in the classroom which had been homogeneously organized at the beginning of the school year.

A glance at Figure 1 will make the fact of the complexity abundantly clear.

The factors listed on the left are in no particular order. Each one will be of serious concern to the conscientious teacher and administrator. For example, whether the class organizational framework provided is an integrated one where learners of L are placed with language learners; or a pull-out program where newcomers to the school are taken out of regular classes for 20 minutes to two hours of instruction daily in the second or foreign language; or a bilingual program--a term which has assumed so many forms and connotations as to have a different meaning for each of its users; or a program in which the native language of the learner is neither used as an instrument for learning other curriculum areas or as a discipline to be respected, developed, and reinforced in its own right, the objectives of the program, the curriculum, the methods and materials, the skills needed by the teacher and the techniques for assessing the program will be contingent not only upon the age level of the learner but also--with older students--on their particular vocational or professional aspirations and hence on their communicative needs.

Let me say in passing that the Council of Europe, working with experts from several countries, is preparing a series of so-called functional-notional syllabuses in all the European languages for use with learners who will move to other countries for short or long periods, for either social or vocational purposes.

Limitations of time will not permit me to go into each of the individual and community factors noted on the figure in any detail. Suffice to say, in general, that modifications and adaptations in our COMET will have to be made, depending on age level and aspirations--whatever the left side of the figure indicates.

It may be desirable, however, to take a few moments to ask seasoned teachers and administrators to consider all the differences that five learners as against 500 would make in a school, and what steps would need to be taken in countries like the United States, Great Britain, and Israel, for example, where language learners may come from 20 or more different ethnic backgrounds. Closely allied to this question are two related ones. First, despite the gains we have made in the last few years in identifying language universals and some basic similarities in the process of language acquisition, whatever contrasts may exist between L1 and L2, there is no doubt that languages stemming from totally different linguistic families will present innumerable learning problems which will generally require more time to overcome. Second, the cultural background of the learners--for example, their attitude toward education and especially education for the female members of the community--will engender conflicts and misunderstandings between home and school, and unfortunately between parents and

Figure 1.

Variables	II. AGE LEVELS			III. TYPE OF PROGRAM		
I. WITHIN SCHOOL SITUATIONS	5-9	10-12	13-16	Continuing Education Program	16 and above III. or Function III.	Special Purpose
Types of organization available in the school or community for newcomers (e.g. integrated, pull-out, bilingual, ESL program)						
Number of learners involved in the school or community						
Variety of languages and cultural backgrounds in the same class						
Linguistic distinction between L1 and L2						
Cultural background of learners (education, customs; e.g. students of both sexes in same class)						
Literacy in L1						
Previous schooling in native country (years, subjects, FL learned)						
Schooling in host country (subjects taught in native language and in second language)						
Availability of bilingual personnel (training and qualifications)						
Community (resources, interest, and involvement of)						
Time of entry into special class						
Age of entry into L2 program						

C O M E T
C - Curriculum
O - Objectives
M - Methods and Materials
E - Evaluation Procedures
T - Teachers (Preparation and Skills)

children; the schools will have to help solve these problems before language learning may be expected to flourish.

Allow me to hurry on to the next group of factors which will necessitate further changes in our COMET. The majority of illiterates or functional illiterates entering into a bilingual program beyond the first year of elementary school will find it difficult to enter the mainstream of the school without intensive tutorial or other kind of help. Moreover, schooling in the native land may not have prepared newcomers to another country for such school practices as tests, grades, homework, and rigid time schedules. Nor, in general, would a knowledge of the host country language gleaned from eight or more years in the elementary and secondary schools of their native land serve as adequate preparation for placement with their age peers and for comfortable participation in the life of the community.

The date of entry into the bilingual program would also force changes in classroom practices. How will the newcomers be brought to the communicative and curricular levels of their peers? I have already mentioned the factor of age, which cannot be ignored or minimized. Let me underscore that it is nonproductive to all of the students and demeaning to the older ones when the age span in a language learning class ranges from 5 to 15 because of the small number of students.

This may be the moment to mention with a sigh of relief the tremendous gain which has been made recently in the field of bilingual and foreign language education. The ban on the learners' use of their native tongue has been lifted. The policy of total immersion of newcomers in a totally foreign culture has at last been reevaluated. This gratifying although belated acknowledgment of the importance of the learners' cultural identity has made it imperative to seek out qualified and empathetic bilingual personnel and to give them further training for the overwhelming task that the solution to some of the problems I have merely touched upon demands. It is imperative, too, in most bilingual programs that the school work with other social agencies to bring about a mutually accepting attitude between entrenched community members and newcomers.

All of the variables I have noted, including the one related to community acceptance, require that classroom practices be directed toward the effective and satisfactory resolution of cognitive and affective problems that will undoubtedly arise as the result of the interaction among the myriad forces impinging upon bilingual education programs.

Having set forth the problems, I regret to say that I will not offer instant solutions which would work with each of us in our different communities or countries, with our students and with our own personalities. What I hope to do is to list first some general guidelines which should be kept in the forefront of our thinking as we plan curricula for bilingual programs and second, several concrete teaching practices which may suggest still others.

I have mentioned cognitive and affective problems. I should like to start the guidelines by indicating to which of the two domains the suggestions made would contribute, although the domain--cognitive or affective--will be obvious to you, I am sure. Again, unfortunately, limitations of time do not permit me to give more than one or two examples of possible classroom procedures under each of the guidelines. You will note that in preparing them I have expanded Maslow's hierarchy of basic human needs since it is language--even noises in the beginning stages of life--which makes the satisfaction and realization of human needs possible.

Permit me, however, before proceeding to the guidelines, to underscore the most crucial underlying need of children or adults in bilingual or foreign language learning programs. Learners must be helped to maintain their ethnic values, cultural identities, and native language. They do not come to us as a tabula rasa. They come with a perfectly adequate language and a set of cultural values which ensures their membership in a community. The message the school must get across is one that Professor Lambert expressed so well: the new language and culture are designed to serve as additives and not as a subtractive.

Teachers and school personnel have a number of responsibilities to fulfill.

(1) They must ensure that learners come to school without fear--fear that they will be segregated; that they may not have understood the assignment; that they cannot pass the daily test because they have been absent; or that they will be laughed at by teacher and schoolmates when they make mistakes.

(2) They must be sure that learners understand the language of requests and directions, the reading, the listening comprehension exercise, or any other classroom activity. Translation, a buddy system, a teacher aide, or paraprofessional, will make this kind of linguistic understanding possible; but the affective meaning of the term 'understanding'--feeling understood when an assignment is not completed or when absence is due to respect for cultural traditions, as in taking care of a younger or older family member--is even more important.

(3) We must ensure that learners are helped to enjoy many language learning and other related experiences. Listening to music, singing, looking at pictures, listening to stories, going on community trips where feasible, lead to desirable and essential cognitive and affective processes.

(4) Learners must be helped to feel loved through praise and a warm accepting attitude even though it may seem to take them an inordinate amount of time to learn a language item.

(5) Learners should be made to feel that they belong to the total class group because every effort is made to involve them in meaningful class, group, or paired activities leading to

communicative competence because they are given opportunities to display their newly acquired knowledge in audience situations.

(6) Teachers and school personnel should help students to sense that they are making daily progress and achieving the goals which the teacher has clarified (in their native language, if necessary) and which are considered worthwhile to them now and in their later life.

(7) Finally, learners should be helped to feel successful--to attain the self-realization and actualization that Maslow considers the supreme human need. They can be helped to feel successful if they are given frequent, brief tests which have been announced in advance and which are preceded by crystal clear directions.

There are numerous other general guidelines culled from the findings of the sciences of linguistics, sociology, anthropology, psychology, and education. I will simply list them, and in no particular order, since all of them are important at some point in the learning process. Many of these guidelines would be equally important in any educational program.

In order to enhance the learners' self-image, it is important that they be encouraged to use their native tongue whenever feasible, that they be invited to talk about their own cultural background--in the second language if possible, or in their native tongue--with the teacher, with a buddy, or a paraprofessional who will interpret where necessary, and that they be encouraged to understand that all human beings have culture. They should be helped to appreciate the fact that differences in culture are generally the result of geographical or historical factors.

Self-images can also be enhanced when the teacher accepts the fact that all individuals have different styles and rhythms of learning, and that he/she does not expect all language learners to master a corpus of knowledge at the same time. Learners can be helped to retain their pride and their feeling that they are capable of learning if teachers also realize that numerous recognition or recall activities must precede a request for production and that no out-of-class assignment--except perhaps at university levels--should be given unless it has been explained and prepared thoroughly in the classroom.

And now let us turn to the all-important element in the learning process--motivation, which must be sustained through the often frustrating, tortuous road leading to communicative competence. Avenues which have been found to promote motivation include: using an integrated approach to learning, stated very simply, blending real-world communicative functions within an utterance or speech act, indicating how the speech function--apologizing, complimenting someone, asking for information, for example, can be used in a variety of everyday situations. This approach includes the learning of structures and vocabulary items which would be appropriate in the message that the speaker or writer wishes to express.

Motivation is also fostered by an interdisciplinary approach. The concept is not new in education. Over the years it has produced the resource unit, centers of interest, or thematic units. Whatever the label, the basic aim of the approach is to give learners an open-ended, broad view of a problem, of a period of history, or of any other interesting slice of life--starting with contemporary life--in harmony with their evolving interests. Information and insights from all curriculum areas--social studies, art, music, literature, science--are woven together in order to give learners a many-faceted, integrated overview of the entire problem or period under study.

An interdisciplinary approach demands the cooperation of all members of the school staff and of resource people in the community--an innovative notion in many countries. Fragmented, compartmentalized knowledge is difficult for native speakers to comprehend. How much more difficult for people who may have language difficulties! The reinforcement of different aspects of knowledge from various points of view, and especially from more than one teacher, can only lead to a more effective restructuring of that knowledge in the learner's mind.

Several other guidelines which seem worth remembering include the following.

(1) Learning should proceed in two parallel streams. We cannot wait until students know all the phonemes of the language or all the sound-symbol relationships, for example, before we help them understand authentic, interesting listening or reading material.

(2) Incidental happenings within the school, the community, and the country should be given precedence over the carefully planned language lesson if they are motivating to learners while reinforcing or presenting pertinent grammatical or lexical items.

(3) A spiral approach should be used to reintroduce, reinforce, and extend previously taught linguistic or cultural materials. Such an approach has the added advantage of ensuring continuity of instruction for language learners. We must not only know 'where they are', an educational cliché which does not really have great significance unless it implies that we know where they came from--in other words, what they have learned before they have entered a particular class or level--but also what they will be expected to know when they progress to the next higher level.

And now I beg your indulgence as I turn to the last section of this paper in which I plan to list some practical suggestions which again would be valid in any educational situation, whether it be in teaching a native language, a second language, or a truly bilingual program. I need not tell this audience that the varieties of bilingual programs run the gamut from teaching concepts of a discipline in the learners' native language and giving the important labels of the concepts in the second language, to teaching all the curriculum areas in one language in the morning and the same curriculum areas in the second language in the afternoon, or to the total immersion programs which are the subject of research in Canada.

Following is a list of some of the practices which have worked for many teachers.

(1) Teachers adapt and modify the existing textbook, making additions and deletions where necessary and changing the sequence of material presentation where logical. For example, the troublesome phoneme which impedes comprehension should be taught before the one suggested in the text unit.

(2) They help the students learn two- or three-line realistic dialogues in which the importance and use of a language function within a particular social situation is emphasized.

(3) They enable learners to recognize and eventually to create alternative but appropriate sentences for each dialogue utterance. Memorizing dialogues found in texts is generally a waste of teachers' and learners' time. Except for formulae like How do you do, the learners may never again hear the dialogue utterances.

(4) They teach the vocabulary that the students need immediately because it is related to places or happenings in their homes and community, and because it enables them to talk about the elements in their environments which are of importance to them.

(5) They help the students acquire the ability to use redundancy clues in listening, speaking, reading, and writing; and contextual clues in listening and reading.

(6) They ensure that the older students especially internalize the rules which underlie grammatical structures in the second language.

(7) They enable learners to keep systematic tables of nouns, verbs, adjectives, and adverbs which would help them to see sound shifts in function shifts if such exist, and to learn how to use different prefixes and suffixes in words having the same roots.

(8) Where these are pertinent, they help learners to recognize and to use cognates in the first and second languages. Parenthetically, these should be placed on the blackboard so that sound differences do not interfere with comprehension.

(9) They use the same passages at different times for listening comprehension, reading, word study, dictation, expansion, outlining, and summarizing, so that students can learn to appreciate the interrelationship of the four major communication abilities.

(10) They proceed from manipulative drills leading to habit formation and fluency to creative activities where learners may select any item in their linguistic repertoire which will be appropriate in the particular speech act.

(11) They use the same listening comprehension passage at three different levels of difficulty at intervals during the

semester: first, deleting all adjectives, adverbs, and clauses, and using only yes/no questions; second, deleting the clauses only and using simply Wh questions; and third, reinserting the clauses and using inferential and personalized questions.

(12) They vary the types of pupil participation--large groups, smaller groups, chain drills, paired practice--leading the students gradually to the essence of communication, an exchange of messages between two people.

(13) They individualize instruction to cope with the complex factors noted, with work sheets and other simple audiovisual materials prepared by boards of education and/or committees of teachers.

(14) They engage in role-playing, problem-solving or community learning activities provided that they are within the language capabilities of the learners and that the community resources available make community learning activities feasible.

(15) They plan classroom activities which have balance and variety, and--particularly in integrated classes--activities in which the newcomers can be actively involved from their first day of entry into the program.

I am afraid I have again opened a Pandora's box, but this was done as a preface to my plea that realistic action research be engaged in--research that is based on proven theories and on classroom teachers' knowledge and legitimate concerns. Moreover, teachers and administrators cannot wait until research studies are completed before they are given materials they must have in order to cope with learners from a variety of ethnic backgrounds who are on different points of the continua of the four major language abilities.

Viable, feasible bilingual education programs leading to communicative competence, to an understanding of cultural pluralism (not merely of biculturalism), to enhanced social values, to enriched personalities, are not only possible but imperative in today's world. They demand, however, the concerted efforts of all social agencies in a country and not the efforts of the ministry or board of education alone.

Conferences such as this, which should be followed by intensive, appropriate action in every country represented here, give rise to many hopes. Foremost among these is the hope that societies will be strengthened as bonds of communication make possible the sharing of knowledge and of moral and social experiences among nations.

Each one of us, like Candide, cultivating his own garden, can--by sharing materials, expertise, interest, and enthusiasm--create the better world in which men and women, secure in their own cultural identity, will be proud to join the larger community. The knowledge of more than one language and of a plurality of cultures will enable them to do this.

We are here because of our special interests and concerns. It is up to each of us, therefore, to encourage the formation and maintenance of carefully designed and evaluated bilingual programs. As our chairman, Dean James E. Alatis, said so well on another occasion: 'If not we, who then?'

VII. Communication and Bilingualism in the Classroom

POSITIVE EFFECTS OF BILINGUALISM
ON SCIENCE PROBLEM-SOLVING ABILITIES

Carolyn Kessler
University of Texas at San Antonio

Mary Ellen Quinn
Edgewood School District, San Antonio

Introduction. The effect of bilingualism on the individual is a research issue with a long history of contradictory findings. The issue of whether the bilingual is cognitively different from the monolingual has generated many studies in this century from those of Ronjat (1913) and Leopold (1949) to those of the present. Early works, particularly before the 1960s, tend to report the poor academic achievement of bilingual children and to argue that bilingualism itself leads to mental confusion and language handicaps. (For a review of the literature, see Darcy 1953, 1963.) More recently, however, a substantial number of studies suggests that bilingualism can accelerate aspects of cognitive growth. These studies cite advantages for bilingual children on a variety of measures of cognitive functioning.
It is the purpose of this paper to examine some of the effects of bilingualism on sixth-grade children's ability to formulate scientific hypotheses or solutions to science problems and to observe the interaction of this ability with linguistic competence by comparing the bilingual children's performance with that of a group of monolinguals of the same age and grade level. The problems are designed to set up discrepant events which trigger the divergent thinking manifested in the generation of scientific hypotheses. Linguistic competence is examined through the syntactic complexity of the language used to express these hypotheses.
That bilingual children have a cognitive flexibility and a more diversified set of mental abilities than monolinguals is a conclusion reached in the benchmark study conducted by Peal and Lambert (1962) working with matched monolingual and bilingual

groups. Their results, indicating that bilingualism may favorably affect the structure and flexibility of thought, have since found further confirmation from many parts of the world: Switzerland (Balkan 1970); Singapore (Torrance, Gowan, Wu, and Aliotti 1970); South Africa (Ianco-Worrall 1972); Israel and New York (Ben-Zeev 1972, 1977); Western Canada (Cummins and Gulutsan 1974); France, Germany, Canadians living overseas (Bain and Yu 1978); the United States (De Avila and Duncan 1979), among others. All of these studies indicate that bilingual children, relative to monolingual controls, show advantages on measures of cognitive flexibility, creativity, or divergent thinking.

Of particular relevance to the study reported in this paper is the work of Scott (1973) with French-English bilingual children in Montreal. Scott studied the effects of bilingualism on children's divergent thinking, an indicator of cognitive flexibility. Assessment measures of divergent thinking provide the subjects with a starting-point for thought and then ask them to generate a whole series of permissible solutions to various kinds of problems. Scott's results show that children who had become functionally bilingual through an immersion program for bilingual schooling scored substantially higher than the monolingual controls equated for IQ and socioeconomic level. Cummins and Gulutsan (1974), testing sixth grade bilingual and monolingual children on a task in which the subjects within a given time limit were to give as many uses as possible for an object named by the experimenter, found that bilinguals responded with greater diversity or originality, indicators of divergent thinking. These studies seem to indicate a causal link between bilingualism and divergent thinking, thus supporting the conclusion of cognitive advantage for bilingual children.

Lambert (1977) has suggested that the consequences of bilingualism may depend upon the dominance of the bilingual's two languages. He proposes the notions of subtractive and additive bilingualism. Subtractive bilingualism refers to situations in which the learning of the second language is at the expense of the first language. Additive bilingualism, on the other hand, occurs in situations where the learning of a second language takes place without loss to the first language. Cummins (1976, 1979) has pointed out that some of the positive effects of bilingualism may depend on the degree of bilingualism attained. He has argued that there may be threshold levels of linguistic competence that bilingual children must reach in order to experience the potentially positive effects of bilingualism on cognitive functioning. This hypothesis assumes that those aspects of bilingualism which exert positive influences on cognitive functioning are unlikely to come into effect until the child has attained a certain minimum or threshold level of competence in two languages. He further makes the claim that there may be two threshold levels, a lower one sufficient to avoid any negative cognitive effects and a higher one which might be necessary for accelerated cognitive growth. For Cummins (1978) linguistic competence refers to the ability to make effective use of the cognitive functions of language. More specifically, it is to use language effectively as an instrument of thought and to represent the thinking processes by means of language. Cummins (1979), in suggesting a developmental interdependence hypothesis, argues that the development of second language competence is a function of the level of the child's first language competence already attained at the time when intensive exposure to the second language begins. In support of this hypothesis, Skutnabb-Kangas and Toukomaa (1976) report that in school subjects such as science, which requires an abstract mode of thought, children educated in a second language with a good level of development of their first language succeed significantly better than children who do not have adequate development of the first language.

One explanation of the hypothesis that bilingualism can influence the development of cognition is found in the theory of cognitive development presented by Piaget (1970). Although Piaget has not specifically addressed the issue of bilingualism, his position on cognitive development and its relationship to language development has implications for an understanding of the effects of bilingualism. And even though Piaget takes a conservative position on the developmental relationship between language and thought, that position does not seem to constitute a denial that bilingualism represents an enriched form of experience capable of influencing cognitive functioning positively. In Piaget's theory discrepant events, such as those presented in science problems, play a central role in setting up the type of internal conflict necessary for intellectual development. Through the equilibration processes of assimilation and accommodation, underlying structures, or schemas, continue to be built up and modified. As Piaget (1952) explains, assimilation is the incorporation of new elements of experience into an internal system, while accommodation refers to modifications of the same system as a result of one or more assimilations. Language learning also involves accommodating activity. Therefore, as Ben-Zeev (1972) points out, bilingualism presents an additional element of conflict within the linguistic environment since the child must adapt to two languages. Furthermore, in learning to manipulate language structures, the child may develop a general cognitive skill useful in other domains. According to Ben-Zeev, the cognitive conflict that triggers accommodation and the cognitive structures necessary for assimilation of new information are enhanced in the bilingual child. Cognitive development itself can then be enhanced for the bilingual.

It is possible, too, that relevant aspects of problem situations may be brought to the bilingual child's attention by the availability of two linguistic codes. This is a basic tenet of the objectification hypothesis drawn from the work of Georgian psychologists in the Soviet Union. Cummins (1976) explains the process of objectification as a process whereby objects become the focus of conscious attention, a process closely linked to language. For example, in science problem-solving situations it may be that certain relevant aspects of the problem situations, or discrepant events, may be brought to the bilingual child's attention by the availability of two different linguistic perspectives. This, then, might predict higher performance levels by bilingual children in science problem-solving situations.

The framework for investigating the ability of children to form hypotheses is set forth in a study by Quinn (1971) and Quinn and George (1975), which evaluated a method for teaching hypothesis formation to monolingual sixth-grade children in two different socioeconomic settings. Under the conditions described in that study, Quinn concluded that hypothesis formation can be taught, that the quality of the hypotheses elicited can be measured, and that there is a significant difference ($p < .001$) between the quality of hypotheses generated by students who received instruction in formulating scientific hypotheses and those who did not. Findings from four groups of sixth-grade children in Philadelphia, Pennsylvania--a control and an experimental group from an upper middle-class suburban socioeconomic level, and a control and an experimental group from a lower working-class urban socioeconomic level-- indicated that the cognitive ability to formulate scientific hypotheses functions independently of socioeconomic level. In a subsequent study with the same population, Kessler and Quinn (1977) found a significant correlation ($p < .001$) between the results of direct instruction in hypothesis formation and written language complexity for both the upper and lower socioeconomic groups.

With socioeconomic level identified as a nonsignificant variable in ability to generate increasingly complex scientific hypotheses, Kessler and Quinn (1979) conducted a pilot study comparing the effects of nonbalanced bilingualism and monolingualism on the ability to formulate scientific hypotheses and the ability to write increasingly more complex expressions of those hypotheses. Holding SES, experimental treatment, and teacher constant, results obtained from 28 sixth-graders indicated that the ability to generate hypotheses favors bilinguals, even when bilingualism is subtractive. The sample included a group of 14 English-speaking monolinguals and 14 Italian-English bilinguals in the process of replacing their first language, Italian, with English. Both groups were matched on IQ scores as measured by the *Otis Quick-Scoring Mental Ability Test, Beta, Form FM*. The mean scores for hypothesis quality and syntactic complexity were significantly higher for the subtractive bilinguals.

In light of the positive effects of bilingualism observed in the pilot study, we hypothesize in the present study that additive bilinguals taught how to approach the discrepant situations presented in science problems will experience greater gains in their hypothesis quality and linguistic complexity scores than their monolingual peers. Additive bilingualism is here operationally defined as the ability to use two languages successfully in school experiences, a characteristic of children who have experienced bilingual schooling for at least four years (K-3). During this period the first language continues to develop while the second language is added. The result is that children who acquire English as a second language in bilingual programs, which provide for continued development of the first language, meet more closely Cummins' conditions of the threshold hypothesis and developmental interdependence hypothesis than second language learners who have not experienced bilingual education.

Subjects. Subjects for this investigation were sixth-grade students in four intact classrooms, two monolingual English-speaking and two Spanish-English bilingual groups.

One control and one experimental group of monolingual children, 32 in each group, were from intact classes in the same school located in an upper-middle class suburban area of Philadelphia. In addition to SES, age and grade level, the two groups were matched on the following variables: (1) IQ as measured by the *Otis Quick-Scoring Mental Ability Test, Beta, Form FM;* (2) reading scores as measured by Part III of the *Pupil Progress Series, Diagnostic Reading Test;* (3) overall grade-point averages.

The bilingual groups were from a Mexican-American neighborhood in San Antonio, Texas. One control and one experimental group of 30 students were from intact classes in the same school in a very low socioeconomic area where Spanish functions as the language of the home and the community. Language proficiency tests designed by the school district and administered at entry to kindergarten had identified the students as Spanish dominant, with little or no proficiency in English. As a result, they were placed in bilingual education programs for grades K-3. By grade 6 all instruction was in English, the second language, but Spanish continued to function in peer interactions, in the home and community. Because of the bilingual program in which they had participated, the children were literate in both Spanish and English. The control and treatment groups were matched on mathematics scores, science scores, and reading scores, all as measured by the *Comprehensive Test of Basic Skills, Level 2, Form S.*

Methodology. The treatment given the experimental monolingual and bilingual groups consisted of 12 science inquiry film sessions and six discussion sessions, each session 40 minutes in length, with all sessions for all groups taught by the same teacher in English. Each film session, based on a

3-minute film loop depicting a single physical science problem, ended with the students writing as many hypotheses as possible in a rigorously controlled 12-minute period. The individual papers were then scored on two criteria: Quinn's Hypothesis Quality Scale (1971) and the Syntactic Complexity Formula developed by Botel, Dawkins, and Granowsky (1973).

An hypothesis is here defined as a testable explanation of an empirical relationship between at least two variables in a given problem situation. The Hypothesis Quality Scale given in Table 1 assigns a numerical value ranging from 0 to 5 for each hypothesis given, with 5 the highest score, awarded for an explicit statement of a test of an hypothesis and 0, the score for no explanation of the problem presented.

Table 1. Hypothesis Quality Scale.

Score	Criterion
0	No explanation, such as a nonsense statement, a question, an observation, a single inference about a single concrete object.
1	Nonscientific explanation, such as '... because it's magic' or '... because the man pushed a button'.
2	Partial scientific explanation, such as incomplete reference to variables, a negative explanation, an analogy.
3	Scientific explanation relating at least two variables in general or nonscientific terms.
4	Precise scientific explanation, a qualification and/or quantification of the variables.
5	Explicit statement of a test of an hypothesis. (An inference is made here that the child who states a test is also able to hypothesize adequately and precisely.

To determine the reliability of the Hypothesis Quality Scale, a set of 50 hypotheses taken from those written by the sixth-grade children in the study were given to three science educators who assigned scores using Quinn's scale. The Nash-Beyers computer program for interjudge reliability, based on Winer (1962), gave an unadjusted coefficient of 0.94, thus establishing the reliability of the scale.

In discussion sessions following each set of two film sessions, the Hypothesis Quality Scale was used to show the children how to judge their own hypotheses and how to make use of their observations and inferences to generate hypotheses of higher quality. Children in experimental groups learned to distinguish between a 0-value hypothesis such as 'Magic did it' and a 5-value one such as 'I could test my idea by putting several little bottles with different amounts of water in them in a tub and then see which ones would sink'.

The Botel, Dawkins, and Granowsky measure of syntactic complexity was selected from among others because of the theoretical basis on which it was developed and because of the ease with which it can be used by the nonlinguist. Derived from transformational-generative grammar theory, it takes into account language development and performance studies which consider the frequency of usage of structures in children's oral and written language as well as experimental data on children's processing of syntactic structures. Syntactic structures are assigned weighted scores ranging from 0 to 3. A 0-count structure is given, for example, to simple sentence structures as 'I hit the ball' and a 3-count structure to clauses used as subjects such as 'What it might do is fall down'. One significant feature of the formula is that syntactic complexity is a function of specific structures rather than sentence length.

To determine the reliability of the Syntactic Complexity Formula the same set of 50 hypotheses used in determining the interjudge reliability of the Hypothesis Quality Scale was given to four language educators for scoring. The Nash-Beyers computer program for interjudge reliability gave an unadjusted coefficient of 0.98.

At the end of the 18 sessions comprising the treatment for the experimental monolingual and bilingual groups, three additional film sessions were presented to elicit hypotheses that were scored for hypothesis quality. This written data was also scored for syntactic complexity. Scores for hypothesis quality and syntactic complexity constitute the criterion variables for the present study. The same three films were presented to the control groups, both monolingual and bilingual, to elicit hypotheses scored for the criterion variables for those groups.

Standardized reading tests were also administered to all four groups in order to have a measure against which correlations for hypothesis quality and syntactic complexity could be compared.

Results. Table 2 summarizes the mean scores attained by the control and experimental monolingual groups on hypothesis quality, syntactic complexity of the written hypotheses, and reading scores on a standardized test.

Closely matched for IQ, reading ability, and grade-point average, the control and experimental groups of the upper socioeconomic monolingual children demonstrate marked differences in their mean scores for hypothesis quality and written language complexity. The group given instruction in science problem-solving situations scored consistently higher than the control group in the quality of their hypotheses and the complexity of the written language used to express them.

Table 2. Means for monolingual groups.

Variable	Control group (N=32)	Experimental group (N=32)
Hypothesis quality	25.4	53.3
Syntactic complexity	52.6	130.0
Reading level	6.7	7.0

Table 3 summarizes mean scores for the bilingual control and experimental groups which were closely matched on standardized tests for mathematics, science, and reading.

Table 3. Means for bilingual groups.

Variable	Control group (N=30)	Experimental group (N=30)
Hypothesis quality	29.5	176.0
Syntactic complexity	39.6	181.8
Reading level	3.4	3.8

The control and experimental groups of the very low socioeconomic bilingual children also demonstrate marked differences in the two variables studied. The bilingual group given instruction in formulating scientific hypotheses scored markedly higher than the control group. Higher scores on language complexity resulted as a by-product of the science instruction.

Figure 1 compares control and treatment groups for monolingual and bilingual children on hypothesis quality scores.

The control bilingual group is slightly above the monolingual control. Both experimental groups show significant gains ($p < .001$) resulting from lessons in formulating scientific hypotheses. Of the two, however, the gain for the bilingual group is far greater than that for the monolinguals.

Figure 2 similarly compares the four groups, monolingual and bilingual control and experimental groups, on syntactic complexity scores.

Scores for written language complexity are slightly higher for the control monolingual group than for the bilinguals. Both experimental groups show significant gains ($p < .001$) in the complexity of the written language used to express their hypotheses, but of the two, the bilingual group scores higher.

To examine the interactions between hypothesis quality scores, language complexity, and reading grade equivalents, Table 4 gives Pearson product moment correlation coefficients for the control monolingual and bilingual groups.

Effects of Bilingualism on Science Problem-Solving /291

Figure 1. Comparison of hypothesis quality scores for monolingual and bilingual groups.

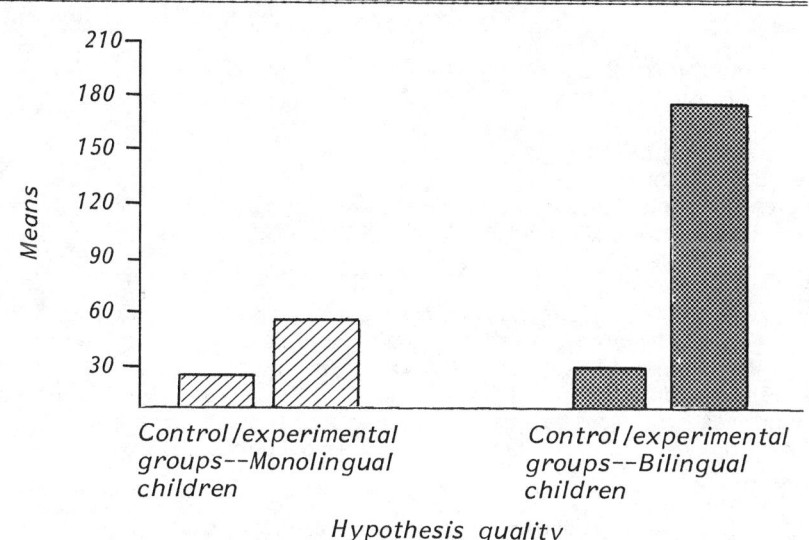

Hypothesis quality

Figure 2. Comparison of syntactic complexity scores for monolingual and bilingual groups.

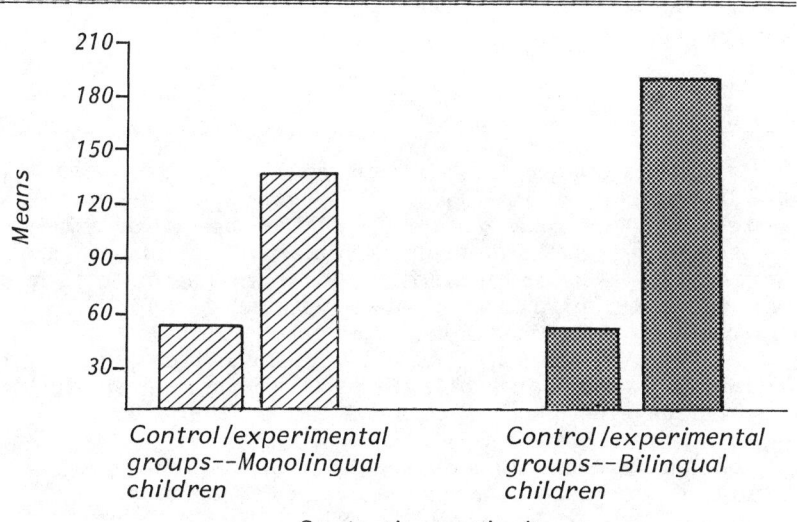

Syntactic complexity

Table 4. Correlation matrix for control groups.

Subjects \ Variable	Hypothesis quality	Language complexity	Reading
Hypothesis quality			
Monolinguals	1.00	0.87	0.62
Bilinguals	1.00	0.74	0.34
Language complexity			
Monolinguals		1.00	0.55
Bilinguals		1.00	0.33
Reading comprehension			
Monolinguals			1.00
Bilinguals			1.00

A consistently higher positive correlation ($p < .001$) is evidenced between hypothesis quality and language complexity than between these variables and reading.

Interactions between hypothesis quality, language complexity, and reading for the experimental monolingual and bilingual groups are indicated in the correlation coefficients given in Table 5.

Table 5. Correlation matrix for experimental groups.

Subjects \ Variable	Hypothesis quality	Language complexity	Reading
Hypothesis quality			
Monolinguals	1.00	0.71	0.44
Bilinguals	1.00	0.98	0.35
Language complexity			
Monolinguals		1.00	0.57
Bilinguals		1.00	0.43
Reading comprehension			
Monolinguals			1.00
Bilinguals			1.00

Hypothesis quality and syntactic complexity again correlate for both groups at the .001 level. These variables correlate more closely with one another than either does with reading.

As a summary of the results of this investigation, Figure 3 gives a comparison of the differences in the means for monolinguals and bilinguals on the two variables of hypothesis quality and syntactic complexity.

It can be observed in Figure 3 that the bilinguals as a group scored markedly higher on both variables (hypothesis quality and language complexity) than did the monolinguals.

Conclusions and implications. In summary, evidence from the study of four sixth-grade classes, two of monolingual English-speaking children and two of Spanish-English bilingual children, indicates a high positive correlation between the quality of scientific hypotheses generated and the syntactic complexity of the language used to express them in writing, suggesting that the cognitive ability to formulate scientific hypotheses and the linguistic competence to express them involve some of the same underlying organizing principles.

Figure 3. Comparison of differences in means for monolinguals and bilinguals.

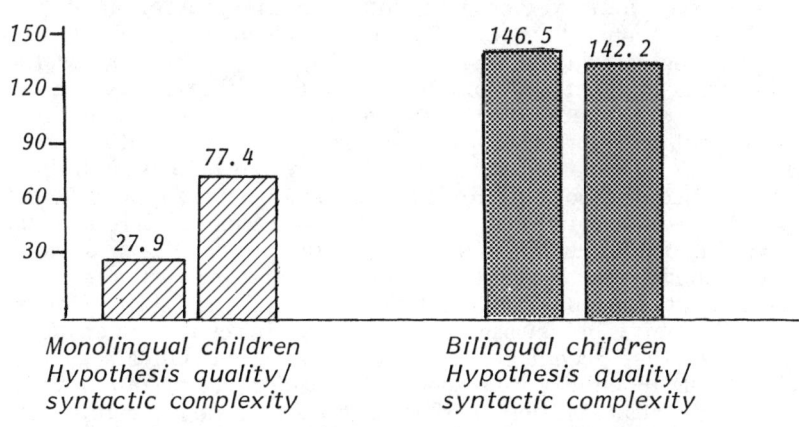

Monolingual children
Hypothesis quality/
syntactic complexity

Bilingual children
Hypothesis quality/
syntactic complexity

As conceptual development takes place, one may expect a facilitating interaction between certain aspects of divergent thinking utilized in formulating hypotheses and aspects of linguistic competence. This is more apparent in levels of syntactic complexity than in reading ability, which introduces semantic variables that reach beyond the kinds of interactive relationships examined here.

Results of this study indicate that bilingual children, given the same instruction by the same teacher in formulating scientific hypotheses in problem-solving situations requiring divergent thinking, consistently outperformed monolingual children both in the quality of hypotheses generated and in their syntactic complexity. Experimental groups were matched for age and grade level, but differed on socioeconomic level. The monolinguals were from a high SES and the bilinguals were from a very low SES. If socioeconomic level were a critical variable, prediction on outcomes would undoubtedly favor the monolingual group. In a previous study, however, Kessler and Quinn (1977) found that the socioeconomic level of the child is not a significant variable in the relationship between the psycholinguistic ability to produce complex syntactic structures and the cognitive ability to formulate scientific hypotheses. Differences do occur, however, between control and experimental groups. The quality of scientific hypotheses and the complexity of the language used to express these hypotheses are significantly higher for both monolingual and bilingual groups given instruction in formulating hypotheses for science problems. The critical variable in the observed difference between the two experimental groups is bilingualism, access to two linguistic codes, together with the cognitive enrichment interactive with it.

Piaget's theory of internal conceptual development offers explanatory power for the differences observed between the monolingual and bilingual experimental groups. In the Piagetian sense, one may view instruction in the generation of hypotheses as an effort to facilitate the learner's movement to a higher cognitive level of inquiry. The higher scores for the bilinguals suggest that bilingual children experience more fully the conceptual conflict that triggers the equilibration processes of assimilation and accommodation operative in cognitive development. Furthermore, results of the positive effects of bilingualism on problem-solving abilities observed here support Piaget's position which attributes an increasingly important role to language in implementing abstract thought in the stages of concrete operational thought and formal operations, stages characteristically represented in 11-year-olds like the sixth-graders in this study. In summary, the research results given here support other recent research findings which indicate that bilingualism in children can accelerate the development of verbal and nonverbal abilities, and that there is a positive interaction between bilingualism and cognitive functioning, such as the type of divergent thinking examined in the context of science problems.

Implications of findings which indicate the positive effects of bilingualism in children are clearly multidisciplinary and of relevance to a wide range of disciplines. Of particular interest here are the implications for education, not only of minority children but of majority children as well. Results of this study imply that a well-organized bilingual program where children develop in two linguistic perspectives can make the positive interactions of cognitive functioning and language development more fully operative.

REFERENCES

Bain, B. C., and A. Yu. 1978. Towards an integration of Piaget and Vygotsky: A cross-cultural replication concerning cognitive consequences of bilinguality. In: Aspects of bilingualism. Edited by M. Paradis. Columbia, S.C.: Hornbeam Press.

Balkan, L. 1970. Les effets du bilinguisme français-anglais sur les aptitudes intellectuelles. Bruxelles: Aimav.

Ben-Zeev, S. 1972. The influence of bilingualism on cognitive development and cognitive strategy. Unpublished Ph.D. dissertation. University of Chicago.

Ben-Zeev, S. 1977. The effect of Spanish-English bilingualism in children from less privileged neighborhoods on cognitive development and cognitive strategy. Working Papers on Bilingualism 14.83-122.
Botel, M., J. Dawkins, and A. Granowsky. 1973. A syntactic complexity formula. In: Assessment problems in reading. Edited by W. H. MacGinitie. Newark, Del.: International Reading Association
Cummins, J. 1976. The influence of bilingualism on cognitive growth. Working Papers on Bilingualism 9.1-43.
Cummins, J. 1978. Metalinguistic development of children in bilingual education programs: Data from Irish and Canadian Ukrainian-English programs. In: Aspects of bilingualism. Edited by M. Paradis. Columbia, S.C.: Hornbeam Press.
Cummins, J. 1979. Linguistic interdependence and the educational development of bilingual children. Review of Educational Research 49.222-251.
Cummins, J., and M. Gulutsan. 1974. Some effects of bilingualism on cognitive functioning. In: Bilingualism, biculturalism, and education. Edited by S. Carey. Edmonton: University of Alberta Press.
Darcy, N. T. 1953. A review of the literature on the effects of bilingualism upon the measurement of intelligence. Journal of Genetic Psychology 82.21-57.
Darcy, N. T. 1963. Bilingualism and the measurement of intelligence: Review of a decade of research. Journal of Genetic Psychology 103.259-282.
De Avila, E., and S. Duncan. 1979. Bilingualism and the metaset. NABE Journal 3.1-20.
Ianco-Worrall, A. 1972. Bilingualism and cognitive development. Child Development 43.1390-1400.
Kessler, C., and M. E. Quinn. 1977. Child language development in two socio-economic environments. Paper presented at the Annual Meeting of the American Educational Research Association, New York. ERIC Report ED 139-253. Arlington, Va.: ERIC Clearinghouse on Languages and Linguistics.
Kessler, C., and M. E. Quinn. 1979. Piaget and the bilingual child. In: Piagetian theory and the helping professions. Edited by M. Poulsen and G. Lubin. Los Angeles: University of Southern California.
Lambert, W. 1977. The effects of bilingualism on the individual: Cognitive and sociocultural consequences. In: Bilingualism: Psychological, social and educational implications. Edited by P. A. Hornby. New York: Academic Press.
Leopold, W. 1949. Speech development of a bilingual child, Vol. 3. Evanston: Northwestern University Press.
Peal, E., and W. Lambert. 1962. The relation of bilingualism to intelligence. Psychological Monographs 76.
Piaget, J. 1952. The language and thought of the child. London: Routledge and Kegan.

Piaget, J. 1970. Piaget's theory. In: Carmichael's manual of child psychology. Edited by P. H. Mussen. New York: Wiley. 703-732.

Quinn, M. E. 1971. Evaluation of a method for teaching hypothesis formation to sixth-grade children. Unpublished doctoral dissertation. University of Pennsylvania.

Quinn, M. E., and K. George. 1975. Teaching hypothesis formation. Science Education 59.289-296.

Ronjat, J. 1913. Le développement du langage observé chez un enfant bilingue. Paris: Librairie Ancienne Honoré Champion.

Scott, S. 1973. The relation of divergent thinking to bilingualism: Cause or effect. Unpublished research report, McGill University, Toronto.

Segalowitz, N. 1977. Psychological perspectives on bilingual education. In: Frontiers of bilingual education. Edited by B. Spolsky and R. Cooper. Rowley, Mass.: Newbury House. 119-158.

Skutnabb-Kangas, T., and P. Toukomaa. 1976. Teaching migrant children's mother tongue and learning of the language of the host country in the context of the socio-cultural situation of the migrant family. Helsinki: The Finnish National Commission for UNESCO.

Torrance, E. P., J. C. Gowan, J. M. Wu, and N. C. Aliotti. 1970. Creative functioning of monolingual and bilingual children in Singapore. Journal of Educational Psychology 61.72-75.

Winer, B. J. 1962. Statistical principles in experimental design. Chicago: McGraw Hill.

VERBAL STRATEGIES IN MULTILINGUAL COMMUNICATION

JOHN J. GUMPERZ

University of California, Berkeley

Abstract. Most scholars have dealt with bilingual communication in terms of the 'code-switching paradigm,' attempting to specify when, and under what conditions, speakers use the varieties in question. The assumption is that one set of forms is specific to certain settings while others are used elsewhere. There are many instances where this is indeed the case. In other cases, however, the correlation between language usage and setting breaks down. This paper is an attempt to give a detailed analysis of several such cases. Bilingual and bidialectal conversations were recorded in Chicano and Afro-American communities and were analyzed as conversational wholes, using anthropological linguistic techniques. Conclusions show that selection among alternate codes is meaningful in much the same way that choice among alternate vocabulary items in meaningful is monolingual societies.

Recent systematic research in the inner city has successfully disproved the notions of those who characterize the language of low income populations as degenerate and structurally underdeveloped. There is overwhelming evidence to show that both middle class and non-middle class children, no matter what their native language, dialect, or ethnic background, when they come to school at the age of five or six, have control of a fully formed grammatical system. The mere fact that their system is distinct from that of their teacher does not mean that their speech is not rule governed. Speech features which strike the teacher as different do not indicate failure to adjust to some universally accepted English norm; rather, they are the output of dialect or language-specific syntactic rules which are every bit as complex as those of standard English (Labov 1969).

It is clear furthermore that the above linguistic differences also reflect far-reaching and systematic cultural differences. Like the plural societies of Asia and Africa, American urban society is characterized by the coexistence of a variety of distinct cultures. Each major ethnic group has its own heritage, its own body of traditions, values, and views about what is right and proper. These traditions are passed on from generation to generation as part of the informal family or peer group socialization process and are encoded in folk art and literature, oral or written.

To understand this complex system, it is first of all necessary to identify and describe its constituent elements. Grammatical analysis must be, and has to some extent been, supplemented by ethnographic description, ethnohistory, and the study of folk art (Stewart 1968; Hanners 1969; Abrahams 1964; Kochman 1969). But mere description of component subsystems is not enough if we are to learn how the plurality of cultures operates in everyday interaction and how it affects the quality of individual lives. Minority groups in urbanized societies are never completely isolated from the dominant majority. To study their life ways without reference to surrounding populations is to distort the realities of their everyday lives. All residents of modern industrial cities are subject to the same laws and are exposed to the same system of public education and mass communication. Minority group members, in fact, spend much of their day in settings where dominant norms prevail. Although there are significant individual differences in the degree of assimilation, almost all minority group members, even those whose behavior on the surface may seem quite deviant, have at least a passive knowledge of the dominant culture. What sets them off from others is not simply the fact that they are distinct, but the juxtaposition of their own private language and life styles with that of the public at large.

This juxtaposition, which is symbolized by constant alternation between in-group and out-group modes of acting and expression has a pervasive effect on everyday behavior. Successful political leaders such as the late Martin Luther King and Bobby Seale rely on it for much of their rhetorical effect. Kernan in her recent ethnographic study of verbal communication in an Afro-American community reports that her informants' everyday conversation reveals an overriding concern—be it positive or negative—with majority culture.

Majority group members who have not experienced a similar disjuncture between private and public behavior frequently fail to appreciate its effect. They tend merely to perceive minority group members as different, without realizing the effect that this difference may have on everyday communication. This ignorance of minority styles of behavior seems to have contributed to the often discussed notion of 'linguistic deprivation'. No one familiar with the writings of Afro-American novelists of the last decade and with the recent writings on black folklore can maintain that low-income blacks are nonverbal. An exceptionally rich and varied terminological system, including such folk concepts as 'sounding', 'signifying', 'rapping', 'running it down', 'chucking', 'jiving', 'marking', etc., all referring to verbal strategies, (i.e. different modes of achieving particular communicative ends) testifies to the importance which Afro-American culture assigns to verbal art (Kochman 1969; Kernan 1969). Yet, inner city black children are often described as nonverbal, simply because they fail to respond to the school situation. It is true that lower-class children frequently show difficulty in performing adequately in formal interviews and psychological tests. But these tests are frequently administered under conditions which seem unfamiliar and, at times, threatening to minority group children. When elicitation conditions are changed, there is often a radical improvement in response (Labov 1969; Mehan 1970).

The fact that bilingualism and biculturalism have come to be accepted as major goals in inner city schools is an important advance. But if we are to achieve this goal, we require at least some understanding of the nature of code alternation and its meaning in everyday interaction. Bilingualism is, after all, primarily a linguistic term, referring to the fact that linguists have discovered significant alternations in phonology, morphology, and syntax, in studying the verbal behavior of a particular population. While bilingual phenomena have certain linguistic features in common, these features may have quite different social significance.

Furthermore, to the extent that social conditions affect verbal behavior, findings based on research in one type of bilingual situation may not necessarily be applicable to another socially different one. Much of what we know about second language learning or on bilingual interference derives from work with monolingual college students learning a foreign language in a classroom. Other research on bilingualism has dealt with isolated middle-class bilinguals residing in monolingual neighborhoods or with immigrant farmers or their descendants. We know least about the kind of situation where—as in the case of big city Afro-Americans or Chicanos—bilingualism has persisted over several generations and where strict barriers of caste limit or channel the nature of communication between the groups in question. Most importantly, we only have a minimal amount of information about the ways in which bilingual usage symbolizes the values of speakers and the social conditions in which they live.

The accepted paradigm for the linguistic study of bilingualism is the code-switching paradigm. Having observed that linguistic alter-

nates exist at the level of phonology and syntax, we proceed to ask
which alternates are used when and under what social circumstances.
The assumption is that the stream of behavior can be divided into distinct social occasions, interaction sequences, or speech events. These
events are assumed to be associated with culturally specific behavioral
norms which, in turn, determine the speech forms to be used. To
some extent this is indeed the case.

In every society there are certain performative occasions, such as
ceremonial events, court proceedings, greetings or formal introductions and the like, where the form of the language used is strictly prescribed and where deviations also change the definition of the event
(Blom and Gumperz 1970). When asked to report about their language
usage, speakers tend to respond in such all-or-none terms. Hence,
language censuses of urban neighborhoods in the U.S. usually indicate
that the minority languages are used for informal, in-group, family
interaction, while the majority language serves for communication
with outsiders.

Tape recordings of conversation in natural settings, however, frequently reveal quite a different picture. A recent study of bilingual
behavior in Texas, for example, reports many instances of what seems
almost random language mixture (Lance 1969: 75-76).

(1) Te digo que este dedo (I TELL YOU THAT THIS FINGER)
has been bothering me so much.
Se me hace que (IT SEEMS THAT) I have to respect her
porque 'ta (BECAUSE SHE IS)
But this arthritis deal, boy you get to hurting so bad you
can't hardly even ... 'cer masa pa tortillas (MAKE DOUGH
FOR TORTILLAS)

In Texas, such language mixture tends to be disparaged and referred
to by pejorative terms such as Tex Mex. It is rarely reported in the
literature and frequently dismissed as abnormal. Nevertheless, such
apparent language mixture is a common feature of informal conversation in urban bilingual societies.

When asked why they use English in situations where, according to
their own reports, the minority language is normal, speakers tend to
respond by stating that the English items in question are loan words,
words for which there are no equivalents in the home language. But
this is not always the case. On a number of occasions, Puerto Rican
mothers in Jersey City could be heard calling to their children as follows:

(2) Ven aquí, ven aquí.

If the child would not come immediately, this would be followed with

Come here, you.

Clearly, it would be difficult to justify such alternation on the grounds of ease of expression. There is more to this message than can be conveyed by usage surveys. The English is used for stylistic effect to convey meaning. An English-speaking mother under similar conditions might respond to her child's failure to obey with something like:

(3) John Henry Smith, you come here right away.

Both the English and the Puerto Rican mothers indicate annoyance, but they use different verbal strategies for doing so.

Let me illustrate this point with some additional examples from conversations recorded in Chicano and Afro-American groups in California, and analyzed in more detail in Gumperz and Hernandez (1969). Recordings in question were made by participants in group discussion, who also assisted in the analysis. The tapes were transcribed by a linguist, using detailed phonetic transcription wherever necessary, in order to isolate instances of code-switching. The contextual meaning of code-switches was then determined by a procedure which derives from the apparatus for conversational analysis developed by ethnomethodologists (Sacks 1970; Schegloff 1970). When in doubt, our hypothesis as to what was meant was checked with other participants in the conversation.

In the first two examples, the speakers are a faculty member at the University of California (E), and (M), a social worker in a day care center where E is working as a volunteer. Both speakers are native Americans of Mexican ancestry. The conversation ranges over a number of topics from the speakers' personal experience.

(4) E. What do you dream in?
    M. I don't think I ever have any conversations in my dreams. I just dream. Ha. I don' hear people talking; I jus' see pictures.
    E. Oh, they're old-fashioned, then. They're not talkies yet, huh?
    M. They're old-fashioned. No. they're not talkies yet. No, I'm tryin' to think. Yeah, there too have been talkies. Different. In Spanish and English both. An' I wouldn't be too surprised if I even had some in Chinese. (Laughter) Yeah, Ed. Deveras (REALLY).

(M. offers E a cigarette which is refused.) Tu no fumas, verdad? Yo tampoco. Deje de fumar. (YOU DON'T SMOKE, DO YOU? I DON'T EITHER; I STOPPED SMOKING) and I'm back to it again.

M breaks into Spanish, just as she is about to offer E a cigarette. The shift is accompanied by lowering of the voice of the type that accompanies confidentiality in monolinguals. She continues to talk about her smoking problem, explaining that she had given up the habit for awhile, but that she had begun again during a period when she was visiting a friend in a local institution. On each visit she would buy a pack of cigarettes; the friend would smoke some and she would take the rest home and smoke them herself. Now notice the passage:

(5) E. That's all you smoked?
 M. That's all I smoked.
 E. An' how about ... how about now?
 M. Estos ... melos halle ... estos Pall Malls me los ... me los hallaron. (THESE ... I FOUND ... THESE PALL MALLS I ... THEY WERE FOUND FOR ME.) No, I mean ... that's all the cigarettes ... that's all. They're the ones I buy.

Later on M goes on to analyze her struggle with the smoking habit as follows:

(6) M. MM-huh. Yeah. An' ... an' ... an' they tell me, 'How did you quit, Mary?' I di'n' quit. I ... I just stopped. I mean it wasn't an effort that I made. Que voy a dejar de fumar porque me hace daño (THAT I'M GOING TO STOP SMOKING BECAUSE IT'S HARMFUL TO ME, OR) this or tha', uh-uh. It just ... that ... eh ... I used to pull butts out of the ... the ... the wastepaper basket. Yeah. (Laughter) I used to go look in the (unclear) ... Se me acababan los cigarros en la noche. (MY CIGARETTES WOULD RUN OUT ON ME AT NIGHT.) I'd get desperate, y ahi voy al basurero a buscar, a sacar, you know? (Laughter) (AND THERE I GO TO THE WASTEBASKET TO LOOK FOR SOME, TO GET SOME, YOU KNOW?) Ayer los (unclear) ... no había que no traia cigarros Camille, no traia Helen, no traia yo, el Sr. de Leon, (YESTERDAY THE ... THERE WEREN'T ANY. CAMILLE DIDN'T HAVE ANY, I, MR. DE LEON DIDN'T HAVE ANY) and I saw Dixie's bag crumpled up, so I figures

> she didn't have any, y ahi ando en los ceniceros buscando a ver onde estaba la ... (AND THERE I AM IN THE ASHTRAYS LOOKING TO SEE WHERE THERE WAS THE ...) I din' care whose they were.

Here again, what someone studying the passage sentence by sentence might regard as almost random alternation between the two languages, is highly meaningful in terms of the conversational context. M is quite ambivalent about her smoking and she conveys this through her language use. Her choice of speech forms symbolizes her alternation between embarrassment and clinical detachment about her own condition. Spanish sentences reflect personal involvement (at least in this particular conversation), while English marks more general or detached statements.

Our next example derives from a discussion session recorded in Richmond, California, by a black community worker. Participants include his wife and several teenage boys. Here we find alternation between speech features which are quite close to standard English and such typically Black English features as lack of post-vocalic r̲, double negation, and copula deletion.

(7) You can tell me how your mother worked twenty hours a day and I can sit here and cry. I mean I can cry and I can feel for you. But as long as I don't get up and make certain that I and my children don't go through the same, <u>I ain't did nothin' for you, brother</u>. That's what I'm talking about.

(8) Now Michael is making a point, where that everything that happens in that house affects all the kids. It does. And Michael and <u>you makin' a point, too. Kids suppose to learn how to avoid these things</u>. But let me tell you. We're all in here. <u>We talkin' but you see</u> ...

Note the underlined phrase in passage seven, with the typically black English phrase <u>ain't did nothin'</u> embedded in what is otherwise a normal standard English sequence. On our tape the shift is not preceded by a pause or marked off by special stress or intonation contours. The speaker is therefore not quoting from another code; his choice of form here lends emphasis to what he is saying. Passage eight begins with a general statement addressed to the group as a whole. The speaker then turns to one person, Michael, and signals this change in focus by dropping the copula <u>is</u> and shifting to black phonology.

It seems clear that in all these cases, what the linguist sees merely as alternation between two systems, serves definite and clearly understandable communicative ends. The speakers do not radically switch from one style to another, but they build on the coexistence of alternate forms to create meanings. To be sure, not all instances of code alternation are meaningful. Our tapes contain several instances where the shift into black English or the use of a Spanish word in an English sentence can only be interpreted as a slip of the tongue, frequently corrected in the next sentence, or where it must be regarded merely as a sign of the speaker's lack of familiarity with the style he is employing. But, even though such errors do occur, it is nevertheless true that code switching is also a communicative skill, which speakers use as a verbal strategy in much the same way that skillful writers switch styles in a short story.

How and by what devices does the speaker's selection of alternate forms communicate meaning? The process is a metaphoric process somewhat similar to what linguists interested in literary style have called foregrounding (Garvin 1964). Foregrounding in the most general sense of the term relies on the fact that words are more than just names for things. Words also carry a host of culturally specific associations, attitudes, and values. These cultural values derive from the context in which words are usually used and from the activities with which they are associated. When a word is used in other than its normal context, these associations become highlighted or foregrounded. Thus to take an example made famous by Leonard Bloomfield (1936), the word fox when it refers to a man, as in he is a fox, communicates the notions of slyness and craftiness which our culture associates with the activities of foxes.

We assume that what holds true for individual lexical items also holds true for phonological or syntactic alternates. Whenever a speech variety is associated with a particular social category of speakers or with certain activities, this variety comes to symbolize the cultural values associated with these features of the nonlinguistic environment. In other words, speech varieties, like words, are potentially meaningful and, in both cases, this is brought out by reinterpreting meanings in relation to context. As long as the variety in question is used in its normal environment, only its basic referential sense is communicated. But when it is used in a new context, it becomes socially marked, by virtue of the fact that the values associated with the original context are mapped onto the new message.

In any particular instance of code-switching, speakers deduce what is meant by an information processing procedure which takes account of the speaker, the addressee, the social categories to which they can be assigned in the context, the topic, etc. (Blom and Gumperz 1970). Depending on the nature of the above factors, a wide variety of contextual meanings can be communicated. In the examples cited in this paper, all contextual meanings derive from the basic meaning inclusion (we) versus exclusion (they). This underlying meaning is then reinterpreted in the light of the co-occurring contextual factors to indicate such things as degree of involvement (items 4 and 5), anger (items 2 and 3), emphasis (item 7), change in focus (8). In the following additional example, taken from a graduate student's recording of a Korean-English family conversation, Korean seems to be used simply as a device to direct one's question to one out of several potential addressees.

(9) A. No, the lady used to know us. Ka mirri saram ya, ku wife-uga, mariji, odi University ... yoginga, odinga ... (YOU KNOW THAT MAN, HIS WIFE, I MEAN, WHICH UNIVERSITY ... HERE, OR WHERE ...)
U. Tokaebbi katchi saenging saram? (YEAH, THE ONE THAT LOOKS LIKE A GHOST?)
A. Unn. Dr. Kaeng katchiin saram. (YEAH, THE ONE THAT IS LIKE DR. KAENG.)
L. Do teachers that teach in Japan have to have teaching credentials?
C. Well, it depends. If you're going to teach in a military installation.

Speakers A and U here are of the older generation of immigrants who are somewhat more imbued with Korean culture. L and C are college students who are probably most at home in English. Thus, A's shift to Korean is interpreted by U as an invitation to respond similarly. L's use of English, along with her topic, mark her message as addressed to C.

On other occasions, switching may simply serve as a sign to indicate that the speaker is quoting someone else:

(10) Because I was speakin' to my baby ... my ex-baby sitter, and we were talkin' about the kids you know, an' I was tellin' her ... uh, 'Pero, como, you know, ... uh ... la Estela y la Sandi ... relistas en el telefon. (BUT, HOW, YOU KNOW ... UH ... ESTELA AND SANDI ARE VERY PRECOCIOUS ON THE TELEPHONE.)

We have chosen examples of code-switching from a number of languages to highlight the fact that the meanings conveyed by code-switching are independent of the phonological shape or historical origin of the alternates in question. The association between forms and meaning is quite arbitrary. Any two alternates having the same referential meaning can become carriers of social meaning.

The ability to interpret a message is a direct function of the listener's home background, his peer group experiences, and his education. Differences in background can lead to misinterpretation of messages. The sentence he is a Sikh has little or no meaning for an American audience. To anyone familiar with speech behavior in Northern India, however, it conveys a whole host of meanings, since Sikhs are stereotypically known as bumblers. Similarly the above-cited statement he is a fox, which conveys slyness to middle class whites, is interpreted as a synonym for he is handsome in black culture. The process of communication thus requires both shared grammar and shared rules of language usage. Two speakers may speak closely related and, on the surface, mutually intelligible varieties of the same language, but they may nevertheless misunderstand each other because of differences in usage rules resulting from differences in background. We must know the speakers' normal usage pattern, i.e. which styles are associated as unmarked forms with which activities and relationships, as well as what alternates are possible in what context, and what cultural associations these carry.

Note that the notion of culture that emerges from this type of analysis is quite different from the conventional one. Linguists attempting to incorporate cultural information into their descriptions tend to regard culture as a set of beliefs and attitudes which can be measured apart from communication. Even the recent work which utilizes actual speech samples by eliciting 'subjective reactions' to these forms or evaluations, going considerably beyond earlier work, does not completely depart from this tradition, since it continues to rely on overt or conscious judgment. Our own material suggests that culture plays a role in communication which is somewhat similar to the role of syntactic knowledge in the decoding of referential meanings. Cultural differences, in other words, affect judgment both above and below the level of consciousness. A person who may have every intention of avoiding cultural bias may, by subconsciously superimposing his own interpretation on the verbal performances of others, nevertheless bias his judgment of their general ability, efficiency, etc.

We know very little about the distribution of usage rules in particular populations. For example, there seems to be no simple correlation with ethnic identity, nor is it always possible to predict usage rules on the basis of socioeconomic indexes. To go back for a moment to the Puerto Rican neighborhood referred to above: While the majority of the Puerto Ricans in our Jersey City block followed usage patterns like those described above, there are others residing among them whose patterns differ significantly. A Puerto Rican college student took a tape recorder home and recorded informal family conversation over a period of several days. It is evident from his recording, and he himself confirms this in interviews, that in his family English serves as the normal medium of informal conversation, while Spanish is socially marked and serves to convey special connotations of intimacy and anger.

It follows that while the usual sociological measures of ethnic background, social class, educational achievements, etc., have some correlation with usage rules, they cannot be regarded as accurate predictors of performance in particular instances. On the contrary, social findings based on incomplete data or on populations different from those for which they were intended, may themselves contribute to cultural bias. The use of responses to formal tests and interviews to judge the verbal ability of lower class bilinguals is a case in point. Rosenthal has eloquently shown that teachers' expectations have a significant effect on learning (1969). When these expectations are effected by misapplied or inaccurate social science findings, education suffers. An incident from a tape-recorded session in Black Language Arts will illustrate the point.

(11) Student: (Reading from an autobiographical essay) This lady didn't have no sense.
Teacher: What would be a standard English alternate for this sentence?
Student: She didn't have any sense. But not this lady: she <u>didn't have no sense.</u>

It happens that in the above case both student and teacher were black, and the classroom atmosphere was relaxed. Thus, the student felt free to give the response she gave. Had the situation been more constrained, she would not have been able to convey what she really wanted to say.

Our final example derives from classroom observation of first grade reading sessions in a racially integrated California school district. Classes in the district include about 60% white and 40% black, chicano, and oriental children. College student observers find that most reading classes have a tracking system such that children are assigned to fast or slow reading groups and these groups are taught by different methods and otherwise receive different treatment.

Even in first grade reading periods, where presumably all children are beginners, the slow reading groups tend to consist of 90% blacks and chicanos. Does this situation reflect real learning difficulties, or is it simply a function of our inability to diagnose reading aptitude in culturally different children? Furthermore, given the need for some kind of ability grouping, how effective and how well adapted to cultural needs are the classroom devices that are actually used to bridge the reading gap?

Recently we observed a reading session with a slow reading group of three children, and seven fast readers. The teacher worked with one group at a time, keeping the others busy with individual assignments. With the slow readers she concentrated on the alphabet, on spelling of individual words, and supposedly basic grammatical concepts such as the distinctions between questions and statements. She addressed the children in what white listeners would identify as pedagogical style. Her enunciation was deliberate and slow. Each word was clearly articulated with even stress and pitch, as if to avoid any verbal sign of emotion, approval, or disapproval. Children were expected to speak only when called upon, and the teacher would insist that each question be answered before responding to further ideas. Unsolicited remarks were ignored even if they referred to the problem at hand. Pronunciation errors were corrected whenever they occurred, even if the reading task had to be interrupted. The children seemed distracted and inattentive. They were guessing at answers, 'psyching out' the teacher in the manner described by Holt (1965) rather than following her reasoning process. The following sequence symbolizes the artificiality of the situation.

(12) Teacher: Do you know what a question is? James, ask William a question.
James: William, do you have a coat on?
William: No, I do not have a coat on.

James asks his question and William answers in a style which approaches in artificiality that of the teacher, characterized by citation form pronunciation of ([ey] rather than [ə]) of the indefinite article, lack of contraction of do not, stress on the have, staccato enunciation as if to symbolize what they perceive to be the artificiality and incomprehensibility of the teacher's behavior.

With the advanced group, on the other hand, reading became much more of a group activity and the atmosphere was more relaxed. Words were treated in context, as part of a story. Children were allowed to volunteer answers. There was no correction of pronunciation, although some deviant forms were also heard. The children actually enjoyed competing with each other in reading, and the teacher responded by dropping her pedagogical monotone in favor of more animated natural speech. The activities around the reading table were not lost on the slow readers who were sitting at their desks with instructions to practice reading on their own. They kept looking at the group, neglecting their own books, obviously wishing they could participate. After a while one boy picked up a spelling game from a nearby table and began to work at it with the other boy, and they began to argue in a style normal for black children. When their voices were raised the teacher turned and asked them to go back to reading.

In private conversation, the teacher who is very conscientious and seemingly concerned with all her children's progress, justified her ability grouping on the grounds that children in the slow group lacked books in their homes and 'did not speak proper English'. She stated they needed practice in grammar and abstract thinking and pronunciation, and suggested that given this type of training they would eventually be able to catch up with the advanced group. We wonder how well she will succeed. Although clearly she has the best motives and would probably be appalled if one were to suggest that her ability grouping and her emphasis on the technical aspects of reading and spelling with culturally different children is culturally biased, her efforts are not so understood by the children themselves. Our data indicates that the pedagogical style used with slow readers carries different associations for low middle class and low income groups. While whites identify it as normal teaching behavior, ghetto residents associate it with the questioning style of welfare investigators and automatically react by not cooperating. In any case, attuned as they are to see meaning in stylistic choice, the black children in the slow reading group cannot fail to notice that they are being treated quite differently and with less understanding than the advanced readers.

What are the implications of this type of situation for our understanding of the role of dialect differences on classroom learning? There is no question that the grammatical features of black dialects discovered by urban dialectologists in recent years are of considerable importance for the historical study of origin of these dialects and for linguistic theory in general, but this does not necessarily mean that they constitute an impediment to learning. Information on black dialect is often made known to educators in the form of simple lists of deviant features with the suggestion that these features might interfere with reading. There is little, if any, experimental evidence that the pronunciations characteristic of urban black English actually interfere with the reading process. Yet the teacher in our classroom, for example, spent considerable time attempting to teach her slow readers the distinction between pin and pen. Lack of a vowel distinction in these two words is widespread among blacks, but also quite common among whites in northern California. In any case, there is no reason why homophony in this case should present more difficulty than homophony in such words as sea and see, and know and no.

It is not enough simply to present the educator with the descriptive linguistic evidence. What we need is properly controlled work on reading as such, work which does not deal with grammar alone. Our data suggests that urban language differences, while they may or may not interfere with reading, do have a significant influence on a teacher's expectation and hence on the learning environment. Since bilinguals and bidialectals rely heavily on code-switching as a verbal strategy, they are especially sensitive to the relationship between language and context. It would seem that they learn best under conditions of maximal contextual reinforcement. Sole concentration on the technical aspects of reading, grammar, and spelling may so adversely affect the learning environment as to outweigh any advantages to be gained.

The problem of contextual relevance is not confined to contact with speakers of black English. It also applies, for example, to the teaching of both English and Spanish in bilingual schools. When interviewed about their school experiences, Puerto Rican high school students in New York as well as Texas and California Chicano students uniformly complain about their lack of success in Spanish instruction. They resent the fact that their Spanish teachers single out their own native usages as substandard and inadmissable both in classroom speech and in writing.

It seems clear, furthermore, that progress in urban language instruction is not simply a matter of better teaching aids and improved textbooks. Middle class adults have to learn to appreciate differences in communicative strategies of the type discussed here. Teachers themselves must be given instruction in both the linguistic and ethnographic aspects of speech behavior. They must become acquainted with code selection rules in formal and informal settings, as well as those themes of folk literature and folk art that form the input to these rules, so that they can diagnose their own communication problems and adapt methods to their children's background.

NOTES

Research reported on in this paper has been supported by grants from the Urban Crisis Program and the Institute of International Studies, University of California, Berkeley. I am grateful to Edward Hernandez and Louisa Lewis for assistance in field work and analysis.

REFERENCES

Abrahams, Roger D. 1964. Deep down in the jungle. Hatboro, Pennsylvania, Folklore Associates.
Blom, Jan Petter, and John J. Gumperz. 1970. Social meaning in linguistic structures. In: John J. Gumperz and Dell Hymes, eds., Directions in sociolinguistics. New York, Holt, Rinehart, and Winston (in press).
Bloomfield, Leonard. 1936. Language. New York.
Garvin, Paul, ed. 1969. A Prague school reader. Washington, D.C., Georgetown University Press.

Gumperz, John J., and Edward Hernandez. 1969. Cognitive aspects of bilingual communication. Working Paper No. 28, Language Behavior Research Laboratory, University of California, Berkeley, December.
Hannery, Ulf. 1969. Soulside. Stockholm.
Holt, John Caldwell. 1964. How children fail. New York, Pitman.
Kochman, T. H. 1969. Rapping in the Black Ghetto. In Transaction, February.
Labov, William. 1969. The logic of nonstandard Negro English. In: Linguistics and the teaching of standard English. Monograph Series on Languages and Linguistics No. 22. Washington, D. C., Georgetown University Press.
Lance, Donald M. 1969. A brief study of Spanish-English bilingualism. Research report. Texas A and M University.
Mehan, B. 1970. Unpublished lecture delivered to the Kroeber Anthropological Society meetings, April 25.
Mitchell, Claudia. 1969. Language behavior in a black urban community. Unpublished doctoral dissertation, University of California, Berkeley.
Rosenthal, Robert. 1968. Pygmalion in the classroom. New York, Holt, Rinehart, and Winston.
Sacks, Harvey. 1970. On the analyzability of stories by children. In: John J. Gumperz and Dell Hymes, eds., Directions in sociolinguistics. New York, Holt, Rinehart, and Winston. (in press)
Schegloff, Emanuel. 1970. Sequencing in conversational openings. In: John J. Gumperz and Dell Hymes, eds., Directions in sociolinguistics. New York, Holt, Rinehart, and Winston. (in press)
Shuy, Roger W. 1964. Social dialects and language learning. Proceedings of the Bloomington, Indiana Conference. N. C. Y. E. Cooperative Research Project No. OE5-10-148.
Song, Linda M. 1970. Language switching in Korean English bilinguals. Unpublished manuscript. University of California, Berkeley.
Stewart, W. 1968. Continuity and change in American Negro dialects. The Florida FL Reporter, spring.
Troike, Rudolph C. 1969. Receptive competence, productive competence and performance. In: James E. Alatis, ed., Linguistics and the teaching of standard English. Monograph Series on Languages and Linguistics No. 22. Washington, D. C.: Georgetown University Press. pp. 63-75.

IMPLICATIONS OF THE ORAL/LITERATE CONTINUUM FOR CROSS-CULTURAL COMMUNICATION

Deborah Tannen
Georgetown University

In pursuit of understanding linguistic phenomena in discourse, I am always in search of factors motivating linguistic choices. A research area that goes far to explain findings of my own and others' scholarly investigations discusses oral vs. literate tradition. Begun in the sixties as an attempt to explore the impact of writing on cognitive and rhetorical processes, work in this area has been advanced by researchers in anthropology, literature, and cognitive psychology. I suggest their findings are enlightening as well for linguists. Elsewhere I have discussed implications for an understanding of the relationship between spoken and written language in various modes (Tannen 1980a and in preparation a) and of communicative style (Tannen 1980b and in preparation b).[1] Here I explore implications for cross-cultural communication.

I briefly outline research in oral/literate tradition and suggest that the key distinction is not between orality vs. literacy as such, but between strategies that have been associated with oral and literate tradition which can be employed in any mode. What has been called 'oral tradition' is language use which emphasizes shared knowledge or the relationship between communicator and audience; what has been called 'literate' emphasizes decontextualized content or downplays communicator/audience interaction.[2] As communication can contain more or fewer of the strategies associated with these traditions, to greater or lesser degrees, I further suggest that the distinction be conceived of not as a dichotomy but rather as a continuum.

In discussing implications of the oral/literate continuum for cross-cultural communication, I draw upon findings of my research on narrative and conversational strategies. I refer to cross-cultural communication on three levels: (1) between natives of different countries (Greeks and Americans); (2) between compatriots of different cultural, ethnic, or geographic backgrounds (Americans of Greek, Jewish, and nonimmigrant parents and grandparents from New York and California); (3) between women and men.

I suggest that nearly all communication is to some degree cross-cultural, in the sense that no two people have exactly the same background and, consequently, precisely the same expectations about interaction. Expectations, however, are more strikingly different when backgrounds diverge more drastically; hence, cross-cultural differences are greater in (1) than (2), and in (2) than (3).[3]

Oral vs. literate tradition. A number of scholars in varying fields pioneered research in the sixties examining the effects of writing on cognitive and social processes (Goody and Watt 1963, Havelock 1963, Ong 1967). The seventies brought continued work by the same scholars (Goody 1977, Havelock 1971, Ong 1977) as well as others (Cole and Scribner 1974, Cook-Gumperz and Gumperz 1980, Kay 1977, Olson 1977, Scribner and Cole 1980).

Lord (1960), following Parry, had demonstrated that oral epics were not memorized but reconstructed at each telling through the imposition of formulaic phrases on the skeleton of a familiar plot. Inspired by this insight, Havelock (1963) surmised that the difference between oral reconstruction and rote memory associated with oral vs. literate tradition, respectively, is not just a habit of expression but represents a difference in approach to knowledge and thought. In literate society, knowledge is seen as facts and insights preserved in written records. As Ong (1967) also points out, in oral culture, formulaic expressions (sayings, cliches, proverbs, and so on) are the repository of received wisdom.

Formulaic expressions function as wholes, as a convenient way to signal knowledge that is already shared. In oral tradition, it is not assumed that the expressions contain meaning in themselves, in a way that can be analyzed out. Rather, words are a convenient tool to signal already shared social meaning. Thus, in an oral tradition, as has been pointed out elsewhere (Tannen and Oztek 1977), it does not matter whether one says 'I could care less' or 'I couldn't care less'. The expression is, in either case, a handy way to make reference to a familiar idea. As Olson (1977) puts it, 'the meaning is in the context'. In contrast, in literate tradition, 'the meaning is in the text'.

Ong observes that in oral tradition, thought is 'exquisitely elaborated' through a stitching together of formulaic language which he calls 'rhapsodic'. In literate tradition, thought is analytic, sequential, linear. Olson notes that truth, in oral tradition, resides in common-sense reference to experience, whereas in literate tradition it resides in logical or coherent argument. It is the oral sense of truth that comes naturally. Hence, says Olson, most people cannot distinguish between a conclusion that is logical and one with which they agree.

Ong explains furthermore that 'knowing' in oral tradition is achieved through analysis. This follows Havelock's assertion that understanding in oral tradition is objective. It explains the fact--puzzling and disturbing to modern scholars--that Plato would have banned poets from participation in education in the Republic. Because of their ability to move audiences emotionally, poets were a dangerous threat to the transition to literacy, by which people were to learn to suspend their emotions and approach knowledge through analytic, logical processes.

Olson points out that children learn language through use of formulas; Wong Fillmore (1979) has demonstrated this for second language acquisition. That is, children do not learn the meanings of individual words and rules for putting them together, like Tinker toys and sticks. Rather, they learn strings of words associated with fixed intonation and other paralinguistic features, to be uttered in certain social settings. By trying the expressions out in various settings, they arrive at correct associations--or at least they approximate correct associations more and more closely.[4]

I hypothesize that when children do learn that words have literal meanings, they go through a stage of overapplication of this principle. This accounts for their inclination, at a certain age, to interrupt their parents during adult conversation with complaints like 'That's not what he said', and offer corrections that do not change the sense at all, to the parents' great annoyance. This stage of language development furnishes Hank Ketcham with numerous Dennis the Menace jokes which derive humor from the boy's literal interpretation of words that were meant formulaically.

In a broad sense, then, strategies associated with oral tradition place emphasis on shared knowledge and the interpersonal relationship between communicator and audience. In this, they 'elaborate' what Bateson (1972) calls the metacommunicative function of language: the use of words to convey something about the relationship between communicator and audience. Literate tradition emphasizes what Bateson calls the communicative function of language: the use of words to convey information or content. This gives rise to the idealization that language can be 'autonomous' (Kay 1977)--that is, that words can carry meaning all by themselves, and that it is their prime function to do so.

Scollon and Scollon (to appear) caution against generalizing the 'bard and formula' notion of orality propounded by scholars whose work I have discussed here. The Scollons note that oral traditions can differ strikingly, and they demonstrate this with Athabaskan examples. They suggest instead a distinction between focused and nonfocused situations. The former is one in which 'there are strong limitations on negotiation between participants'; the latter is one in which 'the highest value is on mutual sense making among the participants'.

Their argument reinforces the awareness that it is not 'orality' per se that is at issue but rather the relative prominence of communicator/audience interaction on the one hand, as opposed to the relative prominence of decontextualized content on the other. For the present discussion, I am going to continue to refer to strategies associated with oral vs. literate tradition, because this is the framework in which the work discussed has been done. However, I do not intend to imply that all oral traditions make use of these strategies nor that they are inherently oral in nature.

All these scholars point out that literate tradition does not replace oral. Rather, the two are superimposed upon and intertwined with each other. Similarly, no individual is either 'oral' or 'literate', but rather uses strategies associated with one or the other tradition in various settings. Goody and Watt (1963) suggest that oral tradition is associated with the family and in-group, while literate tradition is learned and passed on in the decontextualized setting of the school. Certainly this is true, in a prototypical sense. But strategies associated with one or the other tradition can be realized in any setting and in any mode. Literary fiction, for example (Tannen 1980a), uses many strategies that have been considered oral in a written mode.

Cook-Gumperz and Gumperz (1980) point out that strategies associated with literate tradition have been conventionalized in Western countries for oral use in public settings. In fact, it is clear that many middle class families employ strategies associated with literate tradition in the home. This can be seen in their prodding children to 'get to the point' and 'stick to the point'. An outgrowth of such attitudes, too, can be seen when parents and teachers tell children that their talk ought to be 'logical', that, for example, 'two negatives makes a positive', as if sentences can and ought to be analyzable to constituent parts, like mathematical equations. In fact, in interaction, it does not matter how many negative particles a sentence contains, except insofar as more may be better, as in vernacular Black English, which requires negative concord (Labov 1969).

It seems, then, that 'mainstream' middle class Americans have conventionalized verbal strategies and linguistic attitudes associated with literate tradition for use in a wide variety of contexts, whereas Americans of some ethnic and geographic backgrounds, as well as members of other cultural groups (including Greeks), have conventionalized more discourse strategies drawing upon oral tradition for use in a broad range of settings.

It has been suggested that many black children approach school tasks as real-world problems, rather than as decontextualized tasks. Thus, in choosing a word to answer a question on a reading test, they do not limit themselves to the information given in the paragraph presented but choose an answer that takes into account their broader experience (Aronowitz to appear, Nix and Schwarz 1979). The following discussion considers some of the strategies associated with oral vs. literate tradition and shows the effects of their use in cross-cultural communication.

Formulaic language. Ong observes that Americans overvalue strategies associated with literate tradition. 'Most Americans', he says,

> even those who write miserably, are so stubbornly literate in principle as to believe that what makes a word a real word is not its meaningful use in vocal exchange but rather its presence on the pages of a dictionary (1979:2).

In the same spirit, most Americans feel that they ought not to use formulaic language. They feel that fixedness implies insincerity; hence the word 'cliche', with its negative connotation. This attitude persists despite the fact that no one can talk without extensive use of formulaic speech. Fillmore (1979) suggests that 'a large portion of a person's ability to get along in a language consists in the mastery of formulaic utterances'. Nonetheless, many Americans, when uttering formulas, make excuses ('I know this is a cliche, but ...' 'Everyone must say this, but ...') or otherwise mark their expressions with verbal or nonverbal equivalents of quotation marks.

Speakers in many other cultures highly value formulaic use of language. For example, speakers of Greek and Turkish (Tannen and Oztek 1977, Zimmer 1958), Yiddish (Matisoff 1979), Arabic (Ferguson 1976), and other languages seem to be happiest if they can find a fixed way of saying what they mean. For one thing, this lends to their utterance the weight and legitimacy of received wisdom: if everyone says it, it must be true. Second, it assures them that they are making a socially appropriate conversational contribution.

Situational formulas of the type found in Turkish and Greek (Tannen and Oztek 1977, following Zimmer 1958) are rigid collocations that are always said in particular social settings. Their omission carries meaning; it is perceived as a social gaffe or an intended slight, just as in American culture hanging up the telephone without saying 'goodbye' constitutes a positive act that might be reported: 'S/he hung up on me.' Rigid situational formulas are a prototype of formulaic language, or one end of a continuum of fixedness in language use, the other end of which might be a totally new thought expressed in a totally original syntactic pattern. There is a range of relative fixedness and relative novelty along the continuum, including use of familiar combinations of words, familiar syntactic patterns, and so on. As Jarrett (1978) demonstrates for blues lyrics, all utterances are 'inevitably traditional', although the degree of fixedness may range from use of

clearly recognizable formulas to totally new lines which are
formulaic in their adherence to recognizable patterns of rhythm,
metaphor, register, syntax, and so on. Similarly, in everyday
interaction, individuals differ with respect to the relative frequency of their use of more or less formulaic language, and
cultures differ with regard to value placed on relative fixedness vs. relative novelty in expression. These value differences may be seen as expressions of attitudes toward language
associated with literate vs. oral tradition.

What are the consequences in cross-cultural interaction of
differing attitudes toward formulaic use of language? A person
accustomed to using utterly fixed expressions, such as Greek
situational formulas, feels linguistically hamstrung if s/he
cannot find equivalents in the language s/he is speaking. To
understand this effect, one need merely imagine trying to end
a phone conversation without uttering a conversational closing.
What then can a speaker do when feeling called upon to utter
a formulaic expression in conversation in a different language?

One possibility is to borrow the formula from the other language, or to translate it into the language spoken. Zimmer
(1958) notes that Germans residing in Turkey had the habit of
uttering Turkish situational formulas in otherwise monolingual
and monocultural German conversation. Similarly, Jewish Americans, God bless them, often utter Yiddish formulaic expressions
in English conversation--either in Yiddish or in English translation. This strategy, however, is successful only in interaction with others who are familiar with the formulas--in other
words, in communication that is not strictly cross-cultural.

In interaction with others who are not familiar with the situational formulas--or who do not recognize the formulaic nature
of an utterance because they are not familiar with the paradigm
--the speaker may choose to omit them (if possible), thus operating with a reduced linguistic repertoire, with attendant frustrations. However, a speaker often does not realize, or does
not realize in time, that an utterance is 'formulaic', since so
much of speech is habitual and seems self-evidently appropriate.[5] In that case, the formulaic utterance is used, and the
interlocutor may not recognize its formulaic nature. Then, at
the very least, a level of resonance is lost, much as a literary
allusion is lost on someone who is not familiar with the source.
Thus a lack of richness is experienced in cross-cultural communication. Even worse, however, the utterance may be taken
literally and therefore seem odd. At the very worst, its intention can be missed entirely. In the event that an interlocutor perceives correctly the formulaic nature of an utterance,
s/he may find its use charming or quaint, or lazy or insincere,
depending upon his or her attitude toward use of formulaic
language. A final strategy, as pointed out to me by Penelope
Alatis, is to translate the formula and explain its meaning and
use. This, however, enlarges the formula to a topic of talk
rather than simply a vehicle for expression.

I have found that Greeks are more likely to explain motivations, events, and so on with reference to familiar sayings, and that this accounts in part for the fact that they sometimes strike Americans as romantic, trivial-minded, or unsophisticated. But a reverse phenomenon occurs as well. I can recall a time before I knew Modern Greek, when I heard Greeks use expressions in English that I now know are formulaic in Modern Greek. At the time they struck me as highly imaginative, poetic, and charming. I have a suspicion that this phenomenon contributes to the fact that young American women travelling in Greece often find young Greek men inexpressibly charming and poetic. It is an instance of the broader phenomenon pointed out by Sapir (1958) that in communicating with speakers from a different culture, one cannot distinguish between individual and culturally shared style.

Women and men. The phenomenon of using language in a fixed and formulaic way is significant in another kind of cross-cultural communication: talk between women and men. There is a stereotype among Americans that women use language carelessly, that they are not precise, that they talk too much (Lakoff 1975). It has been shown, too, that women pay more attention than men to interpersonal dynamics in conversation--that they are more sensitive than men to nonverbal and paralinguistic cues: the channels that are emphasized in oral tradition. Fillmore (1979) counts as one of four kinds of verbal fluency 'the ability to have appropriate things to say in a wide range of contexts', and he notes that such fluency is often associated with skillful manipulation of fixed expressions. This is the only kind of fluency which he exemplifies with reference to a female (Barbara Walters).

I suggest that in their attention to the interpersonal dynamic of conversation, women are more likely to make use of verbal devices that build upon shared cultural background and context, among them formulaic language. However, since Americans tend to devalue strategies associated with oral tradition, they place more value on the 'precise' and 'analytic' use of language which is prototypically associated with literacy and with men. Thus, the discontinuity in expectations of a 'good person' and a 'good woman' which has been found in other domains (Broverman et al. 1970), may hold as well for the use of formulaic language. As Lakoff (personal communication) has suggested, this may account for the puzzling phenomenon that American women, who clearly have more 'rights' than their counterparts in other cultures, seem to be more disturbed by male/female differences. It may be that in those other cultures a high degree of attention to interpersonal dynamics--as seen, for example, in use of formulaic language--is valued for both women and men.

What to say: Commonplaces, personalizing, philosophizing. The use of formulaic or well-worn language is closely associated with what is said; form and content are intertwined. Just as Greeks find it appropriate to use familiar expressions, so they are more disposed to utter sentiments that are familiar and often reiterated. Just as Americans find it insincere to utter cliches, so they think it better to say something novel than something that has been said often before.

These differing expectations showed up in oral narratives told by Greeks and Americans. Under the direction of Wallace Chafe at the University of California, Berkeley, a film was made which had sound but no dialogue, showing a series of simple events: a man was picking pears; a boy took a basket of pears; he fell off his bike and was helped up by three other boys; he gave the three boys pears; and they ate them as they passed by the pear-picker. The movie was shown to 20 American women and they were asked to tell what they had seen. I took the film to Greece and elicited narratives from 20 Athenian young women.[6] For one thing, in telling about the film, the Greeks in the study were far more likely to try to find a theme or general meaning for the film, and in so doing, they often chose culturally familiar themes, such as the beauty of agricultural life. A readiness to make use of culturally familiar explanations showed up in many ways. For example, in explaining why the boy fell off his bicycle, almost half (nine) of the Greeks made reference to the appearance of a girl, cuing a familiar boy-meets-girl 'script' (see Tannen 1979a for discussion of scripts, frames, schemata). The Americans did not do this. They only mentioned the girl if they were making reference to her in their explanation of causality of the fall.

Another related dimension is the tendency to talk in terms of personal experience and to instantiate rather than talk in abstract or general terms. For example, several of the Greeks followed up their summaries of what happened in the film with their own ideas of what it all meant, in a way that sounds to Americans like 'philosophizing'. One Greek speaker made much of the 'conflicts' in the film, and another focused on the many 'falls', relating this to her pessimistic outlook in general and the difficulty she was experiencing in her own life at the time.

In a comparative study of indirectness in conversation (Tannen 1976), I asked Greeks and Americans, on a questionnaire, for their interpretations of a hypothetical conversation between a husband and wife about whether or not to go to a party. In answering the question, many of the Greeks made reference to their own experience: 'That's the way my husband would do it', or 'That's how it happens in my house'. Others answered by instantiating the conversation: 'The wife is probably home all day while her husband works, so she'd probably want to go to the party.' In contrast, the Americans tended to answer in terms of the dialogue itself: 'The husband said OK, and OK means yes.' Thus, the Greeks were more inclined to instantiate, to personalize, and to answer in terms of broader context. A later study (Tannen 1979c), administering the same questionnaire to Greek-Americans, found that native-born Americans of Greek parents and grandparents exhibited strategies slightly closer to those of the Greeks than those of the Americans. In other words, communication between Americans of different backgrounds is also cross-cultural communication, and those who speak what is ostensibly 'the same language' may nonetheless be using and expecting strategies influenced by those of parents, grandparents, other relatives, or peers of different cultural backgrounds.

Interpretation vs. reporting. Other patterns emerged in the stories about the film which are related to the tendency to personalize. Americans seemed to approach the narrative production as a memory task. They seemed to include as many details as possible, as accurately as possible, and were very concerned with the temporal order of events. In contrast, the Greeks seemed to approach the task as they would storytelling in conversation. Their narratives were shorter, since they included only those details which contributed to the theme they chose to develop. They made more interpretive leaps, such as omitting details or even events which did not contribute to the theme; reporting characters' feelings; calling the man a 'farmer' and the fruit 'harvest'; and adding events that did not occur.

For example, there is a scene in which a boy and girl are seen approaching each other on their bicycles, followed by one in which the boy falls off his bike. Four Greeks say directly and two imply (a total of more than 25 percent) that the boy fell off his bike because he collided with the girl. No Americans say this, although two note that they thought the bikes would collide but did not. I would hypothesize that the expectation that the bikes would collide was present for both groups of viewers, but the Greeks were more likely to commit themselves to the interpretation that (1) followed a familiar script and (2) made a better story. The Americans were more concerned with reporting precisely what the film showed. The commitment to 'stick to facts' is a strategy associated with literate tradition; the tendency to interpret, to make a story fit a familiar form, is associated with oral tradition. Another major difference between the two groups was that Americans tended to tell about the film as a film. They often repeated phrases that reminded the hearer that what was being talked about was a film ('the scene switched', 'the camera panned', and so on). The exercise of their critical faculties was most often aimed at criticizing the film-maker's technique. Thus they said the costumes were unconvincing, the soundtrack unnatural, the action too slow ('He'd never make it as a pear-picker'). In contrast, the Greeks focused their critical acumen on the characters in the film and their actions. They made judgments: the boy should not have taken the pears, he should have thanked his helpers sooner. They often made interpretations of meaning (the scene showed that children love each other). Insofar as all communication is a matter of presentation of self (Goffman 1959), the Americans' concern is to present themselves as able recallers and film critics. The Greeks are concerned with showing that they are good judges of character and film interpreters. Again, the Greeks are employing strategies recognizing personal involvement--hence oral tradition.

Male/female differences surface as well. My comparison of Greek and American women's narratives discovered that the Greek women tended to interpret more, whereas the Americans reported. However, the American women sometimes reported their personal reactions to the film as a film. For example, some reported their ongoing experience as film viewers, as in 'I thought the boy would fall'. The use of adjectives often revealed interpretive processes ('He was really brazen'). In comparing the narratives told by American men and women, Dodge (1980) and Patrick (1980) found that the American women made more interpretive comments than the men. The men tended to tell 'streamlined' narratives in which they stuck to reporting action. Thus, there seems to be a continuum of interpretive personalizing on which American men are at one end and Greek women at the other, with American women in between. Unfortunately, no narratives were collected from Greek men.

Storytelling in conversation. Another dimension of oral and literate strategy differences occurs in storytelling. As Gumperz (1977) and Fillmore (1979) note, to participate in conversation, people need a notion of how conversation is done--they must have a 'schema' for the construction of conversation and its parts. One such element is the telling of stories.

I have analyzed the natural conversation spontaneously generated at a Thanksgiving dinner among Americans of different geographical and ethnic backgrounds (Tannen 1979c, 1980d). Three participants were Jewish and from New York; two were of English/Irish and English/Italian background, both raised as Catholics. The sixth person was British. In the course of two and a half hours of conversation, all participants told stories. Analysis of the structures and the content of the stories told showed that those who were ostensibly from 'the same culture'--middle class Americans--had very different expectations of how stories should be told.

A framework for the analysis of narratives in conversation is provided by Labov (1972), based on stories told by black teenagers. Labov notes that in telling a story, a speaker's main job is to make clear to the audience what the point of the story is--to answer in advance the 'withering question', 'So what?'

Speakers communicate the point of a story--i.e. their attitude toward what is being said--by means of 'evaluation', either external or internal. External evaluation is the obvious kind: the teller steps outside the story to poke the reader verbally and say, 'Hey, here's the point'. This can be done by such comments as 'And this was the incredible thing', or by explaining, for example, 'When he said that, I felt awful'. Internal evaluation is not so obvious. It resides in all levels of verbalization such as expressive phonology, speeding up or slowing down, repetition, lexical choice, and so on. Direct quotation is a common form of internal evaluation. By putting words in the mouth of the characters, the teller communicates what happened from inside the story. Nonetheless, by deciding what words to put in the character's mouth, the teller is building the story toward the desired point.

Labov demonstrates that middle class white speakers tend to use more external evaluation, while inner city blacks use more internal evaluation. He notes as well that internal evaluation makes a better story. I believe this explains the often perceived phenomenon of 'good storytellers' among working-class people, rural people, or members of certain cultures, including Jews and Greeks. I suggest that the phenomenon results from use of strategies associated with oral tradition. Oral tradition depends for its impact on the creation of a sense of identification with characters and tellers of stories, whereas literate tradition depends upon an intellectual understanding of the principles or points to be made. Internal evaluation contributes to the sense of identification, while external evaluation makes explicit what the point is--a feature of literate-based strategies. As Kay (1977) points out, use of language prototypically associated with literacy in an industrial society is 'autonomous'. Whatever is needed for comprehension is included in the words of the text (external evaluation). In contrast, nonautonomous language depends on 'simultaneous transmission over other channels, such as the paralinguistic, postural and gestural'--the basic tools of internal evaluation. Of course, this split is an idealization; what we are dealing with is a continuum: more or less reliance on features of spoken-like vs. written-like language. Lexical choice, by writers as much as by speakers, constitutes internal evaluation. However, a word may be spoken with a certain intonation, tone, gesture, and facial expression that would add to the evaluation, whereas the written word must stand alone.

In the analysis of stories told over dinner, it became clear that the New Yorkers of Jewish background employed more internal evaluation and avoided explicitly stating the points of their stories. Their strategy[8] seemed to be--and this was supported by participants' comments upon hearing the tape, i.e. 'playback' (Labov and Fanshel 1977)--to capitalize upon shared background by not telling the point straight out, simultaneously building upon and reinforcing a sense of 'being on the same wave length'. The fact that the lack of external evaluation seemed inappropriate to the native Californians can be seen in their on-the-spot reactions as well as their comments during playback. For example, one New Yorker told the following story:[9]

(1) K: Í have a little sèven-year-old student ... a little

gírl who wears those. .... She .. is *too*
p
(2) F: ⌊ She wears those? [chuckle]⌋

múch. Can yóu imagine? She's séven years old,
acc

and she síts in her chair and she goes .... [squeals
acc ─────]

and squirms in his seat.]

(3) F: Oh:: Go::d. ... She's only SEVen?

(4) K: And I say well .. hów about let's do sò-and-so. And
acc

she says ... ⌈Okay. ... ⌈Jùst like thát.
─────] [squealing]

(5) F: ⌈Oh:::::
⌊p
(6) D: ⌊What does it méan.
p,acc

(7) K: It's just so ... ⌈she's acting like such a little gírl
p
already.

There are two listener/respondents taking an active part in this story. Their reactions are opposite. Frances (F) responds by showing agreement and understanding, not by saying so, but by responding in like style. In (3) she says, 'Oh: Go::d', using exaggerated tone and lengthened vowels, and repeats a part of Kurt's (K's) story in a 'disbelieving' tone: 'She's only SEVen?' Her tone says 'That really is amazing'. In (4) Kurt continues his story, and in (5) Frances again shows understanding by use of a paralinguistically exaggerated response, 'Oh ::::: '. In contrast, David asks (6), 'What does it mean?'

Here is clear evidence, in the text itself, that Frances, who, like the speaker, is of New York Jewish background,

'got the point' of the story. Part of this evidence lies in her
responding in kind. Kurt's telling of this 'story' is marked by
exaggerated paralinguistic and prosodic features. He uses
marked shifts from high to low pitch; speeding up and slowing
down; postural and gestural cues. In (1) and (4), he mimics
the movements as well as the voice of the girl he is talking
about; he places his hands on his knees and squirms in a
stereotypically female manner. Frances' response is similar
in a number of ways. She picks up on Kurt's words and repeats them back to him, (3) 'She's only SEVen?' with paralinguistically exaggerated phonology. The result is a rhythmically and paralinguistically synchronous and matched speaker/
listener interchange.

In contrast, David's question (6) 'What does it mean?' is
uttered in flat intonation. Not only does the content of his
question make it clear that he does not get the point of the
story. In addition, the rhythm and tone of his question are
in contrast to Kurt's and Frances' utterances. In playback,
David commented that perhaps he did not so much miss Kurt's
point as feel annoyed that Kurt had not made it. That is, he
felt that the point of the story should be *told*--in external
evaluation. He complained that even in answer to his question
(6), Kurt did not tell the point of the story. Kurt's 'explanation' (7) is 'She's acting like such a little girl already'.
David commented that 'such a little girl' means to him 'just like
a person' or 'grown up', as in 'such a little young lady' as
opposed to 'like an infant'. What Kurt meant and should have
said was that she was acting like a 'coquette'. David continued that it made him uncomfortable when Kurt squealed and
squirmed to imitate the girl's manner. This acting-out of the
story seemed to him a breach of good taste.

It is particularly interesting that Kurt, in answering David's
direct question, still did not 'explain' the point of the story.
I submit that it seemed to him self-evident, as it seemed to
Frances.

Thus, Kurt communicated the point of his story through
internal evaluation, by presenting the character in a way that
seemed to him self-evidently demonstrative of the point. He
made much use of paralinguistic and kinesic features--the
essence of oral tradition, building upon shared sociocultural
knowledge and redundancy of channels. David expected something more like Kay's 'autonomous' use of language, in which
the message is carried by and made explicit in words.

Another aspect of cross-cultural differences in storytelling
has to do not only with how the point is communicated but
what the point can be. Thus it becomes clear that for the
New Yorkers of Jewish background, stories were most commonly
told to illustrate the speaker's feelings about something. In
some sense, Kurt's story is about his feelings about little
girls using girly mannerisms. The non-New Yorkers, in contrast, told stories about events in which their feelings were

Implications of the Oral/Literate Continuum /325

not only not dramatized but often not expressed. This led to another set of mismatches: the New Yorkers had trouble getting the point of the non-New Yorkers' stories, since they were looking for meaning in the speaker's attitude toward the events.

At one point the conversation turned to a discussion of heredity vs. environment, as exemplified by adopted children. Kurt told the following story, again about a student:

(1) K: In fact one of my stúdents told me for the first time,

I taught her for over a yéar. .... That she was

adópted. And then I thought .. ?uh? ... that
        acc⎯⎯⎯⎯⎯⎯⎯⎯⎯]   acc
           p

explains .. so many things.

(2) F: What. ⎡That she was ⟶

(3) K: ⎣Cause she's só:: dífferent ⎡from her móther

                                                              ⎣Smarter than she

should have been? or stùpider ⟶

       ⎡than she should've been. [chuckle]

(5) K: ⎣It wasn't smart or stùpid, àctually, it was just she

was so different. .... Just 'dífferent.
F: hm

The point of the story emerges in the first sentence in which Kurt illustrates his emotional reaction to hearing that his student was adopted in the grunt, 'uh', uttered between two glottal stops, accompanied by a facial expression of surprise. This sense of surprise in effect carries the message that the student was different from her parents, and this had been puzzling to Kurt before he learned that she was adopted. I have suggested (Tannen 1980b) that the questions asked by Frances in this interchange do not show lack of understanding or lack of approval of the way the story is being told. Rather, they function as 'cooperative prompts', eliciting information which Kurt would have told anyway. They serve to encourage him to tell what he was planning to tell--a show of enthusiasm on the listener's part. Evidence for this lies in the fact that the story continues over the overlap of the question; the question does not stop the storyteller or interfere with the rhythm of his story; rather the questions and story continue in an interwoven fabric of continuous and rhythmically smooth speech.

In contrast, when David tells a story about a child who is adopted, Kurt reacts with a question that interrupts the flow of David's speech and shows Kurt's impatience.

(1) D: My u::m ... my aûnt's two kids are adopted, and they were both adopted from different .... famili? different móthers.

(2) K: Yeah. And?

(3) D: └ And they're just 'different from each other and dífferent from anyone in my fámily. ....
K hm
They're not like each óther at àll.

All listerners to the tape of this conversation agree that Kurt's 'Yeah. And?' sounds impatient. David himself, during playback, said that it sounded like Kurt was impatient, and David hypothesized that it was his slower pace that was causing the impatience. Indeed, David speaks more slowly than Kurt, and his hesitation over 'families' vs. 'mothers' creates a stalling in the telling. I hypothesize, however, that another part of Kurt's impatience results from the fact that David has not given any hint of how he feels about what he is telling. The flat intonation is in striking contrast to Kurt's storytelling style, although in terms of actual information communicated in the content, David gives no less information than Kurt did, and both are saying that the adopted children are 'just different' from their adopted families. But in David's story there is no element of his own emotional involvement, as there is in Kurt's. This pattern is not limited to these stories but appears in numerous stories told by members of the two groups.

By focusing on personal emotions, and by using internal evaluation through exaggerated paralinguistic and nonverbal cues, the New Yorkers in this study were using strategies associated with oral tradition. By sticking to events and relying on lexicalization, the natives of Los Angeles were using strategies associated with literate tradition. The effect in communication between members of the two groups was slight mutual impatience and annoyance, and incomplete comprehension. Of course, these phenomena were not gross but comparatively subtle and became clear only after microanalysis. All participants left the gathering feeling they had had a good time, and friendships among them endured. However, the nature of their rapport is certainly influenced by such habitual differences, and consequences of such stylistic differences are potentially significant in interaction not favorably biased by ties of friendship and congenial setting.

Conclusion. Kay (1977) suggests that the notion of autonomous vs. nonautonomous speech accounts for Bernstein's (1964) controversial hypothesis of elaborated vs. restricted codes. Kay writes (1977:22) that

> autonomous speech packs all the information into the strictly linguistic channel and places minimal reliance on the ability of the hearer to supply items of content necessary either to flesh out the body of the message or to place it in the correct interpretive context.

I suggest that the addition of background information is a kind of elaboration. Therefore, autonomous or literate-based language is not necessarily always elaborated, nor is oral-based or nonautonomous speech always restricted. Rather, there is a difference in which levels of signalling or which aspects of the communicative channel are elaborated. The use of exaggerated paralinguistic features such as pace, pitch shifts, amplitude shifts, expressive phonology, expressive tone quality, and so on constitutes elaboration of the paralinguistic channel. Similarly, the study of conversational strategies shows that Greeks expected more 'enthusiasm' in expression of preferences and that Jewish American participants in the Thanksgiving dinner expected more active listener participation in the form of expressive reactions, prompting questions, and mutual revelation of personal experience (Tannen 1979c). This is elaboration of another sort. In the autonomous or literate-based mode, the content and verbal channel are elaborated, while the oral-based strategy elaborates paralinguistic channels and emotional or interpersonal dynamics.

Two major conclusions may be drawn from these findings. (1) 'Middle class white' speakers are not a monolithic speech community. Just as we have come to realize that visible ethnic minorities have disparate cultural backgrounds and linguistic norms, so members of middle class white communities come from a variety of ethnic, geographic, and cultural backgrounds. If our goal is to understand the speech behavior of individuals in a multi-ethnic society, we must broaden our notion of ethnicity. (2) The notion of strategies that have been associated with oral and literate tradition explains many of the differences in language use by members of varying ethnic, geographic, class, and cultural backgrounds. Strategies associated with oral tradition place more emphasis on personal topics, personalization, and instantiation. There is some indication, furthermore, that this accounts for some male/female differences as well. In contrast, those who are accustomed, even in casual conversation, to using conventionalized strategies influenced by literate tradition are more inclined to focus on decontextualized content, to expect language to proceed in a linear and logical way, to avoid overlap, and so on.

The consequences of these differences in cross-cultural communication are complex and depend upon the culture in which communication takes place. In communication between members of different cultures, such as nationals of different countries, the mutual stereotyping is likely to be negative both ways. Thus it has been shown (Vassiliou, Triandis, Vassiliou, and McGuire 1972) that Greeks tend to stereotype Americans as cold but organized. This can easily be seen as a consequence of Americans' focus on content, to the exclusion of interpersonal dynamics. In contrast, Americans tend to stereotype Greeks as enthusiastic, spontaneous, but disorganized: a function of their emphasis on the personal and interpersonal. In such settings, each group is convinced that its own norms are based on self-evident assumptions of the qualities of a good person.

The matter is more complicated, however, when communication takes place among people of different cultural backgrounds residing in the same country. Then one set of norms tends to dominate. Those who grow up in a setting in which the norms learned at home are reinforced in the public domain, have attitudes toward their own language that are quite different from those growing up in a culture in which the norms operative at home differ from those endorsed by the society at large. Thus, I found that New Yorkers of Jewish background often were ambivalent about their own speech styles. Those who used strategies associated with literate tradition had a certainty about their convictions. If they proclaimed that it was rude to interrupt or that one ought to state the point of a story, they had no ambivalence about the validity of those values. However, the speakers who tended to overlap in a cooperative way in conversation, on hearing their own conversation on tape, were likely to be critical of themselves. They, too, believe that it is rude to interrupt, to talk loudly, to talk too much. Of course, these negative feelings may be mixed with positive ones: that it is a pleasure to talk to others who talk like them. But at the same time--especially for those who have moved outside homogeneous ethnic communities--they have been influenced by prevalent norms just as much as those who adhere to them. A similar situation obtains for women, in contrast with men.

These are a few of the ways in which an understanding of cross-cultural communication is enhanced by awareness of the oral/literate continuum.

NOTES

1. The summary of research on oral/literate tradition which appears in this paper closely resembles the summary which appears in Tannen (1980a). Here, as there, I thank John and

Jenny Cook-Gumperz for focusing my attention on the importance of this research. I am grateful as well to Ron Scollon for invaluable critical comments and continuing dialogue. Recalcitrant blind spots are mine alone.

2. Such a distinction resembles numerous other theoretical schemata which I do not discuss here, including Hall's (1977) high/low context continuum, field dependency vs. field independency (Cazden and Leggett 1978), and R. Lakoff's (1979) communicative styles camaraderie vs. distance. This last is discussed at length in Tannen (1979c, 1980d).

3. Gumperz and Tannen (1979) present a schema for and discussion of the levels of linguistic signalling at which crosscultural (social) vs. individual differences occur in interaction.

4. My niece, at age nine, was included in the ceremony at her mother's second marriage. At the critical moment in the solemn ceremony, when bride and groom both sipped wine from a ceremonial goblet, the rabbi offered a sip to the little girl as well. She declined politely, saying, 'No, thank you; I don't drink.' The laughter of the wedding guests and the subsequent legendizing of her rejoinder in family lore served as her lesson that she had used the formula in an inappropriate setting.

5. It was not until very recently that I learned that the habit of saying 'Wear it in good health' to someone who has purchased or received a new item of clothing is not in general use among Americans. It is clear that some of my compatriots share this ignorance and it can be a problem for TV producers. A recent episode of a situation comedy presented a scene, taking place in a Midwestern town, in which a character received a gift in a restaurant. Some nice ladies at a nearby table observed the event and gave their blessing as they left the restaurant: 'Wear it in good health.' Jim Drake, a director for CBS, comments (personal communication) that such linguistic egotism is a problem he and his actors must continually correct.

6. No attempt was made to match socioeconomic status or other variables except age and sex. However, it turned out that socioeconomic status, as judged by father's occupation, did not differ markedly. For a detailed comparative analysis of the Greek and American narratives, see Tannen (1980c).

7. An intriguing question is raised whenever I speak about these phenomena: to what extent are culturally determined or associated styles nonetheless personality features? Surely, I do not believe that ways of talking are 'just style'--hence not evidence of personality features. I hypothesize that members of a group have an array of features from which to choose. Personality and communicative style are intertwined, as Sapir (1958) observed.

8. Here, as always, I must note that 'strategy' does not imply a *conscious* choice, but merely a way of achieving a conversational goal.

9. Transcription conventions are a combination of my own and many gleaned from the following sources: the Chafe narrative project, University of California at Berkeley; Schenkein (1978); and the Gumperz project, University of California at Berkeley, based on conventions developed by John Trim.

.. noticeable pause or break in rhythm (less than .5 second)
... half-second pause, as measured by stop watch
an extra dot is added for each additional half-second pause, hence .... full second pause, and so on
ˇ secondary stress
´ primary stress
italics mark emphatic stress
CAPS mark very emphatic stress
⌈ high pitch, continuing until punctuation
⌈⌈ very high pitch, continuing until punctuation
' high pitch on word
, phrase final intonation: 'more to come'
. sentence final falling intonation
→ arrow indicates talk continues without break in rhythm; see next line
? yes/no question rising intonation
: indicates lengthened vowel sound
p under line indicates spoken softly
acc under line indicates spoken quickly, continuing until punctuation unless otherwise indicated
ʔ is the traditional linguistic symbol for glottal stop, as in the expression of warning, ʔuh ʔoh
[brackets] indicate comments on nonverbal characteristics
⌈penned brackets on two lines indicate overlapping speech.
⌊Two people talking at once.
penned brackets with reversed flaps indicate latch.⌉
 ⌊Second speaker begins without pause following first speaker's utterance.

REFERENCES

Aronowitz, Robert. (to appear) Reading tests as texts. In: Spoken and written language. Edited by D. Tannen. Norwood, N.J.: Ablex.

Bateson, Gregory. 1972. Steps to an ecology of mind. New York: Ballantine.

Bernstein, Basil. 1964. Elaborated and restricted codes: Their social origins and some consequences. American Anthropologist 66.6.

Bolinger, Dwight. 1976. Meaning and memory. Forum linguisticum 1.1.

Broverman, Inge, et al. 1970. Sex-role stereotypes and clinical judgments of mental health. Journal of Consulting and Clinical Psychology 34.1.
Cazden, Courtney, and Ellen Leggett. 1978. Culturally responsive education: A discussion of *Lau* Remedies II. Los Angeles: National Dissemination and Assessment Center, California State University.
Chafe, Wallace, ed. 1980. The pear stories: Cognitive, cultural, and linguistic aspects of narrative production. Norwood, N.J.: Ablex.
Cole, Michael, and Sylvia Scribner. 1974. Culture and thought: A psychological introduction. New York: Wiley.
Cook-Gumperz, Jenny, and John Gumperz. 1980. From oral to written: The transition to literacy. In: Variation in writing. Edited by M. F. Whiteman. New York: Erlbaum.
Dodge, Susan. 1980. Male/female differences in oral narrative strategies. Unpublished MS. Linguistics Department, Georgetown University.
Ferguson, Charles. 1976. The structure and use of politeness formulas. Language in Society 5.
Fillmore, Charles. 1979. On fluency. In: Individual differences in language ability and language behavior. Edited by C. Fillmore, D. Kempler, and W. Wang. New York: Academic Press.
Fillmore, Lily Wong. 1979. Individual differences in second language acquisition. In: Individual differences in language ability and language behavior. Edited by C. Fillmore, D. Kempler, and W. Wang. New York: Academic Press.
Goffman, Erving. 1959. The presentation of self in everyday life. Garden City, N.Y.: Doubleday.
Goody, Jack. 1977. The domestication of the savage mind. Cambridge: Cambridge University Press.
Goody, Jack, and Ian Watt. 1963. The consequences of literacy. Comparative Studies in Society and History, 5. [Excerpts reprinted in Language in social context. Edited by P. P. Giglioli. Penguin, 1972.]
Gumperz, John. 1977. Sociocultural knowledge in conversational inference. In: Georgetown University Round Table on Languages and Linguistics 1977. Edited by Muriel Saville-Troike. Washington, D.C.: Georgetown University Press. 191-211.
Gumperz, John, and Deborah Tannen. 1979. Individual and social differences in language use. In: Individual differences in language ability and language behavior. Edited by C. Fillmore, D. Kempler, and W. Wang. New York: Academic Press.
Hall, Edward. 1977. Beyond culture. Garden City, N.Y.: Doubleday.
Havelock, Eric. 1971. Prologue to Greek literacy. Cincinnati: University of Cincinnati.

Havelock, Eric. 1963. Preface to Plato. Cambridge, Mass.: Harvard University Press.
Jarrett, Dennis. 1978. The singer and the bluesman: Formulations of personality in the lyrics of the blues. Southern Folklore Quarterly 42.1.
Kay, Paul. 1977. Language evolution and speech style. In: Sociocultural dimensions of language change. Edited by B. Blount and M. Sanches. New York: Academic Press.
Labov, William. 1972. Language in the inner city. Philadelphia: University of Pennsylvania Press.
Labov, William. 1969. The logic of nonstandard English. In: Georgetown University Round Table on Languages and Linguistics 1969. Edited by James E. Alatis. Washington, D.C.: Georgetown University Press.
Labov, William, and David Fanshel. 1977. Therapeutic discourse. New York: Academic Press.
Lakoff, Robin. 1975. Language and woman's place. New York: Harper and Row.
Lord, Albert. 1960. The singer of tales. Cambridge, Mass.: Harvard University Press.
Matisoff, James. 1979. Blessings, curses, hopes and fears: Psycho-ostensive expressions in Yiddish. Philadelphia: Institute for the Study of Human Issues.
Nix, Don, and Marian Schwarz. 1979. Toward a phenomenology of reading comprehension. In: New directions in discourse processing. Edited by R. Freedle. Norwood, N.J.: Ablex.
Olson, David. 1977. From utterance to text: The bias of language in speech and writing. Harvard Educational Review 47.3.
Ong, Walter. 1979. Literacy and orality in our times. Profession 79. New York: Modern Language Association.
Ong, Walter. 1977. Interfaces of the word. Ithaca, N.Y.: Cornell University Press.
Ong, Walter. 1967. The presence of the word. New Haven, Conn.: Yale University Press.
Patrick, Jane. 1980. Male/female differences in narrative style. Paper presented at Southeast Conference on Linguistics, March. [MS. Linguistics Department, Georgetown University.]
Sapir, Edward. 1958. Speech as a personality trait. In: Selected writings of Edward Sapir in language, culture, and personality. Edited by D. Mandelbaum. Berkeley and Los Angeles: University of California.
Scollon, Ron, and Suzanne Scollon. (to appear) Cooking it up and boiling it down: Abstracts in Athabaskan children's story retellings. In: Spoken and written language. Edited by D. Tannen. Norwood, N.J.: Ablex.
Scribner, Sylvia, and Michael Cole. 1980. The psychology of literacy. Cambridge, Mass.: Harvard University Press.

Tannen, Deborah. (in preparation a) Literary prose as oral and literate language.
Tannen, Deborah, ed. (in preparation b) Spoken and written language. Norwood, N.J.: Ablex.
Tannen, Deborah. 1980a. Spoken/written language and the oral/literate continuum. Proceedings of the Sixth Annual Meeting of the Berkeley Linguistics Society, Berkeley, California.
Tannen, Deborah. 1980b. When is an overlap not an interruption? Papers from the First Delaware Symposium on Languages and Linguistics. Newark, Del.: University of Delaware Press.
Tannen, Deborah. 1980c. A comparative analysis of oral narrative strategies: Athenian Greek and American English. In: The pear stories: Cognitive, cultural, and linguistic aspects of narrative production. Edited by W. Chafe. Norwood, N.J.: Ablex.
Tannen, Deborah. 1980d. Toward a theory of conversational style: The machine-gun question. Working papers in Sociolinguistics. Austin, Texas: Southwest Educational Development Laboratory.
Tannen, Deborah. 1979a. What's in a frame? Surface evidence of underlying expectations. In: New directions in discourse processing. Edited by R. Freedle. Norwood, N.J.: Ablex.
Tannen, Deborah. 1979b. Ethnicity as conversational style. Sociolinguistic Working Paper No. 55. Austin, Texas: Southwest Educational Development Laboratory. [Reprinted in Language and speech in American society: A compilation of research papers in sociolinguistics. Austin, Texas: Southwest Educational Development Laboratory.]
Tannen, Deborah. 1979c. Processes and consequences of conversational style. Ph.D. dissertation. University of California, Berkeley.
Tannen, Deborah. 1976. An indirect/direct view of misunderstandings. M.A. thesis. University of California, Berkeley.
Tannen, Deborah, and Piyale Cömert Öztek. 1977. Formulaic expressions in Turkish and Greek. Proceedings of the Third Annual Meeting of the Berkeley Linguistics Society. Berkeley, California. [Reprinted in Conversational routine. Edited by F. Coulmas. The Hague: Mouton.]
Vassiliou, Vasso, Harry Triandis, George Vassiliou, and Howard McGuire. 1972. Interpersonal contact and stereotyping. In: The analysis of subjective culture. Edited by H. Triandis. New York: John Wiley.
Zimmer, Karl. 1958. Situational formulas. MS. Linguistics Department, University of California, Berkeley.

CROSS-CULTURAL COMMUNICATION IN THE CLASSROOM

Muriel Saville-Troike
Georgetown University

If bilingual/multicultural education is to succeed either in cultivating understanding and respect for social and cultural diversity, or in providing truly equal learning opportunities for students from diverse sociocultural backgrounds, it must be essentially concerned with diversity in language form and use. This is true because language includes among its functions those of serving as a symbol and identifier of group membership and as the principal medium for mediating and manipulating social relationships. Language is unique in its dual role as an intrinsic component of culture and as a medium through which other aspects of culture--including the content of formal education--are expressed and transmitted.

In the identification function, speaking different languages is an obvious marker of differential group membership. By switching languages, bilinguals often have the option of choosing which group to identify with in a particular situation, and thus convey the metaphorical meaning which goes along with such choice as well as whatever denotative meaning is conveyed by the code itself. An example of such metaphorical switching was reported by a student here from Nepal who used three different languages when being questioned by a border customs official: first Hindi as a 'neutral' code for providing information, then English to convey an educated and elite social status when excess tea in her baggage was questioned by the guard and black-marketing motives implied, and finally her native language for 'solidarity' with the guard when he was recognized (because of his accent in Hindi and English) as belonging to the same ethnic group. Bilinguals in the United States frequently use English (even with other speakers of their native language) in formal situations and to convey distance or status, but switch to the other language to express 'solidarity' or ethnic identity.

Diversity of language within a single speech community, such as English or Spanish, also provides a great deal of information about speakers' social identities, and even monolingual speakers (consciously or unconsciously) employ metaphorical switching between regional or social varieties or stylistic registers of the language to signal their role in a particular situation, their relationship to those they are speaking with, and the group identity they wish to convey.

On the receiving end, hearers of English (and other languages) regularly use language variables as a basis for judging others' social background, prestige, and even personality characteristics, as well as their ethnicity. Such concepts as status and role are not permanent qualities of language itself but abstract communication symbols which are always perceived in relation to a particular social context. Children may be characterized as 'good' or 'bad' at least partly in terms of their language use, including not only the employment of politeness rules and 'proper' vocabulary, but even features of pronunciation; e.g. English-speaking children who pronounce *coming* as 'comin_' are judged less well behaved or intelligent than those who say '*coming*' (Fischer 1958). Perceptions of individuals as 'voluble' or 'taciturn' are always in terms of cultural norms, and even expressions of pain and stress are culturally patterned--children in an English speech community learn withdrawal or anger, in Japanese nervous laughter or giggling, and in Navajo silence.

Conflicting attitudes toward language diversity create one of the greatest problems in cross-cultural communication between teachers and students (or their parents), and misunderstandings often occur for this reason. When the differences are understood, they may be used as an educational base; when they are not, they create a formidable barrier to learning. Contributing to an understanding of language diversity (not only in form, but in patterns of use) would clearly be one of the most important possible contributions of bilingual/multicultural education.

No complete inventory exists of different social rules for language usage or of different attitudes toward language even within the United States, but we can think of many examples. One is the difference in voice volume or level normally used by some Native American groups, with Indian students interpreting the non-Indian teachers' louder level as anger and hostility and the teachers interpreting the students' softer level as shyness or unfriendliness. A student who looks directly at the teacher when talking or listening is considered 'honest', 'direct', 'straightforward' by most Anglos and as 'disrespectful' by many Mexican-Americans, blacks, and Indians. The student who averts his eyes would be considered 'respectful' by the latter and 'shifty' or 'dishonest' by many Anglos.

The standard middle-class English speech patterns presented as a model in school are likely to be considered effeminate and thus rejected by lower class boys approaching adolescence, especially since these patterns are used by female teachers. The English of male teachers or of older boys would be much more likely to be adopted by boys wanting to establish a male identity. Studies of the acquisition of English by Puerto Rican adolescents in New York and Mexican-Americans in Chicago document that the variety being learned and used is not the language taught in English classes, but the language of the dominant peer group in the communities--which in these cases is Black English (Wolfram 1974). Even very young children are aware of the function of language in establishing group identity, and use the appropriate variety to identify with friends. One of my former kindergarten students developed a lisp when a best friend lost his front teeth, and many middle-class Anglo parents found during the early years of integration in Southern states that their children were adding the non-standard forms of some black and Spanish-speaking classmates. (Middle-class black parents were often distressed that their Standard English-speaking children were being influenced by the nonstandard speech of lower-class white students.)

Classroom interaction is also affected by language diversity, including sociolinguistic rules regarding who should talk and when. The school supports the convention of talking one at a time (after raising a hand and being called on) and not interrupting; other cultures would consider that rude, a sure sign that no one was interested in what the primary speaker was saying. Some cultures feel it is inappropriate for children to talk at all in the presence of adults, and others that it is inappropriate for women to talk in the presence of men.

Mitigation techniques also differ, and students encounter many problems in our schools when they come from cultures that do not use the same ones that are accepted there. A middle-class student from the dominant culture has learned to avoid unpleasant assignments with such indirect excuses as *I'm tired. Can't I do that later?*, or by nonverbal dawdling or day dreaming until the time is up. While often unsuccessful, the attempt brings no serious reproof. If a student has not learned these cultural strategies and says, *No, I won't*, or just *No*--which have essentially the same meaning--he or she may be considered belligerent or rude.

Language learning for children is an intergral part of their socialization; learning language is also part of learning to be a boy, or a girl, or rich, or poor, or black, or white, or Chinese, or Basque, or Chicano, of dozens of other social roles into which the children are being enculturated. Children learn the social structure of their culture as they learn language, and learning to use appropriate linguistic forms when there is a choice is part of learning one's place in society. The set of sociolinguistic rules learned first through family interaction, then peer group and wider community, involves age, sex, and

social class, as well as ethnic group and larger societal memberships.
  Understanding the roles and identities which others have in the larger society thus minimally involves understanding how language diversity functions in manipulating and maintaining role-relationships, as a boundary marker between social groups, and as an instrument of social change. Ideally, such understanding in the context of multicultural education will also involve the following factors.
  First, it will involve making use of students' native languages as a medium of instruction and assessment. When the educational context is one in which students understand little or no English, this is considered essential by proponents of bilingual education; students who cannot understand the language of instruction clearly cannot learn effectively, and instruction or support in their native language is widely accepted as necessary if they are to have equal opportunity for education.
  Second, it will involve accepting and accommodating the students' language and cultural patterns of language use. The teacher, indeed the whole educational system, should seek to expand and enrich the existing repertoire of teaching styles and instructional activities to provide for the linguistic diversity of students. This is important not only when students speak languages other than English; the essence of the 1979 court decision against the Ann Arbor schools was that although students speaking 'Black English' and their teachers could understand each other, lack of acceptance and accommodation to the language differences resulted in unequal educational opportunity, in violation of the students' constitutional rights (Center for Applied Linguistics 1979).
  Third, it will involve teaching about important and useful components of English and other languages of instruction as they are used in school and in other interactional contexts within American society and an even wider societal context. Students should learn to expand and enrich their repertoire of language-related knowledge, skills, and behaviors, and extend their linguistic and cultural competence. A traditionally recognized function of the school is to 'prepare youth for life'. However, schools have always taken a very narrow view of language as it relates to this function. Only a single 'brand' of language--middle-class formal--has been recognized as legitimate, with bilingual education too often interpreted as the same 'brand' of two languages. This attitude and the language methods which implement it contribute little to fluency in use of sociolinguistically appropriate styles in various contexts.
  The need to take language differences into account is quite obvious when teaching students with limited English proficiency, but accommodation must also be made to social and cultural differences among fluent, even monolingual English speakers. All multicultural education involves cross-cultural

communication. Students may differ in their willingness to ask questions or volunteer information because of cultural differences in the appropriateness of these language behaviors. Teachers should both use and allow a variety of procedures, and be sensitive to which procedures are appropriate for which students, and to which differences in behaviors are due to cultural differences between groups and which to individual personality factors. Many students have been incorrectly stereotyped as 'shy' because the teacher was requiring inappropriate behavior (from the perspective of the students' native language and culture). At the same time, students should be taught, at least by the secondary level, that asking questions and volunteering information is not considered inappropriate or overly aggressive in school, but rather is valued, and often rewarded with a higher grade. Teaching this, and guiding students to behave accordingly, is part of developing the language competence required in school.

Other language-related classroom procedures and behaviors may need to be explained or taught, including some which generally operate below the level of consciousness. We already recognize such behaviors as walking in line, or raising a hand to talk or ask permission to go to the bathroom, as unique to the subculture of the school, and therefore we formally teach them. But many students will also not know the more subtle sociolinguistic rules which are appropriate for school, and these, too, should be made the subject of explicit instruction. These include recognition of indirect instructions and commands, means of verbal mitigation, or even how to prevaricate acceptably or to respond to recognized prevarication. These patterns can be and should be taught as part of teaching school languages.

For older students, instruction in use of appropriate language styles and routines in various practical settings (job interviews, telephone communication, information-seeking procedures) can be an important part of their 'preparation for life'. In the adult world, judgments are continually being passed on people on the basis of their use of language. The ability to style-switch appropriately in different situations, and with different audiences, is a skill which should be recognized and consciously taught to the extent we can do so. Students from different cultural and linguistic backgrounds, including non-mainstream English backgrounds, need at a minimum to know how various linguistic behaviors are perceived and interpreted in the mainstream English-speaking community.

This knowledge needs to be imparted in as objective and sensitive a manner as possible. All instruction should begin with the premise not only that the native language is a valid medium of communication and instruction, but that the language variety spoken by the student is intrinsically as good and valid as the variety which is being taught. Because Standard English is the medium of communication in the larger society, as well as the language of social control, of art, of philosophy, of human services, and of technological development in the United States, competence in its use is of great potential instrumental as well as humanistic significance, but it is no automatic panacea, and false promises or implications should be avoided. Lack of control of Standard English may leave one vulnerable to social and economic exploitation, but American history is replete with counter-examples of nonstandard-speaking leaders of industry and labor, and Ph.D.'s--some in linguistics --working as waiters and clerks. Whitney Young summed up the issue perhaps most succinctly when he once said, 'I would rather say "I is rich" than "I am poor"'.

When language itself becomes a focus in the instructional program, as it does in bilingual programs, it may be the case that the effect of a program results more from the affective impact of using the students' language than from the purely cognitive benefits (though both are surely relevant). Research has shown that students who attend school in their native countries (e.g. Mexico) for several years before coming to the United States tend to do better in English than those who begin school here (Kimball 1968; Troike 1978). In other words, the schools here are at least partly responsible for retarding the students (the alternative explanation--that schools elsewhere are better than United States schools--is unlikely).

The cause of the retardation is to be found both in the school and outside. Where schools have hired members of the students' ethnic group as regular teachers and administrators, and have developed a strong academic program which respects, utilizes, and builds upon the students' native language and culture, achievement has exceeded national norms in English reading and mathematics. Where the school has hired staff from the minority group only in subordinate positions, or not at all, and has given only lip service to the more superficial aspects of the group's culture--food, dress, holidays--the reality of social inequities beyond the school has been telegraphed to minority students, whose achievement has been depressed accordingly. In this context, even the use of the native language may have little positive effect (Cohen 1979).

Social attitudes may thus play a powerful part in determining levels of success in language learning. In Sweden, where Finns are looked down upon and disparged, Finnish children have great trouble learning Swedish and do poorly in school (Skutnabb-Kangas and Toukomaa 1976). In Australia, on the other hand, where Finns are admired and respected, Finnish children usually learn English and do well in school (Ilpola 1979). The 'Pygmalion effect' often manifests itself in our own schools, where Chinese students are expected by teachers to do well, and Hispanic or Filipino students are expected to fail-- and the expectation becomes a self-fulfilling prophecy.

Since language is such a powerful symbol of personal and group identity, direct and indirect attacks on it in the

classroom and outside are attacks on the students' own identities
and their perception of self-worth and the worth of family,
friends, and others they admire. Direct attacks may take the
form of prohibition on the use of another language, or public
corrections of the form of a student's speech. Indirect attacks
are often subtle, and may range from omissions of the students' language from public use (on signs, in announcements,
etc.), to disparagements of its expressive power, negative
evaluations of the intelligence of its users, failure to utilize it
in testing or making home contacts, or restrictive pressures on
its use by staff. Even where the students' language is incorporated into the curriculum, books and materials used may have
an inferior appearance to the English materials, again betraying
a second-class status for the other language, and by extension,
for its speakers.

Education of one kind or another is always going on in the
classroom--students are always learning something, whether it
is what the teacher intended or not. It follows that education
may be either positive or negative, and that what students
learn from school may be beneficial or detrimental. Although
prejudice and ethnocentrism may not be explicitly listed as
objectives of the curriculum, they may be unconsciously transmitted just as surely as if they were. While minority students
are learning to disvalue their language, their culture, and
their social group, the majority students are likewise learning
to disparage their fellow students and to believe in the inferiority of the minority language and culture, and the inherent
superiority of the majority culture and its linguistic medium,
Standard English. Such beliefs, though founded in ignorance,
become deeply engrained to the point that they acquire an almost religious tenacity, and become the basis for perpetuating
inequities and inequality of educational opportunity.

While schools and teachers have understandably focused much
of their attention on raising the achievement level of minority
students (sometimes at the expense of the students' language or
culture), helping nonminority Standard English-speaking students develop an understanding of the nature of language and
linguistic diversity should also form an important part of the
educational program. While the school must prepare students
for coping with the society into which it is graduating them,
it can and should contribute to improving the society of the
future as it prepares today's students to become tomorrow's
adults. Mirabeau B. Lamar, President of the Republic of
Texas, said that 'An educated mind is the guiding genius of
democracy'; teaching respect for linguistic diversity so that
it comes to be considered a characteristic of the educated
mind can thus form a major contribution of bilingual/multicultural education to preserving the future of American
democracy.

REFERENCES

Center for Applied Linguistics. 1979. The Ann Arbor decision: Memorandum opinion and order and the educational plan. [Reproduction of the original plan submitted to the judge.] Arlington, Va.: Center for Applied Linguistics.

Cohen, Elizabeth. 1979. Unpublished research cited by Courtney Cazden at the National Association of Bilingual Education Conference.

Fisher, J. L. 1958. Social influence in the choice of a linguistic variant. Word 14.47-56.

Ilpola, Peija. 1979. Australian suomalainen arvostettu: Kieliolotkin kohentumassa ('The Finns in Australia rated highly'). Suomi Silta 2.8-9.

Kimball, William Lloyd. 1968. Parent and family influences on academic achievement among Mexican American students. Unpublished dissertation. University of California, Los Angeles.

Skutnabb-Kangas, Tove, and Pertti Toukamaa. 1976. Teaching migrant children's mother tongue and learning the language of the host country in the context of the socio-cultural situation of the migrant family. Helsinki: The Finnish National Commission for UNESCO.

Troike, Rudolph C. 1978. Research evidence for the effectiveness of bilingual education. NABE Journal 3(1).13-24.

Wolfram, Walt. 1974. Sociolinguistic aspects of assimilation: Puerto Rican English in New York City. Arlington, Va.: Center for Applied Linguistics.

VIII. *Evaluation and Bilingualism*

THE ROLE OF EVALUATION
IN BILINGUAL EDUCATION

G. Richard Tucker and Gary A. Cziko
McGill University

As several of the other participants at the 1978 Georgetown University Round Table on Languages and Linguistics have observed, the selection, in a particular country, province, or city, of the languages to be taught or to be used as media of instruction clearly constitutes an important aspect of educational and thus of national planning. It seems apparent that despite research, experimentation, or innovation, second language teaching programs or bilingual education (BE) programs will not succeed or thrive unless they are consistent with government policy, whether explicit or implicit, or with the clearly expressed goals of local educational authorities. Educational or national policy, we have observed (Tucker 1977), serves to define the parameters within which language teaching programs can be developed. Furthermore, it seems apparent that social pressures motivated by a diverse array of contributory factors can lead to policy change while the results per se of empirical research rarely do. Nevertheless, it is our basic premise that the notion of an innovative approach to education implies, even necessitates, a comparison of the proposed program with some alternative approach(es).
Before we proceed to examine some of the more specific details or components of typical BE program evaluations, let us first consider a variety of situations in which it would seem appropriate to consider the adoption of some form of bilingual education. Programs involving bilingual education might be desirable in settings where, for example, some foreign language of wider communication (e.g. English, French, Spanish) or an indigenous national language (e.g. Amharic, Pilipino, Swahili) has been adopted as a medium of instruction for all pupils regardless of their mother tongue; or in a country where

immigrant children from diverse backgrounds enter a monolingual school system (e.g. Chicano, Italian, or Portuguese youngsters in the United States or Canada); or perhaps even in a setting where speakers of a nonstandard language variety (e.g. Black nonstandard English, Haitian Creole) attend a school where the teachers and the texts employ a more prestigious standard form. In addition, BE programs have been used in many countries where a serious desire exists to develop pupils' abilities in each of two official languages (e.g. Flemish and French in parts of Belgium; English and French in parts of Canada; Afrikaans and English in parts of South Africa).

On the basis of our personal research experiences during the past ten years in Canada, Haiti, Nigeria, the Philippines, and the Sudan, we conclude that at least five factors provide justification for the implementation of bilingual programs: (1) the rapid spread of universal primary (and in many countries secondary) education; (2) an increasing concern with the validity of educational goals; (3) the desire to develop permanent functional literacy for the greatest possible number of citizens; (4) a belief that language can serve as a vehicle to foster a sense of self-esteem as well as a sense of ethnic awareness, identity, or pride; and (5) recent theoretical insights into the nature of native- and second-language acquisition. Thus, for example, the decision was taken by the Regional Ministry of Education in the southern Sudan, to introduce children to primary education in one of nine vernacular languages in the 1977-78 academic year, and to bridge pupils gradually into Arabic and then ultimately into English as languages of instruction. In this rural agrarian and nomadic setting, where fewer than 17 percent of the children who are eligible-by-age presently attend primary school and fewer than 2 percent who are eligible-by-age attend secondary school; where a need exists to provide access to at least rudimentary education and perhaps to functional literacy for so large a proportion of the population; where a desire exists to forge a united country after a protracted and bitter civil war, some form of bilingual education seems pedagogically and politically sensible.

In the Philippines, despite the existence of longitudinal empirical data which indicated that Filipino children immersed in English with Tagalog Language Arts as a subject for study would become proficient in all aspects of English, would develop a mastery of academic subjects, and would become literate in their mother tongue (Davis 1967; Revil et al. 1968), the National Board of Education decreed in 1973 that 'English and Pilipino serve as media of instruction and be taught as subjects in the curriculum from Grade 1 to the university level ...' The desire to ensure literacy in the mother tongue, to maximize the value of education for those who will likely not complete their schooling, and to enhance national pride and unity, probably far overshadow the goal of developing the highest possible level of second-language proficiency in a select elite.

In Canada, dissatisfaction with the level of French-language proficiency attained by Quebec English-speaking youngsters, despite up to 12 years of formal study of French as a second language, led a number of their parents to demand the establishment of an innovative BE program where the second or target language would be used as the initial medium of instruction. In this case, where the home language was not in jeopardy because of its firmly entrenched ascribed status in North America, it was felt that a teaching program which utilized the target language as the major vehicle for instruction would be pedagogically more effective than a program of study about the language per se.

After a thorough review of the available longitudinal, critical, and empirical assessments of BE programs, Tucker (1977: 39-40) concluded:

> What generalizations can be drawn or what recommendations can be made, if any, on the basis of the present review? I believe that the present review together with the others which have been prepared for this series will permit the conclusion that some form of bilingual education program is desirable in any community where there exists a serious and widespread desire or need for a bilingual or multilingual citizenry; and furthermore, that social rather than pedagogical factors will probably condition the optimal sequencing of languages. Thus, in situations where the home language is denigrated by the community at large, where many teachers are not members of the same ethnic group as the pupils and are insensitive to their values and traditions, where there does not exist a pressure within the home to encourage literacy and language maintenance, and where universal primary education is not a reality it would seem desirable to introduce children to schooling in their vernacular language. For example, the Mexican-American child in many, but not necessarily all communities, the American Indian child and the Canadian Eskimo child would each probably be encouraged to develop to his very fullest potential in such a bilingual program.
>
> Conversely, in settings where the home language is highly valued, where parents do actively encourage literacy and where it is 'known' that the children will succeed, it would seem fully appropriate to begin schooling in the second language.
>
> In conclusion, it now seems apparent to me that no uniform recommendation (such as the UNESCO axiom) can be made that will suffice for all pupils. The available empirical data do not permit universal generalizations. Rather, they highlight the fact that the constellation of

social and attitudinal variables interact in unique ways in diverse sociolinguistic settings to affect the child's ultimate level of linguistic development.

What, then, is the role of evaluation in bilingual education? What type or types of evaluation are desirable or useful? From whom and for what reasons does the pressure to evaluate typically come? What types of evaluation models have been used successfully in the past? How do the results from evaluations filter down to parents, educators, administrators, and decision-makers?

Bilingual education programs: Three illustrative examples. In the sections to follow, we discuss these as well as related questions; and when appropriate, we draw on our experiences with BE programs in various settings. For purposes of the discussion, let us describe briefly programs in three different settings where we have worked.

Canada. Twelve years ago, in September 1965, the South Shore Protestant Regional School Board began its first experimental French 'immersion' classes for a group of English-speaking kindergarten children. This project, designed to promote functional bilingualism through a policy of home-school language switch, was initiated by the Board on an experimental basis in response to numerous requests from parents living in the community. The program, which started out with two kindergarten classes in one school during 1965-66, has expanded throughout the South Shore system. During the school year 1977-78, this innovative program is being offered from kindergarten through Grade 11. This year, approximately 35 percent of all eligible kindergarten pupils have enrolled in an immersion program on the South Shore.

The kindergarten curriculum has been left largely to the discretion of the participating teachers. They stress the development of vocabulary and passive comprehension skills in French along with the other traditional kindergarten activities. They use a direct native language approach, in contrast to the second language methods typically used with English-speaking children. At the end of the kindergarten year, the children are assessed through direct observation by teachers and evaluators; but no attempt has ever been made to test them formally. By the end of the school year, most have built up an extensive recognition vocabulary and attempt to use single French vocabulary items as well as occasional short sentences. Productive skills vary considerably from one child to the next, but all are able to comprehend, without difficulty, simple children's stories as well as their teacher's directions.

At Grade 1, reading, writing, and arithmetic are introduced exclusively via French. No attempt is made to teach the children to read in English, and parents are specifically urged not

to do so in the home. In Grade 2, two daily half-hour periods
of English Language Arts are introduced. The rest of the curriculum remains essentially the same, with reading, writing,
arithmetic, and elementary science being taught via French.
The amount of instruction via English is increased gradually
and by Grade 7 slightly more than 50 percent of the curriculum
is taught in English with the balance in French.

At the request of the Board authorities and the Minister of
Education of the Province of Quebec, we were asked to formally
evaluate the program (see Lambert and Tucker 1972). The progress of the pupils in a Pilot Experimental class and in a
Follow-up Experimental class has been compared each year with
carefully selected Control Classes of French children instructed
via French, and English pupils taught via English. The Control Classes were selected from schools in comparable middleclass neighborhoods. In view of the well-documented influence
of social class on language and intellectual development, and
since the number of students involved was relatively small,
considerable care was taken to equate very carefully the Experimental and Control Classes on intelligence and socioeconomic
factors.

No attempt whatsoever was made to preselect or screen children for the Experimental Classes on the basis of IQ or other
variables; thus, both the Pilot and Follow-up Classes (in fact,
all subsequent classes) contained children with a wide range of
IQ and even had a few pupils with recognized perceptual-motor
deficits.

We have now been following these two separate Experimental
groups of children, the Pilot and Follow-up Classes, since they
began their formal schooling.

Nigeria. Prior to 1970, Yoruba for three years and then
English for the next three years were used as media of instruction in the six-year primary education of all Yoruba-speaking
children in the western part of Nigeria. The Yoruba Six-Year
Primary Project (Fafunwa et al. 1974) was initiated in 1970 in an
attempt to devise a program which would make the primary education of these children more effective and meaningful by using
Yoruba as the sole medium of instruction for the first six years
of school. To test the effects of the exclusive use of Yoruba
as medium of instruction, a research project was initiated.
Experimental and control classes were set up at St. Stephen's
'A' School in Ile-Ife, Western State, Nigeria. Early in the
implementation of the project, however, the project administrators found what they believed to be serious defects in the
primary school curriculum, and so took on the job of creating
a new curriculum incorporating the subjects of Yoruba, English, science, social and cultural studies, and mathematics.
Both the St. Stephen's experimental and control groups have
made use of this new curriculum. In addition, a specialist
teacher of English was used to provide English instruction for

the experimental class, while the usual classroom teacher provided English instruction for the control class.

In 1973, the project was expanded to include ten additional 'proliferation' schools, eight of which were to use Yoruba as the sole medium of instruction (the proliferation experimental group), while the remaining two were to follow the usual pattern of three years of Yoruba followed by three years of English (the proliferation control group). A comprehensive evaluation of the Yoruba Primary Project began in 1976 with the testing of academic achievement, Yoruba- and English-language skills, and intelligence of Grade 3 children in the St. Stephen's and proliferation experimental and control classes, as well as children in selected traditional schools. This large-scale, longitudinal evaluation will continue until these children have completed primary school. It will attempt to determine the effects of using Yoruba as the exclusive medium of instruction, the impact of the new curriculum materials, and the effectiveness of using a specialist teacher for the teaching of English.

Philippines. A number of exciting, innovative BE experiments have been conducted in the Philippines. We will have occasion to refer to work by Davis (1967), and Revil et al. (1968), and by Tucker, Otanes, and Sibayan (1970). For many years, English was the sole medium of instruction in school although Pilipino has been taught as a subject since 1940. In 1957, however, as a result, in part, of a study conducted in the province of Iloilo (see Ramos, Aguillar, and Sibayan 1967), a decision was made to use the prevailing local vernacular as the medium of instruction in Grades 1 and 2, with a shift to English as the major medium in Grade 3 (cf. Fafunwa et al. 1974, Yoruba then English in Nigeria; Modiano 1973, vernacular then Spanish in Mexico; de Ronceray and Petit-Frère 1975, Creole then French in Haiti).

Following this approach, initial instruction and initial reading activities occurred in the child's mother tongue. Oral ESL activities began in Grade 1, followed by English reading-readiness activities in Grade 2. A careful, critical, and longitudinal follow-up experiment was conducted several years later in Rizal province (Davis 1967) to replicate and extend through six grades the findings of the original experiment and to try to determine empirically the most appropriate time to introduce reading in English. The performance of the children was reevaluated at the end of their second year of high school (Revil et al. 1968), so that it is possible to draw a series of rather comprehensive conclusions about the efficacy of this type of educational program.

The Rizal Experiment examined two main questions. The first was designed to provide information that would help Filipino educators to decide when reading activities should be introduced in the teaching of ESL in Tagalog-speaking areas. The second was designed to yield information that would be helpful in deciding when English should be introduced as the medium of classroom instruction. The performance of five groups of pupils was examined. The groups varied according to the grade level at which reading in English and instruction in English was introduced. Thus, pupils in Group 1 began their schooling in English and were introduced to English reading immediately at that grade. They did, however, have one period per day devoted to Tagalog Language Arts. The pupils in Groups 2 and 3 began their schooling in Tagalog, but were introduced to ESL with accompanying English reading activities in Grade 1. The pupils in Groups 4 and 5 likewise began their schooling in Tagalog. They were introduced to oral ESL activities in Grade 1 but English reading activities were postponed until Grade 2. Groups 2 and 4 made the transition from Tagalog-medium to English-medium instruction at Grade 3. Groups 3 and 5 made the transition at Grade 5. Each of the five groups comprised six classes of 50 pupils each. Insofar as was possible, factors such as teacher education and experience, school facilities and community socioeconomic characteristics, were equated. The Tagalog Picture Vocabulary Test was administered as a pretest and criterion variable data were later adjusted using analysis of covariance techniques.

Figure 1. Design of the Rizal Experiment.

Grade in which English-medium instruction began	Grade in which English reading began	
	1	2
1	Group 1	
3	Group 2	Group 4
5	Group 3	Group 5

The language-teaching experiments just described briefly supported the observation of many educators that the exclusive use of one language--either a local vernacular or Filipino--as the chief medium of instruction in the early grades results in transition difficulties for pupils when an abrupt change is made to English as the medium of instruction. (A similar finding has been reported by Douglas 1977, for students educated in Arabic through secondary school when they switch to the English-medium University of Khartoum.) Therefore, it was decided to experiment with an alternate days bilingual approach in an attempt to maximize the advantages inherent in native language instruction coupled with solid grounding in English. It was hoped to reduce the transition difficulties while retaining the advantages of introducing children to schooling in their own vernacular.

Thus, an experiment was designed in which four classes of children participated. Class 1 followed a standard Filipino curriculum; Class 2, a standard English curriculum; Classes 3 and 4 followed an alternate days bilingual approach--i.e. English was the language of instruction on Day 1; Tagalog, Day 2; English, Day 3; Tagalog, Day 4; etc. The material covered on Day 2 was not simply a repetition of that covered on Day 1; but was instead a continuation of the previous day's lesson. The experimental program began in academic year 1968-69 and the results of the first formal evaluation have been published (Tucker, Otanes, and Sibayan 1970). It is our understanding that the project was terminated after the initial two years. We allude to it here because we shall later refer to an interesting feature of the testing program. Let us turn now to a consideration of some of the factors that may lead to the inclusion of an evaluation component in an innovative program.

The pressure to evaluate. The pressure to evaluate a BE program may come from many sources. It may come singly or in combination from parents, professional educators, educational administrators, funding agencies, or other government bureaucrats. Let us consider a few examples. In the early days of planning for the St. Lambert experiment, there was distinct pressure from both parents and administrators of the School Board for an evaluation to be conducted of the effects of the proposed program of home and school language switch on the development of native-language skills, cognitive or intellectual development content-subject mastery, and social or attitudinal development of participating pupils. The parents and board members were actually expressing the fear that their children might not fare as well in this innovative program as peers taught via the mother tongue. Thus, they were asking for what we might refer to as 'summative' evaluation. Essentially, they wanted to know how participating children would compare on a series of tests or measures with a 'control' group of more traditionally educated youngsters. This type of evaluation is frequently called for. Typically, parents, administrators, funding agencies, and government officials all seem to want to know what the cumulative effects will be on children who participate in a particular innovative program for a specified period of time, in comparison with children who participate in the more traditional programs. Furthermore, many such evaluators tend to examine exclusively the product (usually as a series of dependent measures) of such an intervention as opposed to the actual process of the intervention. Thus, it would seem appropriate to encourage the broader application of 'anthropological-type' observational studies of bilingual programs as a valuable adjunct to the usual empirical, summative evaluations (cf. Bruck and Shultz 1977; John and Souberman 1977).

It is interesting to note that despite their apparent popularity, there have been exceedingly few critical, empirical, longitudinal evaluations. The paucity of such studies can be attributed to a variety of sources such as the transience of potential researchers, the unwillingness or liability of funding agencies to commit funds for a multi-year or even decade-long project, and the unfortunate tendency for administration to regard initial results as a major criterion for continuing or terminating a proposed lengthy project (Campbell 1969).

This is unfortunate for it is only by assessing the cumulative impact of a wide variety of innovations such as the St. Lambert program of home and school language switch and the Yoruba Six-Year Primary Project that we can begin to understand the role of language in education. Thus, summative evaluation constitutes, for us, one of the important elements in theory building.

There exists, of course, another type of evaluation referred to as 'formative'. The ostensible purpose of formative evaluation is to provide rapid feedback to classroom teachers or to educators concerning the desirability of introducing curricular or structural modifications in the program. Thus, the results of an analysis of the errors made by participating pupils with certain aspects of the target-language verb system (Harley and Swain 1978) may have important implications for the content or sequencing of the syllabus. Likewise, the results of an analysis which compares the effects of introducing one group of children to reading in their mother tongue (L1) followed by reading in the second language (L2) versus a second group which is first taught to read in the second language (Cziko 1976), may have important and immediate structural implications. These types of assessment have the goal of providing rapid feedback to teachers and administrators, and fall under the rubric of formative evaluation.

It has been our general experience, however, that this type of evaluation is rarely undertaken on any systematic basis, and that even when such research is planned, feedback rarely reaches classroom teachers or administrators rapidly enough or in such a form that it can be utilized to effect change in ongoing programs. For example, in the Philippine alternate days experiment, we regularly videotaped lessons in the four classes; but the tapes were not watched by participating teachers with a view toward modifying their classroom behaviors. In the St. Lambert research, we collected very detailed information about difficulties which participating children had with determining the grammatical gender of French nouns; but we never helped the teachers to devise remedial lessons to correct this persistent problem, despite the fact that we had earlier done so for a university program (cf. Tucker, Lambert, and Rigault 1977). It does seem to us as though a wide variety of individuals or groups for various reasons do ask that some form of evaluation accompany each innovative program. We shall return later to the question of how the results from such evaluations actually affect educational planning.

Choice of an evaluation model. Let us turn now to a consideration of the selection of evaluation strategies for BE programs and of the specific components of various types of evaluation. It should be taken for granted that the goals of the particular BE program dictate the choice of an evaluation strategy. However, it has been our experience in Quebec (and we believe the situation prevails elsewhere as well) that many parents and educators have not yet articulated clearly their expectations for the academic, affective, cognitive, linguistic, or social development of children who participate in bilingual programs. Although it can be assumed that a complex array of personal, pedagogical, social, and political factors will influence the choice of goals, it is absolutely essential that consensual goals be locally agreed upon before the efficacy of bilingual programs can be adequately assessed.

The lack of clearly defined goals raises the important issue of what criteria shall constitute successful educational innovation. Does the performance by a certain proportion of students in an experimental group at a specified level on a standardized norm-referenced test constitute success? Does a mean performance by students in an experimental group equivalent to that of a traditionally instructed group of youngsters on a specific test constitute success? Does ability to understand, speak, read, and write the target language as well as the mother tongue in such a manner (albeit unspecified) as to be able to pursue higher education, or to secure employment, constitute success? Clearly, the choice of evaluation strategy will be determined at least in part by the specific program goals.

There has been some discussion recently concerning the general form BE program evaluations should take (Cummins 1977; Paulston 1975; Tucker 1976). All of the evaluations in which we have been involved have used what may be called the 'standard experimental' approach whereby the type of school program is considered to be the independent variable and a number of measures of academic achievement, language skills, intelligence, and attitude constitute the dependent variables. Paulston (1975) criticizes this approach since she feels that social factors are the most important independent variables and the failure to identify and investigate these (considering type of program as an intervening variable) often leads to contradictory results that lack generalizability to other settings. Cummins (1977) goes a step further in stating that the language abilities of children under evaluation must be carefully measured and also considered to be an important intervening variable affecting cognitive, academic, and linguistic development. Finally, Macnamara (1974) expresses the opinion that the factors affecting the outcome of a BE program are so numerous and complex that it is impossible to generalize the results of any BE program evaluation to other settings, regardless of the research model used. How, then, can we justify our use of a standard experimental approach in the evaluation of BE programs and how can we hope to build a general theory of the role of language in education?

Let us first address the issue of the appropriate research model to be used in BE program evaluations. We agree with Paulston that type of school program is only one of the variables influencing the cognitive, linguistic, and academic development of a particular child, and that social and other factors may be equally, if not more, important. However, in any particular BE program setting it is usually not possible to investigate all of the relevant social factors due to the very fact that the program takes place in one particular social setting. Although it may be possible to study the effect of socioeconomic status (SES) (see, for example, Cziko 1975), or some other factor for which there is variation within the setting under investigation, the evaluator can in most instances do little more than use a standard experimental approach, with program type as the independent variable and test scores of some sort as the dependent variables. The effect of language abilities as intervening variables can be assessed within this approach if care is taken to measure these abilities accurately and thoroughly. It is only after a number of such evaluations are carried out in different settings that one can attempt to investigate the effects of social factors. The very fact that Paulston was able to formulate an elaborate theory of bilingual education based on the results of evaluations which used this approach, may be taken as an indication of its effectiveness.

Note, however, that the formulation of a general theory of BE in no way implies that the results of any one BE program evaluation can be generalized to a program in another setting. The dangers of attempting to generalize evaluation findings were clearly identified by Macnamara (1974), who emphasizes the uniqueness of each research setting. For example, although it has been demonstrated many times that English-Canadian children who take part in French immersion programs gain an impressive mastery of the French language with no adverse effects on the development of English-language skills and academic achievement (Swain 1974), there is no guarantee that a new French immersion program in another setting will be equally effective. The employment of an incompetent or unmotivated teacher, for example, could cause a new program to become a catastrophe. Also, evaluations typically use groups of children as the unit of analysis and do not usually describe the effects of the program on each individual child nor relate success in the program to individual differences (see, however, Genesee 1976; Tucker, Hamayan, and Genesee 1976).

This means that there is always the possibility that a child may flounder badly in a program that has been shown to be successful in other settings for other children. This is no reason to believe, however, that we cannot have an explanatory, useful theory of BE based on the results of program evaluations. Such theories already exist (Lambert and Tucker 1972; Paulston 1975), and it is certain that these will be revised and refined as new data from BE program evaluations become available.

Such theories will never replace the need for careful formative and summative evaluation of innovative BE programs, but rather depend on such evaluations and may serve as guidance and inspiration for administrators and educators considering the implementation of new programs.

We will not discuss at length all of the design considerations that must be taken into account when implementing a BE program evaluation since this is the principal topic of another paper in this monograph. We will, however, discuss some basic methodological considerations and mention how real-life constraints often necessitate the use of research designs which are far from optimal.

By far, the most crucial design component of any objective evaluation is the assignment of children to the experimental and control classes to be evaluated. Optimally, one would like to be able to assign children randomly from some population of interest to the experimental and control classes (see Campbell and Stanley 1965:25, 26). In this way there should be no systematic differences between the classes in intelligence, SES, or any other variables that might otherwise bias test results. In addition, this procedure allows the use of inferential statistics to generalize the results of the evaluation to the population from which the experimental and control children were drawn. Unfortunately, our experience indicates that this procedure is seldom if ever used. The St. Lambert experiment is a case in point. Although originally children were assigned randomly to the experimental and control classes from a population of kindergarten pupils whose parents were willing to have their children participate in the experiment, pressure from certain administrators and influential parents eager to have their children placed in the experimental group resulted ultimately in an assignment that was not random.

The second approach, which is less desirable but often more practical, is the random assignment of preexisting classes to experimental and control conditions (see Campbell and Stanley 1963:47-50). However, since preexisting groups may differ initially in their knowledge of subjects to be later tested, and/or on other potentially confounding variables such as intelligence and SES, pretesting of both experimental and control groups is required. In the St. Lambert experiment, this pretesting took the form of administering tests of nonverbal intelligence and assessing the SES of each child's family prior to the beginning of the treatment. If pretest results show that the groups do differ in ways that might bias later evaluation results, analysis of covariance procedure can be used to analyze the evaluation results controlling for the effects of the pretest variables, i.e. using them as covariates.

It is important, however, that the pretest data be collected before the treatment has had a chance to affect these scores (see Elashoff 1969). This is especially crucial in the case of intelligence since if intelligence is tested after the program has been in effect, adjusting for it or other measures of cognitive or academic skills may actually result in adjusting for the effects of the program while attempting to assess the effects of the program! In the St. Lambert program and in the Philippine research, measures of SES and intelligence were obtained before the program was likely to have an effect and were both used as covariates. In the Yoruba project evaluation, however, SES and intelligence were not determined until the end of Grade 3. It was, therefore, unfortunately not possible to use intelligence as a covariate, although SES was used since we considered it unlikely that the program had affected the SES of pupils' families. That the lack of baseline intelligence data has seriously reduced the power of the Yoruba evaluation to detect the effects of the program is a striking example of the importance of collecting such data for evaluations where preexisting groups are used. Even when it is possible to assign children randomly to the experimental and control groups, the collection of relevant pretest scores and the subsequent use of analysis of covariance can considerably increase the sensitivity of the evaluation to the effects of the program (Campbell and Stanley 1965:26).

There is one remaining design problem that should be mentioned here--the possible confounding effect of class teacher. Since it is inevitable that different teachers be used for experimental and control classes, it turns out that program effect and teacher effect are completely confounded. There is no easy way to untangle these variables and usually the best that one can do is to make sure that experimental and control class teachers are equally qualified. However, if more than one experimental class or more than one control class can be included in the evaluation, it is possible to compare two or more classes within the same treatment condition to investigate the presence of a teacher effect. If, after adjusting for pretest scores, no significant differences are found on the test variables, we can be more confident in attributing any observed differences between the treatment groups to the different educational programs being offered. Such an analysis was done for the Grade 3 and Grade 4 evaluations of the Yoruba project, comparing the test scores of four urban proliferation classes within the same treatment condition but with different teachers. The findings that these four classes did differ significantly on several measures of language skills and academic achievement indicate that the differences observed among the various treatment groups may be due not to the different programs being offered, but rather to teacher effects or other uncontrolled or unmeasured factors.

Content of evaluation. Whenever an evaluation of a BE program is to be undertaken, one of the first decisions to be made is what components of the program are to be evaluated. This decision concerning the number and type of dependent variables to be included in the evaluation will depend not only on the goals of the program but also on the availability of appropriate control groups and test materials. These dependent variables may be divided into four major types: (1) language skills, (2) academic achievement, (3) affective consequences, and (4) long-term effects.

Language skills. It is difficult to imagine a setting where the assessment of language skills in one or both languages would not be of primary concern. In the evaluation of 'transitional' bilingual programs where the L1 of the pupils is used as a bridge to the mastery of the language of the majority, an important measure of the effectiveness of the program lies in the comparison of the L2 skills of pupils in the program with those of comparable pupils not in the program. In the evaluation of 'maintenance' bilingual programs where competence in both languages is desired, the effectiveness of the program is in part indicated by a comparison of both the L1 and L2 skills of pupils in the program with those of pupils not in the program.

Content-subject mastery. The assessment of subject content mastery is also of central importance in BE program evaluations since it is an indicator of the effectiveness of using a particular language as the medium of instruction for a specific particular school subject. There are, however, difficulties in comparing two different languages as media of instruction. These difficulties, discussed by Cummins (1977), result from the inability to separate the effects of instruction in a language from the effects of testing through the language.

Thus, if the control group had been instructed in a subject via L1 and the experimental group via L2, testing through L1 may be inappropriate for the experimental group. Even though L1 may be the experimental group's stronger language, they may be unfamiliar with the subject vocabulary in L1. On the other hand, if the experimental group is tested through L2, these pupils may have difficulty demonstrating their knowledge of the subject through L2, despite having had no difficulty in learning via the language. In the Philippine alternate days study, this problem was handled by dividing the class in thirds and administering Tagalog, English, or bilingual versions of tests to the pupils. In the Yoruba project, approximately 80 percent of the pupils in a class were given the version of the test corresponding to the language through which they had received instruction, while the remaining pupils were given the other language version. In situations where one wants to eliminate completely language of testing effects, the most effective and interesting technique would be to give all pupils bilingual tests such as those used in the Philippine study, so that for any question the pupils would have the choice of answering the L1 or L2 version of the question. In this way not only would the test be equally suitable for both experimental and control groups, but the choice of language for each response would itself be an interesting source of information. Of course, there may be situations where one is particularly interested in the effect of the language of testing, in which case the Philippine model would be most appropriate.

Affective consequences. It is generally agreed that the affective consequences of BE programs are of great importance. Three types of attitudes are of interest to the evaluator. First, attitudes of the pupils toward the program itself reflect the attractiveness of the program and may be considered an indirect measure of the ability of the program to motivate the children and to elicit and sustain their interest in education. Second, attitudes toward the language being taught and toward speakers of the language have been shown to be related to proficiency in the language (Gardner and Lambert 1972), and are therefore also of interest. Finally, since a BE program may also incorporate educational innovations not having to do with language (the teaching of science in the early elementary years, for example), attitudes toward traditional values and beliefs, religion, science, etc. may also be of interest. However, it seems that an assessment of the attitudinal consequences of BE programs are seldom included in program evaluations. This is no doubt at least partly due to the difficulty of measuring attitudes effectively and validly, particularly for young children, and the necessity of constructing appropriate instruments for the program under study.

In spite of these difficulties, an attempt at measuring the affective consequences of a BE program may provide important information that would otherwise be neglected. For example, using interviews and questionnaires to determine the attitudes of the pilot group of St. Lambert students toward Canada's first French immersion program for English-speaking children, it was found that although these graduating secondary school students were generally pleased with the program and considered themselves fortunate to have had the opportunity to participate in it, they also indicated that they were disappointed with certain aspects of it and offered suggestions for improving it. In another study using adjective rating scales (Cziko, Holobow, Lambert, and Tucker 1977), it was found that English-Canadian children who had participated in a bilingual French-English program had more favorable attitudes toward French-Canadians than did English-Canadian children in traditional English programs. This is an encouraging finding when one considers that friction between English- and French-Canadians has appeared to increase recently to the point where the partition of Canada has become a possibility.

Presently, an attempt is underway to measure the affective consequences of the Yoruba primary project. Using a sentence completion task, the influence of the program on the children's pride in Yoruba culture, attitude toward school, the English language, English-speakers, and scientific explanation (among other things) will be investigated. This information, along with measures of language competence and academic achievement of children in the program compared with appropriate controls, should provide a more complete picture of the total impact of the program.

Long-term effects. If we assume that the goals of every BE program are to provide adequate language skills and other fundamental skills for those pupils capable and eager to continue their education to the secondary and university levels, and to provide maximum 'surrender value' for those who will not do so, then a truly complete evaluation of a BE program must include an assessment of the long-term consequences of the program. Although to our knowledge, such 'tracer' studies have never before been carried out, there are two such studies in progress that should provide important information about the long-term consequences of such programs. One of these tracer studies involves maintaining contact with the pilot experimental St. Lambert group as they pursue postsecondary studies, enter the job market, and start families of their own. We are particularly interested in determining whether their experience in the St. Lambert program will have an effect on where they decide to live, their employment opportunities, and their integration into both the English and French communities in Canada.

The other tracer study involves a similar assessment of the long-term effects of the Yoruba project. Here we are particularly interested in determining whether the English-language ability of graduates of the program (in which Yoruba is used as the sole medium of instruction) is adequate for secondary and university study where English is the sole medium of instruction. We are also interested in determining whether the program's emphasis on developing literacy in Yoruba has a lasting impact on the lives of the vast majority of primary school graduates who do not continue their formal education. Let us now consider issues related to the choice of instruments to assess these four major types of skills which we have identified.

Choice and construction of testing materials. The choice and/or construction of testing materials is an important component of any BE program evaluation. For measuring intellectual ability, a good number of standardized group tests are available (see, for example, Anastasi 1968:640, 641), including nonverbal tests such as Raven's Progressive Matrices (1958), which are especially useful when children of different language backgrounds are to be compared. There are also a number of standardized group tests of academic achievement available. These, however, are of limited usefulness since they may not correspond to the curriculum of the program being evaluated;

they are not often available in languages other than English; and they often have been developed to reflect particular world views or cultural perspectives that may not be relevant for the groups being studied. Standardized group tests are also available for testing language skills, although the majority of these tests include only vocabulary and reading comprehension measures. Therefore, the evaluator of a BE program is often faced with the task of constructing his own testing materials if there is a need to assess: (1) the academic achievement of children following any program which uses a special or nontraditional curriculum, regardless of medium of instruction; (2) language skills other than reading comprehension and vocabulary; or (3) the affective consequences of a program.

In spite of the importance of developing reliable and valid testing instruments for use in gauging the impact of a BE program, there is typically little assurance that the tests used are in fact reliable and valid. It has been our experience that even when there has been adequate money and lead time available for careful construction of tests, the basic ingredients of test development, such as pretesting and item analysis, are neglected. Tests of academic achievement must, of course, be constructed by individuals with knowledge of the objectives and content of the program syllabus. It is unlikely, however, that such people will have an adequate knowledge of the principles of psychological testing, nor does it appear that they seek out individuals with such knowledge to aid in the construction of these tests.

In some ways, the construction of tests of language skills poses less of a problem. If, in fact, the ultimate language goal of any BE program is native-speaker competence in all aspects of the target languages, then it follows that for summative evaluation one need not be concerned with the particular language syllabus of the program being evaluated. In addition, research by Oller (1972, 1973) has shown that integrative tests such as cloze and dictation tests, which are relatively easy to construct and score, can serve as reliable and valid measures of general language competence. Our own use of cloze tests and dictation (see Cziko 1975; Cziko, Holobow, Lambert, and Tucker 1977) has shown that these integrative tests are among the most sensitive measures of language proficiency of the many types of language tests (both standardized and 'homemade') we have used in the evaluation of various French immersion programs in the Montreal area. The advantages of integrative language tests were also demonstrated by the results of recent evaluations of the Yoruba project (Cziko and Ojerinde 1976; Ojerinde and Cziko 1978). We found that the scores of a large number of language subtests were highly intercorrelated, suggesting that general language competence, and not distinct language skills, was measured by these tests.

However, while integrative test scores are useful in comparing an individual with a group or a group with another group (i.e. as a norm-referenced test), individual scores in themselves have little meaning. Furthermore, although Group A may perform significantly better statistically than Group B on a cloze test of English, this does not necessarily mean that Group A's English program is 'significantly' better than Group B's. It may be that the cloze test is so sensitive to variations in language proficiency that the meaningful magnitude of a statistically significant difference may be very small indeed. What may be more useful, then, is the development of criterion-referenced tests of language proficiency, i.e. tests constructed in such a way that an individual's score serves as an indication of his absolute language proficiency. This obviates comparing his score with that of other individuals or other groups. If a minimum desirable level of language proficiency can be determined, then the success of a program can be measured by the number of children at or above this minimal level, regardless of the overall group mean on the test.

Of course, this use of criterion-referenced tests is only possible where the goals of the program have been clearly defined. Another disadvantage of cloze and dictation tests is that they require both reading and writing skills. Thus, they may be unsuitable for children in the early primary grades. Also, there may be strong pressure from teachers and administrators to evaluate reading, writing, listening, and speaking skills separately, especially for purposes of formative evaluation. If it is decided to construct tests of these skills, the form such tests will take will depend on the availability of audiovisual equipment.

For example, to measure second-language speaking skills, the St. Lambert evaluation (Lambert and Tucker 1972) employed tape recorders to collect pupil speech samples which were later rated by sophisticated native speakers of the language. For the Yoruba Grade 3 evaluation (Cziko and Ojerinde 1976), however, since neither tape recorders nor electricity were available, performance on a block-stacking task requiring verbal communication in English (see Samuels, Reynolds, and Lambert 1969) was used as an indirect measure of speaking skills. Not only did the unavailability of recording equipment prevent a direct evaluation of these children's speaking skills, but it was also not possible to administer a test of listening comprehension with the same recorded voice as stimulus for each group.

Finally, the construction of measures of the affective consequences of a BE program probably requires even more care and sophistication than the construction of tests of academic achievement and language proficiency. We have worked with teachers who, while appearing quite capable of writing items for tests of academic achievement, attempted to construct affective measures composed of multiple-choice items with one 'correct' choice per item! While outside help was clearly needed in this case, it should be kept in mind that the most competent

psychometrician who does not understand the history, culture, and values of the group under investigation can do no better.
The main idea that we wanted to convey in this and the preceding two sections is that problems of research design and test selection or development confront even the most experienced investigator as he prepares to undertake a new evaluation. Thus, if there does exist a serious desire to include an evaluation component in any BE program, it should be recognized that planning for such an evaluation must begin at the very outset of the program. Once it has been decided to include an evaluation component, the question arises as to where should the responsibility lie for conducting formative or summative evaluation: with staff from the participating schools or boards? with local university or independent consulting groups?

Responsibilities for evaluation. It seems to us that a distinction might usefully be made between the responsibility for formative versus summative evaluation. To date, as mentioned previously, evaluators really seem not to have provided useful formative data to people who must devise curricula, produce materials, train teachers, or implement programs. It is entirely possible, given the general pattern and time frame of most academic research projects, that school boards must themselves assume primary responsibility for formative research. On the other hand, we believe that summative evaluation should be conducted by people who are 'outside' the system, individuals who are interested and informed but who do not have a particular pedagogical or theoretical axe to grind and whose job does not depend upon whether the outcomes are positive or negative (cf. Campbell 1969).
Individuals who undertake to evaluate BE programs must be sophisticated researchers with advanced training in research design, statistics, and applied linguistics, who possess sensitivity for the concerns of their intended audience and for the values, attitudes, and traditions of the groups whom they are studying. They need not necessarily be or have been practicing classroom teachers, but they must certainly be able to communicate their initial questions and later their findings in precise, nontechnical terms to diverse sets of audiences. Furthermore, we would argue that program evaluation in the so-called 'developing countries' can best be done by nationals of the countries, and that one of the greatest challenges we face is preparing language-education researchers from developing countries to undertake these tasks (cf. Sack et al. 1976).
We recommend the provision of a variety of oral and written reports each year concerning the research undertaken. In Montreal, although we have tried to follow this general suggested pattern, we have not always completed each phase. We operate on a testing cycle so that the majority of our summative evaluation is conducted in the spring. We try to analyze the data as rapidly as possible and to present the results of the

evaluation informally to board administrators before the summer
recess begins. Over the course of the summer, we complete
or refine our analyses and write (ideally) two types of reports
--first, a nontechnical summary of the research findings, intended for widespread distribution to parents, teachers, and
board members; and second, a more technical report intended
for Ministry of Education employees, colleagues, etc. We also
make it a practice to send copies of such reports directly to
the office of the provincial Minister of Education--from whom
we usually receive no reply--and also to the office of the
Prime Minister of Canada--from whom we always receive a reply. In addition, we try at least once a year to participate
in an open meeting with parents and teachers to discuss diverse aspects of the evaluation. We have found much to our
chagrin in the past few years that we have not been as conscientious as we should have been in sharing the results or
other information with the actual program participants, who by
now are advanced secondary or junior college pupils.

In Nigeria, a special meeting was held in May, 1977, to discuss the philosophy, the goals, the content, and the test results to date with the Ministers of Education, their assistants,
and the chief inspectors from each of the five Yoruba-speaking
states. This meeting provided an open and candid discussion
of the issues among project staff, consultants, and the key
Nigerian decision-makers. Thus, we conclude that it is extremely important to disseminate information about the program
being scrutinized as broadly and as rapidly as possible.

Repercussions of program evaluations. Let us now turn our
attention to a consideration of the general purposes which can
be served by program evaluation, as well as to a brief consideration of the repercussions of such evaluation in Canada,
Nigeria, and the Philippines. One important general repercussion of the decision to conduct a formal evaluation is the
necessity to specify or to operationalize program objectives.
Thus, individuals are forced to work together to define the
goals of the proposed program and the criteria for successful
implementation. Ideally, parents and educators will work together toward this end. The extent to which such collaboration occurs varies drastically from setting to setting, but
active community involvement would seem to constitute one
necessary ingredient for successful program implementation.

Another general, more negative repercussion of the decision
to involve 'outside' resource people in the task of summative
evaluation is that such evaluation may actually paralyze the
curricular or methodological flexibility that seems to characterize many successful teachers or programs. It is the case that
many community-based or church-based BE programs have
thrived for years despite (or because of) the absence of formal
evaluation. Nevertheless, we do reiterate the position stated
earlier, that an innovative approach to education necessitates

a comparison of the new program with alternative approaches. Thus, it would seem psychologically desirable to view the task of an evaluator ultimately not as one which requires that he decide whether a particular program is one which works or does not work, but rather to evaluate the relative strengths and weaknesses of a variety of program alternatives and to specify the conditions under which each might be more or less successful. In this way, an examination of the results of critical, longitudinal summative evaluations can lead to the formulation of a clearer understanding of the roles of language in individual growth and ultimately in national development.

What role has program evaluation per se played in the spread of BE for English-speaking youngsters throughout Quebec and Ontario, and indeed to every other province in Canada (Swain 1974)? The move to bilingual education occurred in response to a variety of social pressures which today link the development of second-language fluency to the preservation of economic or occupational mobility within Quebec, and in a more general way to the preservation of Canadian national unity. It may be only happy coincidence that the majority of BE program evaluations have been positive and that the number of programs has grown rapidly; however, the results of evaluation studies certainly provide some measure of assurance for parents and for educators, and we can conclude in retrospect that the widespread adoption of this unique--almost radical--approach to elementary education would not have occurred had the results of evaluation studies been unfavorable. The Canadian experience, then, has been one of collaboration among English-speaking parents, educators, and researchers to develop a system of education to better prepare children for an evolving social reality in which a knowledge of French will be essential.

It may be instructive here to compare the Canadian experience with that of the Philippines. Despite a body of longitudinal empirical data to the contrary (Davis 1967; Revil et al. 1968), Filipino educators have adopted programs with increasingly large components of instruction via Pilipino. The desire to ensure literacy in the mother tongue or national language, to maximize the value of education for those who will likely not complete their schooling, and to enhance national pride and unity, probably far overshadow the goal of developing the highest possible level of second language proficiency in a select elite.

Once again, it seems apparent to us that no uniform recommendation concerning the choice or sequencing of languages as media for literacy training or for instruction can be made that will suffice for all pupils in all settings. Rather, the available data highlight the fact that a variety of factors--individual, instructional, and social--interact in unique ways in diverse settings to affect the student's ultimate level of achievement and of development. Because of this diversity, it seems to us that evaluation--both formative and summative--should constitute an important component of each new BE program. The continuing synthesis of data from such programs should eventually yield a clearer understanding of the role of language in education.

In writing this paper we have been forced to consider the problems and flaws of our own evaluation research to date. Insofar as we have been able to come up with ideas and suggestions to improve the quality and usefulness of BE program evaluations, we have--we believe--demonstrated the need for those involved in evaluation research to review periodically and attempt to improve the quality and usefulness of their work.

NOTE

The preparation of this manuscript has been supported in part by a grant from the Canada Council to W. E. Lambert and G. R. Tucker, and by a grant from the Ministry of Education of the Province of Quebec to A. d'Anglejan and G. R. Tucker.

REFERENCES

Anastasi, A. 1968. Psychological testing. Third edition. New York: Macmillan.
Bruck, M., and J. Shultz. 1977. An ethnographic analysis of the language use patterns of bilingually schooled children. Working Papers on Bilingualism 13.59-91.
Campbell, D. T. 1969. Reforms as experiments. American Psychologist 24.409-429.
Campbell, D. T., and J. C. Stanley. 1966. Experimental and quasi-experimental designs for research. Chicago: Rand McNally.
Cummins, J. 1977. Psycholinguistic evidence. In: Bilingual education: Current perspectives, Vol. 4. Arlington, Va.: Center for Applied Linguistics.
Cziko, G. A. 1975. The effect of different immersion programs on the language and academic skills of children from various socioeconomic backgrounds. Unpublished M.A. thesis. McGill University.
Cziko, G. A. 1976. The effects of language sequencing on the development of bilingual reading skills. The Canadian Modern Language Review 32.534-539.
Cziko, G. A., N. E. Holobow, W. E. Lambert, and G. R. Tucker. 1977. A comparison of three elementary school alternatives for learning French: Children at grades 5 and 6. Unpublished research report. McGill University, December.
Cziko, G. A., and A. Ojerinde. 1976. Yoruba Six-Year Primary Project: The June 1976 evaluation. Unpublished research report, November. Available from Institute of Education, University of Ife, Ile-Ife, Nigeria.

Davis, F. C., ed. 1967. Philippine language-teaching experiments. Quezon City, Philippines: Alemar-Phoenix.
de Ronceray, H., and S. Petit-Frère. 1975. Projet expérimental sur le bilinguisme créole-français au niveau de l'enseignement primaire en Haiti. Les Cahiers du CHISS. Revue Haitien de Sciences Sociales 12.1-35.
Elashoff, J. C. 1969. Analysis of covariance: A delicate instrument. American Education Research Journal 6.383-401.
Fafunwa, A. B., et al. 1974. Six-Year Primary Project. Institute of Education, University of Ife, Ile-Ife, Nigeria, December. Multilith.
Gardner, R. C., and W. E. Lambert. 1972. The role of attitudes and motivation in second language learning. Rowley, Mass.: Newbury House.
Genesee, F. 1976. The suitability of immersion programs for all children. The Canadian Modern Language Review 32.494-515.
Harley, B., and M. Swain. 1978. A descriptive approach to French immersion speech: Focus on the verb system. Ontario Institute for Studies in Education. Mimeo.
John, V. P., and E. Souberman. 1977. Educational perspectives on bilingual education. In: Frontiers of bilingual education. Edited by B. Spolsky and R. L. Cooper. Rowley, Mass.: Newbury House.
Lambert, W. E., and G. R. Tucker. 1972. The bilingual education of children. Rowley, Mass.: Newbury House.
Macnamara, J. 1974. The generalizability of results of studies of bilingual education. In: Bilingualism, biculturalism and education. Edited by S. T. Carey. Edmonton, Alberta: University of Alberta.
Modiano, N. 1973. Indian education in the Chiapas highlands. New York: Holt, Rinehart and Winston.
Oller, J. W. 1972. Dictation as a test of ESL proficiency. In: Teaching English as a second language. Edited by H. B. Allen and R. N. Campbell. New York: McGraw-Hill.
Oller, J. W. 1973. Cloze tests of second language proficiency and what they measure. Language Learning 23.105-118.
Ojerinde, A., and G. A. Cziko. 1978. Yoruba Six-Year Primary Project: The June 1977 primary 4 evaluations. Unpublished research report. Available from Institute of Education, University of Ife, Ile-Ife, Nigeria.
Paulston, C. B. 1975. Ethnic relations and bilingual education: Accounting for contradictory data. Working Papers on Bilingualism 6.1-44.
Ramos, M., J. V. Aguillar, and B. P. Sibayan. 1967. The determination and implementation of language policy. Quezon City, Philippines: Alemar-Phoenix Press.
Raven, J. C. 1958. Standard progressive matrices: Sets A, B, C, D, and E. London: Lewis.

Revil, J. T., H. P. Hachero, S. G. Alondogam, E. B. Ortega, and D. B. Demaluan. 1968. A follow-up study of the Rizal experiment relative to achievement in English, Pilipino, and content subjects at the end of second year high school. Unpublished M.A. thesis. Philippine Normal College, Manila.

Sack, R., R. Gahizi, L. Shuvembo, K. Lokombe, O. Okoko, E. Yangoy, and A. Ngay. 1976. La langue d'instruction et ses incidences sur les ecoliers Zairois: Cas du Nord Kivu. Les Cahiers du Cride, Octobre, Série 1, No. 2.

Samuels, M., A. G. Reynolds, and W. E. Lambert. 1969. Communication efficiency of children schooled in a foreign language. Journal of Educational Psychology 60.389-393.

Swain, M. 1974. French immersion programs across Canada: Research findings. The Canadian Modern Language Review 31.117-129.

Tucker, G. R. 1976. Summary: Research conference on immersion education for the majority child. The Canadian Modern Language Review 32.585-591.

Tucker, G. R. 1977. The linguistic perspective. In: Bilingual education: Current perspectives, Vol. 2. Arlington, Va.: Center for Applied Linguistics.

Tucker, G. R., E. Hamayan, and F. H. Genesee. 1976. Affective, cognitive and social factors in second language acquisition. The Canadian Modern Language Review 32.214-226.

Tucker, G. R., W. E. Lambert, and A. Rigault. 1977. The French speaker's skill with grammatical gender: An example of rule-governed behavior. The Hague: Mouton.

Tucker, G. R., F. T. Otanes, and B. P. Sibayan. 1970. An alternate days approach to bilingual education. In: Georgetown University Round Table on Languages and Linguistics 1970. Edited by James E. Alatis. Washington, D.C.: Georgetown University Press. 281-299.

RESEARCH METHODOLOGY
IN BILINGUAL EDUCATION

Robert L. Cooper
Hebrew University of Jerusalem

The Federal Bilingual Education Program has required local recipients of grants for instructional projects to provide annual evaluations of the success of their projects and to submit semi-annual objective measurements of project success. Critics have charged that most of this research is inadequate. They are right. But for the wrong reasons.

Among the faults which critics have noted in the design or reporting of project evaluations are the following: inadequate sampling procedures; insufficient sample size; lack of information about the initial achievement of pupils enrolled in the project, against which their subsequent achievement might be compared; inadequate information about the performance of similar children, enrolled in conventional, monolingual programs, against which the attainments of the bilingually schooled children might be compared; failure to control for variables such as socioeconomic status, pupils' initial language abilities, and teacher preparation when comparing the attainments of control and experimental groups; failure to describe adequately the project's instructional activities; the use of inadequate or inappropriate measurement instruments; the use of inappropriate tests of statistical significance; and failure to guard against the 'Hawthorne effect'.

While these project evaluations have many technical faults, there is a more fundamental if less obvious objection to this research. Even if the technical faults, correctly pointed out by critics, were remedied, much of the research would still be of little use.

Gap between real and stated program aims. One reason for the lack of usefulness of this research is that the stated goal of the Bilingual Education Program appears not to be its real goal (see Rubin 1977 for a discussion of the difference between stated and unstated goals in language planning). The Program, approved by the Congress in 1968, was authorized as a research and demonstration program which would test the effectiveness of various bilingual educational approaches to boosting the educational achievement of poor, ethnolinguistic minority children whose English proficiency is limited. It seems likely, however, that the real goal of the Program is to provide bilingual education for those minority groups which, for varying reasons, want it. What evidence is there for a gap between stated and real aims?

One source of evidence comes from a national evaluation, completed by the American Institutes for Research in 1977, of the Program's Spanish-English projects (about two-thirds of all projects in the Program are designed for Spanish-speaking children). According to that study, fewer than 30 percent of the participating children are actually limited in their ability to speak English and about 85 percent of the projects keep children in bilingual programs long after the children's English proficiency would permit them to move into monolingual English-medium classrooms (Herbert 1977). These figures, if correct, would support the notion that whatever the original intent of the legislation, the underlying goal of the Program is to provide bilingual education per se rather than to study the effectiveness of varying bilingual education approaches for improving the English proficiency of ethnolinguistic minority children.

More compelling evidence of the marginal importance of evaluating the effectiveness of competing bilingual education models as a goal of the Program comes from the manner in which the evaluations have been executed. First of all, the evaluations of local projects have been carried out by the projects themselves, although it is in the best interest both of the project evaluator who wants to be rehired and the project director who wants a renewal of his grant to submit evaluations which are as favorable as credibility permits. Second, having allowed local projects to evaluate themselves, the Program has given the projects wide latitude in deciding what to measure, how to measure it, and how to analyze the data which have been collected (General Accounting Office 1976), with the consequence that project-to-project comparisons are extremely difficult to make. Would the Program have carried out its evaluations in such a manner if evaluation had been a primary goal? If the Program had been a serious research and demonstration enterprise, would the Department of Health, Education, and Welfare fiscal year 1974 report on the Bilingual Education Program have been able to state the following? '... the only current source of data concerning the program's impact on children are the annual individual project evaluation reports whose limitations in the data or methodologies prevent them from being used to draw conclusions about overall program effectiveness' (quoted by General Accounting Office 1976:30). It seems hardly credible that, after the appropriation of half a billion dollars from 1969 through 1977 for the Program, so little would be known about the impact of various bilingual approaches on the attainments of children if the Program had been a serious research and demonstration enterprise. One can only conclude that the Program's real goals lie elsewhere.

It is likely, then, that the Congress passed the Bilingual Education Program and has continued to fund it not so much to determine what types of bilingual education are effective as transitional interventions, but rather in response to the pressures of minority groups who have demanded such education. While it is true that minority group leaders may view bilingual education as a means for improving the education of poor, minority group youngsters (many of whom, in any event, had little to lose inasmuch as their education in conventional monolingual programs can scarcely have been worse), it is also probable that other goals have been more important, particularly the maintenance of ethnic identity, ethnic values, and ethnic languages. Such goals are clearly legitimate, even if unstated for tactical reasons. Indeed, such goals may be far more appropriate ones for bilingual education than transitional remediation. However, if these are the underlying goals of the Program, then research directed towards the relative effectiveness of varying bilingual education approaches for improving the English language skills of pupils seems misdirected.

Difficulties of generalizing from local evaluations. A second reason why much of the research associated with the Bilingual Education Program is not very useful is that even if the Program were being carried out primarily for research and demonstration purposes, evaluations of the effectiveness of individual projects can rarely have more than local significance. There are two bases for this claim.

First, it seems abundantly clear that the sociolinguistic and educational matrix in which the bilingual program is embedded has important (though dimly understood) consequences for the success or failure of the program. Thus, to cite two of the best-known examples, bilingual programs in Ireland appear to have been associated with English mother-tongue children's retardation in problem arithmetic, with no corresponding gain in their Irish language skills (Macnamara 1966), whereas French-English bilingual programs for English mother-tongue children in Montreal appear to have been markedly successful in imparting French language skills, with no ultimate deficits either in subject-matter areas or in English language skills (Lambert and Tucker 1972). Lambert and Tucker's findings are consistent neither with the Irish bilingual experience nor with the failure of poor, ethnolinguistic minority children to achieve well in monolingual English-medium classrooms in the United States. Similarly, Engle's (1975) survey of studies concerned with the relationship between the language employed for teaching beginning

reading and success in reading in a second language suggests
that there is no simple answer as to whether schools should use
the children's mother tongue to teach them to read, when the
ultimate goal is to impart literacy in a second language. The
relative socioeconomic position of the children's families, the
opportunity and need to communicate in the second language
outside the classroom, the attitudes of the children, their parents, and their teachers towards each of the languages involved,
the amount of time and curricular emphases accorded each language of instruction, the size and the composition of the class,
the training and ability of the teachers, the expectations of the
teachers regarding their pupils' ability to succeed, the extent
to which adequate materials can be prepared in each language,
and the similarity between the backgrounds of teachers and
pupils, are all variables which are likely to be related to the
success or failure of bilingual programs. Because the success
of such programs is the outcome of a complex interaction among
many such factors, and because sociolinguistic and educational
contexts differ markedly from locale to locale, the generalizability of local studies is quite limited.

One does not need to invoke the comparison between Dublin
and Montreal to make this point. The bilingual education contexts in the United States alone are quite diverse. Thus, for
example, the Spanish-English programs at the Garfield School
in Redwood City (Cohen 1975a) and the Coral Way School in
Miami (Gaarder 1967) are different with respect to numerous
variables such as the ethnic identity of the Spanish-speaking
children, the relative size and social and economic position of
the Spanish language community, the proportion of Anglo children enrolled, the number of children per class, and the uses
to which English and Spanish are put as media of instruction.
Many more such between-project comparisons can be made. Indeed, it is probably not an exaggeration to claim that each of
the 400 current local projects of the Bilingual Education Program
is unique with respect to the sociolinguistic and educational context in which it operates. Thus, we cannot be sure that a program which works well in one context will work well in another.

A second basis for claiming the doubtfulness of our ability
to generalize from the results of local projects lies in the difficulties involved in attempting to carry out controlled research
in educational settings. The conflict between the requirements
of controlled experimentation and those of administrative convenience and feasibility is well known to anyone who has tried
to carry out experimental research with groups of schoolchildren
at school. As a practical matter, children often cannot be
randomly assigned to experimental and control treatments; where
randomization is not feasible, it is often difficult to find control
groups which appear to be comparable to the children in the
experimental group; where before-and-after measurements are
used in lieu of or in addition to comparisons between control
and experimental groups, it is sometimes difficult to ensure that

the only variable intervening during the period of the project is the project itself (i.e. that there have not been concomitant changes in the community that might account for any observed changes in educational attainment). In addition to problems involved in making comparisons between experimental and control groups or between pre- and post-test data, there are the problems inherent in the relatively small number of classrooms which are typically involved in the study of a local project. Because the influence of particularly good or particularly poor teachers may be pervasive, one would like to observe the experimental program at work with enough teachers so that the influence of exceptional teachers is minimized, but this is rarely possible. Thus, even were we able to find two sociolinguistically similar bilingual projects, it is likely that we would have difficulties in comparing their results either because of differences in their research designs or because of differences in the implementation of their designs, either type of difference occurring as a result of considerations of practical convenience.

Thus, much of the research associated with the Bilingual Education Program is of doubtful usefulness, not only because it is directed towards goals which, though stated as primary, appear in fact to be marginal, but also because the local nature of the programs and the exigencies of educational research make it difficult to generalize from the results of individual projects.

How should research be redirected? If project evaluations have been misdirected, does it necessarily follow that bilingual education projects ought to abandon the gathering of information about the progress of their pupils? Not at all. Parents have a right to know how well their children are performing, and teachers and administrators need this information as well. However, this is equally true with respect to children in conventional programs. It seems doubtful that an elaborate evaluation design or procedure is required to supply such information. Devices (tests, questionnaires, interviews, rating scales, systematic observation procedures) can be periodically administered to children in bilingual programs as they are in ordinary programs. It might be argued that the measurement devices which are appropriate for monolingual programs may not be appropriate for bilingual programs. This is clearly true with respect to goals of instruction in the bilingual program which are not found in monolingual programs, e.g. skills in languages other than English, knowledge of subject-matter areas connected with ethnic identity, and positive attitudes towards ethnic identity. Thus, bilingual projects may require a certain amount of instrument construction not required by conventional programs, although this need appears to be diminishing because of the growing bank of instruments designed by or for local bilingual education projects (see, for example, Silverman, Noa, and Russell 1976). In any case, elaborate and costly research designs are not required to give parents, teachers, and administrators information about the progress of individual pupils in bilingual education projects.

One can also argue that elaborate research designs are not required to show whether a given project is 'working', at least with respect to educational goals. It is reasonable to suppose that the average number of absences per child, the drop-out rate, and the percentage of children who are able to read at specified levels in English and in their mother tongue provide good, rough measures of the success of a program from the point of view of educational outcomes (if not from the point of view of outcomes related to ethnic solidarity). Such measures are not particularly difficult to obtain. In fact, one could argue that if it is necessary to resort to elaborate designs and tests of statistical significance in order to demonstrate the success of a project, the project's impact has been marginal.

While elaborate research may not be necessary to document the success of a given project, some experts suggest that detailed studies of individual projects will help us to develop a theory of bilingual education which will account for the contradictory findings emerging from research in bilingual education. This may be true. However, it can be argued that studies of individual projects are more likely to lead to the development of theory when they have been motivated by theory rather than by the need to assess the success of a given program. This is not to claim that valuable theoretical insights cannot flow from research directed towards practical ends, but only that such insights are more likely to be found if the research has been designed to find them. While there is neither a necessary nor a direct practical payoff for theoretically motivated research, such research will, in the long run, be more useful because it helps us to understand the phenomena underlying the solution to practical problems (Kerlinger 1977). A study evaluating a particular bilingual project may convincingly demonstrate the efficiency of that project's approach to solving a particular set of problems. But it is difficult to transfer that experience to a different setting unless we understand why the approach was successful. To understand why an approach works or does not work for particular children in a particular sociolinguistic and educational context, we must understand better than we do today the many ways in which cognitive, emotional, and sociocultural aspects of learning affect and are affected by the content, context, and language of learning.

What theoretical questions will ultimately lead to better educational practice can be determined only after the event. However, theoretical studies such as the following exemplify sociolinguistic and psycholinguistic research which has some chance to influence educational practice: Gumperz and Hernández' (1972) study of code alternation in classroom interaction; Ervin-Tripp's (1972) comparison of the development of syntactic and morphological features between children learning a second language and those learning their first; Cohen's (1974, 1975b) studies of the phenomenon of forgetting a second language because of limited exposure to it after the onset of learning; Fillmore's (in press) description of the social and cognitive strategies involved in young schoolchildren's learning the medium of instruction as a second language; and Macnamara's (1967) study of children's problem-solving via first and second languages. Studies such as these are likely to influence educational practice because they are addressed to questions about universal mechanisms. Bilingual education offers one context in which such questions can be investigated. It is these questions, rather than the questions about the extent to which given projects have been successful, which are most likely to help us understand such phenomena as second-language learning, the learning of reading, the formation of complex cognitive structures, language maintenance and language shift, and the formation and maintenance of ethnic identity. If we can improve our understanding of such phenomena, we will be in a better position to recommend sound educational policy and practice.

Recommendations. The arguments presented here lead to the following recommendations for the conduct of research within the context of the Bilingual Education Program.

(1) Give greater attention to the unstated goals which apparently underlie the continuance of the Program, particularly the maintenance of ethnic solidarity, ethnic values, and ethnic languages.

(2) Do not require bilingual education projects to go through the motions of experimental design, including the obtaining of comparative measurements from control groups, unless there is a serious intention to study the relative effectiveness of competing bilingual education models.

(3) If there is a serious intention to study the relative effectiveness of different models, give less responsibility to local projects for their own evaluation and impose greater uniformity (to the extent permitted by variability in local goals) with respect to what is measured, how it is measured, and the ways in which data are presented and analyzed.

(4) Continue to gather local data which will permit parents, teachers, and administrators to assess the performance of individual children.

(5) Give greater support to research which asks general questions, i.e. questions whose answers promise to further the development of behavioral or cognitive theory. Here are some examples of promising questions: (a) Are the psychological processes underlying first and second language learning the same? (b) Why do students fail to solve a complex problem couched in their second language

when they can solve each of its components in that language? (c) What cognitive and social strategies underlie second language learning? (d) How does code-switching convey social information? (e) What are the mechanisms underlying language maintenance and language shift? (f) What role does language maintenance play in the maintenance of ethnic identity? The argument here is not that these questions are necessarily the best ones from the point of view of bilingual education (others might suggest different questions as being ultimately more rewarding) but that we should give greater emphasis to the identification and solution of such problems.

Educational policy decisions, of course, are rarely based on rational considerations alone. Political pressures and constraints usually play an important role as well. Nowhere is this clearer than with respect to bilingual education. Nonetheless, decisions are sound to the extent that the evidence on which they are anchored is sound. With respect to bilingual education, the reorientation of research along the lines suggested here ought, in the long run, to give us a firmer basis for formulating educational policy.

NOTE

Andrew D. Cohen's criticisms of an earlier draft of this paper were very helpful.

REFERENCES

Cohen, A. D. 1974. The Culver City Spanish immersion program: How does summer recess affect Spanish speaking ability? Language Learning 24.55-68.
Cohen, A. D. 1975a. A sociolinguistic approach to bilingual education: Experiments in the American Southwest. Rowley, Mass.: Newbury House.
Cohen, A. D. 1975b. Forgetting a second language. Language Learning 25.127-138.
Engle, P. L. 1975. The use of vernacular languages in education: Language medium in early school years for minority groups. Papers in Applied Linguistics, Bilingual Education Series: 3. Arlington, Va.: Center for Applied Linguistics.
Fillmore, L. W. (in press). The second time around: Cognitive and social strategies in second language acquisition. New York: Academic Press.
Gaarder, A. B. 1967. Organization of the bilingual school. Journal of Social Issues 23:2.110-120.
General Accounting Office. 1976. Comptroller General's report to the Congress--Bilingual education: An unmet need. Washington, D.C.: Department of Health, Education and Welfare.

Gumperz, J. J., and E. Hernández-Chávez. 1972. Bilingualism, bidialectalism, and classroom interaction. In: Functions of language in the classroom. Edited by C. B. Cazden, V. P. John, and D. Hymes. New York: Teachers College Press. 84-108.
Herbert, W. 1977. Bilingual education missing the mark? APA Monitor 8:9 and 10.8.
Kerlinger, F. N. 1977. The influence of research on education practice. Educational Researcher 6:8.5-12.
Lambert, W. E., and G. R. Tucker. 1972. Bilingual education of children. Rowley, Mass.: Newbury House.
Macnamara, J. 1966. Bilingualism and primary education. Edinburgh: Edinburgh University Press.
Macnamara, J. 1967. The effects of instruction in a weaker language. Journal of Social Issues 23:2.121-135.
Rubin, J. 1977. Bilingual education and language planning. In: Frontiers of bilingual education. Edited by B. Spolsky and R. Cooper. Rowley, Mass.: Newbury House.
Silverman, R. J., J. K. Noa, and R. H. Russell. 1976. Oral language tests for bilingual students: An evaluation of language dominance and proficiency instruments. Portland, Ore.: Center for Bilingual Education, Northwest Regional Educational Laboratory.

BILINGUAL AND BICULTURAL EDUCATION: THE ROLE OF THE SCHOLAR

Noel Epstein
The Washington Post

I feel greatly honored to be here today. Much of what I know about the subject at hand, after all, comes from the work of those who have assembled for these distinguished Georgetown University Round Table meetings, and I am deeply in their debt.

There are those who think that I have not learned well enough from their work, and there are others who think that I have learned only too well. That is always the case. But my experience in examining national bilingual and bicultural education policy in the United States has confirmed my belief that journalists and scholars have exceedingly important benefits to gain from each other--if only we can overcome some of the strains between us.

That will not always be easy. There are many inherent flaws in journalism, mainly growing out of the limited time and space available for what we write, and that understandably makes some scholars uncomfortable in dealing with us. From the journalist's view, there are also problems with scholars, including the tendency of some to indulge in needless obscurity and jargon. I must say that in trying to understand the bilingual-bicultural issue, I feel that I have become multilingual myself--and all in English.

But there are also deeper problems, and one in particular which has been troubling me for some time. This is the tendency of some scholars, in their eagerness to influence public policy, to confuse rhetoric and research, to blur the critical distinction between their scholarship and their ideologies, between what they know and what they believe.

This tendency is certainly neither new nor peculiar to the bilingual-bicultural education issue, and it has been disturbing a good number of scholars themselves. As Dr. Richard C. Atkinson, director of the National Science Foundation, has remarked, he has heard his fellow psychologists 'too often speaking on issues of education, child rearing, and mental health using what they claim to be research evidence as a disguise for advocating a particular policy'. To his mind, 'some social scientists want to run the goddamn country, and that's an unhealthy attitude'.

But my efforts in the bilingual-bicultural area have served to deepen my concerns. The question that troubles me, it should be emphasized, is not whether scholars should also be advocates; they obviously have as much right as anyone else to press their political views. Rather, the question is when scholars have an overriding responsibility to identify what is research and what is rhetoric, when their scholarly authority ends and their beliefs carry no more or less weight than anyone else's, when they must say there is no reliable evidence to support--or contradict--their personal views. I would go even one step further: Do scholars have an obligation to make available to public bodies information which they fear might damage their personal causes, or are errors of omission permissible?

Let me give you an example. In early 1974, as everyone is aware, the Supreme Court handed down its ruling in Lau v. Nichols. The Court, confirming a guideline of the Health, Education and Welfare Department, ruled that school systems had to provide some kind of special instruction to students who had little or no command of English. It did not specify what that instruction should be, leaving the decision to the school district, in that case San Francisco.

San Francisco then appointed a citizens' task force to devise a remedy, and it also contracted with the Center for Applied Linguistics to provide technical assistance. The task force and the Center worked together. But as I noted in my policy analysis, Language, Ethnicity, and the Schools, there was a problem: The task force did not want the Center to include any studies which raised doubts about the effectiveness of bilingual-bicultural education in improving student achievement. As Dr. Roger Shuy, a distinguished member of this faculty and also associate director of the Center, told me:

> Our instructions from the task force were to give them positive instances. We told them that in terms of reading, there wasn't much evidence to show that bilingual education helped. But they didn't want us to say anything like that. They had a political job to do.

What do scholars do in such circumstances? I am sure that the task force demand caused considerable consternation at the Center.

In the end, the Center essentially went along with the demands. The opening section of the plan developed for the school system and the court listed seven fragile studies which could be used to support bilingual education. No unfavorable studies were included. The listing was then followed by this caveat: 'This survey has focused on projects which have shown (or have tried to show) that bilingual or vernacular education really works'. As Dr. Shuy said, 'It was a concession getting that statement in to protect my integrity'.

Where does the scholars' responsibility lie in such a case? Did not the court have a right to know that, so far as bilingual education's impact on achievement and on the acquisition of a second language are concerned, the evidence is fragmented, largely unreliable, and inconclusive? Did not the school officials have a right to know? Above all, did not the parents of the children concerned have a right to know? Does not it make one wonder why the task force members would not trust parents in their own language groups with the available evidence? Would you accept the same standards from a journalist?

Since completing my brief policy analysis, I have had more reason to wonder about such questions. Among other things, attorneys for several school systems have asked me to testify in court cases involving bilingual education. Why me? Surely there are many scholars more qualified than I am to tell a court what is and is not known about bilingual education. As I stated to begin with, much of what I know about the issue, and certainly everything I know about the research aspects, comes from you and your colleagues. But the attorneys have made it clear to me that they cannot get many, if any, scholars to testify on behalf of the school systems. Presumably, the scholars do not want to appear to be opponents of bilingual and bicultural education, even though one of the school systems challenging the HEW 'Lau remedies' growing out of the Supreme Court ruling is run by a school board made up entirely of Alaskan natives.

That makes me wonder again: Can a scholar seriously claim that telling a balanced version of reality, at least as he or she knows reality, might hurt a cause that one deeply believes in? Again, would the same standards apply to journalists? I think not.

I am not surprised at all when attorneys or politicians try to prove their cases with whatever evidence they can muster. That is generally expected of them, and their words consequently are often greeted with the appropriate skepticism. I am sure you do not want to see the same reception for the words of researchers. I certainly do not. Yet I think that is increasingly, if gradually, becoming the case. It was both distressing and humorous to discover that in one bilingual case, Otero v. Mesa County Valley School District No. 51, the court remarked: 'Listening to these experts causes one to conclude that if psychiatrists' disagreements are to be compared to differences between educators, psychiatrists are almost of a single mind'.

Do not misunderstand. I am aware that the scholarly process demands disagreement. It is also not a swift process that can produce instant answers to pressing social issues. Part of the problem is that the society often expects more from scholars than they can reasonably deliver. The other part of the problem is that scholars often begin to believe that they should oblige.

In the bilingual-bicultural policy area, I believe, one of the problems is that scholars have sometimes let themselves be used and abused by others. They have not emphasized enough in the public arena how little is known about bilingual education. Yet they have often complained, at least to me, about the paucity of research funds available to finance their investigations. Indeed, for nearly a decade now, many persons have been proclaiming that bilingual education is the answer, but, as I have asked in my analysis: What was the question?

To some scholars, of course, the primary question is not what effect bilingual-bicultural education can have on achievement in general. They have stressed that bilingual-bicultural education, in and of itself, should not be expected to make a significant difference in the achievement of poor, limited-English-speaking children. If that is what the evidence shows, those scholars should be stating that specifically, with any appropriate qualifications, to the Congress, the courts, and the parents of those students. If, as some have stated, language barriers do not appear to be the chief cause for the poor achievement of many such students, the policymakers and parents surely have a right to know that.

Statements to this effect are not hard to find in scholarly or professional journals. For example, Dr. Joshua A. Fishman, one of the most forceful bilingual-bicultural advocates in this country, has written that the cumulative evidence on transitional bilingual-bicultural education, which is chiefly what is being funded in this nation, shows that:

> ... on the whole, bilingual education is too frail a device, in and of itself, to significantly alter the learning experiences of the minority-mother-tongue-poor in general or their majority-language-learning success in particular.

But members of Congress, judges, and parents do not read those scholarly and professional journals, and they are the ones responsible for the decisions that are made.

Dr. Fishman, of course, has long believed that enriching these students' lives with two or more languages and cultures, thereby maintaining minority languages and cultures and also enriching the society as a whole, are sufficient justifications

not only for bilingual-bicultural education, but for the federal government to assume responsibility for its financing and promotion. That position, I need scarcely say, does not necessarily rest on scholarship, just as opposing positions need not rest on scholarship, and Dr. Fishman has made this clear.
In the landmark study he headed in the early 1960s, <u>Language Loyalty in the United States</u>, in the eloquent chapter on policy recommendations, Dr. Fishman stated:

> ... these recommendations are not necessarily derived from data reported by the Language Resource Project. Many could have been advanced (and probably would have been) without the data obtained from three years of concerted effort.

That was a refreshing acknowledgment to discover, and I commend Dr. Fishman for it. I only wish that others would include such statements in their public testimony, as well as in their studies, whenever they are expressing their personal views.

I have deep admiration for scholars in general, and I know that what I have said may seem presumptuous to many, particularly coming from a journalist. Journalism, after all, has many problems of its own, and I am only too well aware of them. But I make these remarks with the conviction that the primary search of both scholars and journalists is still for the truth, wherever that may lead. To the extent that this search is compromised, the authority of both is diminished and both we and the nation suffer.

IX. Case Studies

BILINGUAL EDUCATION
FOR THE ENGLISH-SPEAKING CANADIAN

Merrill Swain
Ontario Institute for Studies in Education

It was just eight years ago that participants of the Georgetown University Round Table on Languages and Linguistics heard Professor Lambert discuss the consequences to English unilingual children of being instructed during their early schooling entirely in French (Lambert 1970). Since that time much has happened: students have progressed through the program; many similar programs have been initiated and evaluated across Canada; programs beginning the 'immersion' experience at later grade levels have been planned, implemented, and evaluated, as have other variations of the immersion format. The context within which these programs have developed is a Quebec where French has become the langue de travail, and a Canada where English-French bilingualism has increasingly been required for employment within the Federal civil service. The latter is only one aspect of the Federal government's attempt to promote bilingualism, the ultimate purpose of which is to convince Quebec to remain part of the Canadian confederation.

The purposes of this paper are threefold. The first purpose is to describe three formats of bilingual education for the English-speaking Canadian which have emerged from the 'immersion' model. The second purpose is to provide an overview of the results related to the three programs. Thirdly, based on these results and several theoretical considerations, some implications for bilingual education are suggested. Omitted is a discussion of the political and social forces which underlie the existence, development, and expansion of bilingual education for English-Canadians, and the current economic and political forces which support or militate against their further expansion. These issues will be considered elsewhere (Swain, in preparation).

1. **French immersion education.** The first French immersion class in the public sector began in 1965 in St. Lambert, a suburb of Montreal, prompted by a group of English-speaking parents whose primary concern was that the level of French attained by their children in a traditional French-as-a-second-language (FSL) program would not be sufficient to meet their needs in a community and country that was increasingly emphasizing the importance of French as a langue de travail (Lambert and Tucker 1972). They were convinced that if French was used as a medium of communication in school--as a means to an end rather than as an end in itself--second language learning would be enhanced.

1.1 **Early total immersion.** The program the St. Lambert parents established has come to be known as an early total French immersion program: early because it begins with the first day of schooling; total immersion because all instruction is initially provided through the medium of the second language. Typically, English Language Arts is introduced and taught in English in grades two or three for approximately an hour a day. With each successive year thereafter, a larger proportion of the curriculum is taught in English until an approximately equal balance is reached between the time devoted to instruction in each language. The English and French portions of the day are taught by different teachers.

The term 'immersion' has led to many a misconception of what actually occurs in a French immersion class. Although it is the case that French is the only language used by the teacher, it is not the case that it is the only language used by the children. During much of the first year in an early total French immersion program, the children continue to speak English among themselves and to their teacher, who, although a native speaker of French, is bilingual, and therefore can understand the children when they use their native language. It is not until the second year of the program that the teacher begins to insist that the children attempt to express their ideas in French and, through a gradual transition, French comes to be established as the language of the classroom.[1]

Although the early total immersion program begins as a unilingual one, it is the case that over the students' educational career, instruction occurs in two languages, legitimately placing it within the category of bilingual schooling. Another possible format is that throughout the students' education both languages are used as the medium of instruction. The early partial immersion program is such a program.

1.2 **Early partial immersion.** The early partial immersion program differs from the early total immersion program mainly in that both French and English are used as languages of instruction in each year of schooling. Typically, instructional

time is divided equally between the two languages, with a
different teacher teaching each portion.
   The origin of the early partial immersion program in Canada
stems from parental and administrative concerns. In some communities a total immersion program was considered and rejected
owing to the possible negative effects it might have on the
native language skills, especially reading and writing, of their
children--a concern, discussed further on in this paper, that
appears to be unfounded. School administrators considered
that a program in which half the day was taught in one language and half the day taught in the other language was much
simpler to schedule and organize than the seemingly unwieldy
scheduling involved with the introduction of English for small
portions of the day, which necessarily occurs after several
years of the total immersion program. In fact, one Board of
Education which began in 1969 with a total French immersion
program retreated in 1975 to a partial immersion program to
eliminate the costly 'overlay' difficulties of the existing scheme
and to provide a program which was more acceptable to larger
numbers of parents (Moore 1976).

   1.3 **Late immersion.** Whereas the two programs I have
described begin when schooling begins, late immersion programs begin some years after the students have entered school.
The most common starting point seems to be about grade seven
or eight, although programs exist in Canada where the immersion experience begins as early as grade four or as late as
grade ten. Typically, the program consists of one to two
years of immersion, followed by the possibility of taking
several course options each year in French ('postimmersion').
Prior to entering a late immersion program, students have
taken at least one year of FSL (20 to 60 minutes a day of
formal French instruction), but again this varies considerably,
ranging across Canada from one to six years of previous FSL
instruction.
   These programs are different from the early immersion programs in that teachers in the late immersion programs tend to
insist that their students use French, at least during teacher-student interactions, from the first day of the program. Insistence on the initial use of French is considered feasible
because students have received previous FSL instruction.
Additionally, there is an implicit but largely untested assumption that being denied the possibility of spontaneous expression in their first language will not be as disorienting, emotionally upsetting, or intellectually stultifying for the older
student as it has sometimes been argued to be for the younger
child just entering school.
   Interestingly, the concept of late immersion also originates
from the early immersion program. As results of the early
immersion program came to be more widely known across
Canada, many parents began to believe that their children,

already in the educational system, had missed out on a valuable educational experience (Edwards and Smyth 1976a). Additionally, parents who were concerned that if immersion was introduced too early, native language skills might be impaired, were sympathetic to the notion of late immersion. Administrators, too, were supportive: the program would be less costly because it started later and it would involve less disruption of the total school system (Stanley 1974).

It is important to note that in many instances where an immersion program has been initiated, it has been demanded by parents rather than imposed by administrators. Furthermore, each of the immersion programs I have described is, where offered, optional. Although this does not imply that brighter students will enter the program, it does suggest that students whose home environment is supportive of bilingualism will enter. (See Swain forthcoming b, for a discussion of the implications for program evaluation.)

Total enrollment figures of English-speaking students in French immersion programs in Canada are not known. However, enrollment figures for the Province of Ontario, available from the Ministry of Education, indicate that in 1973 there were approximately 5,000 students enrolled in immersion programs, and in 1976 there were approximately 13,000.

2. **Overview of research results.** Of the three formats of bilingual education I have discussed, the most extensively researched one is early total immersion, in part because it is the most radical departure from unilingual English education. (For a bibliography of immersion education for the majority child, see Swain 1976).

In many of the studies undertaken, at least two successive cohorts--in some cases, three successive cohorts (Swain 1978)--of students are evaluated as they begin their respective program and proceed through it. This allows one to look at the progress of students over time, as well as to determine to what extent the results from one year are replicated by a new group the following year. The performance of each group of bilingual education students is usually compared with the performance of English-speaking students in the unilingual English program in the same school board, and in some cases with French-speaking students in francophone schools. Because details of the methodology and the statistical results have been discussed extensively in published literature, the discussion of program results is limited to summary statements: this inevitably glosses over the occasional finding for which the summary does not hold true.

2.1 **Early total immersion.** The English language skills of the early total immersion students have been monitored over the years and across programs using a variety of techniques, ranging from standardized tests measuring vocabulary knowledge, reading comprehension, punctuation, spelling, and grammar, to the measurement of communicative abilities and sensitivity to the needs of the listener (Genesee, Tucker, and Lambert 1975), to global and detailed scoring of stories written (Swain 1975; Genesee and Stanley 1976) and told (Edwards and Smyth 1976b) by the students.

The results show that the early total immersion students do not do as well as their unilingually educated peers through the end of grade one. This is not particularly surprising as they have had no formal instruction in English. One exception to the inferior performance of the immersion children at this grade level is that they were found to be, in their oral communicative skills, more sensitive to the needs of the listener than were children educated in their native language. Genesee, Tucker, and Lambert (1975:1013) suggest that these findings may be related to the immersion children's experience in school, which 'may have made them more aware of possible difficulties in communicating as well as providing them with some experience in coping with such difficulties'.

Through the end of grade three, the immersion students continue to have some difficulty with such technical skills as spelling, punctuation, and capitalization. But by the end of grade four, the immersion students and their English-educated peers perform equivalently. This appears to be the case even if English is not introduced into the curriculum until grade three, or even grade four. By the end of grade five, the immersion students in some instances out-perform their comparison groups on several aspects of measured English skills, for example, reading comprehension and vocabulary knowledge.

As with English, the French language skills of the early total immersion students have been monitored through a variety of tests and techniques. The results reveal consistently superior performance of the immersion students relative to students following a program of FSL instruction. Furthermore, immersion students perform at least as well as 30 percent of native French-speaking students who served as norming populations for the standardized tests employed. After six or seven years in an immersion program, student performance in the areas of listening and reading approaches native-like levels; whereas in the areas of speaking and writing, many differences between immersion and francophone students still remain (see, for example, Spilka 1976; Harley and Swain 1977).

In a detailed study of the verbal system used by several grade five students, Harley and Swain (1978) concluded that, in general, the immersion children may be said to be operating with simpler and grammatically less redundant verb systems than native speakers of the same age. They tend to lack forms for which grammatically less complex alternative means of conveying the appropriate meaning exist. The forms and rules that they have mastered appear to be those that are the most generalized in the target verb system (for example, the first

conjugation -er verb pattern). In the area of verb syntax, it
appears that where French has a more complex system than
English (for example, in the form and placement of object pronouns), the immersion children tend to opt for a simpler pattern that approximates the one with which they are already
familiar in their mother tongue.

The difference between the speech of the immersion students
and their francophone counterparts may in part be accounted
for by their lack of interaction with native French-speaking
peers. In the French immersion classroom, the students are
for the most part exposed, in any one year, to only one native
French-speaking model, namely, the teacher. Otherwise the
spoken French they hear is largely that of their nonnative
French-speaking classmates--all of whom have the same first
language--in interaction with the teacher or each other. Once
the children have reached a point in their second language development where they can make themselves understood by their
teacher and classmates, there is no strong social incentive to
develop further towards native speaker norms. This suggests
that after several years of an immersion program--once a sufficiently high level of French is attained so that the language
of communication can be French[2]--sustained contact with francophone peers may be essential, if the attainment of native-like
speaking abilities is to be a program goal.[3]

The learning of content material has been measured over the
years through the use of standardized tests in mathematics,
and from approximately grade five, through the use of standardized tests in science and social studies as well. It should
be noted that the tests of content mastery were written in
English, thus potentially handicapping the immersion students
who had been taught the subject material in French. Almost
without exception, the immersion students perform as well as
their unilingually educated counterparts on both computational
and problem-solving tasks in mathematics. Additionally, the
immersion students demonstrate equivalent performance to
their comparison groups in science and social studies (e.g.
Tucker 1975; Swain and Barik 1976).

2.2 **Early partial immersion.** The results reported further
on in this section are based on data associated with two programs. One program involves only one class at each grade
level in Elgin County, beginning at grade one and now extending to grade eight. (Details of the evaluation through grade
six can be found in Barik and Swain 1974; 1976a; 1977; 1978;
Lapkin and Stinson 1978.) The second program involves
virtually all the students in the Ottawa Roman Catholic Separate School Board (ORCSSB), beginning at kindergarten and
now extending to grade three. (Details of the evaluation
through grade two can be found in Edwards, Doutriaux, and
McCarrey 1976; Edwards et al. 1977.)

Based on standardized tests, the results related to the English language skills of the early partial immersion students relative to their comparison groups are similar to those found for early total immersion; that is, the partial immersion students tend not to do as well as their comparison groups until the end of grade three or grade four, even though one-half of their program has been taught through the medium of English as compared to total immersion groups who began the study of English only in grade two or three for an hour a day. Additionally, whereas the total immersion students perform better than their comparison groups in several aspects of English language skills by the end of grade five or six, this is not the case with the partial immersion students relative to their comparison groups.[4]

The results related to the French language skills of the early partial immersion students indicate performance that is not as good as that of the total immersion students at the same grade level but which is, for the most part, better than that of students at the same grade level following a program of FSL instruction. Although partial immersion students do not perform as well as total immersion students of the same grade level, they tend to perform as well as total immersion students in lower grade levels who have had similar amounts of contact time with French.[5]

The learning of content material has been measured by standardized tests of mathematics and science.[6] The results reveal that the early partial immersion students tend to perform equivalently or not as well as their English-educated peer groups. One plausible explanation for these findings is derived from Cummins' (1976) threshold hypothesis. According to this hypothesis, learners must attain a 'threshold' level in their second language if they are to profit from instruction in that language. What defines the threshold level is not known. However, by extrapolation, one might argue that the early partial immersion students have not attained it.

Let us consider a concrete example. The grade six early partial immersion students did not perform as well as their English-educated peers in either science or mathematics. It is also the case that their level of French performance more closely approximated grades three and four early total immersion students. It may thus be the case that their level of French was not adequate to deal with the more sophisticated level of mathematical and scientific concepts being presented to them in French in grade six.

2.3 **Late immersion.** The outcomes of late immersion programs in relation to possible negative effects on the native language, second language learning, and content learning are more difficult to summarize, owing largely to the variation in program formats which have been evaluated. However, from the results related to specific program formats, it seems possible to draw several general conclusions.

In relation to native language performance, it is sometimes the case that late immersion students score lower at the end of the immersion year than their English-educated comparison group. However, their poorer performance is only temporary in that it disappears by the following year (e.g. Barik and Swain 1976b).

The performance of the late immersion students in all aspects of French language abilities is consistently superior to that of students at the same grade level following an FSL program, and typically, it is at least equivalent to FSL students two to three grade levels above them (e.g. Barik, Swain, and Gaudino 1976; Shapson and Kaufman 1978). When students continue after the immersion year to take course options in French throughout secondary school, their achievement in French appears considerable. For example, on a set of leaving examinations designed for native French-speaking students by the Quebec Department of Education--'expression orale', 'compréhension de texte', poésie et roman', and 'théâtre et essai'--the average scores obtained by grade eleven students[7] who had taken a grade seven late immersion program plus postimmersion courses in French each year were higher than the provincial averages except for 'poésie et roman' (Genesee 1976).[8] Results are less impressive, however, when courses are not offered in French throughout secondary school, or when students do not choose the options taught in French. Under these circumstances, postimmersion students appear to maintain an advantage over FSL students in listening comprehension, but otherwise tend towards performance levels similar to those of FSL students[9] (Swain and Lapkin 1977).

To date, no detailed analyses of the French spoken by the late immersion students have been undertaken. A fascinating area for exploration by those interested in second language acquisition lies in comparisons of the French used by the early and late immersion students.

The results associated with the mastery of content by late immersion students are somewhat inconsistent. In some cases late immersion students do not perform as well on tests of subject achievement taught in French and tested in English as do their English-instructed counterparts. The results appear to be related to the subject, and to the amount of prior FSL instruction that the students have had. Where students have had--as in Montreal and Ottawa--FSL instruction each year through to the immersion year, the level of mastery of content taught in French by the immersion students appears to be comparable to that attained by their English-instructed counterparts (Genesee, Polich, and Stanley 1977; Stern et al. 1976). If the amount of prior FSL instruction is more limited, however, poorer performance in some subject areas (science, but not mathematics) has been noted (Barik and Swain 1976). Here

Bilingual Education for the English-speaking Canadian /393

again, Cummins' threshold hypothesis appears useful in accounting for the different results, with perhaps an additional qualifier that the threshold level will vary according to the nature of the content being considered: the threshold level will be higher, the greater the interdependence between language and the content.

Results from Montreal reveal that, for those late immersion students who have continued to take several course options in French throughout secondary school, average scores obtained on leaving examinations are higher than those obtained by their francophone peers in the rest of Quebec. These examinations include 'histoire', 'géographie', 'mathématique', and 'dactylo'.[10]

3. **Implications for bilingual education for the majority language child.** Overall, these results suggest that French immersion programs--early or late--are viable alternatives to unilingual education for English-Canadians. The results also suggest that the early total immersion format may be preferable to the early partial immersion format in that the former develops second language proficiency rapidly, enabling the pupils to assimilate knowledge presented in that language without handicap. Development of second language skills in the partial immersion program proceeds more slowly, allowing for the possibility that students will not have sufficient linguistic skills to be able to deal with the subject material being presented to them in French. Furthermore, the additional time initially devoted to the development of English reading and writing skills in the partial immersion program does not, in the long run, appear to lead to achievement which is superior to that attained by total immersion students. This finding reflects, in part, the fact that English and literacy are integral aspects of the environment in which these students live.

The results related to the late immersion programs suggest that if there is sufficient FSL instruction prior to the program and if sufficient additional courses are taken in French following the program, high levels of French proficiency, at no loss to the mastery of content material or native language proficiency, can be attained. Given these findings, it is appropriate to ask: 'Why have early immersion, given the additional resources needed--both in teachers and materials, and the complete disruption it involves of the system?' The answers are tentative, subject to revision should incoming data be contradictory.

First, it is not yet known how the French of the early and late immersion students will compare at the end of schooling. It would be surprising to all concerned, however, if there were not significant differences favoring the early immersion students. One anticipated difference relates to the feelings of the speakers themselves--their feelings of ease, comfort, and naturalness in using the language.

Secondly, there is the matter of student perception of the programs. Late immersion students recognize after the immersion experience (if not before) that learning a second language involves considerable time and effort--time and energy that they may prefer to spend elsewhere. Learning French becomes one of many competing interests, one which may not be perceived as providing sufficient rewards to choose. Course options which are offered in French may not correspond to the students' interests. Even if they do, some students choose to take the subjects in English in order to get a 'better' or an 'easier' grade. Early immersion students, however, enter into the challenge of learning a second language without an awareness of the challenge. It does not compete with other interests, but rather it is an integral part of school activities.

Thirdly, there exists a number of well-controlled studies which suggest that bilingualism, or the process of becoming bilingual, can positively influence aspects of cognitive and linguistic growth (for a review, see Cummins in press). These studies, for the most part, consider individuals who have learned their second language prior to adolescence. It may be that similar results would be found in relation to individuals who have learned their second language as adolescents or adults. However, since the data already reveal positive effects associated with early bilingualism where proficiency in both languages is high, it becomes a missed opportunity to delay second language learning for those individuals whose first language is sufficiently well developed.

These considerations suggest that the early total immersion program makes bilingualism a possibility for a potentially larger number of students to whom cognitive and linguistic benefits may accrue. As bilingual education for English-Canadians continues to expand, these factors may be important to consider.

NOTES

1. Clearly, this immersion setting differs considerably from that of immigrant and/or minority language children who are mixed together in class with children who already know the school language. For descriptions of the differences, see, for example, Burnaby (1976); Cohen and Swain (1976); Paulston (in press); and Swain (in press a).

2. In most parts of Canada the francophone population is a minority, and assimilation into the dominant English majority is occurring (see, for example, Mougeon, Canale, and Bélanger 1978). Therefore, francophones are legitimately concerned about any suggestion to integrate francophone and anglophone students together in the same class, arguing that it will only hasten assimilation by making English the language of communication in school as well as out of school. It is thus essential that if francophones are to accept anglophones

in their schools, the level of proficiency in French of the anglophone children be such that French can be maintained as the language of the school.

3. It is not clear what parents and educators consider to be the goal of immersion programs in relation to the degree of bilingualism to be attained. My own understanding of the situation, based on listening to many parents and educators over the years, is that they are convinced that immersion programs will lead to 'full bilingualism', that is, native-like proficiency in all four skills. Either parents and educators need to be more realistic about their expectations, or schools need to adapt their programs so that they incorporate interaction with French-speaking peers, if disappointment is not to follow.

4. These findings are based on the Elgin County program only. The English language skills of the students in the ORCSSB were measured and compared with those of students who, although labelled as English language program students, received at least an hour a day of social studies and French instruction in French, whereas the Elgin County comparison students received all instruction in English.

5. These comparisons do not include writing, which has not been examined in any evaluation of the partial immersion program to date. Furthermore, they do not include any detailed comparison of language use by the two groups.

6. Again, the results from the ORCSSB are not considered here because in their program, mathematics was taught in English, and science, which was taught in French, was not tested.

7. Grade 11 is the graduating year from secondary school in Quebec, whereas grade 12 or 13 is the graduating year in other Canadian provinces.

8. The author (Genesee 1976:3) points out that interpretation of these results should be made cautiously 'owing to differences in the characteristics of students who comprise the populations. In particular, it must be borne in mind when interpreting the results that ... there is undoubtedly less variation in socioeconomic and academic ability levels among the students from the school samples under consideration than among the populations of students comprising the provincial groups'.

9. It is important in interpreting these comparisons to be aware of two facts. (1) The FSL students in the comparison groups tend to be highly motivated successful learners, others having opted out earlier. This means that the students who have had the immersion year, plus some postimmersion courses, are at least as proficient in French as the few students who 'make it' in the FSL option. (2) In grades 12 and 13 the postimmersion students studied FSL with the grades 12 and 13 FSL students, respectively. This suggests that the similar performance levels observed may be due to equivalent instruction received by both groups.

10. See note 8.

REFERENCES

Barik, H. C., and M. Swain. 1974. English-French bilingual education in the early grades: The Elgin Study. Modern Language Journal 58.392-403.
Barik, H. C., and M. Swain. 1976a. English-French bilingual education in the early grades: The Elgin Study through grade four. Modern Language Journal 60.3-17.
Barik, H. C., and M. Swain. 1976b. A Canadian experiment in bilingual education at the grade eight and nine levels: The Peel Study. Foreign Language Annals 9.465-479.
Barik, H. C., and M. Swain. 1978. Evaluation of a bilingual education program in Canada: The Elgin Study through grade six. Bulletin CILA 27.
Barik, H. C., M. Swain, and V. Gaudino. 1976. A Canadian experiment in bilingual education in the senior grades: The Peel Study through grade 10. International Review of Applied Psychology 99-113.
Barik, H. C., M. Swain, and E. A. Nwanunobi. 1977. English-French bilingual education: The Elgin Study through grade five. The Canadian Modern Language Review 33.459-475.
Burnaby, B. 1976. Language in native education. In: Bilingualism in Canadian education: Issues and research. Edited by M. Swain. Yearbook of the Canadian Society for the Study of Education, Volume 3. Edmonton, Alta.: Western Industrial Research Centre. 62-85.
Cohen, A. D., and M. Swain. 1976. Bilingual education: The immersion model in the North American context. TESOL Quarterly 10.1.45-53. Reprinted in: English as a second language in bilingual education. Edited by J. E. Alatis and K. Twaddell. Washington, D.C.: TESOL. 55-63.
Cummins, J. 1976. The influence of bilingualism on cognitive growth: A synthesis of research findings and explanatory hypotheses. Working Papers on Bilingualism 9.1-43.
Cummins, J. (in press) The cognitive development of children in immersion programs. The Canadian Modern Language Review.
Edwards, H. P., C. W. Doutriaux, and H. A. McCarrey. 1976. Evaluation of the grade one 50-50 bilingual program. Ottawa: The Ottawa Roman Catholic Separate School Board. Mimeo.
Edwards, H. P., C. W. Doutriaux, H. A. McCarrey, and L. Fu. 1977. Evaluation of second language program extensions offered in grades 1, 2, 7, and 8: Final report. Ottawa: The Ottawa Roman Catholic Separate School Board. Mimeo.
Edwards, H., and F. Smyth. 1976a. Alternatives to early immersion programs for the acquisition of French as a second language. The Canadian Modern Language Review 32.5.524-533.

Edwards, H. P., and F. Smyth. 1976b. Evaluation of second language programs and some alternatives for teaching French as a second language in grades five to eight. Toronto: The Ontario Ministry of Education.
Genesee, F. 1976. Addendum to the evaluation of the 1975-76 grade 11 French immersion class. Montreal: The Protestant School Board of Greater Montreal. Mimeo.
Genesee, F., E. Polich, and M. H. Stanley. 1977. An experimental French immersion program at the secondary school level, 1969 to 1974. The Canadian Modern Language Review 33.3.318-332.
Genesee, F., and M. H. Stanley. 1976. The development of English writing skills in French immersion programs. Canadian Journal of Education 1.3.1-17.
Genesee, F., G. R. Tucker, and W. E. Lambert. 1975. Communication skills of bilingual children. Child Development 46.1010-1014.
Harley, B., and M. Swain. 1977. An analysis of verb form and function in the speech of French immersion pupils. Working Papers on Bilingualism 14.31-46.
Harley, B., and M. Swain. 1978. An analysis of the verb system used by young learners of French. Interlanguage Studies Bulletin 3.1.
Lambert, W. 1970. Some cognitive consequences of following the curricula of early school grades in a foreign language. In: Georgetown University Round Table on Languages and Linguistics 1970. Edited by James E. Alatis. Washington, D.C.: Georgetown University Press. 229-279.
Lambert, W. E., and G. R. Tucker. 1972. Bilingual education of children: The St. Lambert experiment. Rowley, Mass.: Newbury House Publishers.
Lapkin, S., and R. Stinson. 1978. Learning in French for half the day. Orbit 42.
Moore, G. 1976. Comments in general discussion by panel of school board officials and coordinators of second-language departments. The Canadian Modern Language Review 33.2. 276-279.
Mougeon, R., M. Canale, and M. Bélanger. 1978. Rôle de la société dans l'acquisition et le maintien du français par les élèves franco-ontariens. The Canadian Modern Language Review 34.3.
Paulston, C. B. (in press) Bilingual-bicultural education. Review of Research in Education.
Shapson, S., and D. Kaufman. 1978. A study of a late immersion French program in secondary school. The Canadian Modern Language Review 34.2.186-193.
Spilka, I. V. 1976. Assessment of second-language performance in immersion programs. The Canadian Modern Language Review 32.5.543-561.

Stanley, M. H. 1974. French immersion programs: The
experience of the Protestant School Board of Greater
Montreal. The Canadian Modern Language Review 31.2.
152-160.
Stern, H. H., M. Swain, L. D. McLean, R. J. Friedman,
B. Harley, and S. Lapkin. 1976. Three approaches to
teaching French. Toronto: Ontario Ministry of Education.
Swain, M. 1975. Writing skills of grade three French immersion pupils. Working Papers on Bilingualism 7.1-38.
Swain, M. 1976. Bibliography: Research on immersion education for the majority child. The Canadian Modern Language Review 32.5.592-596.
Swain, M. 1978. French immersion: Early, late or partial?
The Canadian Modern Language Review 34.3.
Swain, M. (forthcoming a) Home-school language switching.
In: Understanding second language learning: Issues and
approaches. Edited by J. C. Richards. Rowley, Mass.:
Newbury House.
Swain, M. (forthcoming b) School reform through bilingual
education: Problems and some solutions in evaluating programs. In: Comparative education review. Edited by J.
Simmons and R. G. Paulston.
Swain, M. (in preparation) The political and economical
factors behind French immersion schooling.
Swain, M., and H. C. Barik. 1976. Bilingual Education
Project: Evaluation of the 1975-76 French immersion programs in grades three to five in the Ottawa Board of Education and the Carleton Board of Education. Toronto: The
Ontario Institute for Studies in Education. Mimeo.
Swain, M., and S. Lapkin. 1977. Beginning French immersion
at grade 8. Orbit 39.10-13.
Tucker, G. R. 1975. The acquisition of knowledge by children educated bilingually. In: Georgetown University Round
Table on Languages and Linguistics 1975. Edited by D. P.
Dato. Washington, D.C.: Georgetown University Press.
267-277.

BILINGUAL SCHOOLING
AND FOREIGN LANGUAGE EDUCATION:
SOME IMPLICATIONS OF CANADIAN EXPERIMENTS
IN FRENCH IMMERSION

H. H. Stern
Ontario Institute for Studies in Education

Introduction. The purpose of this paper is to consider the implications for FL education of Canadian experiments and investigations on the so-called 'French immersion programs'. As was explained in the paper by Merrill Swain, these programs provide bilingual education in French and English for anglophone children in Canada within anglophone school systems. They began in Montreal in a single school in the mid-sixties and have spread since to other school systems, first in Quebec, then in Ontario, and also to other provinces in Canada, constituting an alternative form of schooling on a large scale in Ottawa and Montreal and on a much more restricted scale elsewhere. These programs are offered in several forms, principally as 'early full immersion' in which most of the school instruction is given in French as the language of communication from kindergarten or grade 1. In subsequent years, the time allotted to French is gradually reduced and the schooling becomes bilingual. In a 'late immersion program', French immersion is offered for one or two years at a later grade, e.g. in grades 7 and 8. 'Partial immersion' refers to a program in which only part of the day, e.g. 50% of school time, is spent in French, the rest in English. The term 'extended program' has been used to refer to a program which includes, besides a conventional French language class from 20 to 40 minutes per day, one or two subjects taught in French.
  The case I propose to make is that this experiment in bilingual education has important implications for FL teaching in general. First of all, immersion and the studies on it constitute a group of projects comparable in scope and significance to

such other projects as the Pennsylvania Project, the recent Pilot Scheme on Primary French in Britain, or the IEA studies in French and English in various countries. In Section 1, I propose therefore to discuss its implications for research and development in language education. In Section 2, I consider four specific aspects of immersion in relation to FL education: (1) immersion as a form of FL education; (2) immersion and the optimal age question; (3) immersion and the time issue; (4) the formal-functional dimension in immersion teaching and its relevance for FL teaching methodology and curriculum.

1. The immersion experiment and innovation in FL teaching

1.1 The historical context. If we want to locate the immersion experiment in the history of innovation in language pedagogy, Tables 1a and 1b may be helpful. As is widely known, of course, innovation in language pedagogy has a long and rather unhappy history. Decade after decade, battles and debates on methods and other innovations have gone on without basic issues being resolved.

As Table 1 shows, there has been a certain parting of the ways from about the mid-sixties. On one side, there is a continuation of the search for decisive innovations that claim to constitute a major breakthrough in FL teaching. French immersion programs in Canada must be counted among these. In this respect, they can be grouped with other recent inventive approaches such as Individualization, Suggestopaedia, or the Silent Way. On the other side, we observe a trend of development which can be regarded as a break with the global method concept as well as a break in the search for decisive innovations. This new trend began with Mackey's Method Analysis (1965). It also expressed itself in the critical tenor of evaluative studies on the main reform efforts, the audiolingual method (Chastain and Woerdehoff 1968; Smith 1970), the language laboratory (Smith 1970), and FLES (Burstall et al. 1974). It also led to a number of critical studies (e.g. Valdman 1966) and the exploration of new concepts, which are suggested by the arrangement of Table 1 in approximate chronological order from left to right, ending with the most recent empirical studies on second language learning and teaching. This trend has developed out of a scepticism vis-à-vis radical innovation; it seeks to resolve the FL language learning problem by means of better theory and a focus on issues that have hitherto been neglected, as well as by more systematic empirical research on learning and teaching.

I do not think that virtue and vice lie in one or the other of these two directions. I hardly think we could stop attempts to solve problems of language learning by intuition and inspiration and who would want to do so? On the other hand, I can see a great advantage in recent efforts to develop a more solid research basis and better theory for language pedagogy.

Table 1a. Innovation in language teaching: 1840-1950s.

Dates	Developments
From about:	
1840	Grammar Translation method
1880	'Reform'/'Direct' method
1920-1940	'Compromise'/'Oral' method
	Reading method
1940	Linguistic Approach. American Army method: Intensive language teaching
1950s	Audiolingual (USA) and Audiovisual (France/Britain) methods. FLES. The Language Laboratory

Table 1b. Innovation in language teaching: 1964-1978.

1964	Audiolingual Habit theory v. Cognitive Code-Learning theory (Carroll 1966)				
1964-1978	Critique of innovations/ Breakdown of method concept		Recent Innovations Silent Way (Gattegno 1972) IMMERSION Individualization (Altman and Politzer 1971) Suggestopaedia (Racle 1975)		
Method analysis	Evaluations of FL innovations	Curriculum theory	Language syllabus theory	Strategy concept	Empirical language learning research
Mackey (1965) Halliday, McIntosh and Strevens (1964)	Scherer and Wertheimer (1964) Smith (1970) Burstall et al. (1974)	Valette (1971) Stern (1974) Allen (1976)	Corder (1973) van Ek (1975) Wilkins (1976)	Bosco and Di Pietro (1970) Stern (1974) Krashen and Seliger (1975)	Allwright (1975) Fanselow (1977) Chaudron (1977)

In this historical development, the immersion experiment is in many ways unique. While the initiative of most language teaching reforms came from outstanding teachers or other professionals, French immersion in Canada was the creation of a group of parents in the early sixties; and parental initiative and support have played a significant part in the spread and subsequent development of this movement throughout Canada during the past decade and a half.[1] These parents were hoping to respond constructively to the Canadian political, social, cultural, and linguistic situation. They made no claim to have worked out all the practical implications of their demand for immersion programs. What they expressed was a wish that schools should play a more decisive role in creating a new generation of anglophone Canadians who are bilingual in English and French. They were influenced by the positive view of bilingualism that resulted from Lambert's work (e.g. Peal and Lambert 1962). For the development of a practical proposal, they based themselves on existing examples of bilingual schooling such as the Toronto French School, and the various international schools that had sprung up in Western Europe after the war. They were also encouraged by Penfield's claim that the early years of life provide unique opportunities for multiple language education and they drew inspiration from experiments in language teaching for younger children (Stern 1963, 1967), reported just at the time when they were formulating their own ideas and presenting them to their school board. Moreover, the idea of an intensive approach to language learning had become familiar through the widely publicized American 'Army Method' of the war years and similar postwar programs.

1.2 **Immersion and other FL innovations.** As an innovation, immersion began, as many other language teaching innovations do, with an idea, a hunch, an enthusiasm but not too much preparation for implementing this new idea. Immersion, then, was started no more nor less propitiously than many other language teaching innovations. In certain respects, it was less propitious. Compare the British Pilot Scheme with Canadian immersion. As soon as the British Pilot Scheme was planned in 1963, it was supported by a curriculum development project, the Nuffield Foreign Language Teaching Materials Project, and by a teacher in-service training program.[2] Compared to that, the French immersion experiment was much more modest. It had less official backing; and curriculum development was at first a sketchy and improvised affair. Teacher education--at the beginning, at least--was nonexistent. Much depended on the ingenuity and initiative of the immersion teacher and the goodwill and understanding of the school principal.[3]

If immersion did not come to grief in the way many FLES programs or the language labs in many instances did, it is above all due to the robustness of the experiment itself. To a

Bilingual Schooling and Foreign Language Education /403

very considerable extent, immersion really worked. If the results of immersion had been as equivocal as were the results of the British Pilot Scheme or other FLES-type experiments, it is most doubtful whether its growth would have been as spectacular as it has been. Immersion produced a level of second language achievement that is substantially superior to conventional language learning in classroom settings. This was clearly shown in the evaluation studies and was obvious also to casual observers. It is no doubt because of this that the immersion research, although it was not universally accepted, never suffered the kind of angry controversy that surrounded, for example, the Pennsylvania Study, the Gume Project in Sweden, or the recent Primary French in the Balance in Britain.[4]

1.3 The research approach. Another noteworthy feature of the immersion experiment has been that from the outset it has been accompanied by evaluative research. One of the demands --and an important raison d'être of the two UNESCO studies on early language teaching (Stern 1963; 1969)--had been to urge experimenters in FLES-type programs to make provision for systematic evaluation. To this end, a section contributed by J. B. Carroll to the first UNESCO report had dealt with research questions, and the second report included a guide on research methodology, also prepared by J. B. Carroll at the invitation of UNESCO. In spite of this insistent international demand for research, FLES-type programs have produced very little of it. The British ten-year evaluation of the Primary French experiment is a notable exception (Burstall et al. 1974).
   One of the very fortunate features of Canadian immersion programs has been the regular and extensive evaluation that has accompanied it. Here again, the first parents' group in St. Lambert deserves credit for having approached Wallace Lambert and his colleagues, inviting him to undertake an evaluation of the St. Lambert project. From Lambert and Macnamara's first report on immersion in the Journal of Educational Psychology in 1969, the report of the second year in the Georgetown University Round Table on Languages and Linguistics (Lambert, Just, and Segalowitz 1970), down to reports at this meeting, immersion programs across Canada have been fortunate in being systematically evaluated by numerous studies.
   In effect, there are three major and a smaller number of minor groups of studies to date. First, there is the original St. Lambert research and a series of other studies carried out in the Montreal area (e.g. Lambert and Tucker 1972). Second, there is a large volume of studies which have come out of the Bilingual Education Project of the Modern Language Centre of the Ontario Institute for Studies in Education (OISE) in Toronto, mainly carried out by Swain and Barik (e.g. 1976). Third, there is a group of studies on immersion and other types of extended French programs, carried out in Ottawa in 1974 and 1975.[5] The Ottawa experiments had a threefold scrutiny, one

by three local research teams in the Ottawa region, another by
an OISE team which provided the Ontario Ministry of Education
with a kind of synthesis and 'meta-evaluation' (Stern, Swain,
and McLean 1976; Stern et al. 1976), and finally, a review of
the whole group of Ottawa project studies by three international
authorities, Drs. Burstall, Carroll, and Rivers (Harley 1976).

In addition, there are a number of studies in other parts of
Canada and some on certain special issues.[6] These various
evaluations have documented the progress of the project. They
have provided the program participants, teachers, parents, administrators, and various research groups with a constant
stream of information, evaluation, and discussion. They can
be said to have contributed to an increase in sophistication of
the quality of the program. Many innovations decline as they
lose their early impetus and novelty. Immersion has expanded,
has become more diversified, and has enormously strengthened
its curriculum base, its teacher potential, and its theoretical
foundations. The evaluative research has no doubt played an
important part in this.

Fortunately, for the programs, there has been much consensus among research findings; so much so that the funding
of the different research studies by various provincial and
federal government sources has been interpreted by a few
opponents of immersion as a means of pressing immersion upon
the school authorities with a weight of pseudoscience. This I
consider totally unjust. The Ontario Ministry of Education,
for example, with which our team at OISE has dealt most of
the time, has almost fallen over backwards to insure objectivity
of research and to take into account a wide range of opinion,
including views which run counter to the immersion project.[7]

The multiplicity of studies can, in fact, be considered a useful safeguard. Unlike some other innovations, Canadian immersion has been evaluated by several different independent teams.
In this way, the program has not been looked at from a single
perspective. It is in this respect that I feel the immersion research has an advantage over a comparable study, the British
evaluation of the Pilot Scheme. The latter was studied by one
team, that of the National Foundation for Educational Research
(NFER). In retrospect, much as one can find to admire in
this long-term and large-scale study, it might have been better
if several research teams had simultaneously investigated language teaching for younger children in Britain. When the NFER
report came out, it was criticized for not offering the construc-
tive help that was expected from it. However, the critics had
no other data base; all they could do was to reinterpret the
findings offered in the NFER report. More recently, a Nuffield
Foundation committee had a second look at the early teaching of
modern languages in Britain (Nuffield Foundation 1977); but
while this study provides a more positive perspective, a short
review and questionnaire study post hoc does not have the same
weight as a variety of different research studies investigating

the same problems and coming up with a variety of findings, even if they conflict with each other.

1.4 Negative aspects of the research. In retrospect, the Canadian research may be criticized for its too exclusive adherence to the same 'test-and-compare' approach that was initiated by Lambert's team in the St. Lambert study. The diminishing returns of this approach as the major or only research pattern were pointed out in the concluding phases of the Ottawa immersion research (Stern et al. 1976). Moreover, such instantaneous evaluation in the early stages of an innovation is risky from another point of view. It makes no clear distinction between the pilot phase of a curriculum innovation and its establishment as a regular program; in other words, between formative and summative evaluation. In the course of the research it has become increasingly clear that these distinctions should have been made more deliberately and should have been reflected in the organization of the studies (Stern et al. 1976).

1.5 A positive aspect: Research continuity. One final, and in my view important, lesson from the immersion research should be pointed out that distinguishes these studies from other recent research in FL education: that is the value of continuity in research. Although immersion can be described as a reasonably successful innovation, it has not been and is not without problems; it has given rise to a number of questions. For example, is the positive outcome of immersion only applicable as long as immersion appeals to a relatively selected and privileged elite among the population? Is the surprisingly high level of language proficiency that is achieved early maintained later? To what extent does the immersion program help in breaking down social and cultural barriers? Is an early immersion program more effective than a late immersion program? These and other questions that have arisen from immersion could not have been anticipated in the initial stages of the experiment, nor could they have been answered in a single research effort. This has some consequences for the organization of research in bilingual and foreign language education.

Those of us who have been in FL education for some time have welcomed the increase in research since the sixties. However, as I have pointed out, several research projects have given rise to acrimonious debate and they have been quite unpopular with influential sections of the language teaching profession. If we ask ourselves why this should be so, it was, of course, largely because they poured cold water on popular and what seemed promising innovations. But there is more to it than that. An important factor lies in the organization of the research. Most of the language teaching research projects are one-shot affairs, even though they may take quite a long time. They end up with a report, such as Smith (1970) or Burstall (1974). With the report, the commitment of the research team ends. Once the report has been delivered, it is up to the administrators and teachers to pick up the pieces. This is summative evaluation with a vengeance.

In the case of immersion, the two principal research teams, the Language Research Group at McGill and the Bilingual Education Project at OISE, have developed an ongoing commitment to monitor these experiments, changing the research strategy as certain questions were answered and new questions arose. For example, the McGill Group has focused its attention in recent years on the value of immersion for all children, including children with language and learning disabilities or children from minority groups. At OISE there has been a shift towards a better understanding of the classroom processes in immersion and of long-term second language development among children in these programs. A single research on language education cannot be expected to provide definitive answers to all possible questions. The organization of research must permit the to-and-fro between practical experimentation, evaluation, new issues, and research studies. This also has the advantage that an innovation is constantly reviewed in relation to research findings and modified rather than accepted or condemned in toto.[8] I believe the immersion research provides an interesting (positive and negative) object lesson on the possibilities and problems of such an ongoing and formative approach to research applied to one particular type of innovation in language education.

1.6 **Immersion and FL policy.** Finally, the French immersion experiment is interesting as an example of the interaction between a language teaching experiment and the development of language teaching policy. Here the experience of the province of Ontario is specially instructive. In 1973, the Ontario Ministry of Education set up a committee on the teaching of French in Ontario, with a view to developing a new policy for French as a second landuage. This committee, which had a strong research orientation, took into account the immersion experiments and other investigations on language teaching. The report (Ontario 1974) and recommendations of this committee could not have been written without the research evidence from the immersion studies.

The policy on French as a second language which resulted from the committee's recommendations has integrated the immersion alternative into the second language program. It is probably one of the first examples of a second language program anywhere which includes a distinct bilingual education option.

1.7 **Conclusion.** To sum up, the Canadian experiment in French immersion deserves to be considered as an interesting example of experimentation and research in language education which has moved in ten years from a small-scale pilot study in one school to an alternative form of schooling in a number of educational systems across Canada. The main lessons of this experiment for bilingual and FL education generally are fourfold. (1) The studies amply confirm the need to monitor an innovation by systematic evaluation. (2) For educational planners and administrators to have at their disposal the findings from several independent research teams rather than a single one is of great value; however, the advantages would have been greater if the teams had more deliberately adopted complementary but not necessarily identical research strategies. (3) An ongoing commitment to the research on the part of two or three research teams has been valuable because it has enabled these research teams to interact with the experimenters, to respond to the changing demands of the project, to build up expertise and continuity, and to develop coherent research strategies. (4) On the negative side, the danger of a lack of distinction between formative and summative aspects of the evaluation in some of the studies has been pointed out.

2. Implications of some characteristic features of immersion for FL education. In this section I consider the significance of some aspects of French immersion for FL education. When immersion programs were first proposed and then begun, the concept of 'immersion' was a somewhat vague but picturesque and optimistic metaphor of 'immersion into a language bath'. A number of ideas on FL education came together in this concept concerning bilingualism, age, time, and treatment. Each of these is dealt with in turn.

2.1 Bilingualism, immersion, and FL education. The immersion experiment began against a background of dissatisfaction with conventional second language teaching. The parents who proposed this experiment were in no doubt that they wanted their children to be bilingual, and they blamed language teaching in the schools for contributing so little to bilingualism. In many countries, including Canada, language teachers for their part have tended to argue that it is not possible (or even desirable) within a school context to make children 'bilingual' (in the popular sense of the term). The common saying, 'You can't really learn a language in the classroom', is an expression of resigned abdication which many language teachers themselves have accepted. As a consequence, FL education and bilingual education have been treated both theoretically and practically as entirely different and unrelated. The thesis proposed by Fishman (1966), i.e. that FL education inevitably creates bilinguals, has not in fact been widely accepted by the language teaching profession.

The immersion experiment has been a challenge to this conceptual separation of school language teaching from bilingual schooling. For it has shown that it is possible under school conditions to create artificially a high level of bilingual competence in relatively unilingual social settings. The immersion experiment is a bridge between the various forms of bilingual schooling and conventional FL education.

From this point of view, the solution that the Ontario Ministry of Education has proposed for the teaching of French is of particular interest. This proposal has quietly abandoned the old resigned attitude that it is not possible to create bilinguals through the school system; it has argued instead that a school system can and should offer the opportunity to become bilingual, but that not all students would want to or should attempt to do so. In line with this principle, the Ontario educators today propose that schools should offer three second language options of varying intensity: a basic program for a basic command, an extended program for a working knowledge, and an immersion option for the nearest to native-like proficiency. Thus, bilingual schooling and conventional language teaching are seen as a continuum rather than as totally different operations. However, the language teaching profession as a whole --I am speaking here for Canada--is only just beginning to be aware of the fact that the immersion experiment has these far-reaching implications for FL education.

2.2 **Immersion and the optimal age issue.** Immersion began at a time when the belief in early language teaching was at a peak. The St. Lambert parents consulted with Wilder Penfield and found encouragement in his writings for an early start. It was therefore natural to propose immersion in kindergarten and the primary grades.

Meanwhile, as is known, there has been much debate on the optimal starting age for foreign language teaching in a conventional teaching setting. The evidence from research on classroom language learning has not supported the expectation of a substantial gain merely on the strength of an early start. If we accept the views of Carroll (1975) or Burstall (1974), it is total length of learning time rather than an early age which accounts for average proficiency levels reached. What does the immersion experiment contribute to this discussion? If early and late immersion are compared, is one more effective than the other? Such comparisons are notoriously difficult to make, especially as children in early and late immersion are at different levels of cognitive maturity and of social and language development. But if children in early and late immersion programs are compared with native speakers of the same age, as Swain has pointed out, the early start seems to have the edge over the later immersion. In short, while for conventionally taught children Burstall and Carroll were led to the conclusion that prima facie later rather than earlier learning has an advantage, under conditions of immersion it may well be the other way round. If this interpretation is correct, we are led to the hypothesis advanced by Tucker (1976) that the type of treatment that immersion provides may be more effective for younger than older learners.[9] This is, however, and must remain, an interesting speculation until attempts are made to study systematically age or maturity differences in second language learning under different conditions of schooling.

2.3 The time factor. On the time factor the immersion experiment is less controversial. It provides excellent support for Carroll's thesis that the time spent on language learning is the most important ingredient because it provides the opportunity for practice of and contact with the second language. The Ottawa immersion experiments are particularly instructive in that they have tried a whole range of time provisions from small daily amounts, and larger daily amounts of 40, 60, and 90 minutes to half-day, and a full school day of 300 minutes of French immersion. The studies have shown (e.g. Stern et al. 1976) that the measured proficiency of groups of learners under these different conditions increases as the time increases.

The net effect of this experimentation with time variations has been to create an awareness among Canadian language educators of the need to make realistic assessments of total time allowances if certain levels of language proficiency are to be guaranteed within the school systems. The importance of time for language learning has been recognized for some time by linguists elsewhere. For example, in 1960 a table was published in an American book in which time estimates were made for learning different languages to three different levels of proficiency in intensive daily instruction and allowing for differences of learners of lower and higher aptitude. However, these estimates were intended for adult learners taking intensive courses in the U.S. Foreign Service.[10] In Ontario, the Ministry of Education, on the basis of immersion and other experimentation and a thorough review by the ministerial Committee on French, referred to earlier, has made time allowances the key factor in the development of its French programs in schools.[11] I mentioned earlier that three levels of French proficiency are envisaged. For the Basic Level, a minimum of 1,200 hours of 'core program' French of 20 to 40 minutes a day during a student's school career is proposed; for the Middle Level, at least 2,100 hours involving an extended program; and for the Top Level, an immersion program of at least 5,000 hours.

The main implication for FL education of this entire group of studies on various forms of bilingual schooling is that they corroborate other findings in FL education on the importance of sufficient time allowances.[12] The fact that FL education often produces inadequate proficiency levels can be largely accounted for by unrealistically low amounts of time set aside for second language learning.

It is obviously not time alone, but what happens during the time, that matters. Time just provides an opportunity for language learning to occur. The difficulty under school conditions, of course, is that the timetable does not permit foreign language learning to gobble up large portions of curriculum time. It is here that the treatment factor proposed in the immersion program offers an interesting solution.

2.4 The treatment aspect. I now turn to the third and, in my view, most characteristic feature of the immersion program, i.e. the language as a medium of instruction and communication rather than as a subject, or, in other words, the application of a 'functional' rather than a 'formal' strategy of teaching. Teaching the school curriculum fully or partially through the medium of the second language, as the pioneers of immersion proposed, had three advantages: (1) it simulated to a certain extent the experience of a bilingual home or life in the L2 community; (2) it was a way of providing an adequate amount of contact time with the second language; but (3) by teaching other subject matter in the L2, the second language learning process did not take too much time away from the rest of the school curriculum.

What began in the sixties as a useful expedient has in the seventies turned out to be a theoretically highly interesting aspect of the immersion program; and it is in this respect that it has perhaps the most far-reaching implications for the methodology of FL education and the FL curriculum. This can best be explained if we adopt the point of view that the language teacher has a limited number of pairs of strategies at his disposal. These pairs of strategies can be visualized as continua (Table 2). One of these is the formal-functional dimension (Table 3).

In the formal or linguistic strategy, the focus is on code or language. In the functional or communicative strategy, the focus is away from code or language; it is on communication, activity, and content. Most language teaching is formal in this sense. It is openly concerned with features of the language which are studied or practiced through texts, drills, or other exercises. For the purpose of this discussion it does not matter whether the formal strategy can be described as 'cognitive', 'audiolingual', or anything else. Most language teachers who rely on a formal strategy are aware of the problem that there is often too little transfer from formal training to functional use of the language and that opportunities must be created to provide for communicative experiences. The questions have always been: at what point in the learning process is it advantageous to introduce these? What kind can best be arranged, and which are most effective?

Many language teaching theorists in recent years have dealt with the formal-functional distinction in language teaching and learning, among them, Newmark and Reibel (1968), Savignon (1972), Jakobovits and Gordon (1974), Krashen (1976), and others. Some theorists have gone so far as to question the

Table 2. Principal teaching/learning strategies.

crosslingual	intralingual
←――――――――――――→	
crosscultural	intracultural
formal	functional
←――――――――――――→	
(linguistic)	(communicative)
explicit	implicit
←――――――――――――→	
(analytical/rational)	(intuitive)

	productive	receptive
audiolingual	speaking	listening
graphic	writing	reading

timing: concentrated   distributed
←――――――――――――→
(massed)

groupings: individualized   whole class
←――――――――――――→
(small group)   (large group)

---

theoretical validity of any formal language training. A challenging article by Macnamara (1973) illustrates this position: conventional classroom learning is unsuccessful, he argues, because it undertakes the hopeless task of teaching a language by irrelevant analytical methods. They fail because they do not engage the learner's faculté de langage. The faculty becomes active only in real-life situations of language use which, in the early years, typically occur in the nursery or street. In the language class the teacher must therefore create lifelike situations. Macnamara would thus dispense almost entirely with the apparatus of formal language instruction. Other theorists who have also recognized this problem have not taken up such an extreme position of rejection of all formal step-by-step classroom learning. They have argued that a language learned in a formal language lesson does not regularly lead to effective language use; therefore, special steps must be taken to create a transition from the classroom setting to real-life communication. This was, for example, Rivers' plea when she contrasted skill-getting and skill-using techniques (Rivers 1972). With the same issue in mind, language teachers have for many years arranged programs involving the learner in authentic language use through pen-friendships, visits, contact with native speakers of the target language, through

Table 3. Some features of the 'formal-functional' dimension.

Formal (linguistic)	Functional (communicative/experiential)
Code	Communication
Controlled language input arranged in a pedagogical sequence.	Uncontrolled exposure to the language in use as dictated by communicative needs.
Study and practice. Language class.	Language in the field.
Language as a system. Control of language through selection, gradation, presentation and repetition. Classroom techniques. Emphasis on linguistic processes: study and practice of formal properties of sounds, grammar, lexis, discourse, semantic features or sociolinguistic characteristics.	Language in use in its own habitat. Experience approach. L2 as medium of instruction. Residence abroad. 'Immersion'.

radio, television, and film programs, through exchange schemes, residence and study abroad, and so on.
On this continuum, immersion implies a mainly functional strategy. Of course, the immersion teacher may also choose to teach the language by formal techniques. He may, for example, focus on language features, practice, and correct pronunciation or grammar. There is no strict dichotomy between formal and functional procedures. But if a teacher has the responsibility to teach other subject matter through the medium of the second language, then the language in the classroom must--for some, and probably most of the time--be used with focus on content and communication and not on code. The immersion experience has brought functional language use into the language classroom at a very early stage of language learning, and maintains it as such consistently as an indirect means of language learning. The learner in the immersion class is therefore put into a position which has much in common with first-language acquisition and with learning a second language in a natural environment. It is not so much linguistically ordered, but ordered in terms of classroom activities, the content of teaching, and regular communicative events. The learner has to sort out language in relation to persons and events rather than for its formal properties. Language is directly experienced rather than rehearsed for later use. The language learner is not a spectator or onlooker of a language used by other people, e.g. the characters in an audiovisual program. He himself becomes involved in language use through the learning activities of the school.

What, then, are the implications for general foreign language pedagogy of this experiment in mainly functional language teaching? I believe they are considerable. Let me say straightaway that I do not follow those theorists who completely brush aside any formal strategy as theoretically unjustified and practically useless. On the contrary, I align myself with the kind of position that I see Valdman take on this issue: a linguistic selection and gradation is possible and necessary; it can be made in such a way that it is linguistically sophisticated and also accords with the learner's natural progression (Valdman 1977-78). All language teaching, I contend, can offer a mixture of formal and functional procedures. Programs or stages of language instruction may differ in the amount to which they rely on either formal or functional activities. But having said this, I believe that the lesson we can draw from the immersion experiment for regular FL teaching is that the functional component in language pedagogy could be enormously strengthened.

What does this involve? It means that an FL curriculum should be devised so as to include, besides a linguistic syllabus, content of real substance, authentic communicative activities, and specific language-related experiences. The substance of language programs is often so trivial because the focus is on code and not on content. Macnamara is, of course, right: the

teacher and student in the language class have nothing to say
to each other and, therefore, language use is not learned. In
immersion classes, on the other hand, they do have something
to say to each other; the teacher has a content syllabus to convey which the student has to learn, and the language is
acquired through use. If this has a general lesson, the topics
or substance or activities associated with a language class do
not become the more or less pleasant vehicle of language teaching; they assume importance equivalent to the linguistic subject matter. Consequently, language-related activities, residence abroad, exchange schemes, literature, cultural content,
specialist subjects, acquire much greater significance in the
planning of a second language curriculum.

The immersion experience suggests that a language curriculum
should contain a substantive and experiential syllabus which is
not offered as an occasional reward to the language learner but
forms an integral part of the curriculum. Through it a language
learner is given the opportunity to learn to cope with the language in use which a formal syllabus alone can never provide.

It follows from what has been said about the FL curriculum
that the immersion experience has implications also for the development of curriculum materials. At first, the immersion program often simply adopted curriculum materials prepared for
native speakers. However, in the course of time it became evident that students who learn a subject through the medium of
an L2 cannot always use the same curriculum materials as native
speakers do, and new materials for immersion students have begun to be prepared.[13] There is a certain affinity between these
and curriculum materials for language programs for special purposes. The former, however, are more subject-oriented, the
latter more language-oriented. But both types of materials
would be relevant to a new FL curriculum which is designed to
have more substantive content than FL curricula have had up
until now.[14]

The language teacher's task also receives a new direction.
Since the audiolingual revolution, language teachers have become
very much drill masters who occasionally make brief excursions
into culture and civilization. The new language teacher might
well be of a different kind. Thanks to the immersion experience,
there is in Canada already a new type of language teacher emerging who is a language teacher as well as a kindergarten, primary
grade, or subject specialist able to teach kindergarten, primary
grades, mathematics, social studies, and other subjects to anglophone students through the medium of French.[15] Foreign language teachers have, of course, conventionally had one such
substantive area--namely, literature--but I think a greater diversity of fields and activities needs to be associated with language, including sports, outdoor activities, art and music, if
the functional component of language programs is to be developed.

Another consequence of this emphasis would be that the education of language teachers may have to reflect this association of substantive areas with the language. FL teachers in schools, in any case, often have a second field of specialization; it is therefore a relatively small step for teacher training to make it possible for a future teacher to offer this second area or interest to be available in the FL.

The immersion experience has further implications for languages in universities. Traditionally, university language courses are offered outside substantive areas, or are confined to literature. But a few newer university courses, particularly in Britain, are associated with sociology, government, commerce, or technology. In one Canadian university, the ESL program shadows groups of different disciplines; it has therefore become closely associated with the teaching of content in substantive areas. Some recent experiments in languages for special purposes, which have mainly emanated from Britain (Strevens 1977), and career-oriented courses in the United States have an affinity with the immersion experience in that they relate language learning to subject areas of concern to the group of learners. The Middlebury summer language school has offered for many years a combination of formal language instruction with living in the FL environment in which the language comes into functional use.[16] In British university language programs exchanges or prescribed periods of residence abroad are often a necessary part of the degree course. In the United States, extensive study abroad schemes have been in operation since the fifties. In short, the principle of functional activities has been recognized in FL education for a long time. What immersion has done is (a) to bring the functional component into the language program much earlier, in most instances right from the start, (b) to bring it directly into the school setting, (c) to make it thereby accessible to a large and potentially unselected school population (not merely to selected adult students in university programs), and (d) to make it an integral and central part of the curriculum (not an occasional reward rather late in the program).

Last, the functional approach of an immersion program has some interesting implications for the learner. It requires the training of the student in learning techniques which are somewhat different from the step-by-step learning of formal study and practice. They might be described as field techniques. On the receptive side, the learner has to guess and infer more from the situation and context, and on the productive side, he must be prepared to improvise, to circumlocute, and to take risks with the language. These are qualities that the formal strategy generally does not cultivate, but which in an immersion setting, as much as in real-life situations, are constantly needed. To learn such coping techniques seems to me an essential of all effective language learning. Immersion programs offer at least an opportunity for students to gain

experience in these techniques. It may be one of the most
valuable contributions of a functional teaching strategy.[17]

2.5 Conclusion. To sum up, I have examined four implications of the immersion experiment for general FL education. (1) Unlike the majority of American experiences in bilingual education which attempt to provide education for children in a bilingual situation, the Canadian bilingual education through immersion is an attempt to create through bilingual schooling advanced levels of bilingualism in children from unilingual backgrounds. Immersion which has achieved a measure of success in this respect has the potential to close the gap between bilingual schooling and FL education. (2) Immersion has done little to solve the optimal age question. On the contrary, its findings run counter to some conclusions of FL education studies. These contradictions make it appear all the more imperative to study differences in language learning at different maturity levels and in different settings. (3) The immersion experience amply confirms the dominant current view on the relationship between proficiency in a second language and the amount of total time given to language learning. (4) The immersion experiment suggests that the functional or communicative component, i.e. the use of the language for a real purpose, has to be strengthened in FL teaching. Such a new emphasis would have implications for curriculum, materials, the teacher's role, and ultimately, teacher education and university language courses.

3. Final comment. To sum up, it is clear from the foregoing that it would be a mistake to look upon French immersion in Canada as a purely Canadian response to a specifically Canadian language situation. Admittedly, it has unique features. But the principles and experience involved in research and development and certain characteristic features of the program have application to FL education generally. For these reasons I believe the immersion approach deserves the attention of all language educators, particularly those who seek continuity between bilingual schooling and FL education.

NOTES

1. A national association, Canadian Parents for French, was founded in March, 1977.
2. On this point, see the accounts presented at the UNESCO meeting in Hamburg in 1966 (Stern 1969).
3. For the early development of immersion, see Appendix A in Lambert and Tucker (1972): 'Parents as change agents in education', by O. Melikoff. See also Stern (1977).
4. For a brief summary of references to the debate on the British study, see Stern and Weinrib (1977) and Nuffield Foundation (1977).

5. For a brief bibliographical summary on Canadian developments in the context of language education for younger children, see Stern and Weinrib (1977).
6. For examples, see Mollica (1974), particularly Swain (1974), and Swain and Bruck (1976).
7. For example, in 1974 Ministry officials prepared a list of 44 questions which expressed their concerns and misgivings about immersion, and on which they wished to have answers from researchers (see a discussion of these questions in Stern, Swain, and McLean 1976). Another illustration of the attempt to study the question in all its complexity is that, as soon as the British report by Burstall et al. appeared, the Ministry initiated a week-long discussion with Dr. Burstall in Toronto (see on this Stern, Burstall, and Harley 1975).
8. The recent report on the early teaching of modern languages by the Nuffield Foundation in Britain (1977:25) was advocating this kind of formative approach to research when it made the following comment on the NFER report Primary French in the Balance: '... some regrets may be felt that the researchers confined their conclusions to a "profit and loss" account of the experimental work without producing a specific answer to the School's Council's "chief question" ... which could be rephrased, "What are the conditions of success for primary French?" To have done so would have switched the conclusion from the retrospective to the forward-looking, from the depressing factual statement that certain conditions of success had not been fulfilled, to the more inspiriting statement that future success was likely to result from the establishment of identifiable conditions'.
9. Tucker (1976) writes with reference to younger learners: 'A student can more effectively acquire a language when its learning becomes incidental to the task of communicating with someone about an inherently interesting topic'.
10. See Cleveland et al. (1960). The table from this book has been reproduced in an adapted form in Jakobovits (1970) and Ingram (1975), and discussed in some detail by both authors.
11. On this point, see a fascinating short booklet produced by the Ontario Ministry of Education, entitled Teaching and Learning French as a Second Language: A New Program for Ontario Students (1977). This booklet explains the system, illustrates time allowances, and describes a new funding formula which rewards increased time allocations.
12. Particularly the IEA French study, The Teaching of French as a Foreign Language in Eight Countries (Carroll 1975).
13. For a list of materials especially designed for immersion or found useful in immersion programs, see Lapkin and Kamin (1977).
14. See, for example, the Focus Series, published by Oxford University Press, which has such titles as English in

Agriculture, English in Physical Science, English in Social
Studies. See also Strevens (1977).
15. This was clearly revealed at the founding meeting of a
new association of immersion teachers, the Canadian Association
of Immersion Teachers, held in Ottawa in October, 1977, which
attracted some 700 participants.
16. For an account on the Middlebury summer language program and other illustrations of functional strategies in American university language teaching, see 'Report on Teaching' in
Change: The Magazine of Learning, no. 5, 1977.
17. The lack of training in this respect in conventional
language teaching has been pointed out by Naiman et al.
(1978) in a recent study on good language learners.

REFERENCES

Allen, J. P. B. 1976. The applied linguistics interface and
 'EST'. Curriculum Theory Network 5.291-304.
Allwright, R. L. 1975. Problems in the study of the language
 teacher's treatment of learner error. In: New directions in
 second language learning, teaching, and bilingual education.
 Edited by M. K. Burt and H. C. Dulay. Washington, D.C.:
 TESOL.
Altman, H. B., and R. L. Politzer. 1971. Individualizing
 foreign language instruction. Proceedings of the Stanford
 Conference, May 6-8. Rowley, Mass.: Newbury House.
Bosco, F., and R. Di Pietro. 1970. Instructional strategies:
 Their psychological and linguistic bases. IRAL 8.1-19.
Burstall, C., et al. 1974. Primary French in the balance.
 Windsor, England: NFER Publishing Company.
Carroll, J. B. 1966. The contributions of psychological
 theory and educational research to the teaching of foreign
 languages. In: Trends in language teaching. Edited by
 A. Valdman. New York: McGraw Hill. 93-106.
Carroll, J. B. 1975. The teaching of French as a foreign
 language in eight countries. New York: John Wiley.
Chastain, K. D., and F. J. Woerdehoff. 1968. A methodological study comparing the audio-lingual habit theory and the
 cognitive code-learning theory. Modern Language Journal
 52.268-279.
Chaudron, C. 1977. A descriptive model of discourse in the
 corrective treatment of learner's errors. Language Learning
 27.29-46.
Cleveland, H., and G. J. Mangone. 1960. The overseas
 Americans: A report on Americans abroad. New York:
 McGraw Hill.
Corder, S. P. 1973. Introducing applied linguistics.
 Harmondsworth, England: Penquin Books.
Fanselow, J. 1975. Beyond Rashomon. TESOL Quarterly
 11.17-39.

Fishman, J. A. 1966. The implications of bilingualism for language teaching and language learning. In: Trends in language teaching. Edited by A. Valdman. New York: McGraw-Hill. 121-132.
Gattegno, C. 1972. Teaching foreign languages in schools: The silent way. New York: Educational Solutions, Inc.
Halliday, M. A. K., A. McIntosh, and P. Strevens. 1964. The linguistic sciences and language teaching. London: Longmans.
Harley, B., ed. 1976. Alternative programs for teaching French as a second language in the schools of the Carleton and Ottawa School Boards. The Canadian Modern Language Review 33, entire No. 2.
Ingram, E. 1975. Psychology and language learning. In: Papers in applied linguistics (the Edinburgh Course in Applied Linguistics, Vol. 2). Edited by J. P. B. Allen and S. P. Corder. London: Oxford University Press. 218-290.
Jakobovits, L. A. 1970. Foreign language learning: A psycholinguistic analysis of the issues. Rowley, Mass.: Newbury House.
Jakobovits, L. A., and B. Gordon. 1974. The context of foreign language teaching. Rowley, Mass.: Newbury House.
Krashen, S. D. 1976. Formal and informal linguistic environments in language acquisition and language learning. TESOL Quarterly 10.157-168.
Krashen, S. D., and H. W. Seliger. 1975. The essential contributions of formal instruction in adult second language learning. TESOL Quarterly 9.173-183.
Lambert, W. E., and J. Macnamara. 1969. Some cognitive consequences of following a first-grade curriculum in a second language. Journal of Educational Psychology 60.86-96.
Lambert, W. E., M. Just, and N. Segalowitz. 1970. Some cognitive consequences of following the curricula of the early school grades in a foreign language. In: Georgetown University Round Table on Languages and Linguistics 1970. Edited by J. Alatis. Washington, D.C.: Georgetown University Press. 229-262.
Lambert, W. E., and G. R. Tucker. 1972. Bilingual education of children: The St. Lambert experiment. Rowley, Mass.: Newbury House.
Lapkin, S., and J. Kamin, eds. 1977. A survey of French immersion materials (K-6). Informal Series, 2. Toronto: The Ontario Institute for Studies in Education.
Levin, Nennart. 1972. Comparative studies in foreign language teaching: The GUME project. Stockholm: Almquist and Wiksell.
Lewis, E. G., and C. E. Massad. 1975. The teaching of English as a foreign language in ten countries. New York: John Wiley.
Mackey, W. F. 1965. Language teaching analysis. London: Longman.

Macnamara, J. 1973. Nurseries, streets, and classrooms: Some comparisons and deductions. Modern Language Journal 57.5-6, 250-254.
Mollica, A., ed. 1974. Bilingualism in education. Special number of the Canadian Modern Language Review 31.2.
Naiman, N., M. Frohlich, H. H. Stern, and A. Todesco. 1978. The good language learner. Toronto: The Ontario Institute for Studies in Education.
Newmark, L., and D. Reibel. 1968. Necessity and sufficiency in language learning. IRAL 6.145-161.
Nuffield Foundation Committee. 1977. The early teaching of modern languages: A report on the place of language teaching in primary schools. London: The Nuffield Foundation.
Ontario Ministry of Education. 1974. Report of the Ministerial Committee on the teaching of French (Gillin Report). Toronto: The Ontario Ministry of Education.
Ontario Ministry of Education. 1977. Teaching and learning French as a second language: A new program for Ontario students. Toronto: The Ontario Ministry of Education.
Peal, E., and W. E. Lambert. 1962. The relation of bilingualism to intelligence. Psychological Monographs 76, entire no. 546.
Racle, G., ed. 1975. A teaching experience with the suggestopaedic method: Reports, studies, conferences, round table with Dr. Lozanov. Ottawa: Public Service Commission.
Rivers, W. M. 1972. Talking off the tops of their heads. In: Speaking in many tongues. Edited by W. M. Rivers. Rowley, Mass.: Newbury House. 20-35.
Savignon, S. J. 1972. Communicative competence: An experiment in foreign language teaching. Philadelphia: Center for Curriculum Development.
Scherer, G. A. C., and M. A. Wertheimer. 1964. A psycholinguistic experiment in foreign language teaching. New York: McGraw Hill.
Schumann, J. H. 1976. Second language acquisition research: Getting a more global look at the learner. In: Papers in second language acquisition, special issue No. 4 of Language Learning. 15-28.
Smith, P. D., Jr. 1970. A comparison of the cognitive and audiolingual approaches to foreign language instruction. Philadelphia: The Center for Curriculum Development.
Stern, H. H. 1963. Foreign languages in primary education: The teaching of foreign or second languages to younger children. Hamburg: The International Studies in Education of the UNESCO Institute. London: Oxford University Press, 1967.
Stern, H. H., ed. 1969. Languages and the young school child: An international collection of studies. London: Oxford University Press.

Stern, H. H. 1972. Directions in language teaching theory and research. In: Applied linguistics: Problems and solutions, AILA Proceedings. Heidelberg: Julius Groos Verlag, 1974.
Stern, H. H. 1977. French immersion in Canada: Achievements and directions. Keynote address, Canadian Association of Immersion Teachers, Ottawa, October 13-15. To be published in The Canadian Modern Language Review.
Stern, H. H., C. Burstall, and B. Harley. 1975. French from age eight, or eleven? Toronto: The Ontario Ministry of Education.
Stern, H. H., M. Swain, and L. D. McLean. 1976. French programs--some major issues: Evaluation and synthesis of studies related to the experimental programs for the teaching of French as a second language in the Carleton-Ottawa School Boards. Toronto: The Ontario Ministry of Education.
Stern, H. H., et al. 1976. Three approaches to teaching French: Evaluation and overview of studies related to the federally funded extensions of the second language learning (French) programs in the Carleton and Ottawa School Boards. Toronto: The Ontario Ministry of Education.
Stern, H. H., and A. Weinrib. 1977. Foreign languages for younger children: Trends and assessment. Language Teaching and Linguistics: Abstracts 10.5-26.
Strevens, P. 1977. Special-purpose language learning: A perspective. Language Teaching and Linguistics: Abstracts 10.145-163.
Swain, M. 1974. French immersion programs across Canada. The Canadian Modern Language Review 31.117-129.
Swain, M., and H. C. Barik. 1976. Five years of primary French immersion. Toronto: The Ontario Institute for Studies in Education.
Swain, M., and M. Bruck, eds. 1976. Immersion education for the minority child. The Canadian Modern Language Review 32, entire no. 5.
Tucker, R. G. 1976. Cross-disciplinary perspectives in bilingual education: Linguistics review paper. Paper prepared in the Psychology Department of McGill University for the Center for Applied Linguistics.
Valdman, A., ed. 1966. Trends in language teaching. New York: McGraw Hill.
Valdman, A. 1977-78. Communicative competence and syllabus design. Alberta Modern Language Journal 16.2.16-30. Special issue: The language connection.
Valette, R. M. 1971. Evaluation of learning in a second language. In: Handbook on formative and summative evaluation of student learning. Edited by B. S. Bloom, J. T. Hastings, and G. F. Madans. New York: McGraw Hill.
van Ek, J. A. 1976. The threshold level for modern language learning in schools. Strasbourg: Council of Europe.

Wilkins, D. A. 1976. Notional syllabuses. London: Oxford University Press.

TOWARD BILINGUAL EDUCATION FOR PARAGUAY

Joan Rubin
California State University, Northridge

The Paraguayan Ministry of Education has recently been giving increased attention to the language problems of rural monolingual Guarani school children. As cognizance of the role of language skills as an important factor in school repetitions and drop-out grows, consideration of bilingual education as a solution has increased. This paper discusses some of the major issues considered and implicit in implementing such a program. The issues to be discussed include technical, social, and philosophical ones. The relevance of these issues for other multilingual countries, especially in Latin America, is mentioned.

1. Background. In a 1967 paper entitled 'Language and Education in Paraguay', I identified some of the educational problems that seem to arise from the language situation in Paraguay. In contrast to the widely held view there that it is a bilingual country, I noted that it is 'basically a Guarani-speaking nation with a heavy incidence of Spanish-Guarani bilingualism in which each language tends to fulfill distinct functions' (1968a:485-486). This picture is substantiated by the census figures. In 1950, some 95% of the population (three years and older) was reported to know Guarani. Some 52% of the population (three years and older) claimed to be bilingual in Spanish and Guarani. What is noteworthy is that the highest percentage of bilingualism is to be found in the capital, Asuncion, where some 76% claimed to be bilingual.[1] On the other hand, the rural area of Paraguay is largely Guarani-speaking and getting more so. In 1950, 45.7% of the rural area knew only Guarani while according to the 1962 census, some 52.3% knew only Guarani. Despite the high incidence of bilingualism nationally, for most people, Spanish is learned in schools or during employment. It has been estimated that 90%

of rural children begin schools speaking only Guarani. Since for many rural persons their only exposure to Spanish is in the schools, there is a high correspondence between years of school and language ability (Rubin 1968a:483).

Until recently, the Ministry of Education has not really attended to the problem which the language ability of rural school children might present. Until 1973, the policy of the Ministry of Education had been to enforce a rule of Spanish only as the language of the classroom and recreation period. Teachers were given no instruction in how to cope with the problem; indeed, they did not perceive it as one. Even with the inauguration of a new school curriculum in 1973, no differentiation was made in the program for rural children. It is no surprise then that a high correlation between the degree of ruralness and the repetition rate can be observed (Rubin 1968a:485). Since monolingual rural school children have little opportunity or necessity to use Spanish and since the language of schools has been only Spanish, the school repetition rate seems to reflect, at least in part, student frustration and inability to perform in this second (almost foreign) language. Probably also indicative of the language problem is the fact that it takes 7.3 years to produce a fourth grade finisher. A further problem which prevents school success is that most children do not stay in school very long. The average time a rural student remains in school is 3.2 years, hardly enough to acquire a language which is only used in the school setting in the rural areas.

2. **Educational language policy.** When I observed in 1960 that language might constitute a problem for rural children, most Paraguayan educators did not seem to see the problem in that way. The teachers I interviewed said that the problem was that the children simply did not want to learn. An outstanding exception in those days was the late Professor Decoud Larrosa, occupant of the chair of Guarani at the University, who frequently lectured to teachers' colleges about the problem of monolingual school children. I understand he had been doing so for many years.

The policy of the Ministry of Education of insisting that Spanish be used as the only language in schools and on the playground was often strictly enforced throughout Paraguayan history[2] and has changed only recently. In 1812, the governmental junta advised schoolteachers to make sure that Spanish was the language of the classroom and to banish Guarani from school usage (Instrucciones ... 1812). Despite governmental regulations, this turned out to be difficult to implement. Thus arose the now famous use of 'rings' to remind students of the need to use Spanish. A description of this bizarre tactic is given in the memoirs of Juan Crisóstomo Centurión:

In school the use of Guarani in class hours was prohibited. To enforce this rule, teachers distributed to monitors bronze rings which were given to anyone found conversing in Guarani ... on Saturday, return of the rings was requested and each one caught with a ring was punished with four or five lashes (translated from Centurión 1894:62).

The period after the Triple Alliance War, from 1870-1932, was one in which Spanish was especially emphasized. This was due in part to the heavy Argentine influence in the country, the Paraguayan loss of the Triple Alliance War and the subsequent occupation, and to a feeling that whatever came from outside was better than anything that was Paraguayan. In the case of education, this meant a heavier emphasis on Spanish and a greater negation of Guarani. Thus in 1894, the head of the Ministry of Education, Manuel Dominguez, referred to Guarani 'as a great enemy of the cultural progress of Paraguay' (Cardozo 1959:81). Whereas Dominguez clearly recognized the problem posed by the monolingual Guarani speakers, he did not recognize the problem caused to monolingual Guarani speakers by the requirement of Spanish-only instruction.

When the incumbent Colorado party came into power in 1948, some basic change in attitudes toward language began to appear. This change may be due to the basic philosophy of the party, which places emphasis on self-reliance, self-sufficiency, and pride in things Paraguayan. Given this philosophy, Guarani began to be given more acceptance in many spheres including, eventually, education. In 1950, a chair of Guarani was created at the university. Further, starting in 1955, classes in Guarani began to be taught at the high school level. In 1967, a new constitution was approved, naming Guarani and Spanish the 'national languages' of Paraguay, with Spanish as the 'official language'. However, there was no immediate change of policy within the Ministry of Education and the 'Spanish only' rule was reiterated until 1973 when, with the inauguration of the New Curriculum (Curriculum Renovado) in the primary schools, the Ministry of Education, for the first time in its history, authorized the use of Guarani in the classroom to facilitate the transition to Spanish.

3. **Growth of awareness of the language problem in education.** Despite official governmental lack of attention to the language problem until recently, unofficial attempts at resolving it have been made for many years. Teachers, in an effort to help students through the course of studies in Spanish, had recourse to a number of techniques, none of which was too successful. As I indicated in an earlier paper (Rubin 1968a):

In the first few grades, many teachers begin by using a limited amount of Spanish, which is gradually increased as the years progress. Translation into Guarani is the most

frequent technique used to convey the meaning of Spanish.
The teacher says the sentence in Spanish, translates it
into Guarani, and then asks the student to repeat it into
Spanish.

Another technique is the memorization of poems and stories in
Spanish. Unfortunately, for many children these exercises
remain completely rote during the first months or years of
their education.

Another common approach to student language learning was
to try to require the rural parents to speak only Spanish to
their children, a not too successful technique, given it required a change in rural language usage patterns. More recently, the Ministry of Education has begun to recognize the
need to do something about the language problem. In 1962,
with USAID funds, a book entitled Enseñanza Inicial del Español
was published. The 52-page book offers some only general
indications about how to teach language--in particular, use of
poems, games, stories, and description of pictures. Nonetheless, the book represents a significant departure from the
previous lack of attention to the problem.

In 1964, with funds from UNESCO, a Ministry of Education
experimental group worked on techniques and materials to
teach Spanish as a second language at a place called Posta
Gaona. Two products from this experiment were incorporated
into the New Curriculum of 1973: (1) a list of key vocabulary
and (2) a set of basic sentence patterns.

Unfortunately, although the New Curriculum, following the
constitutional changes of 1967, specifically encourages teachers
to use Guarani when and for as long as is deemed necessary,
it offers relatively few suggestions on second language teaching techniques. Further, it does not make a distinction between the language problems of rural and urban students.

Another indication of the growing change of attitude and
awareness of the language problem can be noted in the teacher
training colleges. The 1977 language arts curriculum of ISE,
Superior Institute of Education, introduces its students to the
bilingual nature of the country and encourages recognition of
the value of Guarani.

Most recently, in January, 1976, a new Investigative Unit of
the Ministry of Education organized a study of school achievement of first grade students. One of the principal instruments
of this research focused on language ability. Early results of
the research indicate much lower school performance and language competence in rural areas. The work of this team has
heightened the Ministry's interest in investigating the possibilities of bilingual education as a solution.

From Fall, 1976 to the present, the Investigative Unit of the
Ministry of Education has explored with USAID and several
consultants the possibility of a pilot project in bilingual education. As of this date, the project has not yet received final

approval. Nonetheless, the issues which arose in the process
of considering this project are of considerable interest to those
concerned with implementing bilingual education projects and to
those concerned with both the short- and long-range effects of
bilingual education.

4. **Issues for bilingual education.** In this section, I am going to discuss some issues which arose in the consideration of
bilingual education in technical and social terms of reference.
This separation is somewhat artificial since each hinges on the
other to some extent. Nonetheless, each issue is discussed
under the most relevant rubric. I am also going to discuss
philosophical issues; although these did not arise in the Paraguayan discussions, they seem implicit in that country as well
as in other countries which are considering or implementing bilingual education.

4.1 **Technical issues.** One of the seemingly burning issues
in Paraguay is the question of which orthography to use to
write school primers. Guarani has been a written language for
several centuries, but through the years a number of orthographies have been created. At the present time, there is a
minimum of seven alphabets for the writing of Guarani in Paraguay.[3] Each of these alphabets has its adherents and the
choice of the alphabet seems to have taken on a political tone.

Further, since Paraguay is currently thinking about transitional bilingual education, certain technical problems arise,
given that the learner will need to move from reading Guarani
to reading Spanish. Some of these difficulties were pointed
out by Stark in an unpublished paper. In some cases, Stark
notes, symbols derived from Spanish are used to represent
different sounds in Guarani. For example, in the Guarani
alphabet developed by Padre Guasch, the symbol x stands for
/š/, while in Spanish the same symbol indicates the consonant
cluster /ks/. On the other hand, the same sound in both languages has often been represented by different graphemes.
Thus, in the orthography commonly used by song writers, the
Guarani j and the Spanish y indicate the phoneme /ỹ/. The
problem is further compounded since j represents the phoneme
/x/ in Spanish.

The issue is a very emotional one, as alphabets often seem
to be, and when I suggested an alphabet that would facilitate
the transition, an adherent of one of the alphabets suggested
that I wanted to kill Guarani! At the moment, it is difficult
to assess how resistant some of the groups might be to what
seems to be the technically most appropriate solution, namely,
one suited to the transition approach, as Stark has suggested.
As always, the technical problems of orthography are complicated by attitudes and values attached to language.

The orthography issue has arisen in other parts of Latin
America. The technical problems were especially complex in

the case of Peru (cf. Parker's 1973 discussion of Quechua). Orthography issues are currently under debate in Guatemala. For some Guatemalan languages, two competing orthographies have been created, one written by the Summer Institute of Linguistics and the other by the Proyecto Francisco Marroquin.

A second issue concerns the kind of Guarani to use in school textbooks. Due to the coexistence of the two languages over some 300 years, each has exerted considerable influence on the other. In fact, no one speaks what might be called 'pure Guarani'. A cursory examination of some normal Guarani conversations showed that they could contain between 28 and 54% Spanish loan words (Rubin 1968b). In some cases, Guarani equivalents are still in use but in most, the Spanish borrowing is accepted as being part of Guarani. Some attempts have been made to 'purify' the language, the most notable being that of the late Guarani scholar, Decoud Larrosa, who translated parts of the Bible into as pure a Guarani as he could find or invent. I am told that people have difficulty reading this material. For those concerned with the promotion of Guarani, there is some fear that writing mixed Guarani will lead to a diminution in its value.

However, the issue of the maintenance and elaboration of the purer variety of the vernacular seems even stronger in other countries. A Bolivian bilingual colleague, Pedro Plaza, feels strongly that using a mixed variety of Quechua in schools will kill the language. The strength of Plaza's views reflects the nature of the competition between Spanish and Quechua in Bolivia.

A third and very important technical issue is the identification of the appropriate second language teaching methodology for countries like Paraguay. Something like the immersion method has been used for years unsuccessfully. Given the fact that in the rural area, Guarani is the only language used for communication, the rural student has little or no opportunity to use Spanish outside the classroom. The student rarely observes his/her own parents using the language. Within the classroom, the student never needs to use Spanish to fellow classmates and uses Spanish only to respond to or interpret the teacher's questions or instructions. Thus, despite parental aspirations that children acquire the ability to speak Spanish and the Ministry of Education requirement that the children do so, it would appear that the language has little value for the child. Further complicating the learning problem is the number of years during which the student remains in school, an average of 3.2 years. This figure might be improved if school success were enhanced through bilingual education techniques. But the need to identify adequate methods to improve Spanish language acquisition remains a challenging one, given the limitations of the sociolinguistic setting.

This problem is a common one for many Latin American countries contemplating bilingual education. The more isolated

Toward Bilingual Education for Paraguay /429

or rural the area, the fewer the opportunities are for use of Spanish outside the classroom and the more challenging the task is for the classroom teacher.
It is worthwhile to mention that the question of the kind of Spanish to be taught did arise in discussing the bilingual program. The question took two forms. The first was related to the problem mentioned previously, namely, given the high degree of mixture between the two languages, what kind of Spanish ought to be used in school. Most opted for some sort of 'Paraguayan Spanish', although with some reservations. The second question related to the level of Spanish to be taught Guarani-speaking children. In order to ascertain this, it was suggested that a study be made of the sorts of structures used most frequently by children in this age range whose mother tongue was Spanish. To my knowledge, there is only one study of the language development of Latin American Spanish-speaking children in the age range of 5-10 years, an unpublished one by INIDE, Ministry of Education, Peru.
One last technical question which arose was the important one of which mix of skills to teach, given the Paraguayan setting. Two approaches were considered: (1) literacy and subject matter in Guarani while teaching Spanish as a second language, followed by literacy in Spanish, or (2) subject matter in Guarani while teaching Spanish as a second language, followed by literacy in Spanish only. It was deemed desirable to try out both approaches to determine the cost-benefit of each.

4.2 Social issues. One of the more important social issues was the question of parental attitudes toward bilingual education. Given that schooling has been so exclusively associated with Spanish and that one of the major purposes of attending school was to acquire Spanish, the question arose of what parental reactions would be toward a program which used Guarani as a medium of instruction or which taught literacy in Guarani. The Investigative Unit and I did a small survey of parental attitudes toward bilingual education.[4] The study was conducted in 18 schools in the department of Paraguari and questionnaires were administered to some 193 parents whose children had attended school for at least three years. In addition to asking parents what scholastic goals they had for their children after completing three years of school (parents indicated that reading, speaking Spanish, and writing were important in that order), and what skills their children did in fact have, the questionnaire asked about parental attitudes toward bilingual education. Two differently worded questions were asked; parental agreement to bilingual education was 58% on one question and 50% on the other.[5] That is, despite the fact that learning Spanish was a major goal of these parents and despite the heavy emphasis on Spanish only in the schools, more than half the parents were willing to consider bilingual education.

In addition to asking whether the parents approved of bilingual education for their children, we also asked them to indicate their reasons for their responses. The reasons fell generally into the following categories: socioeconomic, pedagogic, identity, identification of Spanish with school, and psychological.

It is interesting to note that the most frequent reason given both for and against bilingual education was socioeconomic. Of those in favor of bilingual education, 59 said it would help socioeconomically. The reasons were expressed as follows:

'So that my child can work in both the countryside and the city'.
'Because my child will use both in daily life'.

Of those against bilingual education in some form, 77 said they felt it would impede the child's socioeconomic progress. They often responded as follows:

'In order to work anywhere in the world'.
'Because here Guarani can be used without difficulty, but in the city and in other countries one suffers a great deal'.
'In order to improve their economic situation'.
'In order to be able to send the child on errands'.

A second reason given by many parents for accepting bilingual education was identity. Only those persons who were for bilingual education gave this kind of reason. The responses indicate the strength of feelings toward Guarani prevalent in the country.

'Because we're Paraguayans'.
'In order to regain the prestige of the language'.
'Because it's ours'.
'As countryfolk'.

Naturally, this sort of reason was not used against bilingual education. However, instead, several parents did object to bilingual education for reasons which seem related to the idea that Spanish is the normal language of school. The responses took the following forms:

'Because the child needs Spanish and it is his/her opportunity to learn it'.
'They ought to begin directly in Spanish'.
'All the books are in Spanish'.

A third reason given both for and against bilingual education
can be grouped under the category of pedagogical reason. Of
those in favor of bilingual education, the reasons took the
following forms:

'Because the child will learn more'.
'Because the child can understand what is taught in school'.
'Because education is more complete'.
'So that the child can develop and understand more'.

Of those against bilingual education, the pedagogical reasons
took the following forms:

'Because it will confuse the child's learning of Spanish'.
'Because once the child gets used to using Guarani, it is
 doubtful he/she will speak Spanish'.
'Because the child won't learn one or the other'.
'Because when the child doesn't know Spanish the teacher
 has no patience with him/her'.

Only a few parents who were against bilingual education gave a
reason which could be classified as psychological. The reason
given was because the child had already suffered a great deal
with Guarani.
  In summary, we can note that the parents have some fairly
clear reasons why they think bilingual education would or would
nôt be helpful for their child. Any future project would need
to respond to these parental concerns.
  A related social issue is need for teacher's acceptance of bilingual education. Most of the rural teachers come from rural
areas, all have been educated in schools where Guarani was
prohibited (although they themselves may have heard it in the
classroom and may have used it in the classrooms themselves)
and have many of the same kinds of attitudes as the parents.
In addition, they lack training in second language acquisition
psychology and methodology. Any methodology would have to
take this into account and be well organized or the teachers
might return to old methods, given pre-established attitudes
toward the educational process. A further complicating factor
is the widespread belief that Guarani is hard to read. Given
the multiplicity of competing orthographies, most Paraguayans
think it is difficult to read Guarani even though they are
literate in Spanish. If bilingual education were to be implemented, teachers would need to understand and accept the
benefits that bilingual education might bring. They would
have to be able to apply any methods used to teach literacy
and language. Without their acceptance, the success of any
program seems doubtful.

4.3 Philosophical issues. As I have indicated, philosophical
issues did not arise in our discussions in Paraguay; however,

they seem implicit there as well as in other countries in Latin America.
One of the most important philosophical issues hinges on the technical question of the ability to find methodologies suited to the particularly difficult language-learning situation of countries like Paraguay. It is relatively easy for a child to acquire a second language, given both opportunity and the social motivation to do so (cf. Wong Fillmore 1976). However, it is an enormous challenge to do so in a classroom setting, given the size and shape of classrooms, the amount of time the children spend in school, and the lack of immediate need to use this language. I am optimistic that with the use of some newer methods, great strides can be made in improving the amount of Spanish now acquired. But I think it is important that ministries and consultants not exaggerate what can be done, before experimentation with these and other methods. Parents in Latin America are relatively philosophical about what they can expect from schools; nonetheless they are always hopeful. It seems important that bilingual education programs not promise too much.

Another philosophical issue which did not arise in Paraguay but which does arise from time to time in Latin America is the question of whether the bilingual program should be a transitional or a maintenance one. In Bolivia, some speakers of Quechua feel that transitional bilingualism will lead to the elimination of Quechua; that the only way to maintain Quechua is to have bilingual education all the way through high school. These fears seem to fit in with the relatively strong social hiatus existing between Quechua and Aymara speakers on the one hand, and those who use Spanish. Coupled with the fact (mentioned further on) that schooling causes rural peasants to move to the city, where Spanish is dominant in Bolivia, the fears seem well founded. This does not seem to be a problem in Paraguay at the moment, largely because of the functional distribution of the two languages and the relatively positive attitudes toward Guarani (Rubin 1968b). There does not seem to be much fear that Guarani will be lost. However, there is some possibility that if effective teaching of Spanish were implemented and if greater skills in Spanish were acquired, usage patterns might change. There is some indication that with greater knowledge of Spanish, there is a trend toward greater use of Spanish in the rural areas in previously Guarani domains (Rubin 1968c). If this trend accelerated, some pro-Guarani persons might become alarmed at the potential for language loss which bilingual education might portend.

A third more complex philosophical issue is the relationship of increased knowledge of Spanish to socioeconomic development. One of the arguments for bilingual education is that students would better acquire the skills which the schools stand for--reading, writing, arithmetic, and Spanish. The philosophical question is what the relationship of improving acquisition of these school skills is to socioeconomic development. In the case of many Latin American countries, acquisition of Spanish frequently means migration to urban areas. As one Latin American observer said recently, 'La escuela rural es urbanizante' (The rural school urbanizes). Indeed, one of the reasons why parents want their children to learn Spanish is so that they can travel to the city and abroad. On the other hand, making people literate and Spanish-speaking does not automatically enhance socioeconomic development in the rural areas unless these newly acquired skills are used to transmit information which leads to improvement of the rural economy and life style. The fact is that the solution of educational problems must be rationally related to socioeconomic planning.

5. Summary and conclusions. After many years of ignoring the language problem which monolingual Guarani rural school children face when taught through Spanish, the Ministry of Education is now looking at bilingual education as a possible solution to some of the problems which the Spanish-only approach has brought. There are a number of social and technical issues to be resolved--orthography, type of Guarani to use, kind of Spanish to teach, methods of second language teaching, type of teachers and teacher-trainers, in- and preservice training requirements, promotion of positive responses among parents and teachers, and the proper mix of program. None of these issues seems impossible to resolve--indeed, to a large extent they are relatively simple, given the fact that the language issue is not highly politicized in Paraguay. Nonetheless, if bilingual education is to be of benefit, it is essential that all of these issues be attended to in proper order or the program will not prove useful.

A comparison of the Paraguayan situation with that of other Latin American countries considering bilingual education shows many similarities--many of the same issues arise or will arise. Many of these similarities stem from the fact that use of the vernacular language is associated with rural, more isolated, poorer sectors of the society, whereas use of Spanish is associated with the more urban, less isolated sectors of the society. A major advantage which Paraguay has is that the vernacular language is also associated with and used in the urban areas. Unlike much of Latin America, Guarani does not serve to set apart a culturally unique group which is anxious or concerned about assimilating to the urban culture. Therefore, we do not anticipate much resistance to the use of Guarani as a transitional language, nor does it seem that children have as negative a self-image as some more isolated Indian groups in other Latin American countries. All of these factors make some form of bilingual education seem like the most appropriate solution to the current language problems of the rural areas.

NOTES

The most recent information on Paraguay was gathered while
I served as a consultant to a preproject planning period in
March and May-June, 1977, under contract with USAID/Paraguay.
The interpretations of this information are mine alone and do not
represent those of USAID/Paraguay nor the Paraguayan Ministry
of Education. The material herein taken from reports to USAID
is done with the express permission of USAID/Paraguay.
 1. The 1962 census showed that claims to be bilingual increased slightly to 77%.
 2. This account of educational language policy is taken from Rubin 1968, Chapter 2.
 3. Among these are two proposed by the Academia Guarani, one proposed by Padre Guasch, a 'popular' orthography used in song books, and one proposed by Decoud Larrosa.
 4. The questionnaire format and questions were prepared in collaboration with the Investigative Unit of the Paraguayan Ministry of Education. The unit collected all of the data and did all the compilations. Responsibility for the interpretation is mine alone.
 5. The reason for the difference can be explained in part by the form of the two questions. In order to be pro-bilingual education, the correct response was positive for the first question and negative for the second. Questions requiring a negative response to be in favor usually require greater comprehension of the question since the automatic reaction is to say yes. This fact makes the 50% affirmative all the stronger a response.

REFERENCES

Anuario Estadístico de la República del Paraguay 1948-53. 1955.
  Asunción: Ministerio de Hacienda, Dirección General de
  Estadística y Censos.
Cardozo, Efraím. 1959. Historiografía Paraguaya. México:
  Instituto Panamericano de Geografía e Historia--Comisión de
  Historia.
Centurión, Juan Crisóstomo. 1891. Memorias del Coronel Juan
  Crisóstomo Centurión o sea Reminiscencias históricas sobre la
  guerra del Paraguay. Buenos Aires: J. A. Berra.
Instrucciones para los maestros de escuelas por la Junta
  Superior Gubernativa. 1812. Asunción: February 15.
Parker, Gary. 1973. Notes on the linguistic situation and
  language planning in Peru. In: Language planning: Current issues and research. Edited by Joan Rubin and Roger
  W. Shuy. Washington, D.C.: Georgetown University Press.
República del Paraguay. 1962. Censo de Población y Vivienda.
  Ministerio de Hacienda. Dirección General de Estadística y
  Censos.

Rubin, Joan. 1968a. Language and education in Paraguay. In: Language problems of developing nations. Edited by Joshua A. Fishman, C. A. Ferguson, and J. Das Gupta. New York: John Wiley and Sons. 477-488.
Rubin, Joan. 1968b. National bilingualism in Paraguay. The Hague: Mouton.
Rubin, Joan. 1968c. Toward the use of formal methods in the detection of culture change. Seventh International Congress of Anthropological and Ethnological Sciences.
Wong Fillmore, Lily. 1976. The second time around: Cognitive and social strategies in second language acquisition. Unpublished doctoral dissertation. Stanford University.

LEARNING A SECOND LANGUAGE: CHINESE CHILDREN IN THE AMERICAN CLASSROOM

Lily Wong Fillmore
University of California, Berkeley

Doubts about whether existing bilingual programs permit non-English-speaking children to acquire the societal language have worried many educators and educational policy makers in this country. Such programs provide their students much more than English: they offer opportunities to acquire the subject matter and academic skills that their lack of English would prevent them from learning in classes where only English is used. But from all appearances, academic advantages unrelated to the learning of English matter little to many of these policy makers where non-English-speaking children are concerned. Bilingual programs are largely judged on whether or not they succeed in getting the children they serve to learn English. In the past several years, the official nervousness felt by decision makers over this question has been manifested in numerous attempts to curtail or eliminate bilingual education in many areas around the country. For example, there have been at least a half-dozen bills introduced in the California Legislature during this past year or so to repeal or radically change the 1976 legislation that made bilingual education mandatory wherever sufficiently large concentrations of non-English-speaking students are found.
This widespread anxiety over whether bilingual programs make it possible to learn English is puzzling; at least it does not make much sense to researchers who have been studying the language learning that takes place in those programs. One wonders how it could be regarded as a question at all by anyone who has worked with non-English-speaking students in American schools. Once they enter school, whether in a monolingual or bilingual program, children encounter the social forces that will have them learning English before long. Very few children can resist these forces and avoid the linguistic

assimilation that is an inevitable part of growing up in this society. Nevertheless, the anxiety on the part of educational policy makers is real, and therefore the question that causes it ought to be regarded as a problem worth studying. I raise the issue in this paper then: do bilingual classes provide learners with as much exposure to English and as much contact with English speakers as they need in order to learn English as a second language? A question which is fundamental to this issue is this: just how much and what kind of contact with English speakers do non-English-speaking children need in order to acquire English quickly and efficiently as a second language? The research that is being reported here is exploratory; it is work that I expect to follow up with a more formal research effort eventually. This exploratory study was done in connection with my current research on second language acquisition--a longitudinal study examining the sources of individual variation found in the learning of English as a second language by 30 Cantonese and 30 Spanish-speaking children. The study, which is in its first stages, is already showing that it is possible for children to learn English even when the conditions under which they are operating are less than ideal. Ideally, young second language-learners have ample regular contact with speakers of the new language--both age peers and adults.

Prior research indicates that adults and children provide quite different types of linguistic input for young second language learners. Peck (1978) has shown that an adult tends to stress information and meaning in discourse with a child learner, whereas a child interacting with a learner tends to concentrate on social interaction with little concern over informational content. Both kinds of interaction are obviously essential. The type of input learners derive from adults allows them to figure out how meanings and information get expressed in the new language; what they receive from age peers helps them to discover how the language is used socially. My own prior research (Fillmore 1976) indicates that second language learners and speakers of the language to be learned receive the kind of language experience needed to support a language learning effort. It is up to young learners to initiate interactions with the speakers of the language--at least where age peers are concerned--and it is also their responsibility to get these speakers to be willing to provide the kind of language that works as input.

Language that serves as input for acquisition purposes is different from ordinary language. It tends to be less complex, more repetitive and redundant (Ferguson 1977, Snow 1977). Topics tend to be limited to experiences related to the immediate speech situation, or to experiences that are shared by speaker and learner (Phillips 1970), and meanings tend to be overdetermined by a combination of verbal and nonverbal

contextual cues (Fillmore 1976). These adjustments in language
use are made by speakers in response to feedback information
provided by learners (Phillips 1970, Snow 1976, Berko-Gleason
1977). The learners indicate the modifications that are needed
through evidence of their comprehension or noncomprehension
of what has been said; the speakers adjust their speech upward
or downward in linguistic and informational complexity as learners give evidence of being capable of processing more complex
language and information (Cross 1977). The ability to provide
this kind of assistance to learners apparently comes with knowing a language, and it has been shown that even quite young
children are able to adjust their language use for the sake of
younger learners (Schatz and Gelman 1977).

Precisely how much such exposure to a language is needed
before it can be learned is not known. One sometimes finds
estimates in textbooks on language teaching that it takes X
hours of exposure for young children learning a first language,
the figure given based on the number of hours a child is normally awake up to, say, the age of five years; and Y hours
for adults, based on the number of hours adults need to spend
in intensive language programs in order to achieve a certain
level of proficiency. But such estimates are not very informa-
tive either about the amount of input learners need or about
how much they actually get. A child's waking hours are not
filled with talk; and what an adult needs in order to learn a
language through intensive study tells us little about what
child second language learners need or get through ordinary
exposure to a language which is used in school. From experience, we know that the more contact learners have with English speakers, the more English they hear and the faster they
learn it. If only language acquisition is considered, the ideal
situation for learning would be one language learner placed in
a class of perhaps 25 English speakers, with only English
used for communication purposes in the classroom. In such
cases, most children will learn English in a year, or two at
the most. However, experience has shown us that in such
situations, until their knowledge of the new language has become usable, learners frequently derive virtually no benefit
from school other than learning English. This is the best
argument for bilingual education: it permits students to learn
other things during this period.

Ideal conditions for language learning in bilingual classes can
be suggested too, of course. My candidate for a perfect situation is one in which the proportion of non-English speakers is
about equal to that of English-speaking children, where the
two languages are used in about equal parts for instructional
purposes with a clear functional separation between the two,
and where there is ample opportunity for language learners
and English-speaking classmates to work and play together.
Such a situation would insure that the learners receive adequate and varied exposure to the new language. It exists in

some programs (I am conducting research in two classrooms that are very much like that now), but not in all. In reality, circumstances do not permit anything like the ideal to exist in a great many places. In schools with high concentrations of the ethnic group served by the program, there are simply not enough resources available to support the number of bilingual classrooms that would be required in order to achieve this ideal balance between learners and English speakers.

The rule followed in many places at present is a ratio of 2 to 1, or 3 to 1 between non-English and English speakers. But in many of the schools serving non-English speakers, there are often not enough English speakers to be found to provide even that kind of lopsided balance between speakers and learners. Instead, what is quite common, particularly in schools serving Asian children because their families tend to settle in large ethnic communities in urban areas, are classes where the concentration of limited and non-English speakers is as high as 80 percent to 100 percent. In these schools, it is frequently the case that the only native or near-native speakers of English to be found are themselves members of ethnic minorities, who have their own educational problems to keep them busy. At any rate, it is difficult to recruit very many of them for, say, a Cantonese or Vietnamese bilingual program where they can provide the peer language input needed by the non-English-speaking students. And so it is not uncommon, desegregation orders notwithstanding, to find classes where the only English speaker is the teacher. Can a teacher alone provide the necessary language input to support the language learning efforts of a class of 25 to 30 students? The Canadian French immersion programs have shown us that it is possible, but this is done by the teacher using the target language exclusively for instructional and communicational purposes in the classroom, at least during the initial years of learning. However, for sociolinguistic and pedagogical reasons too complex to go into in this paper, we cannot and would not want to do that in this country.

What, then, about the amount of exposure children can get from programs in which only a part of the time is spent learning in the target language, and there are few or no peer age speakers around to provide additional language input? It would seem that even discounting individual differences among children in how much contact with the language is needed in order to learn, there is quite certainly some rock-bottom level of exposure required to sustain a language learning effort at all. Further, if one assumes the necessity of social interaction with speakers for native-like language to be learned, there is most certainly a minimum level of social contact with English speakers that is required in order to achieve this. The question raised in this paper then is whether classes, either bilingual or monolingual, with less than an ideal concentration of non-English speakers, can supply enough exposure to

English and contact with English speakers to permit the children they serve to learn English.

Methods and subjects. This exploratory study consisting of systematic observations of language use in classrooms serving high concentrations of non-English-speaking Chinese students was carried out in two classrooms in a San Francisco Bay Area school. One is a Cantonese bilingual kindergarten, and the other, an English monolingual kindergarten in the same school. The two classes share the same room, with the English one occupying it in the morning and the bilingual one in the afternoon. Both serve Asian children, but as shown in Table 1, the 26 in the bilingual class are all Chinese, while the 21 Asians in the English class consist of 16 Chinese, 4 Vietnamese, and 1 Korean.

Table 1. Students in the two classes by ethnic background and by language proficiency (at the beginning of the school year).

	Ethnicity		English only	Non-English/ Limited ES	Bilingual
Class A*	Chinese	16			
	Vietnamese	4			
	Korean	1			
	Mexican-American	1			
	Black American	1			
	Unknown	1			
	Total	24	2	19	3
Class B*	Chinese	26			
	Total	26		24	2

*Class A = English monolingual; Class B = bilingual

In addition to these Asian children in this class, there are also three non-Asians--a Mexican-American, a black American, and a child of indeterminate background who has at various times claimed to be Mexican, Portuguese, Filipino, and Chinese. Of the 26 Cantonese-speaking students in the bilingual class, all but two were clearly limited- or non-English-speaking when the school year began last September. The other two were bilingual already, and could be described as reasonably fluent in English. In the English class, all but five of the children were limited- or non-English-speaking; the five who came to school with English included the three non-Asians, the Korean child, and one of the Vietnamese. These are classes in which I am conducting the study on individual differences in second language learning, and I therefore have a large amount of data on the language learning taking place there. The classes were selected for the study because they are quite representative of the kind of

classes Chinese children find themselves in, at least in many
parts of California. The English class is taught by a Caucasian
English monolingual teacher who specializes in the teaching of
English as a second language, and teaches special 'pull-out'
ESL classes during the afternoon for upper grade children in
the school. She is referred to here as 'Miss A'. The bilingual
class is taught by a Chinese-American teacher who is fluently
bilingual in Cantonese and English. She is referred to as
'Miss B' in this paper. Miss B is assisted by a bilingual aide
from Hong Kong, while Miss A is assisted by Miss B for a part
of each morning.

The method used for observations for this pilot study was
this: one child was selected from each class for intensive observation of language learning opportunities for a full school
day. Selection was made in the following way: a child's name
was drawn randomly from among the non-English-speaking children we have been following in our longitudinal study in each
of the two classes. The child selected from the English class
was Kim-girl (to distinguish her from the various boy-Kims in
the class), a five and one-half-year-old child whose family only
recently came to the United States. The child selected from the
bilingual class was Tony, also five and one-half years old.
Observations were made in two ways: audio-recordings were
made in which a microphone was placed as close to the child
as possible in order to record as much of what that child said
and could hear said during the day, and on-the-spot observational notes were made by an observer (Fillmore), who watched
and described on an observation form as much as possible of
what was going on around the child, of his or her responses
to what was said or going on, and of the interactions that took
place between the child and his or her classmates and teachers.
Care was taken to note all of the time during which the child
was apparently paying attention, and the times when he or she
was not. Together, the notes and the transcribed audio-
recordings enabled me to reconstruct what took place during
that day, and to determine how much of what went on probably
made sense to the subject. The idea was somehow to get a measure of how much language spoken in the classroom in a given
day could be regarded as usable input for language learning
purposes so far as the child was concerned. The question of
how to distinguish language one could regard as 'usable' input
from that which is just so much background noise to the child
was handled in this way: instances of speech in the target
language to which the child gave some kind of attention, and
chiefly those to which the child made some kind of appropriate
response, whether verbal or nonverbal, were taken as potentially usable input. These recorded speech events were transcribed and the instances of speech noted in the observation
forms as having been noticed by the child were entered into
the tallies. There was a good deal more that went on around
the child that he or she took notice of, but only those that

were fairly obvious were counted. The question of whether or not what the child is getting constitutes adequate support for language learning was answered by examining the language data we have been collecting on their developing speech during the past six months in which we have been following these children.

Results and discussion. A comparison of the manner in which the two classes were organized for activities during the observation day shows that the bilingual class (here designated 'Class B') was somewhat more structured than the English one (henceforth, 'Class A'). As Table 2 shows, both teachers emphasize the development of academic skills; note that there was virtually no time spent on nonacademic activities in either class during this day. The once-a-week 'psychomotor' period for Class A happened to fall on the day of the observations, but otherwise that time, too, would have been devoted to academic work.

A major difference between the two classes is found in examining how much teacher-directed activity goes on in each. The organization shown in Table 2 is typical of the daily schedule for both classes. The psychomotor activity is the one departure from the usual routine in Class A. On other days, there is a structured math group lesson in which Miss B, the bilingual teacher, groups the children by ability level and works with each group for about 15 or 20 minutes each. Notice that in Class B, 105 minutes were spent in teacher-directed activity, compared to 55 minutes in Class A. In other words, very nearly twice as much time is spent in such activities in B as in A. The reverse is true for individual work, with 95 minutes devoted to seatwork in Class A, compared to 45 minutes in Class B. These figures reflect the two teachers' preferred educational approaches: Miss A favors an 'open class' approach, giving the children a degree of choice in how they are to pace their own work, and in how to handle a task. Miss B takes a more structured approach. She times each activity precisely, each period lasting 20 minutes. Each student is assigned to a group, and these groups are assigned activities in a rotating order.

This turns out to be crucial where language learning is concerned. Recall that all but two of the 26 children in Class B began the school year as limited or non-English speakers. By organizing as many of the activities as she has as teacher-directed lessons, Miss B has made it possible to guarantee each child a generous exposure to English. Table 3, comparing language use in the two classes, shows how important this was, given the concentration of non-English speakers in this class. Notice that during the teacher-directed activities (the whole class and group work, with the exception of the Chinese reading and writing lesson), from 77 percent to 92 percent of the teacher talk was in English. The student talk was also largely in English, with 88 percent in the ESL group lesson and

Table 2. Comparison of structure in the two classes.

	Class A (English only)	Class B (bilingual)
Whole class (Teacher directed)	20 mins. Opening (phonics, math, writing instructions) 5 mins Closing 25 mins. total	35 mins. Opening (phonics, writing instructions) 15 mins. Math instruction 15 mins. Closing 60 mins. total
Group work (Teacher or aide directed but less structured than whole class activity)	25 mins. Psychomotor (once per week in auditorium) 5 mins. Transition 30 mins. total	15 mins. ESL 15 mins. Reading readiness 15 mins. Chinese writing, reading 45 mins. total
Seatwork (Individual work at tables with classmates)	95 mins. Math, Phonics, Writing	15 mins. Phonics, Writing 15 mins. Math 15 mins. Chinese writing 45 mins. total
	Total: 150 minutes	Total: 150 minutes

Table 3. Comparison of language use in classes (attended to by subject in each).

	Class A (English only) 25 minutes total		Class B (bilingual) 60 minutes total	
Whole class (Teacher directed)	Teacher talk	100% English	Teacher talk	92% English / 8% Chinese
	Student talk	77% English / 23% Chinese	Student talk	96% English / 4% Chinese
	30 minutes total		15 minutes – ESL	
Group work (Teacher or aide directed)	Teacher/adult	100% English	Teacher talk	88% Eng/12% Chi
			Student talk	89% Eng/11% Chi
	Student talk	46% English / 54% Chinese	15 minutes – Phonics	
			Teacher talk	77% Eng/23% Chi
			Student talk	44% Eng/56% Chi
			15 minutes – Chinese writing	
			Teacher talk	0% Eng/100% Chi
			Student talk	0% Eng/100% Chi
	95 minutes total		45 minutes total	
Seatwork (Individual activities)	Teacher talk	100% English	Teacher talk	72% English / 28% Chinese
	Student talk	28% English / 72% Chinese	Student talk	21% English / 79% Chinese

96 percent in the whole class lessons. During the phonics group work, the student use of English dropped to 44 percent largely because this lesson, which was taught by the aide, was more loosely structured and therefore permitted more informal discussion among the students during the lesson; and as they customarily do, they spoke to one another in their first language, Chinese.

The proportionate use of English for instructional purposes is high, although some Chinese is used during each lesson. It was used chiefly for explaining concepts and instructions that might have been difficult for the children to comprehend, had they been given in English only. At this point of the year, however, the teacher is using Chinese less and less, except during the Chinese lesson. As the figures in Table 3 show, she is able to get by almost exclusively with English, managing somehow in the six months since the beginning of the school year to get the children to handle quite advanced work almost entirely in English. The use of English has been increased gradually since the beginning of the school year, the increase matching the children's developing ability to understand and use English. By the time these observations were made, then (March 12, 1980), the children were hearing and using a great deal of English each day. In fact, the only period in which Chinese was being used exclusively was the Chinese reading and writing lesson. Table 4 shows just how many instances of understandable English each of the two subjects apparently heard and attended to during the opening instructional periods in each class.

In both Class A and B, the teacher talk, especially that directed toward the whole class, tended to be drill-like. The language used in these group lessons can be described as ideal for language learning purposes: it is repetitive, redundant, and clear. Aside from small changes, the same set of expressions was used again and again, and the gestures and demonstrations that accompanied the talk allowed the children to figure out what was being said. In the lesson summarized in Table 4, Miss B drew pictures on the board to illustrate the points she was trying to make as she talked. This device worked in two ways: it captured the children's absolute attention and it helped them to understand what she was trying to communicate. The following excerpts from the transcripts will illustrate how Miss B's language of instruction becomes a language lesson.

Miss B

Miss B is giving the class directions on what to do with a paper on likeness and difference. There are about eight rows of pictures; the left-most one in each row is enclosed in a box. Some of the figures in each row are identical to the one in the box, others vary from it in small ways. The

Table 4. Comparison of language use in whole class opening activity.

Activity	Class A (English only) 20-Minute opening Group instruction in Phonics, Math, and Writing		Class B (bilingual) 35-Minute opening Group instruction in Phonics and Writing	
Language	English	Chinese	English	Chinese
Teacher talk				
Teacher to all	N=77		N=195	N=14
Teacher to individual	N=20		N= 80	N=10
Teacher to subject	N= 0		N= 8	
Total*	N=92	N=0	N=280	N=24
Student talk				
Student-teacher	N=18		N= 43	N= 2
Choral response	N=42		N= 87	
Student-student	N=13	N=22	N= 6	N= 4
Total*	N=73	N=22	N=136	N= 6

*Number of separate utterances in each language.

idea is to write an *S* under the ones that are identical and
a *D* for those that are different from the one in the box.
She has already exemplified the procedure by a series of
drawings she made on the board, eliciting judgments of
'same' or 'different' from the children as she drew each.
She has also explained the idea of same and different in
Chinese to insure the comprehension of these notions. She
also went over the initial sounds in the two words, thus
helping the children understand why *S* is to be used for
'same' and *D* for 'different'. Now she holds up the paper.

Miss B: OK, I'm going to do this paper first. Is this star the same or different?
Class: Same!
Miss B: What should I write?
Class: *S!*
Miss B: Why?
Class: Same!
Miss B: Yes! (She prints an *S* under the first star in the row, and then goes on to the next.)
Is this star and this star the same or different?
Class: No!
Miss B: Are they the same or different?
Class: Different!
Miss B: What should I write for d-d-different?
Class: *D!*
Miss B: (Prints a *D* under the picture and then goes to the next.)
Is this star and this star the same or different?
Class: Different!
Miss B: What should I write?
Class: *D!*
Miss B: Is this star and this star the same or different?
Class: Same!
Miss B: What should I write?
Class: *S!*
Miss B: Yes, *S* for same!

She goes through the rest of the sheet in this manner,
showing the class the procedure for comparing each item
with the one in the box on the left-hand side of the row,
and the reason for using *S* or *D* to indicate the result of
each comparison. (Opening, March 12, 1980)

An excerpt from the transcript of Miss A's opening lesson
during the day of the observations shows her use of the same
technique.

Miss A

Miss A is giving the class instructions for a sheet on which they will be working during the seat work period. She has some geometric forms on the table (orange squares, green circles, red triangles, etc.) which she has already gone over, naming each and eliciting the names and colors of the forms from the class. Now she shows them the sheet and asks them to observe and name the shapes drawn on it. Then, holding the triangle up to the sheet and placing it over a triangle drawn on it, she asks:

Miss A: What color is the triangle?
Class: Red!
Miss A: What color is the circle?
Child: Yellow, no! Green.
Class: Green.
Miss A: What color is the square?
Class: Orange.
Miss A: What color is the rectangle?
Class: Yellow!
Miss A: (Holding up the triangle and placing it on the triangle drawn on the sheet:)
What color will I color this triangle?
Class: Green! (a few scattered other colors such as:) Red! Green!
Miss A: Green! What color will I color the rectangle? (showing them the figure)
Class: Red! No! Yellow!
Miss A: What color will I color this circle?
Class: Red!
Miss A: Yes, red! (Opening, March 12, 1980)

In contrast to the teacher-directed activities where very nearly as much English is used by the bilingual teacher as by the English monolingual teacher, and where the children speak mostly in English, the seatwork activities in which the children work individually with papers and other materials are characterized by far less English in both classes. During these periods, the children work independently on their projects, chit-chatting with one another as they do. Some English is used at such times in both Class A and B, but it is proportionately a lot less than during the teacher-directed activities: 28 percent of the student talk in Class A during seatwork is carried out in English, and 21 percent in Class B, compared with figures of 77 percent in English during teacher-directed activities in A, and 96 percent in Class B. Teachers or teacher-like adults (such as the members of the resident research team) are available to assist and advise the children on their work and the children frequently call on them for help or attention.

These adults use whatever language seems most appropriate, given the child's ability, and their own ability to speak the languages spoken by the children. Hence in Class A, all of the teacher talk during the seatwork was in English, while 72 percent of the teacher talk in Class B was in English. The relatively low use of English among the students in both of these classes reflects the fact that they are, after all, still much more fluent in their first language than they are in their second. They are quite naturally inclined to use a language they can use freely in talking to one another rather than one in which their skills are still limited. In Class A, the few non-English-speaking children who are not Chinese speakers tend to use more English than they do their own language, Vietnamese. They often do use Vietnamese among themselves, but they have to use whatever English they know, if they are to communicate with the other children in the classroom. Whatever English is used by all of these language learners, no matter what their first language, tends to be what I have described as formulaic speech, sentences of the following type: 'Whaddya know!' 'I know how!' 'I'm telling on you!', and 'Take it easy!'

These are expressions that the children have learned as unanalyzed chunks in the context of social use from English-speaking peers, no doubt, and which play an important function in the acquisition process itself (Fillmore 1976). However, a difference is beginning to be apparent between the formulaic chunks being acquired and used by the children in Class B compared with those being learned and used by the children in Class A. In Class B (the bilingual class), these apparently unanalyzed forms tend to be expressions the children have acquired from their teacher in the course of instruction, both in the ESL lesson and in other lessons. These expressions tend to be formal and proper: 'May I go to the bathroom?' 'What should I write?' In fact, the children frequently play with the expressions they have learned through their formal ESL lessons. Consider, for example, this pattern recitation by the child, Tony, who was being observed for this study from Class B.

> While getting settled for the March 12, 1980 ESL lesson, Tony suddenly begins reciting to himself. He gets louder and louder as he does.
>
> What is that? That is a dok (dog)!
> What is that? That is a baseball.
> What is that? That is a telephone.
> What is that? That is a robin!
> (Etc., etc., for 33 turns, including the following:)
> What is that? That is a teenage queen!
> What is that? That is a you.
> What is that? That is a alphabet.
> What is that? That is a Eleanore. Etc., etc.
> (March 12, 1980)

He managed to run through 33 versions of this question-and-answer drill, and he might have come up with 33 more, except that Miss B located his off-switch, thereby preventing him from totally exhausting his English lexicon. The children engaged in this kind of private pattern practice apparently for the fun of it. On the day of the observations, another child recited a litany of apologies to himself as he worked on his math paper: 'I'm solly, William; I'm solly, James; I'm solly, Tony ...' The children in Class A practice in much the same manner, except that their expressions are more usually formulas they have acquired from the English speakers in the class. Consider, for example, Kim-girl's play with the expression 'gip me' (give me) in the following excerpt from the transcripts of the audio-taped observations.

Kim-girl is at the table doing seatwork. Cathy, Sin Man, Suk Wah, and Chui-Wing are at the same table; they have been arguing over the possession of a pink eraser all morning.

Cathy: Gimme 'raser! Eraser! (Takes Kim-girl's eraser.)
Kim-girl: (Looks up crankily. Turns to LWF and complains:)
Can I eraser? Se took my 'raser. Small 'raser. Se want 'raser. This Edlyn gip me.
(She then grabs the microphone which has been placed right in front of her, and says into it:)
Gip me 'raser, yah!
Gip me pencil, yah!
Gip me chopstick, no!
Gip me crayon, yah!
Can I hab color? No way!
That's all! Bye-bye!
Cathy one small $%#&-er! (March 12, 1980)

In summary, then, it appears that the children in both the English monolingual class and the bilingual class are learning English, despite the fact that there are no native speakers in one, and few in the other. Their progress with English has been impressive, but they are not home free yet. Both groups of children need to have contact with more peer age speakers than they presently do in order to acquire a native-like command of English eventually. Impressionistically, since the data are not all in yet, the children in the bilingual class have acquired somewhat more advanced skills in English than have those in the English monolingual class. This has been due largely to the formal ESL instruction the children have been receiving daily from Miss B, and to the emphasis that she has placed on language development in her other instructional activities.

The language exposure that has been available through
these teacher-directed lessons appears to have made up for
the lack of peer age speakers in the classroom. In the absence of these experiences, the children would have heard a
good deal less English, and would have used their first language much more in class during this first school year. What
English they use among themselves is still imperfect--they
have, after all, been speaking English for only six months.
If the class were less structured, the children would probably
be talking more among themselves, relying on their first language for communication purposes, and practicing their newly
acquired English on one another. This just learned and as
yet imperfect English then would function as linguistic input
for the children themselves--it is a kind of input that Selinker
has aptly described as 'junky data'. It can result in the
acquisition of a version of the language which is sufficiently
different from the target language to be described as a special
dialect, which apparently has been happening to some of the
children acquiring French through the Canadian immersion programs (Selinker, Swain, and Dumas 1975). Another reason why
these children need contact with peer age native speakers of
English is that it is only from them that they can discover how
English-speaking children speak. What they are learning from
their teachers now is school talk; it will help them in making
contact with English-speaking children eventually, but only
those children can help them to sound like English-speaking
children.

This study, preliminary as it has been, has shown me that
there are points that educators probably need to keep in mind
in planning programs intended for non-English-speaking children. The first has to do with the relationship between classroom structure and language use. It seems quite clear that
where the concentration of non-English-speaking children is
high, classes need to be as structured as Miss B's in order to
insure that the learners receive an adequate exposure to the
new language. Such teaching is not easy. It calls for the
teacher to take account constantly of how much learners know
and can handle, and to modify the language used for instructional purposes accordingly. A relatively open class format
such as that used by Miss A works only if there are enough
English speakers in the class to make it work. It may be that
the five in Class A constitute the lowest allowable quorum
where language learning is concerned. In such a setting, the
amount of language available to any individual learner as input
will depend on the learner's own ability to seek out the children in the classroom who speak English, and to get into some
kind of sustained interaction with them. Not all children can
do that, and with so few English speakers around, it is not all
that easy to find anyone to interact with. Hence the amount of
contact the children are likely to have with speakers is subject
to variation. Miss A compensates for that variation by

conducting some activities as teacher-directed ones. She also manages to interact with the children on an individual basis frequently enough for that interaction to work for language learning purposes.

How well these children learn English will depend on their continuing to have teachers who are willing to consider their linguistic and social needs. For now, it appears, they are in good hands.

REFERENCES

Berko-Gleason, Jean. 1977. Talking to children: Some notes on feedback. In: Snow and Ferguson, eds. (1977:199-205).
Cross, Toni G. 1977. Mothers' speech adjustments: The contribution of selected child-listener variables. In: Snow and Ferguson, eds. (1977:151-188).
Ferguson, Charles. 1977. Baby talk as a simplified register. In: Snow and Ferguson, eds. (1977:219-236).
Fillmore, Lily Wong. 1976. The second time around: Cognitive and social strategies in second language acquisition. Ph.D. dissertation. Stanford University.
Peck, Sabrina. 1978. Child-child discourse in second language acquisition. In: Second language acquisition: A book of readings. Edited by E. Hatch. Rowley, Mass.: Newbury House. 383-400.
Phillips, Juliet. 1970. Formal characteristics of speech which mothers address to their young children. Ph.D. dissertation. Johns Hopkins University.
Phillips, Juliet. 1973. Syntax and vocabulary of mothers' speech to young children: Age and sex comparisons. Child Development 44.182-185.
Schatz, Marilyn, and Rochelle Gelman. 1977. Beyond syntax: The influence of conversational constraints on speech modifications. In: Snow and Ferguson, eds. (1977:189-198).
Selinker, Larry, Merrill Swain, and Guy Dumas. 1975. The interlanguage hypothesis extended to children. Language Learning 25.1:139-153.
Snow, Catherine E. 1977. Mother's speech research: From input to interaction. In: Snow and Ferguson, eds. (1977).
Snow, Catherine E. 1976. Young children's responses to adult sentences of varying complexity. Paper presented at the Third International Congress of Applied Linguistics, Copenhagen.
Snow, Catherine E., and Charles A. Ferguson, eds. 1977. Talking to children: Language input and acquisition. Cambridge: Cambridge University Press.

This distinguished collection contains 31 articles about the fields of bilingualism and bilingual education, drawn from the annual Georgetown University Round Table on Languages and Linguistics. The editors have here brought together, in a comprehensive, convenient format, the most significant papers from:

Bilingualism and Language Contact (GURT 1970)
International Dimensions of Bilingual Education (GURT 1978)
Current Issues in Bilingual Education (GURT 1980)

ISBN 0-87840-19